MW01697670

Values of Beauty

Historical Essays in Aesthetics

In *Values of Beauty,* Paul Guyer discusses major ideas and figures in the history of aesthetics from the beginning of the eighteenth century to the end of the twentieth century. At the core of the book are Guyer's most recent essays on the epochal contribution of Immauel Kant. The book sets Kant's work in the context of predecessors, contemporaries, and successors, including David Hume, Alexander Gerard, Archibald Alison, Arthur Schopenhauer, and John Stuart Mill.

All of the essays emphasize the complexity rather than the isolation of our aesthetic experience of both nature and art, and the interconnection of aesthetic values such as beauty and sublimity on the one hand and prudential and moral values on the other.

Guyer asserts that the idea of the freedom of the imagination as the key to both artistic creation and aesthetic experience has been a common thread throughout the modern history of aesthetics, although the freedom of the imagination has been understood and connected to other forms of freedom in many different ways.

Paul Guyer is Professor of Philosophy and Florence R. C. Murray Professor in the Humanities at the University of Pennsylvania. He is the author of five books on Kant, most recently *Kant on Freedom, Law, and Happiness,* and he is General Co-Editor of the *Cambridge Edition of the Works of Immanuel Kant,* in which he has contributed to the translation of the *Critique of Pure Reason,* the *Critique of the Power of Judgment,* and Kant's *Notes and Fragments.* He has received fellowships from the John Simon Guggenheim Memorial Foundation and the National Endowment for the Humanities.

Values of Beauty

Historical Essays in Aesthetics

PAUL GUYER
Florence R. C. Murray Professor in the Humanities
University of Pennsylvania

Robert K. Rice

CAMBRIDGE
UNIVERSITY PRESS

CAMBRIDGE UNIVERSITY PRESS
Cambridge, New York, Melbourne, Madrid, Cape Town, Singapore, São Paulo

Cambridge University Press
40 West 20th Street, New York, NY 10011-4211, USA

www.cambridge.org
Information on this title: www.cambridge.org/9780521844901

© Paul Guyer 2005

This book is in copyright. Subject to statutory exception
and to the provisions of relevant collective licensing agreements,
no reproduction of any part may take place without
the written permission of Cambridge University Press.

First published 2005

Printed in the United States of America

A catalog record for this publication is available from the British Library.

Library of Congress Cataloging in Publication Data

Guyer, Paul, 1948–
Values of beauty : historical essays in aesthetics / Paul Guyer.
p. cm.
Includes bibliographical references and index.
ISBN 0-521-84490-8 (alk. paper) – ISBN 0-521-60669-1 (pbk. : alk. paper)
1. Aesthetics – History. 2. Kant, Immanuel, 1724–1804 – Aesthetics. I. Title.
BH81.G89 2005
111′.85′09–dc22 2004024332

ISBN-13 978-0-521-84490-1 hardback
ISBN-10 0-521-84490-8 hardback

ISBN-13 978-0-521-60669-1 paperback
ISBN-10 0-521-60669-1 paperback

Cambridge University Press has no responsibility for
the persistence or accuracy of URLs for external or
third-party Internet Web sites referred to in this book
and does not guarantee that any content on such
Web sites is, or will remain, accurate or appropriate.

For Stanley Cavell,

an exemplar of originality

Contents

Introduction

This volume collects a baker's dozen of my papers in the history of aesthetics. One was published in 1986 and one in 1993, but the rest have all been published or written since 1996. Three have not yet been published elsewhere.

Plato effectively began Western philosophy with an attack on Greek assumptions about the cognitive and practical value of the creation and experience of art, so aesthetics has been both a part of and under attack by philosophy since the outset. In the *Republic*, Plato questioned the claims of poets and their adherents to any important expertise, and cast doubt on the cognitive value of imitations or representations in general by characterizing them as mere copies of ordinary objects that are themselves mere copies of the genuine realities – the Forms. In the *Ion* and *Phaedrus*, he more archly cast doubt on any claims to knowledge that might be made by artists by suggesting that artistic success depends upon divine inspiration, and is therefore incomprehensible to mere mortals. In the *Republic*, he also questioned the practical value of art not only by questioning the cognitive claims on which its practical value might be thought to depend, but also by arguing that the expression of emotion in either the experience or especially the performance of art would be counterproductive for the education of his ideal guardians, who are to learn above all to use their reason to control their emotions, and by extension the emotions of those they are to govern. Yet while doing all of this, Plato was also aware of the spell of beauty, especially beauty in our own kind, and attempted to channel our love of earthly beauty into love of a higher kind of beauty, something not otherwise accessible to the senses, the beauties of the Forms themselves, especially, of course, the Form of the Good or Justice.

Plato has subsequently found few takers for the whole of his critique of beauty and art; indeed, the defense of both the cognitive and the emotional as well as practical value of aesthetic experience began immediately with Aristotle, his student and successor. But the questions that Plato raised – what is the nature and value of beauty? what is the connection between art and knowledge? what is the connection between aesthetics and morality? and what is genius, the source of artistic inspiration? – have always remained at the heart of aesthetics, no less so when aesthetics became a recognized academic discipline early in the eighteenth century than before, and no less so now than at any other time in modernity. Indeed, after several decades in which "analytic" philosophers set these substantive issues aside in favor of supposedly more respectable as well as more tractable questions about the structure and logic of aesthetic language and discourse – just as they attempted to do for a while in other areas of philosophy as well, such as moral philosophy – precisely these ancient questions have recently returned to the forefront of debate in Anglo-American aesthetics, with all their allure and all their difficulty.

Among the liveliest issues in recent aesthetics have been questions about the importance of beauty, the cognitive significance of fictions, the links between aesthetics and morality, and even the nature of genius and artistic creation. The essays in this volume, although they directly engage ideas and figures from the eighteenth, nineteenth, and twentieth centuries, touch upon all of these issues. These essays discuss the sources of the value that we place on the experience of the beautiful, the sublime, and other aesthetic merits in both nature and art; how aesthetic values can be distinctive from and yet connected to and supportive of the range of values in our lives that we group under the rubric of the moral; conceptions of the creation of aesthetic values, traditionally discussed under the name of genius; and continuities between traditional and recent theories of beauty and of art in spite of drastic changes in the arts themselves between the beginning of the eighteenth century and the end of the twentieth. The figure of Kant is central to many of the essays and entirely absent from none of them, although the first two essays focus on writers before Kant and the last three on some successors to Kant, because in my opinion, Kant's analyses of aesthetic experience, aesthetic creativity, and the connections between the aesthetic and the moral responded to the complexity of all of these in ways that ensure their continuing interest and fruitfulness.

Chapter 1, "The Origins of Modern Aesthetics: 1711–1735," looks at alternative accounts of aesthetic pleasure in the foundational quarter-century of the discipline that was named by Alexander Baumgarten at its end. Here I consider the formalist account of beauty of the Earl of Shaftesbury and Francis Hutcheson (although their views are by no means identical), the account of aesthetic experience as controlled emotional arousal advocated by the Abbé Du Bos, and the cognitivist account of Baumgarten, and also suggest that Joseph Addison's famous essays on "The Pleasures of the Imagination," although in some ways they anticipate the associationism of subsequent British aesthetics, which would culminate in the work of Archibald Alison that is contrasted to Kant's in Chapter 8, also recognize the complexity of the sources of those pleasures in a way that would not be seen again until Kant.

Chapter 2, "The Standard of Taste and the 'Most Ardent Desire of Society,'" is an essay on Hume that I originally published in a Festschrift for Stanley Cavell in 1993. Cavell's invocation of Kant in his early essay "Aesthetic Problems of Modern Philosophy" was certainly part of the inspiration for my dissertation on Kant's approach to the problem of taste; the same essay includes a pregnant remark about Hume's concept of the critic, which I take up in this chapter. The central question of this chapter is why we should care about the aesthetic preferences of others, even if they might be critics who are more learned and more practiced than ourselves. I argue that in his major works, Hume outlined a complex theory of beauty, on which we can take pleasure in many aspects of and associations with works of art that go far beyond their form, about which we can learn from critics both present and past; but Hume also recognized that we value the very fact of agreement with our fellows itself, and thus that the existence of a shared critical tradition in a community is an additional source of value in aesthetic experience. Hume's analysis of taste thus suggests a complex analysis of the nature and conditions of community in general, therefore of the conditions for the possibility of human action and thus morality as well, which is surely what caught Cavell's interest. The way in which an individual is part of a community by means of standards or criteria that both constrain how the individual can think and talk, yet must also be actively affirmed and developed by the individual, has been an issue throughout Cavell's work, and indeed the presentation of a conception of the social contract, in response to Hume, that can serve as a model for the comprehension of human linguistic and cognitive interaction and community is the starting point of his magnum opus, *The Claim of Reason* (1979). Cavell does not discuss Hume's essay "Of the Standard of Taste" there, but Cavellian issues about individual and community were in my mind as I wrote about Hume for Cavell. I am happy not merely to reprint this essay here but to dedicate the present volume to my teacher and friend of almost forty years.

The next eight essays focus mainly but not exclusively on Kant. Chapter 3, "The Harmony of the Faculties Revisited," addresses the central concept in Kant's account of our experience of both natural and artistic beauty, which is also the key to his model of how we can value such experience both for its own sake and also for its manifold moral significance. I argue for an interpretation of Kant's conception of the "free play" of imagination and understanding, or in the case of the sublime imagination, understanding and reason, which it is compatible with but goes beyond ordinary cognition and thus strikes us as an unexpected gift in addition to such cognition rather than as an alternative to it. Such a conception of the basis of aesthetic experience, I maintain, is necessary not only to make Kant's theory of the judgment of taste plausible – for after all, we are, indeed on Kant's own account in the *Critique of Pure Reason*, never simply devoid of knowledge in the experience of any object, objects of natural or artistic beauty or sublimity included – but it is also necessary to understand Kant's view of both the varieties of beauty and sublimity as well as the connections between aesthetic experience on the one hand and both cognition and morality on the other.

The variety of both the sources of aesthetic value themselves and of their connections to other forms of value are then explored in ensuing essays. In Chapters 4 and 5, I consider Kant's conception of "dependent" or "adherent" as contrasted with "free" beauty, first in the context of the eighteenth-century debate about the relation between beauty and utility from Shaftesbury through Burke (Chapter 4) and then in Kant alone (Chapter 5). In these two essays, I suggest that Kant, like many other eighteenth-century thinkers, recognized that the human concern for utility is just as natural and inescapable as the human desire for society as well as pleasure in pure form, and that it is therefore only natural – as well as entirely plausible – for him to think that the experience of the beauty of objects, again natural or artifactual, is not always or even usually an alternative to the appreciation of utility in them, but typically exists in interaction with the latter, indeed as Chapter 5 argues, in a variety of forms of interaction.

In Chapter 4, on beauty and utility, I show that whereas previous aestheticians tended to think that the value of beauty must lie either in pure form or in utility alone – a debate between Hutcheson and George

Berkeley, not otherwise known as an aesthetician, is illustrative here – and Hume reconciled these alternatives only superficially by simply supposing that there are two unrelated kinds of beauty, only Kant recognized the teleological character of human mentality, which leads us to make the satisfaction of utilitarian concerns in an object that we think ought to satisfy them a necessary condition for any further aesthetic satisfaction with the object. Indeed, I could have made explicit here that there is a parallel between Kant's general analysis of the harmony of the faculties and the special case of adherent beauty: just as any beautiful object must both satisfy the general conditions of cognition and also give us a sense of unity that goes beyond what is necessary to satisfy those requirements, so in the case of an object that has a readily recognizable purpose we must be able to see the object as satisfying its purpose before being able to take pleasure in the way that it goes beyond merely doing so. The "modest proposal" of Chapter 5 is then that the variety of interpretative approaches to Kant's concept of adherent beauty actually reflects the variety of ways in which purpose and form can interact to give us pleasure: in some cases, the object's satisfaction of its intended purpose may be just a necessary condition for our pleasure in its form; in some cases, our separate pleasures in the function and in the form of the object may be additive; and in some cases, we may take pleasure in a genuine interaction between function and form. But I also argue that such a *variety* of sources of pleasure should not be taken as a *scale* of pleasure and value; it does not automatically follow that a more complex pleasure is a more valuable pleasure. The value of any particular experience will no doubt have to be left to, well, experience.

I have also assumed, if not made as explicit as I might have, that there is a similar structure to Kant's thought about the relation between aesthetic and moral value: as the moral theorist he was, surely Kant must have assumed that the moral permissibility of the creation and the experience of any particular object in the actual circumstances of both that creation and experience is a necessary condition of our taking even a purely aesthetic pleasure in it, but that there is also a variety of ways in which aesthetic experiences may go beyond mere compatibility with morality to actually support it – without losing what makes them distinctively aesthetic. In any case, the complex relations that Kant recognizes to obtain between our appreciation of beauty and the demands of morality are the themes of the next group of essays.

In Chapter 6, "Kant on the Purity of the Ugly," I argue that for Kant, a judgment of ugliness is not typically a purely aesthetic judgment, but rather an expression of the sensible presentation of something that is physiologically, but even more typically morally, repulsive. Thus we cannot understand the full range of what we consider to be aesthetic judgments unless we are prepared to consider the complex relations between aesthetic and moral experience. So again we see that what we may tend to think of as the single category of the aesthetic thus includes a variety of values. Here I also argue that when Kant thinks about aesthetic pain rather than pleasure, he is thinking of the experience of the sublime rather than of the ugly, but that the experience of the sublime must also be thought of as a complex experience with both aesthetic and moral aspects. But that, I conclude, is no real objection to Kant's putting the experience of the sublime on the same plane as the experience of the beautiful, because even though Kant begins his analysis of beauty with the case of pure or unmixed beauty, in fact he recognizes that the vast majority of our actual experiences of beauty are complex experiences with both aesthetic and moral elements.

Indeed, what I argue in Chapter 7, "Beauty, Freedom, and Morality: Kant's Lectures on Anthropology and the Development of His Aesthetic Theory," is that although much of the structure of Kant's analysis of aesthetic experience and judgment had been in place since the mid-1770s, including his key ideas of the subjective origin yet intersubjective validity of judgments of taste in the free play of our cognitive powers, it was only when he finally saw how to relate the aesthetic to the moral without sacrificing what is essential to either that it suddenly became important and perhaps even possible for him to write a third critique in the brief period from 1788 to early 1790. Kant had long toyed with the idea of writing a critique of *taste* like dozens of his predecessors and contemporaries, but it was not until he saw how to write a critique of the power of *judgment* that could both differentiate and yet link aesthetic and moral judgment that the work finally had a uniquely Kantian *raison d'etre*. Kant's discovery of parallels between the connection of aesthetic to moral judgment and the connection of teleological to moral judgment is also what accounts for his startling linkage of aesthetics and teleology in the third critique.

In Chapter 8, "The Ethical Value of the Aesthetic: Kant, Alison, and Santayana," I offer a systematic review of the complex of relations between the aesthetic and the moral that Kant recognized, but go beyond my previous work on this subject (the preceding two essays as well as those collected in my 1993 volume *Kant and the Experience of Freedom*) by contrasting Kant's views on this matter with those expressed by the Scot Archibald Alison in an exactly contemporaneous work, his *Essays on the*

Nature and Principles of Taste of 1790. I use Alison to point up something that is missing in Kant's theory, the real presence of emotion in aesthetic experience and its value for morality, indeed the presence of love in aesthetic experience, although Alison surely goes overboard in reducing every aspect of aesthetic experience to an emotional association. I therefore argue that some sort of synthesis between the two sorts of views is needed, and I suggest that such a synthesis is precisely what George Santayana provided a century later in *The Sense of Beauty* (1896). Santayana tried to disown this book as a product of his youth, and it has certainly been out of fashion lately, but I present it as a work of enduring interest that should be considered in the contemporary debates about the relations between aesthetics and cognition on the one hand and aesthetics and morality on the other. In particular, while many participants in this debate may assume that moral value is in some sense more fundamental than aesthetic value, and while Kant himself assumes that a good will is the only thing of unconditional value, thus that moral value is certainly a constraint upon if not the basis of all other sources of value, Santayana makes the contrasting suggestion that morality is in fact of merely instrumental value: its mission is merely to make it possible for people to enjoy that which is of positive value, such as the aesthetic itself. There is a striking parallel here between Santayana's *Sense of Beauty* and G. E. Moore's *Principia Ethica*, although Moore's book appeared only seven years later than Santayana's; but I do not explore this parallel in the chapter.

Finally, in Chapter 9, "The Symbols of Freedom in Kant's Aesthetics," I further explore the relations between the beautiful and the sublime, also touched upon in Chapter 6, and in particular try to resolve the confusion that Kant creates when he suggests that *each* of these is the *only* paradigmatic aesthetic symbol of the moral. Obviously this cannot be quite right, so what I suggest is that our experiences of the beautiful and the sublime each symbolize different aspects of moral freedom: appealing to a distinction between negative and positive conceptions of freedom that Kant makes in the *Groundwork for the Metaphysics of Morals*, I suggest that the sublime offers us a palpable experience of freedom negatively understood, that is, of our power of resistance to mere nature, while the beautiful offers us a symbolic representation of freedom understood positively, as something that can be achieved only through adherence to universally valid laws. Lying behind both of these connections, of course, is Kant's idea that we *need* sensible symbols of freedom and morality even though, as he puts it in the *Critique of Practical Reason*, we are supposed to be able to understand the demands of morality and prove our freedom to live up to them as a pure "fact of reason." This is not a paradox, however; I suggest throughout these essays that Kant's recognition that we are *rational animals*, both sensible and embodied on the one hand and rational on the other, is the key to much of his thought, both within aesthetics and indeed without it.

Chapter 10, "Exemplary Originality: Genius, Universality, and Individuality," turns to a subject that was of great interest to Kant's predecessors as well as to his successors well into the twentieth century, namely, genius. Here I argue that Kant's conception of this source of artistic production represents a significant departure from both preceding views, such as those of the Abbé Du Bos and Alexander Gerard, but also some succeeding views, such as those of Samuel Coleridge and Ralph Waldo Emerson: while those thinkers conceive of genius as primarily a special gift of *perception*, the ability to see more easily what is both there to be seen and what all can ultimately come to see, Kant treats genius as a power for the *creation* of aesthetic value, indeed of the creation of syntheses of aesthetic and moral value through "aesthetic ideas" – and thus introduces an idea of originality that is itself original. But even Kant may place too much value on the universal validity of originality – what he calls "exemplary originality" – so I turn to someone who usually does not get much attention in the historiography of aesthetics, namely, John Stuart Mill, for a model of how we can value originality and the diversity it creates while being part of a community, indeed a community that prizes intellectual – and ultimately other – forms of diversity.

The final three essays discuss one more nineteenth-century writer, Arthur Schopenhauer, and then three twentieth-century aestheticians, Monroe Beardsley, Arthur Danto, and Mary Mothersill. In Chapter 11, "Pleasure and Knowledge in Schopenhauer's Aesthetics," I argue that while Schopenhauer might seem to offer an entirely negative view of the moral value of aesthetic experience – the experience of beauty simply enables us to escape from the pains of ordinary existence for a time, just as the moral attitude of resignation enables us to escape from it for good – in fact he also recognized a positive pleasure in the exercise of our cognitive powers, indeed a pleasure in the perception through both natural and artistic beauty of what he called the "Platonic Ideas," although these Ideas as Schopenhauer conceives them are diametrically opposed to the Forms as Plato conceived them – Schopenhauer's Ideas are the paradigmatic forms of the realm of appearance, while Plato's Forms are the ideas of a reality that transcends all appearance. (But while Schopenhauer is usually the first to tell us when he's trying to be humorous or ironic, maybe there's an irony in his choice of Plato's name for his own conception that for once he's subtle enough not to point out to us.) I also consider the charge that Schopenhauer is guilty of the cardinal sin of "aesthetic attitude" theorists, namely, allowing that if beauty is just a matter of how we approach an object, then we can make *any* object beautiful just by approaching it in the right frame of mind. That is supposed to be a self-evident knock-down objection to any theory of beauty, which should discriminate between what is beautiful and what is not; but for Schopenhauer, the idea that we might find beauty, and thus both positive pleasure and relief, in any object, is not a flaw but a virtue, although he also points out that it is not so easy to put ourselves into this frame of mind – indeed, we might just need a genius to show us how to find the beauty in an object where it is not immediately apparent.

In Chapter 12, "From Jupiter's Eagle to Warhol's Boxes: The Concept of Art from Kant to Danto," I argue that although the idea that art must ultimately be pleasurable has not been explicit in many recent theories, and indeed for many decades of the twentieth century it seemed as if beauty were simply irrelevant to art, Kantian assumptions in fact continue to play a major role in Monroe Beardsley's theory of beauty and even Arthur Danto's definition of art. Danto has certainly made much of how our image of the *objects* of art has undergone radical changes over the last century, but his own definition of art shows that we find many of the same values in our *experience* of art that our predecessors did. (In his 2003 book *The Abuse of Beauty*, Danto has acknowledged that beauty can be at least a possible if not a necessary aim of art; this too places him squarely in the tradition of modern aesthetic theory, if not exactly in the camp of Kant, then certainly in the camp of many like Addison and Gerard who recognized beauty as just one of the various "pleasures of the imagination" that may be found in our experience of art.)

Finally, Chapter 13 discusses Mary Mothersill's *Beauty Restored* (1984), a work that was willing to connect itself explicitly to some of the key figures of eighteenth-century aesthetics, and was perhaps the earliest of the recent attempts to restore credit to the value of beauty in our experience of art. Mothersill argues that we can indeed acknowledge a continuing *concept* of beauty even while our *conception* of what beautiful objects look like undergoes radical change, and thus that the value we find in beautiful objects need not undergo a revolution even while the objects themselves do. I think this point is a valuable accompaniment to the arguments of her long-time colleague Danto, and worth remembering. But I also suggest we might go further than Mothersill, and that both producers and consumers of art might need not just a concept but also a theory of beauty, because even if we cannot *command* that others find the same things beautiful that we ourselves do, we are always *commending* what we find beautiful to each other, and this is not something we can responsibly do without having some well-grounded expectation that those to whom we commend the objects we have found beautiful may also do so, an expectation that we might well ground in a theory of beauty.

My final comments in this book thus once again suggest that there are inescapable connections between aesthetic and moral values, for that we make our aesthetic recommendations responsibly is itself a moral responsibility.

Acknowledgments

I would like to thank the original publishers of Chapters 1, 2, 4, 5, 7, 9, 10, 11, 12, and 13 for granting me permission to reprint my previously published essays.

Chapter 1, "The Origins of Modern Aesthetics: 1711–1735," was first published in *The Blackwell Guide to Aesthetics*, edited by Peter Kivy (Malden and Oxford: Blackwell Publishing, 2004), pp. 15–44, and is reprinted here with the permission of the publisher.

Chapter 2, "The Standard of Taste and the 'Most Ardent Desire of Society,'" first appeared in Ted Cohen, Paul Guyer, and Hilary Putnam, eds., *Pursuits of Reason: Essays in Honor of Stanley Cavell* (Lubbock: Texas Tech University Press, 1993), pp. 37–66, and is reprinted here with the permission of the publisher.

Chapter 3, "The Harmony of the Faculties Revisited," appears here for the first time. It will also appear in Rebecca Kukla, ed., *Reflecting on Sensibility: Aesthetics and Cognition in Kant's Critical Philosophy* (Cambridge University Press, forthcoming).

Chapter 4, "Beauty and Utility in Eighteenth-Century Aesthetics," first appeared in *Eighteenth Century Studies* 35 (2002): 439–53, and is reprinted here with the permission of The Johns Hopkins University Press.

Chapter 5, "Free and Adherent Beauty: A Modest Proposal," first appeared in the *British Journal of Aesthetics* 42 (October, 2002): 357–66, and is reprinted here with the permission of Oxford University Press.

Chapter 6, "Kant on the Purity of the Ugly," appears here for the first time. It will also appear in Heiner D. Klemme, Michael Pauen, and Marie-Louise Raters, eds., *Im Schatten des Schönen* (Bielefeld: Aisthesis Verlag, forthcoming).

Chapter 7, "Beauty, Freedom and Morality: Kant's Lectures on Anthropology and the Development of His Aesthetic Theory," first appeared in Brian Jacobs and Patrick Kain, eds., *Kant's Anthropology* (Cambridge: Cambridge University Press, 2003), pp. 135–63.

Chapter 8, "The Ethical Value of the Aesthetic: Kant, Alison, and Santayana," appears here for the first time.

Chapter 9, "The Symbols of Freedom in Kant's Aesthetics," appeared first in Herman Parret, ed., *Kant's Ästhetik/ Kant's Aesthetics/ L'esthétique de Kant* (Berlin: Walter de Gruyter, 1998), pp. 338–55, and is reprinted here with the permission of the publisher. It also appeared in Portuguese as: "Os Símbolos da Liberdade na Estética Kantiana," *O que nos faz penser* **9** (1995): 73–92.

Chapter 10, "Exemplary Originality: Genius, Universality, and Individuality," first appeared in Berys Gaut and Paisley Livingstone, eds., *Creation in Art* (Cambridge: Cambridge University Press, 2003), pp. 116–37, and is reprinted here with the permission of the editors.

Chapter 11, "Pleasure and Knowledge in Schopenhauer's Aesthetics," first appeared in Dale Jacquette, ed., *Schopenhauer, Philosophy and Art*, (Cambridge: Cambridge University Press, 1996), pp. 109–32.

Chapter 12, "From Jupiter's Eagle to Warhol's Boxes: The Concept of Art from Kant to Danto," first appeared in *Philosophical Topics* **25** (1997): 83–115, and is reprinted here with the permission of the publisher.

Chapter 13, "The Value of a Theory of Beauty: Mary Mothersill's *Beauty Restored*," first appeared in the *Journal of Aesthetics and Art Criticism* **45** (1986): 245–55, and is reprinted here with the permission of Blackwell Publishing.

For their generous assistance with proofreading, I would like to thank Jody Beck, Lucy Collins, Adrian Daub, Carrie Golden, Thomas Hilgers, Samantha Matherne, Mariachiara Piccinotti, Elena Polegnova, Kimmia Pourrezaea, Jessica Slaven, and Scott Straud.

Abbreviations Used in the Text

Ak	Kant: *Gesammelte Schriften*
CPJ	Kant: *Critique of the Power of Judgment*
CPrR	Kant: *Critique of Practical Reason*
DV	Kant: "Doctrine of Virtue" in *Metaphysics of Morals*
ENPT	Alison: *Essays on the Nature and Principles of Taste*
EPM	Hume: An Essay Concerning the Principles of Morals
FI	Kant: "First Introduction" to *Critique of the Power of Judgment*
G	Kant: *Groundwork of the Metaphysics of Morals*
I	Hutcheson: *An Inquiry into the Origin of Our Ideas of Beauty and Virtue*
SB	Santayana: *The Sense of Beauty*
ST	Hume: "Of the Standard of Taste"
T	Hume: *A Treatise of Human Nature*
WWR	Schopenhauer: *The World as Will and Representation*

PART I

MOSTLY BEFORE KANT

1

The Origins of Modern Aesthetics

1711–1735

It is well known that the subject of aesthetics, as a recognized and customary subject within the academic practice of philosophy, received its name in 1735. In that year, in his dissertation *Meditationes philosophicae de nonnullis ad poema pertinentibus* ("Philosophical considerations of some matters pertaining to the poem"), the twenty-one-year-old Alexander Gottlieb Baumgarten introduced the term to mean "a science of how things are to be known by means of the senses" (*scientiam sensitive quid cognoscendi*) (*Meditations*, §§cxv–cxvi). (Four years later, in his *Metaphysica,* Baumgarten would expand this definition to include the "logic of the lower cognitive faculty, the philosophy of the graces and the muses, lower gnoseology, the art of thinking beautifully, the art of the analogue of reason"; and another decade later, in his monumental fragment *Aesthetica,* the first treatise to bear the title of the new subject, he would combine his two previous definitions to form his final definition of the subject: "Aesthetics (the theory of the liberal arts, lower gnoseology, the art of beautiful thinking, the art of the analogue of reason) is the science of sensitive cognition" (*Metaphysica,* §533; *Aesthetica,* §1). It is equally well known that although Baumgarten was the first to name the new subject and perhaps the first German philosophy professor to give it a regular place in his lectures and treatises, he by no means invented the subject itself. Of course, philosophers since antiquity had at least occasionally argued about the nature of beauty and the value of what we now group together as the fine arts, such as literature, visual arts such as painting and sculpture, and music. But around the beginning of the eighteenth century, there began a torrent of writing about the character and value of beauty and other properties, notably the sublime, in both art and in nature itself, a flood to which professional philosophers as well as other men of letters (of course the writers were without exception male) contributed and which has since hardly abated. In particular, the second and third decades of the eighteenth century have a real claim to be the moment of the origin of modern aesthetics. This moment was marked by the appearance in the first of those decades of the *Characteristics of Men, Manners, Opinions, Times* by Anthony Ashley Cooper, third Earl of Shaftesbury, in 1711; Joseph Addison's eleven essays "On the Pleasures of the Imagination" in the *Spectator* in June and July 1712; and finally by the 1719 *Critical Reflections on Poetry, Painting and Music* by the Abbé Jean-Baptiste Du Bos, a work that went through at least five editions in French in the next two decades and was widely circulated in Britain long before its translation into English in 1748, and then in the second by the first treatise of Francis Hutcheson's *Inquiry into the Original of our Ideas of Beauty and Virtue* in 1725. None of these writers except Hutcheson was a professor of philosophy. But the issues they raised and the positions they took in these books prepared the way for the more professional philosophical work of much of the rest of the century, and beyond, and thus modern aesthetics should not be conceived of as if it sprang full-grown from the brow of Baumgarten in 1735, but rather as having developed much of its eventual programs and positions in the years from 1711 to 1735. It is thus this period that will be the focus of the present chapter.

Is there a common idea that marks this foundational epoch of modern aesthetics? Some have argued that it was this period which first saw the invention of the idea that what we now almost unwittingly lump together as the "arts" or the "fine arts"; for example, the "poetry, painting and music" of Du Bos's title, constitute some sort of system, an assumption that was necessary to supply a subject for the discipline of aesthetics as the philosophy of art.[1] Others have focussed on the addition of the idea of the sublime to the traditional idea of beauty,[2] or on the emergence of the idea of artistic genius as a special form of human mentality.[3] More

[1] See Paul Oskar Kristeller, "The Modern System of the Arts" (1951), reprinted in his *Renaissance Thought II: Papers on Humanism and the Arts* (New York: Harper & Row, 1965), pp. 163–227.

[2] See Samuel Monk, *The Sublime* (1935), revised edition (Ann Arbor: University of Michigan Press, 1960), and for a recent sampler of eighteenth-century writing on the sublime, Andrew Ashfield and Peter de Bolla, eds., *The Sublime: A Reader in British Eighteenth-Century Aesthetic Theory* (Cambridge: Cambridge University Press, 1996).

[3] See M. H. Abrams, *The Mirror and the Lamp: Romantic Theory and the Critical Tradition* (Oxford: Oxford University Press, 1953).

recently, it has been argued that it was in the eighteenth-century writings on aesthetics that modern ideas of subjectivity and individuality first came to the fore,[4] while yet others have argued that it was in the aesthetics of this period that the modern practice of ideology, masking the claims of a single class to domination of society behind a sham claim to universal validity, first emerged.[5] But without rejecting any of these claims outright (although I think the last one tells us more about the preoccupations of the late twentieth century than of the eighteenth), I will pursue a different tack. As I see it, the central idea to emerge in eighteenth-century aesthetics is the idea of the freedom of the imagination, and it was the attraction of this idea that provided much of the impetus behind the explosion of aesthetic theory in the period.

However, the idea of freedom, whether of the imagination or anything else, is notoriously vague and ambiguous. Later in the eighteenth century, Kant was to make famous a distinction between negative and positive conceptions of freedom, that is, a conception of freedom as consisting simply in the absence of determination or control of some specified type as contrasted to a conception of freedom as consisting precisely in the determination or control of action by one specified kind of agent or agency rather than another. Kant introduced this distinction, of course, in his practical philosophy, where he described a negative conception of freedom as the independence of the will from determination by causes alien to the true self, especially determination by merely sensory impulses or inclinations, and the positive conception of freedom as the determination of the will by the legislation of pure reason;[6] a central theme of Kant's moral philosophy is then that the freedom exercised in and valued by human morality is never simply freedom negatively conceived, but positive freedom, the freedom to conduct ourselves autonomously by a law legislated by pure reason, which is the most distinctive feature of our selves and whose law is thus the purest expression of our own autonomy. But we may also understand Kant's aesthetic theory as dominated by an

4 See Luc Ferry, *Homo Aestheticus: The Invention of Taste in the Democratic Age*, translated by Robert de Loaiza (Chicago: University of Chicago Press, 1993). An older work which emphasized *Individualität* as the key idea in eighteenth-century aesthetics is Alfred Bäumler, *Das Irrationalitätsproblem in der Ästhetik und Logik des 18. Jahrhunderts bis zur Kritik der Urteilskraft* (1923), second edition (Tübingen: Max Niemeyer, 1967), although Bäumler, who later became a notorious Nazi spokesman, linked individuality to irrationalism, and thus saw the development of aesthetics as a locus of opposition to rationalist universalism rather than associating it with the origins of modern liberalism as does Ferry.

5 See Terry Eagleton, *The Ideology of the Aesthetics* (Oxford: Blackwell, 1990).

6 Kant, *Groundwork for the Metaphysics of Morals*, 4:446.

apparent tension between negative and positive conceptions of freedom of the imagination and the effort to resolve this tension.

In the initial phase of his analysis of what he calls the aesthetic judgment of the beautiful, or more properly the reflective rather than merely sensitive aesthetic judgment, Kant begins with the purported disinterestedness of the judgment of taste, its independence from any merely sensory agreeableness of an object on the one hand and from any recognition of it as good in light of its classification under a determinate concept on the other. This is, of course, a purely negative conception of the nature of aesthetic response and judgment in the straightforward sense that it tells us what it is not, not what it is. Kant goes on to give a more informative characterization of aesthetic response as based on a harmony or free play between the cognitive faculties of imagination and understanding, in which the subjective conditions of cognition are satisfied apart from the satisfaction of what is ordinarily the objective condition of cognition, namely, the subsumption of an object under a determinate concept (e.g., the recognition of a three-sided, closed plane figure as a triangle or a four-footed mammal with a certain pattern of dentition as a dog). But this may still be regarded as a negative conception of the freedom of the imagination in aesthetic response, for it emphasizes that the imagination satisfies our general objective in all cognition without being determined or constrained by any particular concept – where Kant takes the concept of a concept itself quite broadly, to include representational content and intended purpose as well as classification, as in ordinary concepts like *triangle* or *dog*.

Just as in his moral theory, however, Kant is not content with a negative conception of the freedom of the human will, but argues that human freedom can only be fully realized as the positive expression of a self-legislated law of reason, so in his aesthetic theory Kant moves from a negative conception of the basis of aesthetic response and pleasure, the free play of imagination and understanding, to one or indeed several positive conceptions of the basis of our pleasure in both natural and artistic beauty – to a conception of art as the expression of aesthetic ideas, and of the experience of beauty itself as a symbol of morality, thus as both the manifestation of the freedom of the imagination and the representation of freedom more broadly understood by means of the works of imagination. And just as the trick in Kant's moral theory is to show that the negative and positive conceptions of freedom are not in fact two competing conceptions of human freedom, but rather two sides of the same coin – for freedom from domination by mere inclination can in fact be achieved only by self-governance in accord with the law of pure reason instead[7] – so the key to Kant's aesthetics is his reconciliation of his negative and positive conceptions of the freedom of the imagination – his theory that it is precisely in virtue of the freedom of the imagination in aesthetic response from determination by ordinary concepts of the understanding that this response is itself suited to serve as a symbol of morality, because it can thereby represent the freedom that is the essence of morality, yet which is not otherwise made palpable to us in the world of our senses.[8]

Just as in his moral philosophy, and for that matter in his critique of pure reason in general, Kant found a way to put together what previous philosophers had held apart – Kant's most general argument in philosophy, of course, was that intuition and concept, sensory input and intellectual classification, on which previous thinkers had erected two competing schools of philosophy, could only provide human knowledge when firmly yoked together – so in aesthetics Kant found a way to tie together what for many (although, as we will see, not all) earlier writers had been alternative and competing conceptions of the freedom of the imagination in the experience of art and beauty. At the outset of the eighteenth century, we find thinkers excited by a new sense of the freedom of the imagination, but in many cases torn between competing conceptions of this freedom. On the one hand, we find a conception of aesthetic judgment as disinterested, as independent from any of our other practical and cognitive concerns and instead linked most closely to the sheer perceptual form of objects. It was Shaftesbury who introduced the idea of disinterestedness into aesthetic discourse, but it was not in fact he who introduced a truly negative conception of the nature of aesthetic response; this was left to Francis Hutcheson in the following decade, who borrowed the idea of disinterestedness from Shaftesbury but used it to ground a very different theory from that of his supposed master. On the other hand, we find a conception of the imagination as taking a very positive delight in the symbolization of important ideas, a train of thought epitomized by Addison's claim that we enjoy images of grandeur because the imagination delights in symbols of human freedom. And we find complicated cases like that of Du Bos, whose theory looks as if it begins with a

7 See my *Kant on Freedom, Law and Happiness* (Cambridge: Cambridge University Press, 2000), especially chapter 9, "Moral Worth, Virtue, and Merit."

8 I have argued for this interpretation of Kant's aesthetics in my *Kant and the Experience of Freedom* (Cambridge: Cambridge University Press, 1993), especially chapter 3.

purely negative conception of aesthetic response, as a mere release from tedium and *ennui*, but who transforms that into a positive account of the pleasure that we take in the engagement of our emotions. But, although both Addison and Baumgarten were to anticipate him, not until Kant do we find within professional philosophy a fully achieved synthesis of the negative and positive conceptions of the freedom of the imagination in aesthetic experience, but especially in the experience of art – a synthesis that was to prove quite fragile, and largely came apart again in the nineteenth century, as witnessed by a contrast like that between Schopenhauer's conception of aesthetic contemplation as offering a release from the pain of quotidian existence on the one hand and Ruskin's conception of Gothic architecture as an image of the freedom of everyone involved in its production on another.

But that would be a story for another occasion; here, my attention will be confined to the first two decades of modern aesthetics, the period from 1711 to 1719 already mentioned, and the ensuing years from 1725 to 1735, which will bring us to the first works of Hutcheson and Baumgarten. What I will argue is that in this period we find evidence of the competing conceptions of the freedom of the imagination that I have described, which would eventually be reconciled by means of Kant's appropriation of Baumgarten's conception of the character of specifically artistic representation, although Baumgarten himself, while clearly recognizing the complexity of aesthetic objects and our response to them, had not used this recognition to reconcile the two conceptions of the freedom of the imagination developed by his immediate predecessors.

I. Shaftesbury and Hutcheson

Anthony Ashley Cooper, third Earl of Shaftesbury (1677–1713), grandson of the leader of the Whigs in their struggle against the ascension of James II and tutee of John Locke, his grandfather's physician, secretary, and political operative, is widely credited with having introduced disinterestedness as the criterion of aesthetic response and judgment.[9] Shaftesbury did not actually use the terms "interest" or "disinterestedness" in connection with what we now call aesthetic phenomena, but Francis Hutcheson (1694–1746), who invoked the name of Shaftesbury

9 See Jerome Stolnitz, "On the Origins of 'Aesthetic Disinterest'," *Journal of Aesthetics and Art Criticism* 20 (1961): 131–43, and Jane Kneller, "Disinterestedness," in Michael Kelly, ed., *Encyclopedia of Aesthetics* (New York: Oxford University Press), Vol. 2, pp. 59–64.

in the preface to his 1725 *An Inquiry into the Original of Our Ideas of Beauty and Virtue,* did when he wrote:

> The Ideas of Beauty and harmony, like other sensible Ideas, are *necessarily* pleasant to us, as well as immediately so; neither can any Resolution of our own, nor any *Prospect* of Advantage or Disadvantage, vary the Beauty or Deformity of an Object: ... in the external Sensations, no View of *Interest* will make an Object grateful, nor View of *Detriment,* distinct from immediate *Pain* in the Perception, make it disagreeable to the Sense ...
>
> (*Inquiry,* Sec. I, §xiii)

Hutcheson's statement seems a natural extension of passages in Shaftesbury where the earlier writer argues that our pleasure in something beautiful is distinct and independent from all thoughts of *control* and *use* of the object and of the *possession* on which our ability to control and use an object might depend. Thus, in the dialogue *The Moralists, a Philosophical Rhapsody,* which together with the earlier *Inquiry Concerning Virtue or Merit* constitutes the heart of his *Characteristics,* Shaftesbury's spokesman Theocles argues to his interlocutor Philocles:

> 'Imagine then, good Philocles, if being taken with the beauty of the ocean, which you see yonder at a distance, it should come into your head to seek how to command it and, like some mighty admiral, ride master of the seas. Would not the fancy be a little absurd?'
>
> ...
>
> 'Let who will call it theirs,' [continued] Theocles, 'you will own the enjoyment of this kind to be very different from that which should naturally follow from the contemplation of the ocean's beauty....
>
> But to come nearer home and make the question still more familiar. Suppose, my Philocles, that, viewing such a tract of country as this delicious vale we see beneath us, you should, for the enjoyment of the prospect, require the property or possession of the land.'
>
> 'The covetous fancy,' replied [Philocles], 'would be as absurd altogether as that other ambitious one.'
>
> 'O Philocles!,' said he, 'may I bring this yet a little nearer and will you follow me once more? Suppose that, being charmed as you seem to be with the beauty of those trees under whose shade we rest, you should long for nothing so much as to taste some delicious fruit of theirs and, having obtained of nature some certain relish by which these acorns or berries of the wood became as palatable as the figs or peaches of the garden, you should afterwards, as oft as you revisited these groves, seek hence the enjoyment of them by satiating yourself in these new delights.'
>
> 'The fancy of this kind', replied [Philocles], 'would be as sordidly luxurious and as absurd, in my opinion, as either of the former.'
>
> (*Characteristics,* pp. 318–19)

So Shaftesbury certainly proposes that our pleasure in the beauty of objects, here natural objects or views thereof, is independent of any expectation of the use or consumption of those objects that might in turn be dependent upon the possession of the objects. But it would be a mistake to suppose that he means to restrict himself to a negative characterization of the nature of aesthetic response, let alone to a negative characterization of the free play of the imagination as the foundation of aesthetic response, and thus that he means to separate the sources of aesthetic response from other fundamental forms of human thought and action. On the contrary, Shaftesbury means his insistence upon the independence of aesthetic response from promises of personal use or advantage to associate or even identify our response to beauty with our response to other forms of value, above all with the response to goodness which constitutes the moral sense. Shaftesbury discusses the sense of beauty in order to introduce his account of the moral sense, but his view is not at all what Hutcheson's was to be, namely, that there is a sufficient analogy between the sense of beauty and the moral sense to make the evident immediacy and necessity of the former a good argument for the immediacy and necessity of the latter; his view is rather that our sense of beauty is an instance of the very same sensitivity to the wonderful order of the universe that is also manifested by the moral sense. As Philocles observes, "beauty . . . and good with you, Theocles, I perceive, are still one and the same" (*Characteristics*, p. 320), or as Theocles says, with Shaftesbury's own italics, "with us, Philocles, it is better settled, since for our parts we have already decreed that *beauty and good are still the same*" (p. 327).

Shaftesbury's introduction of the criterion of disinterestedness, then, is not the beginning of an argument for the freedom of the imagination in aesthetic response from any form of external constraint, but rather the beginning of an elaborate argument for a disinterested pleasure in the order of the cosmos that is manifested in our feeling for both beauty and virtue. The key claims in this argument are, first, that what we love in all forms of beauty and virtue, free from the limits of personal interest, is order and proportion, but, second, that what we really admire in admiring order and proportion is not so much the manifestation of order and proportion in the object in which they are manifested itself, but rather the creative intelligence which is behind them, ultimately the divine intelligence which is behind all order and proportion, even when the immediate manifestation thereof might be produced by a human agent, for the latter is itself nothing but a product of the underlying divine intelligence. The first step of this argument is stated when Shaftesbury locates the object of our sense of the beauty of works of both nature and art in the order and proportion they manifest:

Nothing surely is more strongly imprinted on our minds or more closely interwoven with our souls than the idea or sense of order and proportion. Hence all the force of numbers and those powerful arts founded on their management and use! What a difference there is between harmony and discord, cadency and convulsion! What a difference between composed and orderly motion and that which is ungoverned and accidental, between the regular and uniform pile of some noble architect and a heap of sand or stones, between an organized body and a mist or cloud driven by the wind!

He makes it explicit that we have an immediate sense for such order, and that it is the same sense that is at work in our appreciation of art and of nature:

Now, as this difference is immediately perceived by a plain internal sensation, so there is withal in reason this account of it: that whatever things have order, the same have unity of design and concur in one, are parts constituent of one whole or are, in themselves, entire systems. Such is a tree with all its branches, an animal with all its members, an edifice with all its exterior and interior ornaments. What else is even a tune or symphony or any excellent piece of music than a certain system of proportioned sounds?

(*Characteristics*, pp. 272–4)

Having in this last passage identified order with design, Shaftesbury then goes on to argue that what we really love in loving order is the designer, the mind or intelligence which we take to be the source of such order:

[T]*he beautiful, the fair, the comely, were never in the matter but in the art and design, never in body itself but in the form or forming power.* Does not the beautiful form confess this and speak the beauty of the design whenever it strikes you? What is it but the design which strikes? What is it you admire but mind or the effect of mind? It is the mind alone which forms. All which is void of mind is horrid, and matter formless is deformity itself.

(*Characteristics*, p. 322)

Shaftesbury does not actually explain why if we are struck by the beauty of a design we must also or even ultimately exclusively love the designer, but perhaps this seems to him a natural and inevitable transition of the mind from effect to cause. In any case, the same assumption that our sense of beauty naturally follows the chain of effects and causes is at work in the concluding flourish of his argument, in which Theocles argues that there are actually "three degrees or orders of beauty": first, the "*dead forms*... which bear a fashion and are formed, whether by man or nature, but have no forming power, no action or intelligence"; second, "*the forms which form,* that is, which have intelligence, action and operation"; and finally, "*that third order of beauty, which forms not only such as we call mere forms but even the forms which form.*" Shaftesbury's justification for recognizing this third order of beauty is precisely his assumption that each of the causes of our feelings of beauty, whether proximate or ultimate, is itself an order of beauty, that is, an object of our admiration: "that which fashions even minds themselves contains in itself all the beauties fashioned in those minds and is consequently the principle, source and foundation of beauty." To all these assertions, Philocles, like one of Socrates's interlocutors, can only respond meekly "It seems so" (*Characteristics,* pp. 323–4).

Shaftesbury's conception of the disinterestedness of our sense of beauty is thus not yet a modern conception of the freedom of imagination in aesthetic response; far from it, it is but a step toward his deeply traditional, neo-Platonic identification of beauty and goodness (with truth thrown in for good measure) (*Characteristics,* p. 65). In the hands of Francis Hutcheson, however, Shaftesbury's idea is transformed into a modern conception of aesthetic response as consisting in an immediate gratification in perceptual form that is free of the influence of all other forms of thought and value. Hutcheson thus introduces a clearly negative conception of the freedom of the imagination in aesthetic response.

Hutcheson presents himself as a follower of Shaftesbury – indeed, in the first edition of his *Inquiry* the title page stated that in it "The Principles of the late Earl of Shaftsbury [*sic*] are explain'd and defended," although by the fourth edition this statement had disappeared. But his differences with Shaftesbury are as great as his similarities. Whereas Shaftesbury supposed the underlying identity of the beautiful and the good, Hutcheson treated them as fundamentally distinct, although sufficiently alike that the indisputable innateness of a natural sensibility for beauty could serve to introduce the more controversial idea of a moral sense not founded on rational calculations of self-interest:

> In the first Treatise, the Author perhaps in some Instances has gone too far, in supposing a greater Agreement of Mankind in their *Sense* of *Beauty,* than Experience will confirm; but all that he is sollicitous about is to show 'That there is some *Sense* of *Beauty natural* to Men; that we find as great an Agreement of Men in their Relishes of *Forms* which all agree to be *natural*; and that Pleasure or Pain, Delight or Aversion, are *naturally* join'd to their Perceptions.' If the Reader be convinc'd of this, it will be no difficult matter to apprehend another *superior Sense, natural* also to Men, determining them to be pleas'd with *Actions, Characters, Affections.* This is the *moral sense,* which makes the Subject of the second Treatise.
>
> (*Inquiry,* pp. xv–xvi)

The very fact that Hutcheson divides his work into two separate treatises, the first "Concerning BEAUTY, ORDER, HARMONY, DESIGN" and the second "Concerning MORAL GOOD and EVIL" (*Inquiry*, p. i), already argues for a difference between his view and that of Shaftesbury: the division of the unitary subject of the beautiful and the good into two separate treatises would never have occurred to the earlier writer.

Indeed, Hutcheson proceeds to demonstrate that our response to beauty should be conceived of as a sense in a way that Shaftesbury could not have, by inferring that this response can only be a sense precisely because of its distinction from any form of either cognition or volition. First, he argues that aesthetic response is not a form of cognition: "This superior Power of Perception is justly called *a Sense*, because of its Affinity to the other Senses in this, that the Pleasure is different from any *Knowledge* of Principles, Proportions, Causes, or of the Usefulness of the Object; we are struck at the first with the beauty; nor does the most accurate *Knowledge* increase this Pleasure of Beauty" (*Inquiry*, pp. 11–12). Then, in a passage that has already been partially quoted, Hutcheson distinguishes the response to beauty from any form of desire that necessarily determines the will to action:

> And farther, the Ideas of Beauty and Harmony, like other sensible Ideas, are *necessarily* pleasant to us, as well as immediately so; neither can any Resolution of our own, nor any *Prospect* of Advantage or Disadvantage, vary the Beauty or Deformity of an Object: For as in the external Sensations, no View of *Interest* will make an object grateful, nor View of *Detriment* distinct from immediate *Pain* in the Perception, make it disagreeable to the Sense; so propose the whole World as a *Reward*, or threaten the greatest Evil, to make us approve a deform'd Object, or disapprove a beautiful one; Dissumulation may be procur'd by Rewards or Thretnings, or we may in external Conduct abstain from any *Pursuit* of the Beautiful, and pursue the Deform'd; but our *Sentiments* of the Forms, and our *Perceptions*, would continue invariably the same.
>
> (*Inquiry*, pp. 11–12)

Now Hutcheson does not mean by this that aesthetic responses are necessarily without any effect on the will. In fact, he argues much later that since it takes so little to satisfy our basic "external" or material needs, such as our needs for food and shelter, it is actually desires for the sorts of pleasure that can be afforded by such things as "*Architecture, Musick, Gardening, Painting, Dress, Equipage, Furniture*, of which we cannot have the full Enjoyment without *Property*," that "are the *ultimate Motives* of our pursuing the greater Degrees of *Wealth*" (*Inquiry*, pp. 94–5). Rather, his starting point is simply the idea that our pleasure in beautiful things does not have a necessary and immediate effect on the will, since any effect it might have can be stayed by other considerations of the advantages or detriments of action; and thus the response to beauty cannot be identified with volition any more than it can be identified with cognition, whether of the choiceworthiness of its object or of any other property of it. Hutcheson then infers that our response to beauty should be conceived of as a sense of beauty by means of elimination: once cognition and volition have been excluded, sense is the only locus left for this response. Of course, the sense of beauty is not restricted to any one of the five senses ordinarily recognized, nor does it have any obvious organ, so for these reasons Hutcheson classifies it as an internal rather than external sense. It is not, to be sure, the only member of that class: the moral sense will also be characterized as an internal rather than external sense.

Hutcheson's basic characterization of aesthetic response is thus a negative one: it is classified as a sense on the basis of what it is not. Hutcheson then argues that there are three main kinds of objects for this sense: uniformity amidst variety in perceptual forms, which is the source of "Original or Absolute Beauty" (*Inquiry*, p. 16); uniformity amidst variety in conceptual contents, which is the source of the "Beauty of Theorems" (p. 30); and "Relative or Comparative Beauty," which is "that which is apprehended in any *Object*, commonly considered as an *Imitation* of some Original," and our pleasure in this beauty too "is founded on a *Conformity* or a kind of *Unity* between the Original and the Copy" (p. 39). However, Hutcheson does not conceive of these three classes of the objects of beauty as providing a more positive characterization of the sense or feeling of beauty itself; rather, he conceives of them as three different causes of the idea of beauty, identified by empirical and inductive arguments – throughout this part of his work, he explicitly appeals to example to establish his theses (pp. 17, 19, 73). Hutcheson's view is thus that we can say something specific about the objects of the sense of beauty, but the sense or feeling itself remains characterized essentially by what it is not – it is not a form of cognition or volition.

Thus, Hutcheson emphasizes the non-cognitive character of the sense of beauty even as he makes room for the beauty of theorems, stressing that our pleasure in this form of beauty has nothing to do with the true contents of the propositions which make up theorems, but simply "with the most exact Agreement [of] an infinite Multitude of particular Truths" in a theorem (*Inquiry*, p. 30). He also makes clear his departure from the neo-Platonism of Shaftesbury in his concluding section "Of the *Importance* of the *internal Senses* in Life, and the *final Causes* of them" (p. 93). Hutcheson was a pious Christian, most probably more pious than Shaftesbury, but his piety did not take the form of the latter's argument that our feeling of beauty is a direct perception of the overarching order of the universe established by its intelligent author. Instead, Hutcheson argues that it is precisely the distinction between the sense of beauty on the one hand and cognition and volition on the other that grounds a proof of God's benevolence: God did not have to constitute us so as to take an immediate pleasure in uniformity amidst variety, which also turns out to be so important for our effective thought and action, so the very fact that he did so is another proof of the goodness of God:

> And hence we see 'how suitable it is to the *sagacious Bounty* which we suppose in the DEITY, to constitute our *internal Senses* in the manner in which they are; by which Pleasure is join'd to the Contemplation of *those Objects* which a finite *Mind* can best imprint and retain the Ideas of with the least Distraction to *those Actions* which are most efficacious, and fruitful in useful Effects; and to *those Theorems* which most inlarge our *Minds*.'
>
> (*Inquiry*, p. 101)

Hutcheson is by no means the secular thinker that Hume would be even a few years later. Nevertheless, the core of his aesthetic theory is secular and modern: the object of aesthetic response is not characterized in theological terms, although the existence of our capacity for aesthetic response can be given a theological explanation.

I have emphasized that Hutcheson characterizes aesthetic response in negative terms, by its contrast with cognition and volition. Does this mean that he has a negative conception of the freedom of the imagination in aesthetic response? This might seem a stretch, for Hutcheson does not make much of the concept of imagination at all. But he does in fact consider two forms of mental activity that Kant would later group together under the rubric of imagination, namely, the sensory perception of present objects and the representation of absent objects through imitations of them. And in each case, his characterization of the basis of our pleasure in such objects is, to say the least, minimalist, and might well be taken to imply that a good part of our enjoyment lies in the freedom of our mental activity from external constraints. In the case of original beauty, we enjoy uniformity amidst variety in perceptual form unhampered by any other cognitive or practical concern. In the case of comparative beauty, the beauty of imitations, we enjoy the relation of conformity or correspondence between imitation and original, but do so quite independently of any other content or significance to what is imitated. Indeed, Hutcheson stresses this point in explaining how we can enjoy a beautiful representation of an original that is itself ugly: "it is by Resemblance that the *Similitudes, Metaphors* and *Allegorys* are made *beautiful* whether either the Subject or the Thing compar'd to it have *Beauty* or not" (*Inquiry*, p. 41). In enjoying resemblance, the imagination enjoys something of significance to itself alone, independent of any other concern with the content or value of what is represented. In this sense, I think, it is fair to see Hutcheson as introducing a negative conception of the freedom of the imagination.

II. Du Bos

Jean-Baptiste Du Bos (1670–1742), diplomat and historian as well as critic and aesthetician, produced one of the most widely circulated aesthetic treatises of the eighteenth century: his *Critical Reflections on Poetry, Painting and Music* went through five French editions and was widely circulated in Britain long before Thomas Nugent's 1748 translation. It may seem as if Du Bos employs a merely negative conception of aesthetic experience as any form of escape from *ennui*, whether by watching gladiatorial combat in the coliseum or tragedy in the theater. But in fact he introduces a positive conception of the imagination as a powerful capacity to stir genuine emotions by means of representations or, as he calls them, imitations, rather than by beliefs held to be true. Du Bos's conception of aesthetic response is thus diametrically opposed to Hutcheson's: instead of conceiving of our pleasure in beauty as an autonomous or even anomalous response to perceptual form, unrelated to the rest of our cognitive and practical concerns, he sees the imagination and its paradigmatic objects, artistic imitations, as distinctive means for engaging the same emotions that are relevant throughout the rest of our activities and conduct, although only too rarely aroused in quotidian life, and aroused there at too great a cost. Even in cases that would seem good candidates for Hutcheson's formalist treatment, such as beautiful representations of indifferent or ugly objects, Du Bos's strategy is to find a genuine emotion that can be aroused by the engagement of the imagination. Du Bos's positive conception of the power of the imagination is an important precursor of later romanticism in spite of the antiquarian style and references of his writing.

Du Bos begins his work with the claims that boredom or mental inactivity is one of the most unpleasant of human conditions, and that the arousal of the passions is one of the most effective means to dispel boredom. First, he posits that

The soul hath its wants no less than the body; and one of the greatest wants of man is to have his mind incessantly occupied. The heaviness which quickly attends the inactivity of the mind, is a situation so very disagreeable to man, that he frequently chuses to expose himself to the most painful exercises, rather than be troubled with it.

(*Reflections*, I, p. 5)

Then he states that

In fact, the hurry and agitation, in which our passions keep us, even in solitude, is of so brisk a nature, that any other situation is languid and heavy, when compared to this motion. Thus we are led by instinct, in pursuit of objects capable of exciting our passions, notwithstanding those objects make impressions on us, which are frequently attended by nights and days of pain and calamity; but man in general would be exposed to greater misery, were he exempt from passions, than the very passions themselves can make him suffer.

(*Reflections*, I, p. 9)

Thus, all sorts of "frightful spectacles," from public executions and gladiatorial combats to bull-fights, as well as less bloody diversions such as gambling, will draw great crowds eager to escape boredom and lassitude (*Reflections*, I, pp. 10, 18–19). But such stimulations come at a high cost in suffering, if not directly to ourselves, then to others to whom we can be linked by the natural mechanism of sympathy,[10] and in any case such violent stimulation of our passions is rarely available in ordinary life. So humans have hit upon the use of imitations in art to engage the passions and escape *ennui* without the costs that would otherwise be paid:

Since the most pleasing sensations that our real passions can afford us, are balanced by so many unhappy hours that succeed our enjoyments, would it not be a noble attempt of art to endeavour to separate the dismal consequences of our passions from the bewitching pleasure we receive in indulging them? Is it not in the power of art to create, as it were, beings of a new nature? Might not art contrive to produce objects that would excite artificial passions, sufficient to occupy us while we are actually affected by them, and incapable of giving us afterwards any real pain or affliction?

(*Reflections*, I, p. 21)

[10] See Du Bos, *Reflections*, Vol. I, p. 32. Some time ago, Peter Jones argued for the influence of Du Bos on Hume's conception of criticism and the standard of taste; I think he could also have argued for the influence of Du Bos on the more general concept of sympathy in Hume's moral psychology. See Peter Jones *Hume's Sentiments* (Edinburgh: Edinburgh University Press, 1982), Chapter 3, "Scepticism in Criticism," pp. 93–106.

But one must be clear that by calling the passions aroused by works of artistic imitation "artificial" rather than "real," Du Bos by no means intends to dissociate these emotions from those induced by executions, bull-fights, gambling or any of the more customary events of daily life, our successes and failures in love, work, and everything else, or to imply that works of art arouse a distinct kind of feeling – such as a sentiment of beauty – that is unrelated to our other passions. Rather, his meaning is perhaps more clearly expressed in the description of the contents of the chapter that opens with the paragraph just cited: "The principle merit of poems and pictures consists in the imitation of such objects as would have excited real passions. The passions which those imitations give rise to, are only superficial." That is, the impression made by an artistic imitation is of an "inferior force" to that which would be made by the real existence of the object or events depicted,[11] it does not have the same duration as the latter, and it is "quickly therefore effaced, without leaving any permanent vestiges, such as would have been left by the impression of the object itself, which the painter or poet hath imitated" (*Reflections*, I, p. 23) – whether those permanent vestiges be simply unpleasant memories of excessive emotion, or other kinds of damage that might be suffered in the pursuit of passion, such as physical injury or damage to one's fortune at the gaming-table. "The pleasure we feel in contemplating the imitations made by painters and poets, of objects which would have raised in us passions attended with real pain, is a pleasure free from all impurity of mixture. It is never attended with those disagreeable consequences, which arise from the serious emotions caused by the object itself" (p. 24). Yet in spite of these qualifications, which make the emotions aroused by art both more accessible and more tolerable than those aroused by exceptional occurrences in real life, it is crucial to Du Bos's whole argument that these emotions be instances of the real thing, genuine passions of love and hate, fear and joy, which may be experienced without their usual costs. Otherwise, Du Bos has no account of how art relieves the tedium of everyday life.

This is evident much later in Du Bos's argument, when he rejects the theory that the effect of the theater depends upon illusion, that is, being induced by the presentation of the play to believe to be true what is actually false. Du Bos claims that everything that goes on in the theater "shews itself there in the nature of a copy . . . we have a thousand things

[11] Du Bos, *Reflections*, Vol. I, p. 22. Here too there seems to be another anticipation of one of Hume's most central ideas.

continually before our eyes, which remind us constantly of our real circumstances with respect to place and condition," so that not even the most inexperienced theater-goer is deluded into believing that something is really happening which is not (*Reflections*, I, p. 350). Nevertheless, the theatergoer is "touched in almost as lively a manner as he would have been, had he really seen Roderigue at the feet of his mistress after he had killed her father" (p. 351). The pleasure of going to the theater depends precisely upon the fact that there we can experience the very same sorts of emotions we would experience if our own lives were not so humdrum, although without the great costs that we would then have to pay. And this can only happen if the imagination is a powerful alternative to cognition, but one which engages the very same emotions that would be engaged by true belief and lead to real action, not some unrelated sentiment such as a sense of the beauty of uniformity amidst variety.[12] It is in this sense that I claim that Du Bos introduces a positive conception of the imagination and its freedom: on his view, our capacity to respond to imitations – what I am perhaps slightly anachronistically referring to as the imagination – is free from the constraints of ordinary cognition and action but has a power of its own to engage our most fundamental emotions.

Du Bos draws a variety of critical conclusions from his basic conception of the function of art. Precisely because works of art engage our emotions through the imagination, but do so less forcefully than real events would, the artist must seek to make his work as engaging as possible within its natural limits. This is ordinarily done by the choice of maximally engaging subject matter or material for imitation. Thus, masters like Poussin and Rubens "are not satisfied with giving a place in their landskips to the picture of a man going along the high road, or of a woman carrying fruit to market; they commonly present us with figures that think, in order to make us think; they paint men hurried with passions, to the end that ours may be also raised" (*Reflections*, I, p. 45). The strength of the effect of a work of art does not depend upon formal properties, such as the degree

[12] Du Bos's theory must thus be distinguished from what might seem to be its current counterpart, Kendall Walton's theory of mimesis as make-believe. Walton's theory is that we respond to works of art by engaging in games of make-belief, using the artworks as props, and thereby experience *analogues* of ordinary emotions, or "fictionally" rather than really experience emotions; see Walton, *Mimesis as Make-Believe* (Cambridge, Mass.: Harvard University Press, 1990), e.g., p. 271. Du Bos's theory is that we really experience the same emotions in observing a work of art that we would in observing or undergoing the events depicted, though in a more tolerable and less costly form, and that only the fact that we do experience such real emotions in art explains our interest in it.

of conformity between imitation and what is imitated; it depends upon the emotional force of what is imitated, upon the strength of its effect on the imagination. And even in a case where it might seem as if a formal relation of some sort must be the object of a special sense of beauty, such as in a painting of some emotionally indifferent subject, Du Bos rejects that approach: unlike Hutcheson, he does not explain our admiration of still-life by appeal to the conformity of representation and object, but rather by appeal to the skill of the artist that is manifested in such an exercise: "when we contemplate curiously any pictures of this kind, our principal attention is not fixt on the object imitated, but upon the art of the imitator" (*Reflections*, I, p. 57). This is because the exercise of human skill or artistry is something that can engage our emotions in the way that neither dead hares and copper pots nor a formal relation of resemblance between such things and images of them can.

Since the function of art is to engage our emotions by the presentation of imitations, the different possibilities for imitation that different media and genres within them afford dictate what sorts of subjects and means of representing them will best attain that end. This is the subject to which Du Bos devotes the greatest part of his book, and here too his work looks toward the future. Much of the book is devoted to a contrast between the representational potentials of painting and poetry and the emotional effects of these differences, the underlying principle of which is that "The subject of imitation ought not only be interesting of its own nature, but moreover should be adapted to painting, if intended for the pencil; and proper for poetry, if designed for verse" (*Reflections*, I, p. 69). Du Bos observes that "A poet can tell us several things, which a painter would find impossible to exhibit," because the latter can only present those emotions which are "particularly marked in our attitude, or precisely characterised in our countenance"; painting must therefore aim to engage just those sorts of emotions in the observer, while poetry can aim to arouse others. Further, anticipating at least part of the famous argument of Lessing's *Laocoön* by nearly half a century, Du Bos observes that because the poet can depict the evolution of an action over a period of time or a succession of actions, "he may use several strokes to express the passion and sentiment of one of his personages," and thereby to engage ours (p. 75), whereas the medium of the painter confines him to the representation of a single moment of action, and therefore he "can only make use of a single touch in the expressing of a passion on each feature of the countenance, where he intends to make this passion appear," and likewise must engage the passion of the observer by means of this single touch (p. 76).

Du Bos even goes so far as to extend his theory of the engagement of the passions by means of imitation to music (*Reflections*, I, ch. XLV, pp. 360–75). He does not reject purely instrumental music in favor of vocal music on the ground that only the latter but not the former can represent human passions; instead, he argues that non-verbal music or the non-verbal aspects of music imitate the inarticulate expressions of human emotion rather than the verbal expressions of human emotion; but in both cases, whether it imitates natural signs or artificial signs, music works by engaging the imagination and arousing the represented passions in its audience.

The limits of this theory may become obvious in its application to music, which cries out for a synthesis of Hutcheson's theory of a special sense of pleasure triggered by formal relationships with Du Bos's theory of the pleasure in the arousal of our passions. A sophisticated version of such a synthesis of that sort would have to wait for Kant's work at the end of the century. But at least an adumbration of such a more complicated theory had already been suggested several years before the publication of Du Bos's treatise by Joseph Addison's popular essays on the multiple "Pleasures of the Imagination" at the very start of modern aesthetics.

III. Addison

Addison explicitly employs the concept of imagination and argues that the exercise of the imagination affords us multiple possibilities for pleasure. The different kinds of pleasure afforded to us by the imagination include both those that are unique and independent from the rest of our cognitive and affective economy and those that are intimately connected with our deepest interests in knowledge and action. Further, the pleasures of the imagination include both those that depend chiefly upon freedom from constraint from anything outside the imagination and those that are produced by images of our freedom in areas outside of the imagination itself, presumably our freedom of action in moral and political arenas. We may consider these as freedoms of the imagination in negative and positive senses. In his complex conception of the pleasures of the imagination, Addison thus puts together negative and positive conceptions of the freedom of the imagination in a way that will not be done within more professional philosophy until Kant's synthesis at the end of the century.

Early in the series of eleven papers "On the Pleasures of the Imagination" that Addison published in the *Spectator* from Saturday, June 21, to Thursday, July 3, 1712, he observes, in words very similar to those published by Shaftesbury a year earlier, that the imagination can afford us pleasure independent of the possession and therefore the use of an object:

A man of a polite imagination is led into a great many pleasures that the vulgar are not capable of receiving. He can converse with a picture, and find an agreeable companion in a statue. He meets with a secret refreshment in a description, and often feels a greater satisfaction in the prospect of fields and meadows, than another does in the possession. It gives him, indeed, a kind of property in every thing he sees, and makes the most rude uncultivated parts of nature administer to his pleasures . . .

(*Spectator* 411, 6:123–4)

Addison's claim that a view of a landscape can give a properly sensitive person a pleasure independent of and greater than any to be derived from the possession of it can be counted as another early appeal to the idea of disinterestedness, but, as is also the case with Shaftesbury, the kind of disinterestedness he has in mind is not supposed to entail the independence of the pleasures of the imagination from all other sources of pleasure in our lives. If anything, what Addison has in mind is that the imagination is a power that can amplify other sources of pleasure in our lives, affording us pleasure without the costs of possession and other costs of ordinary experience. To this extent, his view is also similar to that of Du Bos.

Addison clearly takes himself to be breaking new ground in his account of the imagination, and thus pauses "to fix and determine the notion" of the fancy and imagination before setting out his theory. By pleasures of the imagination, he states, he means "only such pleasures as arise originally from sight," and these are of two kinds: "primary pleasures of the imagination, which entirely proceed from such objects as are before our eyes"; and "secondary pleasures of the imagination, which flow from the ideas of visible objects, when the objects are not actually before the eyes, but are called up into our memories, or formed into agreeable visions of things that are either absent or fictitious" (*Spectator* 411, 6:122–3). The pleasures of the imagination are thus those that we take in the visual appearance of things and in ideas of visual appearances conveyed by non-visual media. In the account of the pleasures afforded to us by various arts that Addison goes on to provide, he includes primarily visual media such as painting, sculpture, architecture, and landscape gardening, and all forms of literature, which he conceives of as employing verbal means to call up visual imagery. He does not include music in his account of the arts, although presumably he could have given an associationist account of music, as Du Bos was to do a few years later.

Before discussing the pleasures afforded by the different arts, Addison divides the primary pleasures of the imagination into three fundamental kinds – a division that would remain influential for decades to come. The three main primary pleasures of the imagination are the pleasures in grandeur, novelty, and beauty. I will discuss these in the opposite order from that in which they are discussed by Addison. Pleasure in beauty can come first, because in at least one of its forms, it seems to be the most autonomous of the pleasures of the imagination, that is, that form which is least connected to any of our other cognitive or conative interests. This is the beauty "which immediately diffuses a secret satisfaction and complacency through the imagination, and gives a finishing to any thing that is great or uncommon . . . modifications of matter, which the mind, without any previous consideration, pronounces, at first sight, beautiful . . . " (*Spectator* 412, 6:129). Addison illustrates this sort of beauty with the example of a male bird who may be "determined in his courtship by the single grain or tincture of a feather," which might seem to suggest that the origin of pleasure in this sort of beauty lies in the gratification of sexual desire – a common enough theory of beauty, to be sure.[13] But he does not mean to derive the sense of beauty from the sexual drive. Rather, his view is that in its most fundamental form, our pleasure in beauty is simply an autonomous response to properties discerned by vision, no doubt in principle explicable by something in our individual or generic physiology, which is independent of any other drive or interest that we might have, although it can affect the direction of our choice and action due to other drives and interests. On this account, the male bird's interest in finding a female partner would not be due to the phenomenon of beauty, although his choice of a particular partner might be affected by his individual or avian conception of beauty.

Addison recognizes a "second kind of beauty that we find in the several products of art and nature," which "consists either in the gayety or variety of colours, in the symmetry and proportion of parts, in the arrangement and disposition of bodies, or in a just mixture and concurrence of all together." Without any argument, Addison claims that this sort of beauty "does not work in the imagination with that warmth and violence as the beauty that appears in our proper species," but he goes on to suggest

[13] See e.g., Edmund Burke, *A Philosophical Enquiry into the Origin of our Ideas of the Sublime and the Beautiful*, second edition (London, 1759), Part III, sections xiii–xv.

that the paradigmatic cases of beauty in both nature and art are of this form, and also, in passing, to illustrate his associationist conception of the beauty of verbal rather than visual media:

> We nowhere meet with a more glorious or pleasing show in nature, than what appears in the heavens at the rising or the setting of the sun, which is wholly made up of those different stains of light that show themselves in clouds of a different situation. For this reason we find the poets, who are always addressing themselves to the imagination, borrowing more of their epithets from colours than from any other topic.
>
> (*Spectator* 412, 6:130)

On Addison's theory of the primarily visual nature of beauty, all of the poets' "epithets" must ultimately be "borrowed." The main point to note here, however, is that on Addison's account this kind of beauty, which may be secondary in some order of explanation but seems primary at least in its importance in the arts, is, like Hutcheson's account of beauty, due to uniformity amidst variety, similar to but not dependent on a principle of cognition. The perception of beauty is not a form of cognition, although what it responds to, symmetry and proportion, arrangement and disposition, may also be important in cognition. Whether in its simpler or more complex form, the perception of beauty is an autonomous power of the imagination

The next pleasure of the imagination that Addison recognizes is the pleasure in novelty. Here he says that "Every thing that is new or uncommon raises a pleasure in the imagination, because it fills the soul with an agreeable surprise, gratifies its curiosity, and gives it an idea of which before it was not possessed" (*Spectator* 412, 6:127). These could seem like positive characterizations, but much of what Addison goes on to say suggests a negative account of our pleasure in novelty, an account which, like that of Du Bos, stresses our need for relief from boredom:

> We are, indeed, so often conversant with one set of objects, and tired out with so many repeated shows of the same things, that whatever is new or uncommon contributes a little to vary human life, and to divert our minds, for a while, with the strangeness of its appearances. It serves us for a kind of refreshment, and takes off from that satiety we are apt to complain of, in our usual and ordinary entertainments.
>
> (*Spectator* 412, 6:127–8)

The sources of our boredom or exhaustion may come from elsewhere in our lives – "our usual and ordinary entertainments" may include a great deal – but works of the imagination have a distinctive power to relieve us from those ills that arise elsewhere, a power that is not dependent upon other interests but is unique to the imagination. But it does not seem to matter much for this purpose what the form and content of the works of the imagination are, as long as they are new. This power of the imagination works by contrast, and seems neither to require nor generate any unique or characteristic sort of form or content – this is what I mean by calling this a negative conception of the imagination or its freedom. It is a conception of the imagination simply as free from the constraints of our usual and ordinary entertainments, or of the imagination as our ability to free ourselves from those entertainments.

But Addison also recognizes a third primary pleasure of the imagination, its pleasure in greatness or grandeur. This is, of course, what would become one of the twin pillars of almost all later eighteenth-century theories under the name of the sublime. Addison really has two accounts of our pleasure in the great or sublime. In his first treatment of it, he names the usual suspects – "prospects of an open champaign country, a vast uncultivated desert, of huge heaps of mountains, high rocks and precipices, or a wide expanse of waters" – and explains our pleasure in such vistas by saying that "We are flung into a pleasing astonishment at such unbounded views" because "The mind of man naturally hates everything that looks like a restraint upon it, and is apt to fancy itself under a sort of confinement, when the sight is pent up in a narrow compass" (*Spectator* 412, 6:126–7). This could look, again, like a negative account of the freedom of the imagination: we hate constraint as much as we hate boredom (perhaps boredom is just constraint by the familiar), so we love anything that liberates us from constraint. But as Addison continues, his account takes a subtle turn: he says that

> a spacious horizon is an image of liberty, where the eye has room to range abroad, to expatiate at large on the immensity of its views, and to lose itself amidst the variety of objects that offer themselves to its observation. Such wide and undetermined prospects are as pleasing to the fancy, as the speculations of eternity or infinitude are to the understanding.
>
> (*Spectator* 412, 6:127)

Addison compares the imagination in the experience of the sublime to a kind of understanding or cognition, without reducing the former to the latter. So what he seems to have in mind is that we enjoy a certain sensuous – or we might say symbolic – representation of an idea that is important to us, the idea of freedom itself. Here the imagination is not just a negative capacity to free ourselves from constraint, but a positive capacity to represent the fact or possibility of our freedom itself. In the experience of grandeur or the sublime, the imagination and its works finally acquire a special content of their own.

Addison at least tacitly recognizes a second form of pleasure in greatness ten essays later, when he writes that

> Nothing is more pleasant to the fancy than to enlarge itself by degrees, in its contemplation of the various proportions which its several objects bear to each other, when it compares the body of man to the bulk of the whole earth, the earth to the circle it describes around the sun, that circle to the sphere of the fixed stars,

and so on (*Spectator* 420, 6:171). Now as he continues in this vein, Addison begins to speak of "the proper limits, as well as the defectiveness of the imagination," and he notes that "The understanding, indeed, opens an infinite space on every side us," although "the imagination, after a few faint efforts, is immediately at a stand"; "our reason can pursue a particle of matter through an infinite variety of divisions; but the fancy soon looses sight of it" (*Spectator* 6:172). Yet he does not say that the imagination is frustrated by its limits in comparison to the understanding or reason, or that we are pained rather than pleased by this discovery of its limits. Instead, he continues to treat the fancy of immensity as the source of a pleasure of the imagination. Perhaps his idea here is that this exercise of the imagination is pleasing to us precisely because it launches us upon a path that needs to be completed by understanding or reason, but that we might not start upon at all were it not for the power of the imagination. In this case, then, the imagination does not please us entirely independently of our other cognitive faculties, but it plays a unique role in engaging those other capacities.

In both of these forms of the pleasure of the imagination in greatness, that where it enjoys an image of freedom and that where it starts us on the path to speculation about infinitude – which it is hard to read except as an anticipation of Kant's later distinction between the dynamical and mathematical sublime – Addison pictures the imagination as working in conjunction with rather than in complete independence from our other faculties, but as playing a distinctive role in such cooperations, and as it were doubling our pleasure by means of such cooperations. This is also true in his account of the secondary pleasures of the imagination. "This secondary pleasure of the imagination proceeds from that action of the mind which compares the ideas arising from the original objects with the ideas we receive from the statue, picture, description, or sound, that represents them." Again, Addison does not reduce this pleasure in representation or imitation to a straightforward satisfaction in cognition, but regards it as an independent effect of the autonomous imagination: "It is impossible for us to give the necessary reason why this operation of the mind is attended with so much pleasure . . . but we find a great variety of entertainments derived from this single principle" (*Spectator* 416, 6:151). At the same time, Addison clearly envisages this principle of pleasure as working in tandem with the primary pleasures of the imagination to produce complex responses to objects and intensified pleasure in them, responses in which figure both our primary pleasures in what is depicted or imagined as well as our secondary pleasure in its depiction or image. Thus, in comparing Homer, Virgil, and Ovid, he states that "The first strikes the imagination wonderfully with what is great, the second with what is beautiful, and the last with what is strange" (*Spectator* 417, 6:156–7): each combines the secondary pleasure of the imagination generated by his skill at depiction with a different primary pleasure in what is depicted.

The same combinatory principle is also at work in Addison's treatment of the relations between nature and art. Addison describes at least one dimension in which each of these affords greater pleasure than the other. Thus,

> If we consider works of nature and art as they are qualified to entertain the imagination, we shall find the last very defective, in comparison with the former; for though they may sometimes appear as beautiful or strange, they can have nothing in them of that vastness or immensity which afford so great an entertainment to the mind of the beholder. The one may be as polite and delicate as the other, but can never show herself so august and magnificent in the design. There is something more bold and masterly in the rough, careless strokes of nature, than in the nice touches and embellishments of art.

This might seem to say just that nature is more sublime than art, but as Addison continues, it appears that his point is rather that the immensity and variety of nature means that it exceeds art as a source for all the primary pleasures of the imagination:

> The beauties of the most stately garden or palace lie in a narrow compass, the imagination immediately runs them over, and requires something else to gratify her; but in the wide fields of nature, the sight wanders up and down without confinement, and is fed with an infinite variety of images, without any certain stint or number.
>
> (*Spectator* 414, 6:138–9)

However, because of the imagination's ability to combine images in ways never found in nature, at least certain kinds of art, the fantastic, or what Addison cites John Dryden as calling the "fairy way of writing" (*Spectator* 419, 6:165), afford possibilities of pleasure not found in nature:

> Thus we see how many ways poetry addresses itself to the imagination, for it has not only the whole circle of nature for its province, but makes new worlds of its own, shows us persons who are not to be found in being, and represents even the faculties of the soul, with her several virtues and vices, in a sensible shape and character.
>
> (*Spectator* 419, 6:168)

Thus art outstrips nature, at least in its potential for the pleasure of the imagination in novelty. Finally, however, Addison observes that there is the greatest potential for pleasure when the special strengths of both nature and art are fully exploited:

> But though there are several of those wild scenes that are more delightful than any artificial shows, yet we find the works of nature still more pleasant, the more they resemble those of art; for, in this case, our pleasure rises from a double principle; from the agreeableness of the objects to the eye, and from their similitude to other objects. We are pleased as well with comparing their beauties, as with surveying them, and can represent them to our minds, either as copies or originals.
>
> (*Spectator* 414, 6:139–40)

In observing nature as well as in creating and responding to art, the primary and secondary pleasures of the imagination can be combined.

What more professional philosophers of the same and succeeding decades held apart, Addison the popular essayist put together. He offered a complex picture of the imagination, as a capacity of mind to take pleasure in both the matter and form of objects directly present to the senses and in both the form and content of images of objects not immediately present. The imagination is also characterized as enjoying freedom from constraint whether by nature outside us or other interests within us, but at the same time as a positive power to create and enjoy images of our own liberty. It would take most of the rest of the eighteenth century before a professional philosopher, namely Kant, could achieve a synthesis as complex as that which Addison here achieved so gracefully.

IV. Baumgarten

What Kant would need to reconstruct in his more technical terms the synthesis that Addison had achieved in his popular essays eighty years earlier would be an account of the imagination that allows it to take on symbolic and ideational content while preserving the freedom of its play with the understanding, its defining avoidance of constraint by determinate concepts. The idea that Kant would need to do this was supplied by Alexander Gottlieb Baumgarten (1714–62), who in his *Philosophical Meditations* of 1735, *Metaphysics* of 1739, and *Aesthetics* of 1750 did not merely coin the term "aesthetics," but also provided a conception of the imagination as a cognitive capacity, but one whose products are marked by the richness and density of their contents rather than by logical criteria such as economy and simplicity. It is tempting to use Kant's later language to characterize Baumgarten's distinction between logical and aesthetic representation, contrasting them as determinate and indeterminate, but one has to be careful here: Baumgarten's idea is actually that in order to achieve the determinacy in conception that is the ultimate desideratum of logical thought, concepts have to be kept spare and general, which means that they will apply to indeterminately many individuals; while to achieve the representation of a determinate individual that is the aim of aesthetic thought, the replete determinacy of the object can only be captured by an image that is rich, dense, and, in a sense, indeterminate. This is the origin of Kant's notion of an aesthetic idea, that is, a product of the imagination which has genuine cognitive content, paradigmatically representing an idea of reason otherwise incapable of direct sensory presentation, but which is at the same time so rich and indeterminate that it preserves our sense of the freedom of the imagination from constraint by the understanding.

Baumgarten initially introduces his idea in characterizing a poem as a "sensorily perfect form of discourse."[14] Sensory perfection consists in representing the maximal number of attributes of an object that is compatible with clearly representing that object as distinct from others at all. Thus, "The more the things are determined, the more do the representations of them comprehend; the more that is heaped up in a confused representation, the more is it extensively clear, and the more poetic is it. Thus it is *poetic to determine as much as possible about the things that are to be represented in a poem*" (*Meditations*, §xviii). But achieving a maximally determinate or concrete representation of things is not, contrary to what

[14] Baumgarten, *Meditations*, §vii. Baumgarten's term *sensitiva*, translated into German as *sinnlich*, could easily be translated as "sensitive" or "sensitively." But since in contemporary English that term might connote a special degree of refinement in discernment, I have instead adopted the translation "sensory" or "sensorily," which does not have that connotation.

it might seem, a purely cognitive aim. Rather, Baumgarten's view is that it is the ultimate aim of poetry to arouse affects – here he stands in the tradition of Du Bos – while affects are more richly aroused by richer representations of affecting things. Thus he writes that "Since affects are notable degrees of displeasure and pleasure, their sensations are those that confusedly represent something as good and bad; thus they determine poetic representations; hence it is *poetic to arouse affects*" (§xxv). And then he draws the conclusion that "*Stronger sensations* are clearer, hence *more poetic* than those that are less clear and *powerless*. . . . Hence it is *more poetic to arouse stronger affects rather than less forceful ones*" (§xxvii). Baumgarten's idea is thus that poetry aims to stir the emotions, a conative rather than cognitive objective, but does so through a distinctive form of cognition, the rich, dense, and "confused" imagery of the imagination rather than the spare, general, and "distinct" concepts of science.

Four years after his dissertation on poetry, the twenty-five-year-old Baumgarten published the first edition of his *Metaphysics*, which Kant would still use as his classroom textbook half a century later. Most of this work, of course, does not concern the new discipline of aesthetics, but Baumgarten does touch upon his aesthetic theory in the chapter on psychology.[15] Here he generalizes what he had earlier said about poetry into a general theory of the perfection of sensory representation. He argues that there are two main kinds of representation, intellectual and sensory, and that the perfection or ultimate aim of representation, namely clarity, takes on a different form in each. He holds that the primary virtue of clear intellectual representations is the clarity of their component "marks" – characters or predicates – and that such clarity contributes to the "intensive" clarity of the representation, while the primary virtue of sensory representations is clarity through the number of marks, or "extensive" clarity. He then argues that extensive clarity produces liveliness: "The extensively more clear representation is lively." This is the special feature of aesthetic representations or works of the imagination: "The liveliness of representations and of speech is brilliance (splendor), its opposite is dryness (thinking and speaking in a hair-splitting manner). Both kinds of clarity signify comprehensibility. Hence comprehensibility is either lively or suitable for the understanding or both together" (*Metaphysica*, §531). This passage is interesting because it shows that Baumgarten, first, distinguished imagination and ordinary cognition

[15] This chapter would later be the basis for Kant's lectures on anthropology, so in fact the only place in his lectures where Kant dealt with aesthetic theory was in his lectures on anthropology. See Chapter 7.

within a generally cognitive framework; second, marked the exercise of imagination by its effect on the affects, thus breaking down any simplistic barrier between cognitive and conative analyses of aesthetic response; and, third, held that even within the response to a single work, multiple kinds of cognition, *a fortiori* both cognitive and conative effects, could be involved. Like the more popular writer Addison,[16] Baumgarten avoided a reductionist account of the pleasures of the imagination, and undoubtedly provided a model for Kant in this regard.

Finally, Baumgarten returned to aesthetics in the first volume of his *magnum opus* under that title, published in 1750.[17] I cannot describe here the ambitious plan for this work or the wide range of topics covered even in the fragment that was completed, but will confine my commentary to the key point that would later enable Kant to complete his aesthetic synthesis. Baumgarten sums up the conception of the density of the aesthetic object developed in his earlier works by stating that

> The perfection of every kind of cognition grows from the richness, the magnitude, the truth, the clarity and certainty, and the liveliness of cognition, insofar as these harmonize within a single representation and with each other, e.g., richness and magnitude with clarity, truth and clarity with certainty, all of the rest with liveliness . . . ; when all of these perfections of cognition appear together in sensory appearance, they yield universal beauty . . .
>
> (*Aesthetica*, §22)

Here Baumgarten does not use his earlier term "confused," with its potentially negative connotations; he simply stresses that when a representation accessible to the senses is sufficiently rich and complex while still being clearly apprehensible, we have the foundations for beauty.

In the *Aesthetica*, Baumgarten also stresses that there are three dimensions of complexity in a beautiful sensory representation – the three dimensions that were to found the division of the whole work into a "heuristic," a "methodology," and a "semiotic" (§13). According to Baumgarten, the "general beauty of sensory cognitions" consists, first, in "the harmony of the thoughts, insofar as we abstract from their order and

[16] Although an incurable academic, Baumgarten himself briefly tried his hand at what was intended to be a popular moral magazine along the lines of the *Spectator*, the *Philosophical Letters of Aletheophilus*. The only surprise is that with a title like that it lasted as long as twenty-six numbers in 1741!

[17] There were two volumes published, in 1750 and 1758. These two volumes were an incomplete presentation of the "Heuristic," which was itself to be only one of three parts of the intended work. The massive text that we have is thus only a fragment of what Baumgarten planned to write. Unfortunately, Baumgarten never had robust health, and died in 1762, at the age of forty-eight, leaving only the present fragment.

their means of expression, that is, the consensus of the thoughts among themselves into a unity that in appearance, the beauty of the things and thoughts . . . " (§18); second, "since no perfection is conceivable without order, in the harmony of the order and the sequence in which we consider the beautifully conceived of things, in the internal consensus of the order with itself and in its consensus with the things" (§19); and finally, "since the signified cannot be grasped without signs, in the consensus of the means of expression among themselves as well as with the order and with the things, insofar as they appear" (§20). In other words, the beauty of an aesthetic representation or work of the imagination lies in the richness of the objects represented, in both the syntax and the semantics of the representation, that is, the coherence of the complex representation both with itself and with the things represented, and with the richness of the other dimensions of the representation, such as its diction and style (*dictio et elocutio*) (§20). At this point, it cannot fail to escape one's notice that Baumgarten's aesthetics is based on and most clearly applicable to literary works, and that it is by no means obvious how well either purely visual media or other non-verbal arts such as music would fit his account. This might well be thought to be true of Kant's fully developed conception of fine art in the later sections of the "Critique of the Aesthetic Power of Judgment" as well.

Finally, Baumgarten makes explicit the fundamental implication of his account: "The beauty of sensitive cognition and the elegance of its objects are composite perfections" (*perfectiones compositae*) (*Aesthetica*, §24). Far from attempting to reduce beauty to a single dimension, whether perceptual form or significant content, Baumgarten insists that successful works of art – the elegant objects of perfected sensory cognition – are always complex, pleasing us by means of both their form, content, and material or means of expression. By this last category, Baumgarten clearly has in mind verbal means of expression, where style and diction can add to the interest and coherence of the thoughts expressed; but the category could also be taken to apply to many other media where the materials of the object can add to its other beauties, as does the choice of materials in architecture, the handling of paint in painting, or instrumentation in music.

V. A Glimpse Ahead: Kant

This is hardly the place for a detailed discussion of Kant's conceptions of aesthetic judgment and fine art, although this history of the first decades of modern aesthetics has obviously been written with an eye to Kant. But a closing comment on Kant is necessary, for I have stressed that writers like Hutcheson and Du Bos severally anticipated several of the ideas that Kant was to put together, and that writers like Addison and Baumgarten anticipated the complexity of Kant's synthesis of these ideas, all of which may seem surprising given the common caricature of Kant's purported reduction of aesthetic response, whether in the case of works of nature or works of art, to perceptual form apart from all content and significance. Of course, as caricatures usually do, this one has a basis in reality: there can be no denying that in his initial analysis of aesthetic response and judgment, that is, in the "Analytic of the Beautiful," Kant characterizes paradigmatic cases of pure aesthetic response and judgment as responses to and judgments of perceptual form alone. A "pure judgment of taste" is one "on which charm and emotion have no influence . . . which thus has for its determining ground merely the purposiveness of the form" (*CPJ*, §13, 5:223). Thus, "Flowers, free designs, lines aimlessly intertwined in each other under the name of foliage, signify nothing, do not dependent on any determinate concept, and yet please" (§4, 5:207); "designs *á la greque*, foliage for borders or on wallpaper, etc., signify nothing by themselves; they do not represent anything, no object under a determinate concept" (§16, 5:229); and, for example, "In painting and sculpture, indeed in all the pictorial arts, in architecture and horticulture insofar as they are fine arts, the *drawing* is what is essential, in which what constitutes the ground of all arrangements for taste is not what gratifies in sensation but merely what pleases through its form" (§14, 5:225). Yet as those who continue past the "Analytic of the Beautiful" cannot fail to discover, such comments may represent Kant's analysis of *pure* judgments of taste or their objects, "free beauties" (§16, 5:229), but they hardly represent his analysis of paradigmatic works of art and our response to them. On the contrary, in Kant's view works of art are multidimensional and our response to them is complex, much as Addison and Baumgarten had earlier argued.

As Kant states in concluding the "Analytic of the Beautiful," all aesthetic response is an expression of the freedom of the imagination: "It turns out that everything flows from the concept of taste as a faculty for judging an object in relation to the *free lawfulness* of the imagination" (*CPJ*, General Remark following §22, 5:240), that is, a sense that a manifold of representations presented by the imagination satisfies the understanding's general interest in coherence or lawfulness but without any constraint by a determinate concept of the understanding. But when Kant turns to his explicit discussion of the fine arts – buried in the sections following the "Analytic of the Sublime" and the "Deduction of Pure Aesthetic Judgments" without the benefit of a heading of its own – it becomes clear that the free play or "free lawfulness" of the imagination is not induced by perceptual form alone, but is also induced by the content or significance of works of art and the materials of the means of expression, and above all by the harmonious relationship among all of these elements – just as Baumgarten had asserted forty years before the third *Critique.* This is the import of Kant's conception of fine art, the product of genius, as the expression of "aesthetic ideas." Kant characterizes an aesthetic idea, as the content of a work of artistic genius, as "that representation of the imagination that occasions much thinking without it being possible for any determinate thought, i.e., *concept,* to be adequate to it, which, consequently, no language fully attains or can make intelligible" (*CPJ,* §49, 5:314). In a work of artistic genius,

> we add to a concept a representation of the imagination that belongs to its presentation, but which by itself stimulates so much thinking that it can never be grasped in a determinate concept, hence which aesthetically enlarges the concept itself in an unbounded way... in this case the imagination is creative, and sets the faculty of intellectual ideas (reason) into motion.
>
> (§49, 5:315)

In other words, in the case of aesthetic ideas there is a free play of the imagination with content rather than form, with ideas rather than with shapes or patterns. Content is not, after all, excluded from the aesthetically relevant aspects of works of art; all that is ruled out is the constraint of content as well as of form by determinate concepts functioning as rules for the creation of and response to works of art.

Finally, Kant stresses that artistic genius is expressed in the creation of content as well as form and matter in works of art and in the creation of harmony among all these dimensions of the work of art:

> If, after these analyses, we look back to the explanation given above of what is called *genius,* then we find, *first,* that it is a talent for art...; *second,* that, as a talent for art, it presupposes a determinate concept of the product, as an end, hence understanding, but also a representation (even if indeterminate) of the material, i.e., of the intuition, for the presentation of this concept, hence a relation of the imagination to the understanding; *third,* that it displays itself not so much in the execution of the proposed end in the presentation of a determinate *concept* as in the exposition or the expression of *aesthetic ideas,* which contain rich material for that aim, hence the imagination, in its freedom from all guidance by

rules, is nevertheless represented as purposive for the presentation of the given concept...

(*CPJ*, §49, 5:317)

Genius lies in the invention of aesthetic ideas, which is a free expression of the imagination, and in the creation of vehicles for the expression of these ideas in intuition, which in turn will involve both form and matter, drawing and color, composition and instrumentation, order but also diction and style. This is Kant's development of Baumgarten's remark, "The beauty of sensory cognition and the elegance of its objects display composite perfections... no simple perfection is given to us by the phenomenon" (*Aesthetica*, §24).

We can now, in conclusion, explicate Kant's conception of fine art as a complex conception of the freedom of the imagination.[18] In his initial analysis of aesthetic response and judgment, Kant, like Hutcheson before him, characterizes aesthetic response in negative terms: what is essential to it is the freedom of the imagination in its play with form from constraint by determinate concepts of the understanding. The pleasure of aesthetic response

can express nothing but its [object's] suitability to the cognitive faculties that are in play in the reflecting power of judgment, insofar as they are in play, and thus merely a subjective formal purposiveness in the object... Such a judgment is an aesthetic judgment on the purposiveness of the object, which is not grounded on any available concept of the object and does not furnish one.

(*CPJ*, §VII, 5:189–90)

Or, a beautiful object provides the imagination "with a form that contains precisely such a composition of the manifold as the imagination would design in harmony with the *lawfulness of the understanding* in general if it were left free by itself" (*CPJ*, General Remark following §22, 5:240–1). But as Kant fills in the bare bones of his initial analysis, he provides a positive as well as a negative characterization of the freedom of imagination. Indeed, he provides several positive conceptions of the freedom of the imagination. First, as we have just seen, in his doctrine of aesthetic ideas, Kant makes it clear that artistic imagination and aesthetic response can play freely with content as well as form. In particular, Kant maintains that the paradigmatic contents of aesthetic ideas are *ideas of reason*

[18] For a fuller treatment of Kant's conception of fine art, see my "Kant's Conception of Fine Art," reprinted in the second edition of *Kant and the Claims of Taste* (Cambridge: Cambridge University Press, 1997), as chapter 12.

(§49, 5:314), and ideas of reason are in turn moral ideas. But for Kant, moral ideas are ultimately ideas of human freedom, of its conditions and consequences; thus, the contents of aesthetic ideas are ultimately ideas of human freedom. So without sacrificing its negative freedom, its freedom from constraint by determinate concepts of the understanding in its free play, works of imagination have as their paradigmatic content ideas of human freedom, of its scope and limits. Second, Kant concludes the "Critique of the Aesthetic Power of Judgment" with the argument that because aesthetic response itself is an experience of the freedom of the imagination from constraint by anything external to it, aesthetic experience itself, and derivatively the objects that induce it, can be taken as a symbol of the morally good, because the essence of the latter also consists in freedom, although freedom regulated by a self-given law rather than by a merely indeterminate harmony with the understanding. The key to Kant's claim that the beautiful is the symbol of the morally good is the analogy between the "*freedom* of the imagination . . . in the judging of the beautiful" and the "freedom of the will . . . conceived as the agreement of the latter with itself in accordance with universal laws of reason" (§59, 5:354). This too can be seen as a positive rather than negative characterization of the freedom of the imagination.

Thus, Kant's complex and delicate interpretation of the freedom of the imagination in the experience of beauty can be seen as the summation and synthesis of ideas set forth at the outset of the flowering of modern aesthetics in the first decades of the eighteenth century. Kant transformed the idea of the autonomy of aesthetic response that Hutcheson derived from Shaftesbury's much more limited conception of the disinterestedness of judgments of taste into his basic conception of the free play of the imagination. At the same time, he developed Baumgarten's conception of the complexity of aesthetic representation into an elaborate conception of the content of art and the symbolic significance of aesthetic response itself into a structure that could make room for Du Bos's conception of the engagement of the emotions through the imagination and Addison's idea of our love for images of liberty without sacrificing his guiding idea of the free play of the imagination. In much of the history of aesthetics after Kant, the several threads in Kant's complex fabric would often become unraveled again – but that is a long story, for another occasion.

2

The Standard of Taste and the "Most Ardent Desire of Society"

In his early essay, "Aesthetic Problems in Modern Philosophy," Stanley Cavell considered the connection between the traditional problem of taste and his own fundamental question about what was then called ordinary-language philosophy: whence comes the authority of ordinary speakers, or even ordinary philosophers, to deliver authoritative pronouncements about the meaning of terms in their natural language? The basic idea of his answer to this question, which has been central to so much of his subsequent work, is that meanings are not like natural phenomena waiting to be discovered, but are *constituted* by the shared attunements of the speakers of the language, who thereby have an, as it were, legislative authority over their meanings – although of course, like other legislators, they are hardly infallible. He found a figure of this thought in Hume's idea of the critic, who does not just discover good taste but is part of the means whereby a community of taste can constitute itself: the critic is presented with some extant history of taste, to be sure, but "the critic's worth is not at the mercy of the history of taste"; rather, "his value to us is that he is able to make that history a part of his data, knowing that in itself, as it stands, it proves nothing – except popularity. His value to art and culture is not that he agrees with its taste – which would make him useful for guiding one's investments in the art market – but that he sets the terms in which our tastes, whatever they happen to be, may be protected or overcome."[1] This suggests that Hume's critics are not merely specially qualified scientists of taste whose role could

[1] Stanley Cavell, "Aesthetic Problems of Modern Philosophy," in *Must We Mean What We Say?* (New York: Charles Scribner's Sons, 1969), p. 87.

easily be dispensed with but part of the means by which a community constitutes and acknowledges its own identity. The following systematic interpretation of Hume's aesthetics can be seen as an effort to sustain Cavell's suggestion.

The Problem of Taste

We are all familiar with the paradox which opens Hume's essay "Of the Standard of Taste"[2] and the strategy which is proposed for its solution; indeed, it is hard to avoid being so numbed by this familiarity that we fail to ask the most important questions about Hume's assumptions. On the one hand, we are told, one "species of philosophy" makes an easy inference from the ontological subjectivity of beauty to a thoroughgoing relativism in our judgments about it. Since "Beauty is no quality in things themselves [but] exists merely in the mind which contemplates them," there is no reason why we may not also suppose that "each mind perceives a different beauty," and therefore that "To seek the real beauty, or real deformity, is as fruitless an inquiry, as to pretend to ascertain the real sweet or real bitter" (*ST*, pp. 234–35). This argument simply assumes that because the beauty of an object neither appears in nor can be inferred from even a paradigmatic description of the properties that an object has objectively or independently of its perception by one or another sort of sentient being –

> Euclid has fully explained every quality of the circle, but has not, in any proposition, said a word of its beauty. The reason is evident. Beauty is not a quality of the circle. It lies not in any part of the line, *whose* parts are all equally distant from a common centre. It is only the effect, which that figure produces upon a mind, whose particular fabric or structure renders it susceptible of such sentiments ("The Sceptic," pp. 167–68) –

apparent judgments of beauty are just expressions of idiosyncratic preferences for objects. In fact, there may be more or less similarity among the preferences of different persons; but since such preferences are grounded in what is in principle the "particular fabric or structure" of each perceiver's mind, there is no reason to expect any particular degree

[2] Citations of this essay, abbreviated "*ST*," will be to the text printed in David Hume, *Essays Moral, Political and Literary* (Oxford: Oxford University Press, 1963), pp. 231–55. Other essays will also be cited from this edition. Further works by Hume will include *A Treatise of Human Nature*, ed. L. A. Selby-Bigge, 2nd. ed. revised by P. H. Nidditch (Oxford: Clarendon Press, 1978) ("*T*") and *An Enquiry Concerning the Principles of Morals*, ed. L. A. Selby-Bigge, 3rd. ed. revised by P. H. Nidditch (Oxford: Clarendon Press, 1975) ("*EPM*").

of convergence in such preferences, let alone any rational basis for seeking to establish such convergence by means of the customary tools of discourse and argument. Thus, "the proverb has justly determined it to be fruitless to dispute concerning tastes" (*ST*, p. 235).

But although such a philosophical axiom – that ontological subjectivity implies preferential idiosyncrasy – has found expression in a proverb – *de gustibus non disputandum est* – and by that means "attained the sanction of common sense," there is also what is from the outset "a species of common sense which opposes it, at least serves to modify and restrain it." Thus, Hume says, "It is natural for us to seek a *Standard of Taste*; a rule by which the various sentiments of men may be reconciled; [or] at least a decision afforded confirming one sentiment, and condemning another." It is the assumption of such a standard which leads us to discriminate among what should be incorrigible expressions of subjective preference as if they were true or false assertions of objective fact, thus to maintain that "Whoever would assert an equality of genius and elegance between Ogilby and Milton, or Bunyan and Addison, would be thought to defend no less an extravagance, than if he had maintained a mole-hill to be as high as Teneriffe, or a pond as extensive as the ocean." The first species of philosophy just assumes that because beauty concerns mind-dependent sentiments rather than purely objective properties, all sentiments of beauty are equally valid; but the present species of common sense rejects that inference, and supposes that even subjective sentiments or preferences are fit objects of criticism in light of intersubjective standards: "Though there may be found persons, who give the preference to the former authors: no one pays attention to such a taste; and we pronounce, without scruple, the sentiment of these pretended critics to be absurd and ridiculous" (*ST*, pp. 234–35).

Hume's understated use of what are in fact his most fundamental terms of art makes his position in this dialectic clear. The relativist conclusion that *de gustibus non disputandum est* is not in fact genuine common sense, but only an apparently common-sensical inference from what is actually a typically unreliable axiom of skeptical philosophy, that ontological subjectivity must entail preferential relativism. The discrimination of preferences into those which are absurd and ridiculous and those which are not, however, is well-grounded in the genuinely common-sensical assumption that there is a standard of taste. This standard, however, is "natural" – that is, it is an empirically discoverable fact that there is agreement about the validity of some preferences and absurdity of others. The existence of a standard of taste is not something which can itself be known by any *a priori* means nor does it obviously give rise to any determinate rules for the discrimination of preferences which can be discovered *a priori*:

> It is evident that none of the rules of composition are fixed by reasonings *a priori*, or can be esteemed abstract conclusions of the understanding, from comparing those habitudes and relations of ideas, which are eternal and immutable. Their foundation is the same with that of all the practical sciences, experience; nor are they anything but general observations, concerning what has been universally found to please in all countries and in all ages (*ST*, pp. 235–36).

Such unblinking acceptance of the purely natural and thus contingent existence of the standard of taste itself as well as any precepts it may ground separates Hume not only from Kant and his rationalist predecessors but also, as we shall see, from many of Hume's contemporaries on his own side of the English Channel, indeed on his own side of the river Tweed.

How is the empirical discovery of the standard of taste, or the "catholic and universal beauty" (*ST*, p. 237), of which common sense assures us, to be accomplished? It might seem as if it is a simple matter of majority rule: that is naturally pleasing which is usually pleasing. Just as the true color (or other secondary quality) of an object, though it is also a characteristic of our response to an object rather than an ontologically objective property of it, is that which is usually perceived, so the standard aesthetic response to an object would seem to be the most common response to it:

> If, in the sound state of the organ, there be an entire or considerable uniformity of sentiment among men, we may thence derive an idea of the perfect beauty; in like manner as the appearance of objects in daylight, to the eye of a man in health, is denominated their true and real colour, even while colour is allowed to be merely a phantasm of the senses (*ST*, pp. 235–36).

The ontological subjectivity of aesthetic as well as other secondary qualities does not undermine the "reality" of these qualities, because "There is a sufficient uniformity in the senses and feelings of mankind, to make all these qualities the objects of art and reasoning" ("The Sceptic," p. 168n). However, Hume does not reduce the normative to the normal, or the standard of taste to usual preferences. Rather, the "finer emotions of the mind are of a very tender and delicate nature, and require the concurrence of many favorable circumstances to make them play with facility and exactness, according to their general and established principles" (*ST*, p. 237); and it is not the preferences which are normally found but only those found in such favorable circumstances which determine the norm or standard of taste. Only "the joint verdict" of those whose preferences are formed in maximally favorable circumstances – which may be minimally frequent – "is the true verdict of taste and beauty." Hume's strategy is then to discover the conditions which "entitle critics to this valuable character," or give normative significance for the rest of us to their preferences; the standard of taste is represented not by majority rule but by the preferences of the most qualified critics (*ST*, p. 247).

Most discussions of Hume's essay have focussed on disputing or defending the criteria by which Hume proposes to make the identification of such valuable critics a question "of fact, not of sentiment" (*ST*, p. 248). For my purposes, however, a straightforward account will do. First, Hume specifies conditions under which a particular response to a particular object must occur if that response is to be standard-setting: "A perfect serenity of mind, a recollection of thought, a due attention to the object: if any of these circumstances be wanting, our experiment will be fallacious, and we shall be unable to judge of the catholic and universal beauty" (*ST*, p. 237). Next, he specifies general capacities and abilities that qualified critics must possess. First, a qualified critic must possess what Hume variously calls "*delicacy* of imagination" (*ST*, p. 239), "delicacy of taste" (p. 240), or "a quick and acute perception" (p. 241). This is the capacity for accurate perception of all those qualities of an object, no matter how "mixed or confounded with each other," which may produce an aesthetic response, or that perfection of our taste, whether "literal or metaphorical," which obtains "Where the organs are so fine as to allow nothing to escape them, and at the same time so exact as to perceive every ingredient in the composition" (p. 240); it is this perfection of perceptual discrimination, of course, which is illustrated by the famous story of Sancho Panza's kinsmen, able to discern the faint tastes of an iron key and its leathern thong even in a huge hogshead of wine (pp. 239–40). But of course, responding to a work of art[3] is not just a matter of severally perceiving its various ingredients or components. A work of art is an object created in specific circumstances for specific ends, and "every work of art, in order to produce its due effect on the mind, must be surveyed in a certain point of view." The critic's talent to adopt such a point of view in lieu of any which might otherwise suggest itself is what Hume calls his talent "to preserve his mind free from all *prejudice*, and [to] allow nothing

[3] Hume does not use the term "aesthetic," invented in Germany two decades before the publication of "Of the Standard of Taste," let alone make the Hegelian assumption that aesthetics is the theory of art. Nevertheless, it is clear that in his essay he is concerned with the judgment of works of art, rather than with a mode of judgment (as in Kant) paradigmatically directed to natural beauty and only derivatively directed to art.

to enter into his consideration, but the very object which is submitted to his consideration" (p. 244). This second requirement, it should be clear, does not call for an utterly presuppositionless attitude to a work of art, but rather an appropriate attitude, that is, that attitude intended by the author of a work and assumed by its intended audience, whether that is identical with the natural attitude, i.e. prejudice, of the critic or not.[4]

The capacity to free oneself from inappropriate prejudice, however, is but one application of the third, more general capacity which Hume ascribes to the qualified critic, namely, "*good sense*" (p. 245). Good sense checks the influence of prejudice, but it is also that talent of mind which supplements delicacy of taste by taking in both the formal and functional relations among the various individual components discriminated by the latter. Thus, good sense is the talent possessed by one whose thought is "capacious enough to comprehend all those parts, and compare them with each other, in order to perceive the consistence and uniformity of the whole"; and it is that by which one can determine that a work of art "is more or less fitted to attain" the "certain end or purpose for which it is calculated" (p. 246). Thus, delicacy of taste, freedom from prejudice, and good sense in its more general forms qualify a critic as one whose sentiments, though ontologically just as subjective as anyone else's, may nevertheless set a standard for others. These capacities of mind, however, are not just natural gifts. Rather, they must be cultivated. Such cultivation requires two forms of exercise. First, "nothing tends further to increase and improve" these talents "than *practice* in a particular art, and the frequent survey or contemplation of a particular species of beauty" (p. 242). Such practice makes "clear and distinct" the sentiment which occurs when "objects of any kind are first presented to the eye or imagination," which would otherwise be "obscure and confused." Second, and more specifically, "it is impossible to continue in the practice of contemplating any order of beauty, without being frequently obliged to form comparisons between the several species and degrees of excellence, and estimating their proportion to each other" (p. 243). A person "who has had no opportunity of comparing the different kinds of beauty, is indeed totally unqualified to pronounce an opinion with regard to any object presented to him." Conversely, a critic who is gifted with delicacy of taste,

4 Cf. Peter Jones, *Hume's Sentiments: Their Ciceronian and French Contexts* (Edinburgh: Edinburgh University Press, 1982), p. 110. The present account of the five constraints on qualified criticism is much indebted to that offered by Jones.

freedom from prejudice, and good sense, and who has developed these talents through practice, especially practice in comparisons, is qualified to put forth his own responses as standards for the taste of others.[5] And though no *a priori* rules for compositions, or for the objective properties of excellent works of art more generally, may be formulated, it is an empirical question, and indeed one of no great difficulty, whether any person has and has developed these talents (p. 248), and thus whether his preferences should be counted among those which can maintain a "universal, undisputed empire over the minds of men" (p. 249).

The question usually asked "Of the Standard of Taste" is whether these criteria are really matters of fact rather than sentiment – for instance, whether we can determine that a purported critic has indeed made adequately "frequent survey or contemplation of a particular species of beauty" without already possessing a standard of taste and thus begging the question which the non-controversial identification of qualified critics is supposed to answer.[6] But there are deeper questions to be asked. First, why are Hume's criteria to be applied to critics rather than to oneself? That is, why does Hume apparently specify a procedure for isolating a body of qualified critics, whose preferences may then be allowed to determine a standard of taste, rather than simply recommending procedures or criteria for the improvement of one's own taste?[7] This question

5 Jones has supported the present interpretation of Hume's list of the five conditions for qualified critics, on which it is divided into three terms characterizing the critic's talent and two addressing his development of them, by a discussion of the literary source for Hume's essay, the *Reflexions critique sur la poesie et sur la peinture* (1719) of J.-B. Du Bos (*Hume's Sentiments*, pp. 93–106). But evidence for the interpretation is also to be found in the way Hume's essay was interpreted by his immediate successors. This passage from Hugh Blair is illustrative: "From these two sources, then, first, the frequent exercise of Taste, and next the application of good sense and reason to the objects of Taste, Taste as a power of the mind receives its improvement. In its perfect state, it is undoubtedly the result both of nature and of art. It supposes our natural sense of beauty to be refined by the frequent attention to the most beautiful objects, and at the same time to be guided and improved by the light of the understanding." (*Lectures on Rhetoric and Belles Lettres* (London: W. Strahan, 1783), Vol. I, p. 23.)

6 On this point, see Harold Osborne, "Hume's Standard and the Diversity of Taste," *British Journal of Aesthetics* 7 (1967): 50–56, and Peter Kivy, "Hume's Standard: Breaking the Circle," *British Journal of Aesthetics* 7 (1967): 57–66, reprinted in his *The Seventh Sense: A Study of Francis Hutcheson's Aesthetics and its Influence in Eighteenth Century Britain* (New York: Burt Franklin & Co., 1976), pp. 139–49. The issue is further considered in Carolyn Korsmeyer, "Hume and the Foundations of Taste," *Journal of Aesthetics and Art Criticism* 35 (Winter, 1976), especially pp. 205–06, and in Noël Carroll, "Hume's Standard of Taste," *Journal of Aesthetics and Art Criticism* 43 (Winter 1984), especially pp. 189–91 and note 34, pp. 193–94.

7 This question has been raised by Noël Carroll, in "Hume's Standard of Taste," p. 191.

is particularly puzzling in view of the fact that Hume's contemporaries typically *did* interpret the requirement that the natural faculties of delicate sensibility and sound judgment be sharpened by practice – which they all derived from Du Bos[8] – as principles for self-improvement rather than for the identification of a body of qualified critics. Thus, Alexander Gerard, whose *Essay on Taste* was virtually simultaneous with Hume's own essay,[9] identifies the two chief components of taste as "exquisite *sensibility* and delicacy" (p. 106) and "*Judgment*," which is not only "the faculty which distinguishes things different, separates truth from falsehood, and compares together objects and their qualities" (p. 90) but also "finds out the general characters of *each art*, and, by comparing them, draws conclusions which subsist between *different arts*" (p. 91); he then describes the perfection of sensibility and judgment, that is, refinement and correctness, as being produced precisely by custom and exercise:

> It may be observed farther, that taste, being a faculty of a derivative kind,[10] implies in it's [*sic*] exertion mental actions, which are strengthened by use and exercise. And *their* improvement tends to support the delicacy and liveliness of *it's* [*sic*] perceptions. . . . Custom enables us to apply our minds more vigorously to objects, than we could at first (pp. 110–11);
>
> But refinement and elegance of taste is chiefly owing to the acquisition of *knowledge* and the *improvement* of judgment (p. 118).
>
> Custom enables us to form ideas with exactness and precision. By studying works of taste, we acquire clear and distinct conceptions of those qualities, which render them beautiful or deformed: we take in at one glance all the essential properties; and thus establish in the mind a criterion, a touchstone of excellence and depravity (p. 139).

Gerard clearly conceives of use, custom, and exercise as means by which any one may improve the natural capacities of sensibility and judgment and thereby establish his own "touchstone of excellence," an internal standard of taste. There is no suggestion that the principles of taste can only be used to identify a body of qualified critics whose preferences establish a canon of taste and thereby a model for those who would acquire good taste. Why does Hume apply the conditions for taste in this

[8] See note 5.

[9] The *Essay on Taste* (London: A. Millar, 1759), was published two years later than "Of the Standard of Taste," but was written in response to a prize offer by the Edinburgh Society first offered in 1755 and re-offered in 1756; it was thus presumably composed independently of Hume's essay.

[10] That is, composed of the underlying capacities of sensibility and judgment.

indirect manner rather than simply prescribing the customary methods for self-improvement?

But beyond this lies an even deeper question. Why does Hume suppose that the preferences of great critics *should* "maintain an universal, undisputed empire over the minds of men"? Why must we seek a standard of taste at all, whether by straightforwardly improving our own taste or less directly by seeking to conform our preferences to those of the imperial critics? As we saw, Hume says "It is natural for us to seek a *Standard of Taste*" (*ST*, p. 234); and this might be taken to express his view that there is no justification or even explanation of our pursuit of agreement in subjective preferences, that this pursuit is just one of those points at which the explanations that can be offered by a Newtonian science of man must come to an end, one of those points where "we perceive that we can give no reason for our most general and most refined principles, beside our experience of their reality" (*T*, p. xviii). More cynically, one might even suggest that this is a question Hume never even raised – that he just adopted the essay on taste as one of the literary conventions of his time (by 1757 indeed at least half a century old), and as a man of letters made his own, none too original essay in this genre as a matter of profession rather than philosophy. Either of these answers, however, would be too hasty. In fact, what underlies the essay "Of the Standard of Taste" – which, it must always be remembered, is just an essay and far from a systematic, let alone complete presentation of Hume's views about the matters it touches upon – is a complicated analysis of our aesthetic experience, in which a standard of taste, or canon of agreed upon objects of taste, plays not just a regulative role in the individual pursuit of pleasure – which, to be sure, it does – but also a constitutive role in both aesthetic response and aesthetic judgment; that is, agreement in taste actually turns out to be a crucial factor in both our pleasurable experience of beautiful objects and our meaningful discourse about them.

In what follows, I will analyze Hume's – at least – quadripartite explanation of *why* it is natural for us to seek after a standard of taste, and then return to the question of why he offers us a procedure for identifying competent critics rather than a method for aesthetic self-improvement. But both parts of this discussion must be prefaced by an explanation of Hume's actual theory of beauty, his account of various relations between objects and ourselves which are suited, by the particular fabric and structure of our minds, to cause the characteristic pleasures of beauty, for this theory is in fact entirely omitted from "Of the Standard of Taste."

Hume's Theory of Beauty

Even in his most systematic work, *A Treatise of Human Nature*, Hume never offers a systematic account of his conception of beauty; rather, in both the *Treatise* and the subsequent popularization of its third book, *An Enquiry Concerning the Principles of Morals*, claims about beauty or other aesthetic sentiments are generally made only in illustration of claims about the moral sentiments. Nevertheless, Hume's passing comments on beauty reveal a fairly elaborate theory.

The foundation of this theory is the division of beauty into two classes, the first that of pleasurable sentiment caused by an immediate response – that is, a response not mediated by the intervention of imagination or judgment – to the form or other perceptual qualities of an object, and the second that of pleasurable sentiment, which arises only when the perception of the form of an object is supplemented by a concept or concepts brought to bear on it by imagination or judgment. Ontologically speaking, "beauty is nothing but a form, which produces pleasure, as deformity is a structure of parts, which conveys pain" (*T*, p. 299), but such "an order and construction of parts" may be "fitted to give a pleasure and satisfaction to the soul" either directly by the "*primary constitution* of our nature" (*loc. cit.*) or else only with the additional perspective afforded by imagination or judgment. Hume encapsulates this distinction at the conclusion of the *Treatise*, although in a formulation that can be verbally confusing and that certainly simplifies the diversity of ways in which the immediate perception of formal beauty can be supplemented by the imagination and judgment: "Thus the beauty of all visible objects causes a pleasure pretty much the same, tho' it be sometimes deriv'd from the mere *species* and appearance of the objects; sometimes from sympathy, and an idea of their utility" (*T*, p. 617). This general statement comes immediately after a discussion of the ways in which the fine possessions of a rich man can provide pleasure for the rest of us, which includes, besides the obvious case of the direct "advantage, which we hope to reap from him by his generosity and liberality," the two distinct cases of "the immediate pleasure, which a rich man gives us, by the view of the beautiful cloaths, equipage, gardens, or houses, which he possesses," and the mediated or indirect pleasure which we derive "from the pleasure and advantage which he himself reaps from his possessions, and which produce an agreeable sympathy in us" (*T*, p. 616).

This distinction simplifies, as we shall shortly see, because the sympathetic enjoyment of another's actual use of a particular object is only one among at least three different ways in which imagination may supplement the more immediate pleasure afforded by the perception of "the proportion, relation, and position of parts, [on which] all natural beauty depends" (*EPM*, p. 291). And it can confuse, because while Hume here uses the term "*species*" in its medieval sense to connote purely perceptual form or appearance, he elsewhere uses the same term – but without italics – in its modern sense, connoting a classification, even though the distinction he is propounding is precisely that between immediate pleasures of the imagination which are independent of any conceptual classification of the object and those less direct pleasures of the imagination which depend upon an appropriate classification of the object.[11] To put it with a typographical pun, Hume's distinction is precisely that between beauty of *species* and beauty of species.

Hume's commitment to this basic distinction is clear, even though he often writes as if the immediate beauty of form could be taken for granted and only that sentiment of beauty which is dependent upon the mediation of such processes of the imagination as sympathy needs emphasis. Thus, immediately after stating his fundamental thesis that "Pleasure and pain . . . are not only necessary attendants of beauty and deformity, but constitute their very essence," he goes on to write:

> And indeed, if we consider, that a great part of the beauty, which we admire either in animals or in other objects, is deriv'd from the idea of convenience and utility, we shall make no scruple to assent to this opinion. That shape, which produces strength, is beautiful in one animal; and that which is a sign of agility in another. The order and convenience of a palace are no less essential to its beauty, than its mere figure and appearance (*T*, p. 299).

Hume's basic explanation of the connection between beauty and sympathy seems to give the mediated perception of beauty even more explicit priority. Observing the "force of sympathy thro' the whole animal creation," Hume adds:

> This conclusion from a general view of human nature, we may confirm by particular instances, wherein the force of sympathy is very remarkable. Most kinds of beauty are deriv'd from this origin; and tho' our first object be some senseless inanimate piece of matter, 'tis seldom we rest there, and carry not our view to its influence on sensible and rational creatures. A man, who shews us any house or building, takes particular care among other things to point out the convenience

[11] Hume's fundamental distinction in the theory of beauty is obviously a forerunner of Kant's distinction between free and dependent judgments of beauty (*Critique of the Power of Judgment*, §16).

of the apartments, the advantages of their situation, and the little room lost in the stairs,[12] antichambers, and passages; and indeed, 'tis evident, the chief part of the beauty consists in these particulars. The observation of convenience gives pleasure, since convenience is a beauty. But after what manner does it give pleasure? 'Tis certain our own interest is not in the least concern'd; and as this is a beauty of interest, not of form, so to speak, it must delight us merely by communication, and by our sympathizing with the proprietor of the lodging. We enter into his interest by the force of imagination, and feel the same satisfaction, that the objects naturally occasion in him (*T*, pp. 363–64).

We will return to the details of the sympathetic mechanism which Hume is invoking shortly; at this point, we are only concerned with the general distinction between what Hume calls here beauty of interest and beauty of form. This remark from the second *Enquiry* likewise seems to give statistical preponderance to the former rather than the latter kind of beauty:

It is evident, that one considerable source of *beauty* in all animals is the advantage which they reap from the particular structure of their limbs and members, suitably to the particular manner of life, to which they are by nature destined. . . . Ideas of its utility and its contrary, though they do not entirely determine what is handsome or deformed, are evidently the source of a considerable part of approbation or dislike (*EPM*, pp. 244–45).

But this emphasis on the beauty of convenience and utility is clearly to be explained by the fact that in these books, devoted after all to the subject of morality, Hume discusses beauty at all only to illustrate the similar roles of the ideas of utility and sympathy in the causation of our moral sentiments; so of course the less direct kind of beauty must be emphasized. Nevertheless, it is clear that Hume remains committed to a basic distinction between the immediate beauties of form, beauties which can, "on their first appearance, command our affection and approbation" precisely because they involve nothing but the perception of form, and those "many orders of beauty" such as beauties of interest, for which, because of the ideas which the imagination has to bring to bear on what is more directly afforded by the senses, "it is requisite to employ much reasoning, in order to feel the proper sentiment" (*EPM*, p. 173).

The basic distinction between beauty of form directly perceived by the senses and the other forms of beauty which require the mediation of the

[12] The urban as well as the urbane Hume clearly has in mind Edinburgh townhouses rather than Berwickshire country houses!

imagination and its variety of concepts is also illustrated by this oft-cited passage:

> 'Tis evident, that nothing renders a field more agreeable than its fertility, and that scarce any advantages of ornament or situation will be able to equal this beauty. 'Tis the same case with particular trees and plants, as with the field on which they grow. I know not but a plain, overgrown with furze and broom, may be, in itself, as beautiful as a hill cover'd with vines or olive-trees; tho' it will never appear so to one, who is acquainted with the value of each. But this is a beauty merely of imagination, and has no foundation in what appears to the senses (*T*, p. 364).

This passage has been taken to express the view that the description of the land that is seen as a "plain" necessitates a certain conceptualization of it, in a certain community at least, as arable land, and thus necessitates approbation of it only if properly utilized while excluding appreciation of the beauty of form it might otherwise have even if overgrown with furze and broom.[13] But this misreads Hume. In saying that "This is a beauty of imagination," Hume does not mean to refer back to the formal beauty of an overgrown plain "in itself" and thereby deny that one who is really acquainted with the potential utility of the land can actually appreciate such formal beauty; it is rather the beauty of the land covered with vines and olive trees that is a beauty of imagination, "and has no foundation in what appears to the senses." That is, regardless of the possibility that a certain description of an object may privilege a particular sentiment in response to it – a point to which we shall return – the point which Hume is actually making here is precisely that the approbation of intrinsic or formal beauty is founded immediately "in what appears to the senses," while other forms of beauty, prevalent though they may be, require the supplementation of the senses by the imagination and the concepts it may bring to bear on perceptible structures, relations, and positions.

We may now proceed to the more detailed classification of the varieties of beauty which Hume recognizes. About immediate beauty of form there is actually little more that can be said. This seems to be one of those places where Hume is content to adopt the pose of the Newtonian scientist, refraining from making undue hypotheses: "Some of these qualities produce satisfaction in [us] by particular *original* principles of human nature, which cannot be accounted for" (*T*, p. 590).[14] Just as we

[13] See Jones, *Hume's Sentiments*, pp. 125–26.

[14] This remark has also been cited by Carolyn Korsmeyer ("Hume and the Foundations of Taste," p. 206), but she holds that Hume does not intend it to apply even to the case of formal beauty, for which, she holds, Hume does suggest a general explanation. I will

inevitably but inexplicably form an impression of necessity from repeated continuity, so, it seems, we inevitably but inexplicably feel pleasure in the perception of certain forms.

About those sentiments of beauty which require the intervention of the imagination and specific (in the modern sense) conceptions of the object, however, Hume has a great deal to say. Here I think we may properly distinguish at least three different cases employing in significantly different ways imagination's capacity to supplement the immediate perceptions of the senses with more extended views.

First, however, one candidate mechanism for a concept-connected perception of beauty should probably be rejected. Some traditional theories of beauty considered an individual unusually representative of the characteristics of its class or species beautiful just because of its representativeness; this is the kind of theory that Kant rejects by distinguishing between genuine beauty and "internal objective finality" or "perfection."[15] Hume frequently mentions the influence of a principle of "*comparison*" on the sentiments objects produce in us, our tendency to "judge more of objects by comparison, than by their intrinsic worth" (*T*, p. 593, see also pp. 372, 375),[16] and it might be thought that he too accepts the view that the recognition of a paradigmatic member of some class induces the sentiment of pleasurable approbation characteristic of beauty just because the object is a paradigm. As evidence of such a view, one might attempt to adduce a passage in which he criticizes as "thoughtless" people who observe "that there are few women possessed of beauty in comparison of those who want it: not considering that we bestow the epithet of *beautiful* only on such as possess a degree of beauty that is common to them with a few" ("Of the Dignity or Meanness of Human Nature," *Essays*, p. 85), the thoughtlessness of such observers apparently consisting in their failure to recognize that there is some sort of analytical connection between being beautiful and being a paradigmatic representative of a class. However, it seems more likely that Hume rejects any account on which beauty is connected directly to a cognitive consideration or relation accessible to understanding alone. Thus, for instance, he implies rejection of the idea that beauty can be associated with any objective mean – "It is allowed on all hands, that beauty, as well

argue later that the mechanism she uses is not sufficiently general to explain all the cases of formal beauty which Hume seems to recognize.

[15] See *Critique of the Power of Judgment*, §15.

[16] These passages are also cited by Jones, *Hume's Sentiments*, p. 127.

as virtue, always lies in a medium; but where this medium is placed is a great question, and can never be sufficiently explained by general reasonings" ("Of Simplicity and Refinement in Writing," *Essays*, p. 199) – and more generally any such theory would seem to be excluded by Hume's fundamental rejection of the supposition that beauty can ever lie in ontologically objective properties of objects alone:

> It is on the proportion, relation, and position of parts, that all natural beauty depends; but it would be absurd thence to infer, that the perception of beauty, like that of truth in geometrical problems, consists wholly in the perception of relations, and was performed entirely by the understanding or intellectual faculties. In all the sciences, our mind from the known relations investigates the unknown. But in all decisions of taste or external beauty, all the relations are beforehand obvious to the eye; and we thence proceed to feel a sentiment of complacency or disgust, according to the nature of the object, and disposition of our organs (*EPM*, p. 291).

Rather, the import of Hume's remarks about "comparison" seems to be that quantitative factors such as rarity or cognitive factors such as representativeness may *distort* our perceptions of the "intrinsic worth and value" (*T*, p. 593, cf. p. 375) of objects, that is, that sentiment of approbation that would be induced by an object in the absence of comparison with others in its class; at the least, he clearly seems to suppose that some direct reason for valuing a particular object must be presupposed by any more comparative judgment of its value, but that comparison alone is not a direct source of approbative sentiment. Or, as we shall see in the three cases now to be considered, correct classification of an object may well be a necessary condition for recognition of its beauty; but Hume does not seem to suppose that such a classification is ever a sufficient condition for beauty.

This case excluded, let us now consider the three kinds of mediated perception of beauty which Hume clearly does recognize.

(1) The first of these cases is that most explicitly intended by Hume's general distinction between beauty of form or *species* and beauty of interest, the case in which the mechanism of sympathy transfers a particular possessor's pleasure in the actual utility of an object to another observer of it who cannot himself derive pleasure from his own use of the same object. In cases such as this, objects such as houses, "tables, chairs, scritoires, chimneys, coaches, sadles [*sic*], ploughs" please because of "their fitness for that purpose, to which they are destin'd." That is, they please because they are particularly well-suited to the end for which they were designed and acquired, precisely because they are actually useful for the successful

attainment of that end. But, Hume supposes, this means that they can give pleasure directly only to the possessor or other actual user of the object, who is pleased in virtue of the fact that such an end, itself intrinsically valued, is actually attained, and "this is an advantage that concerns only the owner" (*T*, p. 364). There would thus be no reason for anyone else to take any pleasure at all in the perception of the object – were it not for the operation of the first of "two principles, which are conspicuous in human nature," and which is even more basic than the principle of comparison, namely, that of sympathy (*T*, p. 592). Sympathy functions to transmit to an observer or to replicate in him another person's actual sentiment in the circumstances perceived by the observer; thus even one who does not possess a convenient house nevertheless takes pleasure in it and calls it beautiful because its possessor's pleasure in its actual utility is transferred to him by the mechanism of sympathy:

The observation of convenience gives pleasure, since convenience is a beauty. But after what manner does it give pleasure? 'Tis certain our own interest is not in the least concern'd; and as this is a beauty of interest, not of form, so to speak, it must delight us merely by communication, and by our sympathizing with the proprietor of the lodging. We enter into his interest by the force of imagination, and feel the same satisfaction, that the objects naturally occasion in him (*T*, p. 364).

Hume also describes his theory in a second passage, which also introduces a distinction between the communication of pleasure grounded in any special interest in the feelings of another individual, such as friendship, and the more general interest in the feelings of others which he intends by "sympathy":

Our sense of beauty depends very much on this principle, and where any object has a tendency to produce pleasure in its possessor, it is always regarded as beautiful; as every object that has a tendency to produce pain, is disagreeable and deform'd. Thus the conveniency of a house, the fertility of a field, the strength of a horse, the capacity, security, and swift-sailing of a vessel, form the principle beauty of these several objects. Here the object, which is denominated beautiful, pleases only by its tendency to produce a certain effect. That effect is the pleasure or advantage of some other person. Now the pleasure of a stranger, for whom we have no friendship, pleases us only by sympathy. To this principle, therefore, is owing the beauty, which we find in everything that is useful. How considerable a part this is of beauty will easily appear upon reflection. Wherever an object has a tendency to produce pleasure in the possessor, or in other words, is the proper *cause* of pleasure, it is sure to please the spectator, by a delicate sympathy with the possessor. Most of the works of art are esteem'd beautiful, in proportion to their fitness for the use of man, and even many of the productions of nature derive their beauty from that source. Handsome and beautiful, on most occasions, is not an absolute but a relative quality, and pleases us by nothing but its tendency to produce an end that is agreeable (*T*, pp. 576–77).

Thus, although ideas of utility are preponderant in our perceptions of beauty (*EPM*, pp. 244–45), where it is the actual utility of objects that pleases it is "but sympathy, which can interest the spectator" (*T*, p. 364). An object possesses utility if it is well-suited to an end; it will in the first instance please a possessor who can actually use it to attain that end, to which he must even more directly attach value; his pleasure in the object can then be transferred to others by sympathy. On this account, what pleases the spectator is not any use he might himself make of the object, but the possessor's own pleasure in it – this is why Hume carefully distinguishes "the advantage, which we might hope to reap from [a rich man] by his generosity and liberality" from that "pleasure and advantage, which he himself reaps from his possessions, and which produce an agreeable sympathy in us" (*T*, p. 616). Sympathy does not please us by hinting at the satisfaction of our own ends; rather, by its means we directly take pleasure in the actual satisfaction of others.[17]

This principle of sympathy is the most direct way in which pleasurable sentiment may be communicated from one person to another, but as Hume describes its working in cases of utility and convenience, he presupposes that at least one person is in a position to make actual use of an object called beautiful because of such utility. However, he also introduces mechanisms of the imagination which should not be confused with straightforward cases of sympathetic enjoyment of possessions because they do not presuppose any actual use or even any actual usefulness, i.e., potential use.

(2) There are two clearly distinct ways in which the imagination may go beyond the sympathetic communication of pleasure in actual utility to create more general beauties of interest. Though Hume does not entitle these two mechanisms, we may call them the production of pleasure in beauty by *generalization* and by *association.*

(a) On Hume's account, the imagination has a fundamental tendency to fill in the gaps in our experience by processes of generalization – "*General rules* create a species of probability, which sometimes influences the judgment, and always the imagination" (*T*, p. 585). His most famous use of this tendency, of course, is in his account of our belief in the

[17] In spite of Hume's emphasis on the principle of comparison in human nature, he does not seem to suppose that *envy* is the normal response to our frequent comparisons between ourselves and others.

continuous existence of external objects, where the imagination is seduced into transforming our experience of the similarity of several perceptions into a belief in the continuous existence of a single object represented by them – "The imagination is seduc'd" (*T*, p. 209) into telling us "that our resembling perceptions have a continu'd and uninterrupted existence, and are not annihilated by their absence" (*T*, p. 215). But he also supposes that the imagination is induced, if not seduced, into producing appropriate moral and aesthetic sentiments in cases in which virtues or objects may not actually be used to attain specific ends by its tendency to complete incomplete experiences or to assimilate experiences in which there are certain gaps to a general pattern lacking those gaps. This tendency inclines the imagination to produce pleasure where there is a general potential for use and not just to communicate pleasure in actual use by sympathy:

> ... where any object, in all its parts, is fitted to attain any agreeable end, it naturally gives us pleasure, and is esteem'd beautiful, even tho' some external circumstances be wanting to render it altogether effectual. 'Tis sufficient if everything be compleat in the object itself. A house, that is contriv'd with great judgment for all the commodities of life, pleases us upon that account; tho' perhaps we are sensible, that no-one will ever dwell in it. A fertile soil, and a happy climate, delight us by a reflexion on the happiness which they wou'd afford the inhabitants, tho' at present the country be desart and uninhabited. A man, whose limbs and shape promise strength and activity, is esteem'd handsome, tho' condemn'd to perpetual imprisonment. The imagination has a set of passions belonging to it, upon which our sentiments of beauty much depend. These passions are mov'd by degrees of liveliness and strength, which are inferior to *belief*, and independent of the real existence of their objects.[18] Where a character is, in every respect, fitted to be beneficial to society, the imagination passes easily from the cause to the effect, without considering that there are still some circumstances wanting to render the cause a complete one (*T*, pp. 584–85).

In these cases, we take pleasure in the fitness of an object to some general end of humanity even though it is clearly recognized that there is no one for whom the object actually satisfies a particular end. Thus, such cases must clearly be distinguished from both the case in which we expect our own advantage from a rich man's liberality as well as that in which we

[18] This remark cannot be supposed to be the source for Kant's definition of interest as "*das Wohlgefallen, ... was wir mit der Vorstellung der Existenz eines Gegenstandes verbinden*" (*Critique of the Power of Judgment*, §2), but could well be the source for Meredith's translation of the definition as "The delight which we connect with the representation of the real existence of an object" (J. C. Meredith, tr., *Critique of Aesthetic Judgment* [Oxford: Clarendon Press, 1911], p. 42).

sympathetically share in his own enjoyment of his well-designed possessions. At the same time, however, these cases, as ones in which the objects *are* actually well-suited to satisfy a certain objective even though for some reason they are not or perhaps even cannot be put to use by anyone, must also be distinguished from cases in which objects are *not* actually suited to the satisfaction of any real objective but rather just *suggest* the satisfaction of an end and thus produce pleasure by the *association of ideas.*

(b) Hume's example of the latter kind of case is one of the few he draws from what we would normally consider the subject matter of aesthetics, that is, the fine arts:

> There is no rule in painting more reasonable than that of ballancing the figures, and placing them with the greatest exactness on their proper centers of gravity. A figure, which is not justly ballanc'd, is disagreeable; and that because it conveys the ideas of its fall, or harm, and of pain: Which ideas are painful, when by sympathy they acquire any degree of force and vivacity (*T*, pp. 364–65).

Hume writes as if it were also sympathy which produces pleasure (or, in the example actually used, pain) in such a case, but it is clear that the mechanism is not the same as that in the cases previously described. Since the object is a painting, there is obviously no one who is actually hurt by a fall, or pleased by avoiding one, whose pleasure might be communicated to another person; and, again since the object is a painting, it is also clear that we are not perceiving an object "compleat in itself" and wanting only "some external circumstances" to actually produce some pleasure or pain which could be sympathetically enjoyed. Rather, it is only some more general resemblance between an object such as painting of a well- or ill-balanced figure and a well- or ill-balanced person, which, by association of ideas, suggests the pleasure or pain to which the person might actually be liable even on perception of the painting. Hume at least tacitly draws this distinction by omitting the final clause with its reference to sympathy from an otherwise identical passage in the second *Enquiry* (*EMP*, p. 245).[19]

[19] In attempting to reduce all the forms of beauty recognized by Hume to the three cases just described, which she characterizes as actual "usefulness" (my case 1), "utility [as] a broader, more general category which includes not only qualities which are immediately practical, but those which appear in a general way to benefit society or mankind" (my case 2(a)), and "our perception of formal qualities which are associated with pleasurable or painful situations traceable to a broad concept of utility" (my case 2(b)), Carolyn Korsmeyer appears to suggest that Hume intended to explain *all* of our pleasure or pain in "immediately and naturally agreeable" or disagreeable lines, shapes, colors, proportions, compositions, etc. as due to this associative suggestion of pleasure or pain grounded in mimetic or unintentional resemblance ("Hume and the Foundations of

By means of sympathy, generalization, and association of ideas, then, the imagination supplements those pleasures inexplicably caused by the immediate perception of certain formal properties with an additional range of pleasures. These pleasures are akin to moral sentiments in the mechanisms which produce them, but they are phenomenologically akin to the more immediate pleasures of form and thus suitably expressed by the same terms of approbation:

> Thus the beauty of all visible objects causes a pleasure pretty much the same, tho' it be sometimes deriv'd from the mere *species* and appearance of the objects: sometimes from sympathy, and an idea of their utility. . . . On the other hand, a convenient house, and a virtuous character, cause not the same feeling of approbation; even tho' the source of our approbation be the same, and flow from sympathy and an idea of their utility (*T*, p. 617; see also *EPM*, p. 213n.).

(3) Finally, we must note that Hume also countenances cases in which our approbation of works of art is grounded in a recognition of the fitness of the object to a purpose, requiring imagination and judgment in addition to immediate perception, where, however, the purpose is not one external to the work of art sympathetically or associatively enjoyed by the spectator of the latter, but is rather more internal to the work of art or the art-form. These cases are not obviously reducible to the enjoyment of utility, but seem to involve a more direct enjoyment of a work's fitness to an artistic end. Hume suggests this further mechanism of aesthetic response in "Of the Standard of Taste," when he argues that "good sense" is required not just to check the influence of prejudice or to adopt the prejudices appropriate to a particular work, but also to "comprehend all those parts, and compare them with each other, in order to perceive the consistence and uniformity of the whole" (*ST*, p. 246). This suggests that we have a general desire for consistence and uniformity, the satisfaction of which produces pleasure independently of any further utility though its recognition obviously requires judgment and not just immediate perception. Further, Hume continues, there may be a variety of further artistic purposes, the successful accomplishment of which is also satisfying independently of such external utilities as those actually served

Taste," pp. 207, 209). I find no justification for this reductive interpretation. While Hume clearly supposes that ideas of "utility and its contrary . . . are evidently the source of a considerable part of approbation or dislike," and then exploits the association of ideas to subsume mimetic objects under this explanation (*EPM*), he never suggests that all naturally agreeable "proportion, relation, and position of parts" (*EPM*, p. 291) are associated with any other objects at all and thus that utility is not just a considerable but the exclusive source of our approbation of works of natural or artistic beauty.

or suggested by convenient houses, swift and capacious merchantmen, and the like:

Every work of art has also a certain end or purpose for which it was calculated; and is to be deemed more or less perfect, as it is more or less fitted to attain this end. The object of eloquence is to persuade, of history to instruct, of poetry to please, by means of the passions and imagination. These ends we must carry constantly in our view when we peruse any performance; and we must be able to judge how far the means employed are adapted to their respective purposes (*ST*, p. 246).

Such adaptation is obviously not immediately perceived, but requires the mediation of judgment and imagination. But the purposes mentioned are also not identical to the more ordinary grounds of utility to which Hume otherwise traces such a considerable part of our aesthetic approbation.

With these four distinct kinds of beauty in mind – the immediate beauties of sensible form, the sympathetic enjoyment of actual utility, the imaginative suggestion of pleasure by generalization or the association of ideas, and the approbation of fitness for both general and specific artistic ends – we are now in a better position to consider why Hume should assume that we naturally pursue a standard of taste.

The Standard of Taste

Why did Hume feel it so natural – if not indeed urgent – for men to seek a standard of taste? At a sociological level, of course, the answer should be obvious. In a society like that of eighteenth-century Britain, rampant and, if anything, increasing economic divisions among the populace could no longer be masked by any of the ideological justifications of feudalism; political unity could not readily be found in the crown, which was shared by three forcibly united nations and which had sat for a century upon Scottish, Dutch, then German heads, or in a parliament for which only a few were franchised to vote; and, perhaps above all, the sectarian struggles of the previous century had shattered the role of religion as a common source of culture. Though only at the end of the century did a writer such as Friedrich Schiller offer a fully programmatic foundation of political unity in the aesthetic, at some level intellectuals throughout the century must already have assumed that the only hope for a common culture lay in a common taste. One of the few places where such an assumption becomes explicit is in Lord Kames:

The separation of men into different classes, by birth, office, or occupation, however necessary, tends to relax the connection that ought to be among members of the same state; which bad effect is in some measure prevented by the access all ranks of people have to public spectacles, and to amusements that are best enjoyed in company. Such meetings, where every one partakes of the same pleasure in common, are no slight support to the social affections.[20]

This passage, of course, goes far in the direction of Plato or the French revolutionaries, suggesting that political unity be fostered not just by shared sensibilities but by specific shared events; but there is no reason not to suppose that the broader thought, that shared taste can foster "the connection that ought to be among members of the same state," was not shared by many including Hume.

However, a number of elements in Hume's philosophy, including aspects of the specific theory of beauty which we have just analyzed but also assumptions about desirable forms of sentiment and the nature of language, ground more specific roles for a standard of taste. In what follows, I shall consider what might first be thought of as a regulative role a standard of taste might have, that is, the benefit of a common canon of admired objects on an individual's pursuit of aesthetic pleasure, and then a variety of ways in which such a standard might be described as having a constitutive role, that is, not merely redirecting an individual's pursuit of aesthetic pleasure but actually figuring in the origination of his pleasure or in related matters.

(1) Let us first consider the beneficial effect the existence of an approved canon of taste may have on the individual's pursuit of pleasure. Although Hume begins his exposition of the paradox of taste with the remark that "All sentiment is right; because sentiment has a reference to nothing beyond itself, and is always real, wherever a man is conscious of it" (*ST*, p. 234), it is clear that he does not accept any maxim like Bentham's "pushpin as good as poetry." That is, although it is undoubtedly tautologous that an individual does feel pleasure when he thinks he feels pleasure, Hume does not suppose that all pleasures are equally pleasing and thus simply passively accepted by those who feel them as not only the pleasures they currently feel but also the only ones worth feeling. Instead, Hume clearly supposes that some pleasures, even within a single class such as those of visible objects (see again *T*, p. 617), are preferable to others, that most individuals are both capable of recognizing this and inclined to seek the most preferable forms of pleasure available to them,

[20] Henry Home, Lord Kames, *Elements of Criticism*, ch. 25; in the edition by Abraham Mills (New York: Huntington & Savage, 1849), p. 470.

and that a standard of taste can serve the purpose of redirecting any individual toward more satisfactory forms of pleasure.

That most individuals are not only capable of experiencing more valuable pleasures than they often do but are also inclined to seek such pleasures when alerted to their existence by a standard of taste are both implied in the following remarks:

> Though men of delicate taste be rare, they are easily to be distinguished in society by the soundness of their understanding, and the superiority of their faculties above the rest of mankind. The ascendant, which they acquire, gives a prevalence to the lively approbation with which they receive any productions of genius, and renders it generally predominant. Many men, when left to themselves, have but a faint and dubious perception of beauty, who yet are capable of relishing any fine stroke which is pointed out to them (*ST*, p. 249).

For Hume, to be capable of perceiving beauty and, even more obviously, of relishing a fine stroke, means to be capable of receiving pleasure from an object; so the last sentence of this passage clearly means that many who would not otherwise receive pleasure from an object can do so if pointed toward it (and perhaps instructed in their approach to it) by a canon of good taste assembled by the rare men of delicate taste. But the ascendancy of the latter that Hume describes also means that people are not only capable of relishing finer strokes than they would if left entirely on their own, but are inclined to pursue such finer pleasures as well, and thus generally inclined to follow the lead afforded by the lively approbation of the most qualified critics. Beauty is merely a sentiment of pleasure, but we also recognize that some such sentiments are preferable to others and seek them out when given the opportunity.

The normative force attaching to "finer" objects of taste is even more evident in another essay, where Hume overcomes the scruples of ontology and speaks of "true" and "false" tastes:

> It is seldom or never found, when a false taste in poetry or eloquence prevails among any people, that it has been preferred to a true, upon comparison and reflection. It commonly prevails merely from ignorance of the true, and from the want of perfect models to lead men to a juster apprehension and more refined relish of those productions of genius. When *these* appear, they soon unite all suffrages in their favour, and, by their natural and powerful charms, gain over even the most prejudiced to the love and admiration of them ("Of Eloquence," *Essays*, pp. 107–08).

This passage clearly implies that some aesthetic pleasures are preferable to others, a fact expressed by normative language such as "juster" and "true" rather than "false," and also that a canon of taste – "perfect models" – has a natural role in leading the many, even "the most prejudiced," to the enjoyment of the more refined relishes originally enjoyed only by a few. On this account, it is clearly natural for men to seek a standard of taste because it is natural for them to seek the most refined relishes available to them. On Hume's view, humans do not remain content with pushpin when exposed to poetry.

What makes some pleasures within the class of sentiments of beauty preferable to others? Hume does not spare many words on this issue – so far, perhaps, is he from seeing relativism as a really serious issue – but he does suggest a number of reasons for preferring some forms of pleasure over others. Lending an appearance of systematicity to what Hume merely touches upon in scattered passages, we might say that the pleasures that can be afforded by the canonical objects of good taste are to be preferred to those pleasures which are obvious to less well-formed tastes because they are more numerous, more refined, more stable and more durable.

(i) By the first of these categories, I mean to refer to Hume's view that a well-formed taste affords its possessor opportunities for pleasures of form but even more of sympathy which will escape others. Works of genius, Hume suggests in "Of Eloquence," have the capacity to touch upon the widest variety of our feelings: "The principles of every passion, and of every sentiment, are in every man; and, when touched properly, they rise to life, and warm the heart, and convey that satisfaction, by which a work of genius is distinguished from the adulterate beauties of a capricious wit and fancy" (*Essays*, p. 108). Thus, a genuine taste for such works rather than a "capricious wit and fancy" offers greater opportunity for being so satisfyingly touched. In "Of the Delicacy of Taste and Passions," which he regarded as important enough to place at the opening of the whole collection of *Essays Moral, Political and Literary*, Hume seems to concede that "delicacy of taste" affords greater opportunity for disappointment as well as satisfaction:

When you present a poem or a picture to a man possessed of this talent, the delicacy of his feeling makes him be sensibly touched with every part of it; nor are the masterly strokes perceived with more exquisite relish and satisfaction, than the negligences or absurdities with disgust and uneasiness. A polite and judicious conversation affords him the highest entertainment; rudeness or impertinence is as great punishment to him. In short, delicacy of taste has the same effect as delicacy of passion. It enlarges the sphere both of our happiness and misery, and makes us sensible to pains as well as pleasures which escape the rest of mankind (*Essays*, p. 4).

However, since Hume immediately continues to argue that aesthetic experience is self-controlled in a way in which the "good or ill accidents of life" are not – "we are pretty much masters of what books we shall read, what diversions we shall partake of, and what company we shall keep" – the painful negligences of the aesthetic realm may easily be avoided. The net result then is that good taste can enlarge the sphere of our happiness and make us sensible to pleasures which escape the rest of mankind without exposing us to an increase of pain.

(ii) Second, Hume suggests that the pleasures afforded by good taste are more refined than others. By this he seems to mean that they are less adulterated with painful accompaniments, and even that good taste can transform – or refine – what might otherwise be painful into something pleasant. Hume suggests the first of these points in arguing that "a cultivated taste for the polite arts . . . improves our sensibility for all the tender and agreeable passions; at the same time that it renders the mind incapable of the rougher and more boisterous emotions":

> . . . nothing is so improving to the temper as the study of the beauties either of poetry, eloquence, music, or painting. They give a certain elegance of sentiment to which the rest of mankind are strangers. The emotions which they excite are soft and tender. They draw off the mind from the hurry of business and interest; cherish reflection; dispose to tranquility; and produce an agreeable melancholy, which, of all dispositions of the mind, is the best suited to love and friendship ("Of the Delicacy of Taste and Passion," *Essays*, pp. 5–6).

The second and stronger claim, that good taste does not merely attune us to a greater number of pleasurable sentiments while allowing us to screen out those which are painful, but that it can even transform what might otherwise be occasions for pain into occasions for pleasure, is implied by Hume's solution to the ancient paradox of tragedy. Since the "force of imagination, the energy of expression, the power of numbers, the charms of imitation" are "naturally, of themselves, delightful to the mind," the artistic application of such qualities to a subject intrinsically painful, *a fortiori* the capacity to appreciate such artistry, can produce pleasure out of pain: "The passion, though perhaps naturally, and when excited by the simple appearance of a real object, it may be painful; yet is so smoothed, and softened, and mollified, when raised by the finer arts, that it affords the highest entertainment" ("Of Tragedy," *Essays*, pp. 227–28). The alchemistry of good taste refines pleasure out of pain.

(iii) The stability of canonical pleasures of taste follows closely from the qualities just mentioned. In part, this stability lies in our ability to control our exposure to objects of taste ("every wise man will endeavor to place his happiness on such objects chiefly as depend upon himself" ["Of the Delicacy of Taste and Passion," *Essays*, p. 4]); in part, it means that these refined pleasures have no innate tendency to transform themselves into pain by becoming excessive or to bring a variety of pains and fears along with them. Delicacy of passion gives its possessors "a lively joy upon every prosperous event," but also "a piercing grief when they meet with misfortune and adversity" (p. 3); but delicacy of taste carries no such liability.

(iv) Finally, Hume emphasizes that the pleasures of good taste are not only free of inevitably painful accompaniments but are also durable: "The very sensibility to these beauties, or a delicacy of taste, is itself a beauty in any character; as conveying the purest, the most durable, and most innocent of all enjoyments" (*EPM*, p. 260). Hume does not expand on the value of durability of sentiments, but then again he does not need to: in a world in which the reality of objects but even more of self lies in nothing other than the continuity of mental content, nothing can be of greater significance than durability itself. Durable sentiments must make a fundamental contribution to the perception of one's own identity.

For all these reasons, Hume clearly considers that although every sentiment is "real," some are far more valuable than others. Conforming one's taste to the highest possible standard clearly maximizes one's yield of such valuable sentiments. Thus, it is obviously natural for any individual to seek a standard of taste, for the model it offers can be used to regulate his emotional life in ways of considerable importance.

(2) It should be noted, however, that *agreement* in taste plays at most a contingent role in such an argument. That is, perhaps maximizing the purity, durability, and innocence of one's enjoyments to obtain the various benefits just described will also maximize the agreement of one's taste with that of others; but such increased agreement is not necessary for the individual benefits thus far described. A more profound aspect of Hume's view lies in his assumption that agreement with others is intrinsically valued, thus that a standard of taste constitutes a social source of pleasure and does not just regulate the individual pursuit of satisfaction.

At the most fundamental level, it is Hume's view that the natural urge to find a standard of taste is a direct result of the natural urge to share our sentiments, but especially our pleasures, with each other. Hume actually invokes this general tendency in order to explain the special case in which sympathy leads us to appreciate the fine possessions of another, but clearly the principle is entirely general, working to magnify our immediate pleasures in beauties of form as well as to create beauties of interest. Hume's magnificent profession of faith is worth quoting in full – even in the optimistic eighteenth century few can have held such a generous view of human nature:

> . . . take a general survey of the universe, and observe the force of sympathy thro' the whole animal creation, and the easy communication of sentiments from one thinking being to another. In all creatures, that prey not upon others, and are not agitated with violent passions, there appears a remarkable desire of company, which associates them together, without any advantages they can ever propose to reap from their union. This is still more conspicuous in man, as being the creature in the universe, who has the most ardent desire of society, and is fitted for it by the most advantages. We can form no wish, which has not a reference to society. A perfect solitude is, perhaps, the greatest punishment we can suffer. Every pleasure languishes when enjoy'd a-part from company, and every pain becomes more cruel and intolerable. Whatever other passions we may be actuated by; pride, ambition, avarice, curiosity, revenge, or lust; the soul or animating principle of them all is sympathy: nor wou'd they have any force, were we to abstract entirely from the thoughts and sentiments of others. Let all the powers and elements of nature conspire to serve and obey one man: Let the sun rise and set at his command: The sea and rivers roll as he pleases, and the earth furnish spontaneously whatever may be useful or agreeable to him: He will still be miserable, till you give him some one person at least, with whom he may share his happiness, and whose esteem and friendship he may enjoy (*T*, p. 363).

Or as Hume even more bluntly concludes in the second *Enquiry:*

> Reduce a person to solitude, and he loses all enjoyment, except either of the sensual or speculative kind; and that because the movements of his heart are not forwarded by correspondent movements in his fellow-creatures (*EPM*, p. 220).

The literal implication of these last remarks is that even the immediate pleasures of sensible form, which would not seem to depend upon the actual agreement of others in the way in which beauties dependent upon sympathy more obviously do, must nevertheless be reduced to nothing in the absence of a company of like-minded others with whom to share them. But even if such a strong conclusion follows more from Hume's rhetoric than from his logic, it is clear that he believes that our natural desire to share our feelings with others can add immeasurably to our enjoyment of any object of taste, and thus naturally creates a strong urge for agreement in taste:

> A man who enters the theatre, is immediately struck with the common view of so great a multitude, participating of one common amusement; and experiences, from their very aspect, a superior sensibility or disposition of being affected with every sentiment, which he shares with his fellow-creatures (*EPM*, p. 221).

Even the rich man, who already has so much to enjoy, can have his enjoyment considerably increased by the knowledge that his pleasurable state of mind is shared:

> ... the minds of men are mirrors to one another, not only because they reflect each others [*sic*] emotions, but also because those rays of passions, sentiments and opinions may be often reverberated ... Thus the pleasure, which a rich man receives from his possessions, being thrown upon the beholder, causes a pleasure and esteem; which sentiments again, being perceiv'd and sympathiz'd with, encrease the pleasure of the possessor; and being once more reflected, become a new foundation for pleasure and esteem in the beholder (*T*, p. 365).

So, to every form of pleasure there may be added the pleasure of agreement in the enjoyment of that pleasure,[21] and for every form of pleasure, whether or not sympathy is necessarily involved in its original etiology, it thus becomes natural to seek a standard in order to increase this additional pleasure of agreement.

For some, such as Kant, the strength of our pleasure in the sheer fact of agreement itself seems to threaten the collapse of true taste into mere trend or fashion; Kant scorns what he calls the "empirical interest in the beautiful" at least in part precisely because what he also recognizes as "the drive toward society ... natural to man" can "almost infinitely magnify the value" of an object which is in itself "inconsiderable and without noticeable interest" (*Critique of the Power of Judgment*, §41, pp. 196–97). So the question naturally arises, if our "ardent desire of society" is so strong that solitude must destroy our pleasure in any form of beauty, is there any reason why it should not also be strong enough to make fashion prevail over any genuine standard of taste?

Kant was not alone in seeking an *a priori* solution to this problem. Hume's cousin Kames sought to avoid it by explaining our satisfaction in agreement as pleasure in the conformity of individual members to the ideal for their species rather than as pleasure in agreement among those individuals *per se*; thus for him even the spectacle of considerable agreement about a mere matter of fashion would not produce any additional pleasure of sympathy. That is, for Kames, for whom the genuine naturalism of Hume remained totally incomprehensible, whatever "is universal, must have a foundation in nature," specifically a normative foundation or "common nature ... conceived to be a model for each individual that

[21] Hume suggested that the absence of agreement does not detract from the special cases of sensual and speculative pleasures, but even here there is no reason not to think that these may be augmented by being shared (where that is logically or physically possible).

belongs to the kind" (*Elements of Criticism,* p. 467). Thus, what universally appeals to us (or should so appeal) appeals to us in virtue of the model or standard set by our nature, to which we properly feel "that individuals *ought* to be made conformable" (p. 468). Further, it is natural to us – part of this very nature – to approve of conformity to the standard for our species, to take pleasure in it, and to disapprove of disconformity with it:

> Every remarkable deviation from the standard makes, accordingly, an impression upon us of imperfection, irregularity, or disorder: it is disagreeable, raises in us a painful emotion: monstrous births, exciting the curiosity of a philosopher, fail not at the same time to excite a sort of horror.
>
> This conviction of a common nature or standard and of its perfection, accounts clearly for that remarkable conception we have of a right and a wrong sense or taste in morals. It accounts not less clearly for the conception we have of a right and a wrong sense or taste in the fine arts. A man who, avoiding objects generally agreeable, delights in objects . . . , is condemned as a monster: we disapprove his taste as bad or wrong, because we have a clear conception that he deviates from the common standard (*ibid.*).

Kames admits that we will commonly take pleasure in the fact that others agree with ourselves, and be displeased when they do not, but that is for the contingent reason that we always assume that our own responses accord with the norm; we thus take pleasure in the agreement of others *qua* conformity to the norm rather than *qua* agreement with ourselves: "every man, generally speaking, taking it for granted that his opinions agree with the common sense of mankind, is, therefore, disgusted with those who think differently, not as differing from him, but as differing from the common standard" (*ibid.*).

But there is no hint of such an essentialist solution to the threat of false taste in Hume. For Hume, it is simply one of the "general principles" of empirical science, "beyond which we cannot hope to find any principle more general," that "No man is absolutely indifferent to the happiness and misery of others" (*EPM,* p. 220n.) Thus it is simply an empirically evident but metaphysically inexplicable fact about us that we are pleased by agreement with others as such, and also such a fact that we will lose our taste for what would otherwise please us for the simple reason that others do not like it. There is no underlying standard for human nature, and thus for what we ought to find pleasing, to which we can appeal to distinguish our pleasure in sharing the genuine standard of taste from the pleasure of mere fashion.

Indeed, given the variety of factors of culture, belief and education as well as individual constitution that can confound the operations of the whole delicate machine of taste (cf. *ST*, p. 237), it is clearly the case on Hume's view that in any given society there will inevitably be errors of taste that will nevertheless be generally shared and thus genuinely produce the additional pleasure of agreement in taste. Hume simply searches for no *a priori* argument by which to exclude this possibility, and instead just puts his faith in the entirely empirical fact that in the long run, "though prejudices may prevail for a time, they never unite in celebrating any rival to the true genius, but yield at least to the force of nature and just sentiment." About the undue endurance of unjustified speculations, Hume is not deceived, but he firmly believes that civilized nations "never have been found long to err, in their affection for a favorite epic or tragic author" (*ST*, p. 249). Or as Hugh Blair, obviously writing under Hume's influence, put it: "Authority or prejudice may, in one age or country, give a temporary reputation to an indifferent poet, or a bad artist; but when foreigners, or when posterity examine his works, his faults are discerned, and the genuine Taste of human nature appears. . . . Time overthrows the illusions of opinion, but establishes the decisions of nature" (*Lectures on Rhetoric and Belles Lettres*, vol. I, p. 35).

This issue cannot be left, however, without allowing one dissenting voice to speak. Although for philosophically distinct reasons, both Hume and Kames have held not merely that agreement in matters of sentiment is of profound importance to us, but also that we find such agreement of equal urgency in matters of taste as well as morals. Another view is that while agreement itself is always an occasion for satisfaction, we simply do not attach as much weight to such agreement – or at least to disagreement – in matters of taste as in matters more directly affecting our sense of welfare. Thus Adam Smith writes:

> . . . I can much more easily overlook the want of this correspondence of sentiments with regard to such indifferent objects as concern neither me nor my companion, than with regard to what interests me so much as the misfortune that has befallen me, or the injury that has been done me. Though you despise that picture, or that poem, or even that system of philosophy, which I admire, there is little danger of our quarrelling upon that account. . . . But it is quite otherwise with regard to those objects by which either you or I are particularly affected. Though your judgments in matters of speculation, though your sentiments in matters of taste, are quite opposite to mine, I can easily overlook this opposition; and if I have any degree of temper, I may still find some entertainment in your conversation, even upon these very subjects. But if you have either no fellow-feeling for the misfortunes that I have met with, or . . . no indignation at the injuries I have suffered . . . we

can no longer converse upon these subjects. We become intolerable to one another.[22]

So the pains of disagreement do not necessarily correspond to the pleasures of agreement; indeed, it might even be suggested that the realm of taste affords us a welcome outlet for our appreciation of the diversity rather than similarity of our fellows. But these observations are not inconsistent with the general premise that we do take pleasure in the fact of "fellow-feeling" sufficient to explain our interest in a standard of taste. After all, as even the opening of Hume's eponymous essay implies, our attraction to such a standard, while natural, is not unalloyed.

(3) We may now turn from the general fact of sympathy to the special case in which sympathy actually creates "beauty of interest" by communicating one person's pleasure in the fitness of a particular object to his end to spectators who would otherwise remain indifferent to the object. Here we should note that this mechanism both presupposes some commonality of response but also works to create it. On the one hand, this operation of sympathy presupposes that both owner and spectator share certain conceptual as well as affective dispositions. That is, if I am to share your appreciation of your handsome writing-table, I must categorize it similarly to you and likewise appreciate not only fitness of objects to ends generally but also the more specific ends, such as being able to compose in comfort, for which the object is so admirably fit. If I do not share these attitudes to some degree, your pleasure will be too incomprehensible to be communicated to me, or even to be perceived *as* pleasure by me. This last point is particularly clear from Hume's supposition – to which we shall return later – that we are not immediately acquainted with the mental states of others, but understand them at least in part precisely by understanding their objects:

No passion of another discovers itself immediately to the mind. We are only sensible of its causes or effects. From *these* we infer the passion: And consequently *these* give rise to our sympathy (*T*, p. 576).

Unless I already perceive the object – the cause of your passion – to some extent like you do, and unless I would myself take pleasure in the possession of such an object – thus understand the effect of such an

[22] *The Theory of Moral Sentiments*, eds. A. L. Macfie and D. D. Raphael (Oxford: Oxford University Press, 1976), p. 21.

object – I cannot recognize that your state of mind is pleasurable, and thus have its pleasurability communicated to me by sympathy.[23]

On the other hand, it should also be clear that this mechanism of sympathy will also work to produce a standard of taste. For if some "considerable" part of our pleasure in objects arises from the fact that others are already pleased with them, then of course it will not just be contingent that we all take pleasure in the same objects but rather causally necessitated – sympathy itself creates shared tastes. Again, as in the more general case, there will be no metaphysical necessity that there should be a standard of taste – there is no Kamesian norm for human nature which will determine that we should all find certain objects fit for certain natural human ends – but, within the limits of inductive reliability, it will be naturally inevitable that our several pleasures in beauties of interest will be communicated to each other and thereby create a common canon of such beauties.

(4) The three bases for a standard of taste thus far described all depend upon psychological rather than linguistic assumptions. Indeed, unlike so many of his predecessors and contemporaries, Hume essays no general theory of language. But he does suggest some particular theses about the language of sentiments. As usual, his primary concern is with moral rather than aesthetic sentiments. Nevertheless, these linguistic assumptions also explain the necessity of a standard of taste.

Hume emphatically insists that linguistic agreement requires the adoption of general rather than peculiar points of view:

> ... every particular man has a peculiar position with regard to others; and 'tis impossible we cou'd ever converse together on any reasonable terms, were each of us to consider characters and persons, only as they appear from his particular point of view. In order, therefore, to prevent those continual *contradictions*, and arrive at a more *stable* judgment of things, we fix on some *steady* and *general* points of view; and always, in our thoughts, place ourselves in them, whatever may be our present position (*T*, pp. 581–82).

And:

> ... every particular person's pleasure and interest being different, 'tis impossible men cou'd ever agree in their sentiments and judgments, unless they chose some common point of view, from which they might survey their object, and which might cause it to appear the same to all of them (*T*, p. 591; see also *T*, pp. 582, 603, and *EPM*, p. 229).

[23] The necessity of common classification for shared perception of beauties of interest is also suggested by Peter Jones (*Hume's Sentiments*, pp. 128–32).

But these remarks might seem to beg the fundamental question: to be sure, *if* we will issue similar judgments, then we must issue our judgments from similar positions or on the basis of similar conditions; but *why* must we wish to agree in judgments in the first place?

Of course, Hume's italics reveal a part of his answer. Stability and steadiness are of fundamental value, not just in society but in the self; and as a matter of fact, adopting a general point of view from which to issue verdicts of approbation and disapprobation is necessary not just for the stability of society but for steadiness of individual sentiment as well. For as Hume makes clear, we must not only contend with other persons who are responding to a particular virtuous man or beautiful object from a different position in time or space; "we ourselves often change in our situation in this particular" (*T*, p. 603; *EPM*, p. 229), and if we were to simply express our immediate responses to the "momentary appearances of things" (*T*, p. 582) without correcting these by more general points of views, we would introduce an intolerable instability even into our "internal sentiment." It would be as if we accepted as true the apparent size of every image of an external object without taking into account our changing distance from it. Fortunately, we do not do this:

> The judgment here corrects the inequalities of our internal emotions and perceptions; in like manner, as it preserves us from error, in the several variations of images, presented to our external senses.... And, indeed, without such a correction of appearances, both in internal and external sentiments, men could never think or talk steadily on any subject (*EPM*, pp. 227–28).

Given the very dependence of self-identity on continuity of mental states, without this generalizing tendency our very sense of self would be threatened.

But there are also more specifically linguistic assumptions behind Hume's insistence upon the general point of view. Most explicit is his assertion that certain terms of approbation, or its contrary, directly connote the expectation of general concurrence, and therefore can reasonably be used only if momentary appearances are corrected by a general point of view. This supposition is briefly employed in the *Treatise:* " 'Tis only when a character is considered in general, without reference to our particular interest, that it causes such a feeling or sentiment, as denominates it morally good or evil" (*T*, p. 472). But the point is made more fully in the second *Enquiry*:

> When a man denominates another his *enemy*, his *rival*, his *antagonist*, his *adversary*, he is understood to speak the language of self-love, and to express sentiments,

> peculiar to himself and arising from his particular circumstances and situation. But when he bestows on any man the epithets of *vicious* or *odious* or *depraved*, he then speaks another language, and expresses sentiments in which he expects all his audience are to concur with him. He must here, therefore, depart from his private and particular situation, and must choose a point of view, common to him with others... (*EPM*, p. 272).

As does Kant with his distinction between "agreeable (to me)" and "beautiful" (*Critique of the Power of Judgment*, §7), Hume supposes that some terms of praise are understood by competent speakers of the language simply to report the feeling of the speaker, while others are understood by all to express an expectation of the general validity of what the speaker has felt – it is to mark this distinction that language "must invent a peculiar set of terms, in order to express those universal sentiments of censure or approbation" (*EPM*, p. 274). And while the general expectation of truthfulness may impose a requirement of sincerity in the use of the first sort of terms, in the case of the second it clearly requires the evaluation of one's own response from a general point of view.

Unlike Kant, Hume does not expressly assert this thesis about explicitly aesthetic terms. But it seems clear that he intends it to hold for many terms besides those of character appraisal (thus, "a peach-tree is said to be better than" another because it generally produces a good crop, even if this year's was destroyed by "snails or vermin" [*EPM*, p. 228n]). And the opening observation of "Of the Standard of Taste" makes it clear that aesthetic terms are included among those intended to express universal sentiments. The problem of taste arises precisely because although such terms of praise as "elegance, propriety, simplicity, spirit in writing" are understood to be included among the "certain terms in every language which import... praise; [so that] all men who use the same tongue must agree in their application of them," specifications of the actual extensions of these terms may differ "when critics come to particulars" (*ST*, pp. 231–32). A standard of taste is thus required if we are to use the aesthetic terms to which we help ourselves responsibly, because these terms do connote the existence of agreement in response.

Hume hints at another consideration about language's necessitating a standard of taste. Leaving aside the connotation of general validity just ascribed to them, one might have supposed that aesthetic terms were just meant to designate particular species of pleasure that we all have, just as "toothache" is supposed to connote one sort of pain and "itch" another. One might then suppose that such terms could be used to report our internal sentiments to each other, and that these reports could be understood even if the responses were induced by quite different objects – just as I can understand your report that sucking an ice-cube gives you a toothache even if it does no such thing to me. But Hume's general supposition that the passions of others must be inferred from their causes or effects (*T*, p. 576), which we have already encountered, must at least raise suspicion about this easy assumption. For it at least suggests that I cannot learn what internal state you intend by any particular term, but must infer your meaning from public evidence – in part, perhaps, such cues as your accompanying or subsequent behavior (i.e., "effects"), but in part at least from the objects which appear to induce your inner states and their corresponding expressions (i.e., the "causes" of your passions). Thus, unless there is some similarity in the objects which produce our aesthetic sentiments, I may not even be able to understand your remarks as meant to report aesthetic sentiments at all.

Obviously, Hume's thought had to wait two centuries for any fuller elaboration.[24] But what has been said here should suffice to demonstrate that Hume's assertion that it is natural for men to seek a standard of taste is far from an unthinking assumption, let alone a merely conventional literary pose, but is deeply rooted in his understanding of aesthetic language as well as in his explanation of aesthetic response.

"Where are Such Critics to be Found?"

We are now in a position to consider briefly the other question with which we began. Why did Hume conceive of his rules for establishing the standard of taste as conditions for identifying a body of actual critics whose preferences would then determine the standard of taste, as opposed to a set of rules by which any individual could improve his own taste directly and thereby discover universally valid beauties for himself – especially when such contemporaries as Gerard sought precisely such means for the improvement of the taste of any and all?

In part, the answer must be that there is no reason in principle, but deep reasons in practice for this assumption – there is no *a priori* bar to the individual discovery of the standard of taste, but considerable empirical evidence that in fact such a standard can only be discovered by the

[24] Wittgensteinian strains in Hume have also been noticed by Peter Jones; see *Hume's Sentiments*, pp. 176–84, and "Strains in Hume and Wittgenstein," in Donald W. Livingston and James T. King, eds., *Hume: A Re-evaluation* (New York: Fordham University Press, 1976), pp. 191–209.

combined efforts of generations of individuals specially qualified both to criticize and also to transmit their criticisms of the actual products of human artistry. But even this may concede too much to a tacitly formalistic conception of the objects of taste, for it is also clearly part of Hume's view that our appreciation of much art depends upon specific historical knowledge which could not be discovered by an ideal aesthetic observer but which must really be transmitted to posterity by an actual body of critics. I will briefly explicate three factors lying behind these comments.

(1) One point on which Hume insists is that even though "many men . . . are capable of relishing any fine stroke which is pointed out to them" (*ST*, p. 249), even once one is pointed in the right direction such fine strokes may not be self-evident, but may require repeated study to discover. "There is a flutter or hurry of thought which attends the first perusal of any piece, and which confounds the genuine sentiment of beauty. . . . The several perfections and defects seem wrapped up in a species of confusion, and present themselves indistinctly to the imagination" (*ST*, p. 243). The most immediate bearing of this is that while in principle one could overcome such confusion and obscurity by adequately repeated scrutiny of any given work, in practice one cannot devote such attention to every work one encounters and would often see no reason to devote such effort to many initially off-putting though ultimately satisfying works without the promises made in their behalf by critics who have gone before. Further, it is often the case that the true merits and – perhaps even more often – the true demerits of a work are not obvious to anyone in the first generation of its audience as well as its producer, and that only the actual judgments of subsequent critics – not the timeless conclusions of an ideal observer – will establish the work's canonical status. As Blair said, "Time overthrows the illusions of opinion," or, as a more recent writer has put it, "Time is a reliable filter for passing fads and poor judgments,"[25] but time does not work this effect by itself, but only by the cumulative efforts of generations of actual critics.

At the most general level, however, Hume's remark reminds us of the epistemological point that we do not have incorrigible knowledge of our own sentiments and responses, and certainly not immediate knowledge, but must often revise our first blush of pleasure as well as assessment of its significance in order to introduce even internal consistency into our sentiments. Yet it is surely unrealistic to suppose that the reflection so required can always be motivated and conducted in isolation from

[25] Carolyn Korsmeyer, "Hume and the Foundations of Taste," p. 205.

the opinion of others, indeed without the even more direct guidance of socially sanctioned critical norms. But this surely means that the taste of the individual cannot be improved entirely by self-guided "practice," as Hume might be thought to mean, but only with the assistance of societally recognized critical practices.

(2) The second point to be made is that while the qualifications of the Humean critic can ideally be acquired by anyone of adequate delicacy and sense who undertakes the requisite exercises of practice and comparison, the socio-economic reality is simply that few actually have the means and leisure to become such qualified critics, and that the rest of us must indeed depend on those privileged few to point out those finer strokes that we can follow them in relishing. I suspect that this fact was so obvious to the author of essays which were, after all, moral and political as well as literary that he saw no need to make it explicit; but the equally worldly Kames makes it explicit indeed:

> Those who depend for food on bodily labor, are totally devoid of taste . . . The exclusion of classes so many and numerous, reduces within a narrow compass those who are qualified to be judges in the fine arts. Many circumstances are necessary to form such a judge: there must be a good natural taste . . . that taste must be improved by education, reflection, and experience: it must be improved in vigor by living regularly, by using goods of fortune with moderation, and by following dictates of improved nature . . . This is the tenor of life which of all contributes most to refinement of taste (*Elements of Criticism*, pp. 472–72).

As any observer of society such as Hume obviously recognized, such goods of nature are not distributed bountifully, and the goods of fortune actually necessary to support extensive practice and comparison in the several species of beauty – the money and leisure required for extensive and repeated study of the arts, that is – are even rarer. So of course we must actually rely on the canon discovered by the generations of real critics who have enjoyed these goods; to think of our criteria for identifying them as procedures we can readily use to improve our own taste more directly is not just an abstraction, but a gross idealization of social reality.

(3) Finally, Hume's qualified critics cannot be understood as an unnecessary substitute for the ideal qualifications of any individual because by a standard of taste Hume does not mean just some ideal types of aesthetically pleasing form which could be discovered by a qualified observer at any time and place, but rather the actual accumulation of the finest products of human art which provide the truest models for continuing production as well as appreciation – "The same Homer who pleased at Athens and Rome two thousand years ago, [and] who is still admired

at Paris and London" (*ST*, pp. 237–38). Such canonical objects of taste must obviously be transmitted from generation to generation, and are unlikely to be so transmitted in the absence of an express or tacit critical tradition that recognizes their greatness and can point succeeding generations to their specific merits. Further, as Hume makes clear in his discussion of "prejudice" and "good sense," the canonical virtues of such works will not be "fully relished by persons whose situation, real or imaginary, is not conformable to that required by the performance." "An orator addresses himself to a particular audience, and must have a regard to their particular genius, interests, opinions, passions, and prejudices" (*ST*, p. 244), and his oratory cannot be appreciated without an understanding of these matters; and the same goes for other forms of artistry. But such interests, opinions, and prejudices are objects of actual, historical knowledge, and cannot, especially if they involve special views about artistic intentions, be communicated to even ideally qualified observers in successive generations except by an actual body of historical and critical material transmitted along with the artistic artifacts themselves. Any supposition otherwise could hardly be explained, except perhaps by a tacit limitation of the objects of true taste to the merest beauties of form, such as Kant's notorious "free patterns" and "lines aimlessly intertwining" (*Critique of the Power of Judgment*, §4). And as we have amply seen by now, such things form the least "considerable" part of Hume's conception of even the truest objects of taste.

PART II

MOSTLY KANT

3

The Harmony of the Faculties Revisited

1. The concept of the free yet harmonious play between the cognitive powers of imagination and understanding is the central concept in Kant's explanation of the experience of beauty and analysis of the judgment of taste. In Kant's view, when I make a judgment of taste I assert that the pleasure I take in a particular object is one that under ideal circumstances should be felt by any other observer of the object as well. Such a judgment therefore asserts the "subjectively universal validity" of my pleasure in the object (*CPJ*, §8, 5:215),[1] thus making a claim about that pleasure; but it also makes this claim on the basis of the feeling of pleasure itself rather than on the basis of the subsumption of its object under any determinate concept – this is indeed what makes the judgment an "aesthetic" judgment (*CPJ*, §1, 5:203–4; *FI*, VIII, 20:229). In order for me justifiably to claim subjectively universal validity for my feeling of pleasure, Kant supposes, that pleasure must be based in some condition of cognitive powers that are themselves common to all human beings. But since, as Kant assumes, the judgment of taste and the feeling of pleasure that grounds it cannot be determined by the subsumption of its object under any determinate concept, that pleasure cannot be due to the ordinary cognition of an object, which consists precisely in the subsumption of the manifold of sensibility induced by the object and presented to the understanding by the imagination under a determinate concept, but must instead arise from some relation of the imagination and understanding that does not

[1] All translations from the *Critique of the Power of Judgment* and its "First Introduction" are from Immanuel Kant, *Critique of the Power of Judgment*, edited by Paul Guyer, translated by Paul Guyer and Eric Matthews (Cambridge: Cambridge University Press, 2000).

depend upon such a subsumption. These two conditions, Kant supposes, can be satisfied only by a state of free yet harmonious play between those cognitive powers.

2. But the concept of the harmonious free play of imagination and understanding is obscure, and Kant's central attempts to explicate it do not obviously succeed:

(i) In the first draft of the introduction to the *Critique of the Power of Judgment*, Kant distinguishes an "aesthetic judgment of sense," which merely asserts that the subject who makes it takes pleasure in an object because of some "sensation . . . immediately produced by the empirical intuition of the object" that does not involve the higher powers of cognition and therefore cannot ground a claim of subjectively universal validity, from an "aesthetic judgment of reflection," which can claim such validity because it is grounded on a sensation of pleasure "which the harmonious play of the two faculties of cognition in the power of judgment, imagination and understanding, produces in the subject insofar as in the given representation the faculty of the apprehension of the one and the faculty of presentation of the other are reciprocally expeditious" (*FI*, VIII, 20:224). Here, everything turns on the mysterious phrase "reciprocally expeditious."

(ii) In the published version of the introduction, Kant writes that the feeling of pleasure that is both the subject-matter and the ground for a judgment of beauty "can express nothing but [the object's] suitability to the cognitive faculties that are in play in the reflecting power of judgment, insofar as they are in play," a condition that obtains if in the "apprehension of forms in the imagination" and their "comparison" to the "faculty for relating intuitions to concepts" "the imagination (as the faculty of *a priori* intuitions) is unintentionally brought into accord with the understanding, as the faculty of concepts, through a given representation" (*CPJ*, VII, 5:189–90). This statement, like those in the first draft of the introduction, does nothing to cash in the concept of a harmonious play or accord between imagination and understanding.

(iii) In the section of the "Analytic of the Beautiful" that he labels the "key to the critique of taste" (*CPJ*, §9, 5:216), in which he argues that the feeling of pleasure that grounds a judgment of taste must itself be the product of some form of judging if it is to be universally valid,[2] Kant first repeats the language of play, saying that "The powers of cognition that are set into play by" the "representation" of a beautiful object "are hereby in a free play, since no determinate concept restricts them to a particular rule of cognition," and "Thus the state of mind in this representation must be that of a feeling of the free play of the powers of representation in a given representation for a cognition in general" (5:217). He then adds two new terms when he says that "The animation of both faculties (the imagination and the understanding) to an activity that is indeterminate, but yet, through the stimulus of the given representation, in unison, namely that which belongs to a cognition in general, is the sensation whose universal communicability is postulated by the judgment of taste," a "sensation of the effect that consists in the facilitated play of both powers of the mind (imagination and understanding), enlivened through mutual agreement" (*CPJ*, §9, 5:219). These statements claim that the free, harmonious, or as Kant here says "facilitated" play of the cognitive powers "animates" or "enlivens" them, but do not explain in what facilitation or animation consist.

(iv) In the "General Remark" that follows the "Analytic of the Beautiful," Kant sums up what he has argued to that point by saying that "it turns out that everything flows from the concept of taste as a faculty for judging the object in relation to the **free lawfulness** of the imagination," the condition that obtains when an object provides the senses "with a form that contains precisely such a composition of the manifold as the imagination would design in harmony with the **lawfulness of the understanding** in general if it were left free by itself," a state in which the imagination is both "**free** and yet **lawful by itself**" (*CPJ*, §22, 5:240–1). This varies the previous accounts of free play by suggesting that this free play is located *within* the imagination rather than in a relation *between* the imagination and the understanding, while adding that this free play within the imagination is somehow *consistent* with the "lawfulness" that is characteristic of the faculty of understanding, but still does not make clear what play is.

[2] For my earlier discussions of the complexities of this section, see my "Pleasure and Society in Kant's Theory of Taste," in Ted Cohen and Paul Guyer, eds., *Essays in Kant's Aesthetics* (Chicago: University of Chicago Press, 1982), pp. 21–54, and my *Kant and the Claims of Taste*, second edition (Cambridge: Cambridge University Press, 1997), pp. 133–41.

(v) Finally, in the section that is to prepare the way for the "Deduction of pure aesthetic judgments," which will argue that if our pleasure in beauty is grounded in a condition of cognitive faculties that are universally shared, then it must be universally shareable itself, by explaining how our pleasure in beauty is in fact grounded in a condition of the cognitive faculties, Kant puts all his previous terms together. Here he writes that "the judgment of taste must rest on a mere sensation of the reciprocally animating imagination in its **freedom** and the understanding with its **lawfulness**, thus on a feeling that allows the object to be judged in accordance with the purposiveness of the representation (by means of which an object is given) for the promotion of the faculty of cognition in its free play" – and then adds one more unexplained idea when he writes that "taste, as a subjective power of judgment, contains a principle of subsumption, not of intuitions under concepts, but of the **faculty** of intuitions or presentations (i.e., of the imagination) under the **faculty** of concepts (i.e., the understanding), insofar as the former **in its freedom** is in harmony with the latter **in its lawfulness**" (*CPJ*, §35, 5:297). This idea of the subsumption of the faculty of imagination under the faculty of understanding is not transparent, since the only conception of subsumption that Kant uses elsewhere in his works is that of the subsumption of a manifold under a determinate concept, whether a manifold of empirical intuitions under an empirical concept or a manifold of specific concepts under some more generic concept. So this notion of subsumption could hardly explain all of Kant's previous accounts of the free and animating play of the cognitive powers.

3. The opacity of all these attempted elucidations of the idea of the free yet harmonious play of imagination and understanding has naturally brought forth numerous attempts to interpret them. These interpretations can be divided into two main classes.

(a) Many interpretations of Kant's concept of the free play of the faculties interpret this as a state of mind in which the manifold of representations furnished by the perception of an object satisfies all of the conditions for normal cognition of an object *except for that of the actual application of a determinate concept to the manifold.* If cognition itself is equated with the subsumption of a manifold of intuitions under a determinate concept – as Kant suggests when he famously states that "Intuition and concepts therefore constitute the elements of all our cognition, so that neither concepts without intuition corresponding to them in some way nor intuition without concepts can yield a cognition" (*Critique of Pure Reason*, A 74/B 50) – then on this interpretation, the harmony of imagination and understanding would be a state of mind that satisfies all the conditions for cognition except the final condition that would transform it into actual cognition. For this reason, I propose to call such interpretations "precognitive" interpretations of the harmony of the faculties. The key task for all such interpretations, of course, is to explain why we are pleased, indeed especially pleased, with a state of mind that falls short of satisfying all of the conditions for ordinary cognition.

(b) An alternative sort of interpretation maintains that the free play of the faculties does not satisfy all but one of the normal conditions for cognition, but rather that it satisfies *all* of them, although only in an indeterminate way: instead of suggesting *no* determinate concept for the manifold of intuition that it furnishes, a beautiful object suggests an indeterminate or open-ended *manifold* of concepts for the manifold of intuition, allowing the mind to flit back and forth playfully and enjoyably among different ways of conceiving the same object without allowing or requiring it to settle down on one determinate way of conceiving the object. We can call such interpretations "multicognitive," in order to convey that on this sort of account the free play is precisely among a multiplicity of possible concepts and hence cognitions suggested by the beautiful object.[3]

A particularly clear statement of the precognitive interpretation of the harmony of the faculties is offered by Dieter Henrich when he writes that since on Kant's account we must be able to assert a judgment of taste "without having a description of the object at our disposal," this ability "is readily explained in terms of a cognitive process that precedes the process

[3] Andrea Kern suggests a somewhat similar division of interpretations of the concept of free play, calling them the "material" and "hermeneutical" interpretations, the former after Paul de Man, who describes seeing an object free of any conceptual admixture at all as "purely material," and the latter after Hans-Georg Gadamer, who understands Kant's concept as a precursor of his own "hermeneutic" model of understanding, on which any object is always seen against a background of possible interpretations even before we settle down on one, as we ordinarily do. See Kern, *Schöne Lust: Eine Theorie der ästhetischen Erfahrung nach Kant* (Frankfurt am Main: Suhrkamp Verlag, 2000), pp. 51–3. Her references are to de Man's article, "Phenomenality and Materiality in Kant," an English version of which may be found in Hugh J. Silverman and Gary E. Aylesworth, eds., *The Textual Sublime: Deconstruction and Its Differences* (Albany: SUNY Press, 1990), pp. 87–109, and to Gadamer's *Wahrheit und Methode*, English translation *Truth and Method*, Garrett Barden and John Cumming, eds. (New York: Seabury Press, 1975).

of concept formation in principle although it is compatible with it."[4] But other interpreters in the recent literature on Kant's aesthetic theory have also offered similar accounts. In 1974, Donald Crawford wrote that "Pleasure in the beautiful results when such an ordering" of the manifold of intuition presented by an object "is achieved that the cognitive powers are in harmony: it is as if the manifold has a unity to which a concept ought to apply, even though there is no definite concept applicable."[5] In 1979, I wrote that on Kant's account "there is a subjective state in which the conditions of judgment are met" and that "this state may obtain independently of the making of an actual knowledge claim about the object,"[6] and then proposed that this be interpreted as a state in which the *goal* of cognition subjectively described, namely the unification of our manifold of intuition, is felt to be achieved independently of the satisfaction of the ordinary *objective* condition for cognition, namely, the application of a concept – "the harmony of the faculties produces pleasure because it... represents a state in which a general cognitive objective... is fulfilled without the guarantee ordinarily provided by the subsumability of intuitions under concepts."[7] I further suggested that this state could be interpreted as one in which the first two syntheses that Kant describes in the theory of threefold synthesis in the "Transcendental Deduction" of the categories in the first edition of the *Critique of Pure Reason*, namely, the "synthesis of apprehension in the intuition" and the "synthesis of reproduction in the imagination," are felt to take place even without the completion of the final form of synthesis, namely, the "synthesis of recognition in the concept":[8] as I put it, "The harmony of the faculties is then a state in which, somehow, a manifold of intuition is run through and held together as a unity by the imagination without the use of a concept."[9] And in 1982, Ralf Meerbote wrote that "the object of a pure

4 Dieter Henrich, "Kant's Explanation of Aesthetic Judgment," in his *Aesthetic Judgment and the Moral Image of the World: Studies in Kant* (Stanford: Stanford University Press, 1992), p. 38. Henrich here equates Kant's requirement that the judgment of taste and hence the underlying experience of beauty be free of any *concept* that determines it with the thought that we cannot even *describe* the object of taste; this depends upon the assumption that any description of any object by means of concepts is necessarily sufficient to determine our response to it, which is certainly debatable.

5 Donald W. Crawford, *Kant's Aesthetic Theory* (Madison: University of Wisconsin Press, 1974), p. 90.

6 *Kant and the Claims of Taste*, second edition, p. 66.

7 *Kant and the Claims of Taste*, second edition, p. 74.

8 *Critique of Pure Reason*, A 98–103.

9 *Kant and the Claims of Taste*, second edition, p. 76.

judgment of taste is the presence . . . of conformity of the apprehended features of manifold to the *invariant* features of the understanding" although "this is to *differ* from reflection toward the production of a specific concept."[10]

All of these statements[11] suggest an interpretation of the harmonious play of imagination and understanding as a state in which the mind grasps the unity of the manifold of intuition presented by an object, which would ordinarily both lead to and depend upon the application of a determinate concept of the object to that manifold, without actually applying such a concept.

There are variants of this straightforward version of the precognitive interpretation as well. Hannah Ginsborg has argued that "in the experience of an object as beautiful . . . I take my imaginative activity in the perception of the object to be as it ought to be in the primitive sense, which means that I have no conception of *how* it ought to be except that afforded by the example of my activity itself: namely, the indeterminate conception that it ought to be *this* way,"[12] but also that the ability to have such an indeterminate sense that an object is as it ought to be is a precondition of the general ability to learn to apply concepts to objects, which express in a determinate way how objects falling under those concepts ought to be. Thus, on her account, the ability to have aesthetic experience is a precondition for having ordinary cognitive experience.[13] Her account is unusual in not merely describing aesthetic experience as a precognitive state, but in also insisting that this precognitive state is a precondition for any ordinary cognition.

[10] Ralf Meerbote, "Reflection on Beauty," in Cohen and Guyer, *Essays in Kant's Aesthetics*, pp. 55–86, at p. 72. Where I have indicated an ellision in the quotation from Meerbote, he had written "or absence"; these words express the assumption that negative as well as positive aesthetic judgments are pure judgments of taste. This has been the subject of an extensive controversy in recent literature, which I will not discuss in this essay; for my view, see "Kant on the Purity of the Ugly," Chapter 6 in the present volume.

[11] As well as the more recent statement by Jürgen Stolzenberg that Kant can only mean "that in the manifold elements of an individual object given in intuition a certain connection of these elements can be perceived, which is not producible or alterable at will or in accordance with contingent rules of association, but for which there is nevertheless no general conceptual expression applicable to other objects"; see "Das Freie Spiel der Erkenntniskräfte: Zu Kants Theorie des Geschmacksurteils," in Ursula Franke, ed., *Kants Schlüssel zur Kritik des Geschmacks: Ästhetische Erfahrung heute – Studien zur Aktualität von Kants "Kritik der Urteilskraft," Sonderheft des Jahrgangs 2000 der Zeitschrift für Ästhetik und allgemeine Kunstwissenschaft* (Hamburg: Felix Meiner, 2000), pp. 1–28, at p. 10.

[12] Hannah Ginsborg, "Lawfulness without a Law: Kant on the Free Play of Imagination and Understanding," in *Philosophical Topics* 25/1 (1997): 37–83, at p. 70.

[13] Ginsborg, "Lawfulness without a Law," pp. 53–9, 73–4.

Another variant on the precognitive view is that offered by Rudolf Makkreel. Makkreel is concerned with the compatibility of Kant's explanation of the experience of beauty with his general epistemology (as are of course other advocates of the precognitive interpretation as well), and addresses this issue thus: interpreting the "Transcendental Deduction" of the first *Critique* to demonstrate the applicability of the *categories* or "pure concepts of the understanding," that is, such completely general and abstract concepts as magnitude, substance, causation, and so on, to the objects of empirical intuition, Makkreel proposes that "The 'free conformity' of the aesthetic imagination to the laws of the understanding means that the imagination may not violate the categorial framework of the understanding, although it may explicate possibilities left open by that framework,"[14] and then that in the experience of beauty "the imagination schematizes without using *empirical* concepts," so that "The aesthetic judgment directly compares the apprehended form of an object with the way categories are generally schematized in relation to the form of time."[15] On this account, the idea is not that in the experience of beauty we are simply conscious of some sort of unity in the manifold of intuition prior to and independently of the application of any determinate and thus presumably empirical concept to the object; rather, we are somehow conscious that the manifold satisfies one of the particular temporal structures that "schematizes" the pure concepts of the understanding – for example, the rule-governed succession of states of affairs in time that is the pattern of causation that schematizes the pure category of ground and consequence – but without applying any determinate, empirical causal concept to the manifold. It is as if we somehow feel that the manifold satisfies the general concept of causation without being subsumable under any particular causal concept, such as the concept of combustion or digestion as a type of causation.[16]

The main alternative to the precognitive interpretation is the multicognitive kind of interpretation of the harmony of the faculties. Gerhard

[14] Rudolf Makkreel, *Imagination and Interpretation in Kant: The Hermeneutical Import of the Critique of Judgment* (Chicago: University of Chicago Press, 1990), p. 47.

[15] Makkreel, *Imagination and Interpretation*, p. 56.

[16] In his book, Makkreel goes on to argue that the categories in fact must be schematized through empirical concepts, and that this is accomplished through the discovery of empirical concepts within a *system* of such concepts, which is accomplished by the reflecting use of judgment (pp. 58–9). But this use of reflecting judgment, which Kant describes in the Introductions to the *Critique of the Power of Judgment* but not in the "Critique of Aesthetic Judgment," is clearly entirely distinct from the *aesthetic* use of this power of judgment.

Seel, for example, wrote in 1988 that on Kant's account "the harmony of the cognitive powers is nothing other than the simulation of a successful attempt at cognition,"[17] and then proposed that such stimulation would be best understood – although in this he supposed he was going beyond Kant's *ipsissima verba* – as if "In the case of the *aesthetic* function the intuitively given is not subsumed under *a determinate* concept, but under a multitude of concepts playfully applied to it."[18] Two prominent interpreters writing in 2001 have also advocated versions of this approach, although without evincing Seel's scruple that they might be reconstructing rather than merely interpreting Kant. Fred Rush writes that in the case of "aesthetic reflection and the harmony of the faculties . . . perception is a taking of the manifold as having one among many potential possible characters . . . a state in which it is implicitly registered that what is perceived is one way, but that does not foreclose, and indeed it rests upon, other ways it might be subject to synthesis."[19] "What Kant envisions is a potentially endless ranging over the manifold of intuition by the imagination, engaged in the activity of modeling it as unifiable in any of the multifarious ways that the spatial and temporal properties of that manifold permit."[20] And although Henry Allison's attempts to characterize the harmony of the faculty are not obviously univocal, he seems to be attracted primarily to the multicognitive interpretation of the harmony of the faculties. He writes that the free play of the imagination "does not issue in the exhibition of a determinate concept," but rather in "what might be described as the exhibition of the form of a concept in general (but not any concept in particular)." It is not clear what "the form of a concept in general" might be thought to be, and perhaps it could be understood as whatever degree of spatio-temporal organization or unity of a manifold might be thought to be a necessary condition for the application of a concept to it, thus linking Allison's interpretation to what I have called the precognitive approach. But Allison continues that "the basic idea is presumably that the imagination in its free play stimulates the understanding by occasioning it to entertain fresh conceptual possibilities, while, conversely, the imagination, under the general direction

[17] Gerhard Seel, "Über den Grund der Lust an schönen Gegenständen: Kritische Fragen an die Ästhetik Kants," in Hariolf Oberer and Gerhard Seel, eds., *Kant: Analysen – Probleme – Kritik* (Würzburg: Königshausen & Neumann, 1988), pp. 317–56, at p. 344.

[18] Seel, "Über den Grund," p. 349.

[19] Fred L. Rush, Jr., "The Harmony of the Faculties," *Kant-Studien* 92 (2001): 38–61, at p. 52.

[20] Rush, "The Harmony of the Faculties," p. 58.

of the understanding, strives to conceive new patterns of order."[21] This seems clearly to fall on the side of the multicognitive interpretation of the harmony of the faculties: read literally, Allison's statement suggests that both the imagination and the understanding *conceive* of the object of taste in a variety of different possible ways, although somehow each faculty stimulates the other to do so.[22]

4. Now, before I suggest some reasons why we should not simply choose between these two approaches but should instead look for a third alternative, I want to concede that Kant's texts certainly provide some basis for each of these approaches. In fact, we can find support for each of these approaches in a single text, namely, in Kant's first draft of the Introduction to the third *Critique.* In Section VIII of this text, Kant surely provides a basis for the precognitive approach when he writes that

> A merely **reflecting** judgment about a given individual object, however, **can be aesthetic** if (before its comparison with others is seen), the power of judgment, which has no concept ready for the given intuition, holds the imagination (merely in the apprehension of the object) together with the understanding (in the presentation of a concept in general) and perceives a relation of the two faculties of cognition which constitutes the subjective, merely sensitive condition of the objective use of the power of judgment in general (namely the agreement of those two faculties with each other).
>
> (*FI*, VIII, 20:223–4)

Here Kant's statement that the imagination is involved "merely in the apprehension" of the object, since apprehension is the first stage of the threefold synthesis involved in ordinary cognition, as well as his statement that the power of judgment "has no concept ready for the given intuition," both suggest that the harmony of the faculties is a state that logically and even temporally precedes ordinary cognition, and should thus be understood as a state in which the manifold is unified prior to the application of any concept to it. If so, then the "subjective, merely sensitive condition of the objective use of the power of judgment in general" would be precisely the satisfaction of all the conditions for cognition of an object in a manifold of intuition short of the application of a concept

[21] Henry E. Allison, *Kant's Theory of Taste: A Reading of the Critique of Aesthetic Judgment* (Cambridge: Cambridge University Press, 2001), p. 171.

[22] Malcolm Budd may also suggest the multicognitive approach when he writes that "the imagination's freedom consists in its not being adequate to some particular empirical concept – all that is necessary is that it should be adequate to some empirical concept or other"; "The Pure Judgment of Taste as an Aesthetic Reflective Judgment," *British Journal of Aesthetics* 41 (2001): 247–60, at p. 255.

to the manifold. Similarly, Kant's eventual statement in the preparation for the deduction of pure aesthetic judgments that the "subjective formal condition of a judgment in general" that is satisfied in the case of a judgment of beauty consists "only in the subsumption of the imagination itself (in the case of a representation by means of which an object is given) under the condition that the understanding in general advance from intuitions to concepts" (*CPJ*, §35, 5:287) might be interpreted to mean that the "subjective formal condition" of the cognitive powers that is the ground of the experience and judgment of beauty consists in the fact that the imagination responds to a manifold of intuition as if it satisfied all the conditions of cognition short of the application of any determinate concept of an object to that manifold.

Yet advocates of the multicognitive approach can equally well appeal to another statement in Section VII of the first Introduction in behalf of their position:

> If, then, the form of a given object in empirical intuition is so constituted that the **apprehension** of its manifold in the imagination agrees with the **presentation** of a concept of the understanding (though which concept be undetermined [*unbestimmt welches Begriffs*]), then in the mere reflection understanding and imagination mutually agree for the advancement of their business, and the object will be perceived as purposive merely for the power of judgment, hence the purposiveness itself will be considered as merely subjective; for which, further, no determinate concept of the object at all is required nor is one thereby generated . . .
>
> (*FI*, VII, 20:220–1)[23]

Here, Kant's phrase "though which concept be undetermined" or "undetermined which concept" suggests that the aesthetically pleasing manifold does not merely suggest the satisfaction of some precondition for cognition, but rather suggests *some* concept for the object it presents without suggesting or "generating" *any particular* concept, something that we could most readily understand if we take it to mean that it suggests *multiple* concepts without forcing or allowing us to choose between them.

5. In spite of the fact that there is textual evidence for both the precognitive and multicognitive interpretations of the harmony of the faculties, however, there is also a variety of problems with each. The most

[23] The first part of this passage is cited by Budd immediately following the sentence previously quoted from him; see "The Pure Judgment of Taste," p. 255, and by Rush immediately preceding the second sentence previously quoted from him; see "The Harmony of the Faculties," p. 58.

obvious – and often recognized[24] – problem with the precognitive approach is that on this approach it may seem as if *everything* ought to be beautiful, or at least capable of being found beautiful: that is, if our feeling of beauty in a given manifold is a response to the fact that it satisfies a condition that must be satisfied in every case of cognition, even if it does not satisfy *all* of the conditions that must be satisfied for actual cognition, then why don't we experience beauty in every case of cognition?

A variety of answers to this obvious problem have of course been suggested, or suggest themselves. One proposal would be that the ubiquity of beauty is not a problem for Kant at all – that Kant embraces the conclusion that we do, or at least should be able to, find every object beautiful. This proposal would see Kant as anticipating "aesthetic attitude" theories from Schopenhauer to the mid-twentieth century, that is, the view that with the right – typically, disinterested – attitude any object *can* be found to be beautiful, although, as Schopenhauer argues, the difference between the artistic genius and the rest of us may be the ease with which the former can adopt this attitude.[25] However, there seems to be no evidence that Kant ever held this view: while his paradigms of free beauties of nature are certainly ordinary objects – hummingbirds and crustacea – rather than exalted works of human artistry, he never suggests that *every* ordinary object can be found to be beautiful.[26]

A second proposal has been that Kant thinks that every object *has* been found beautiful by us on our way to cognition, but that ordinarily we forget this, and have to turn to art in order to *recover* this experience of pleasure.[27] This proposal might initially seem to have a textual basis in Kant's remark that "we no longer detect any noticeable pleasure in the comprehensibility of nature and the unity of its division into genera and species, by means of which alone empirical concepts are possible through which we cognize it in its particular laws; but it must certainly have been there

[24] See, for example, Meerbote, "Reflection on Beauty," p. 81; Anthony Savile, *Aesthetic Reconstructions: The Seminal Writings of Lessing, Kant, and Schiller* (Oxford: Backwell, 1987), pp. 137–41; and Budd, "The Pure Judgment of Taste," p. 251n6.

[25] Arthur Schopenhauer, *The World as Will and Representation*, §41; in the translation by E. F. J. Payne (Indian Hills, Colorado: The Falcon Wing's Press, 1958). Vol. I, p. 210.

[26] He does eventually assert that virtually every object – except those which arouse loathing – can be the object of a beautiful *representation* in art (*CPJ*, §48, 5:312), but that is quite a different point; it does not imply that every object can be found beautiful in its own right, that is, directly rather than through a representation of it, which is a numerically and qualitatively distinct object from it.

[27] See Jay M. Bernstein, *The Fate of Art: Aesthetic Alienation from Kant to Derrida and Adorno* (University Park: Pennsylvania State University Press, 1992), pp. 55–63.

in its time, and only because the most common experience would not be possible without it has it gradually become mixed up with mere cognition and is no longer specially noticed" (*CPJ*, VI, 5:187). However, in this passage from the Introduction, Kant is not describing aesthetic judgment at all, but a different application of the power of reflecting judgment, its role in finding determinate concepts of species and genera by means of which to classify the particular objects of nature,[28] and he gives no hint that he thinks that this pattern of an initial pleasure that is forgotten but may then be recovered is characteristic of the judgment of beauty.

Finally, the most common solution proposed for this problem is that not every object of ordinary cognition is or even can be found to be beautiful, because the satisfaction of the precondition for ordinary cognition that is characteristic of the experience of beauty occurs only in special circumstances. There are two ways in which this solution can be developed. One idea is that the mind ordinarily proceeds through all the necessary conditions of cognition, right through and past the preconceptual conditions and up to the application of a determinate concept to the object, but that in some cases it is possible for the mind to abstract from the application of a concept to the object – to turn its attention away from a concept, or away from the task of applying determinate concepts to objects – and to become aware of the unity that the manifold of intuition has even apart from this concept.[29] However, it is by no means clear that Kant thinks that it is always in our own power to adopt the "aesthetic attitude" of disinterestedness and thereby perceive beauty where we otherwise would not. In his discussion of the distinction between free and adherent beauty in §16, he states that "A judgment of taste in regard to an object with a determinate internal end would be pure only if the person making the judgment either had no concept of this end or abstracted from it in his

[28] See also note 16.

[29] For example, Budd writes that "the only viable interpretation of Kant's view is that in judging an object's beauty, its being an instance of that kind must not be allowed to figure in the process of reflection, which must focus solely on the object's form. In fact, it is easy to see that the reflection involved in a judgement of taste must allow the subject to abstract from what the object is seen to be" ("The Pure Judgment of Taste as an Aesthetic Reflective Judgment," p. 253). Anthony Savile clearly formulates the danger that on a precognitive account, everything might turn out to be beautiful, and then seems to suggest that we have a choice about how judgment is to be "conducted," either by determining judgment, in accordance with the guidelines imposed by some concept, or by reflecting judgment, free from such guidelines (*Aesthetic Reconstructions*, p. 140), a freedom that presumably depends upon its being in our power to abstract from any determinate concept that applies to the object.

judgment," and then seems to suggest that it is always possible for anyone to abstract from such a concept because a dispute between one person who is making a judgment of free beauty about an object and another who is making a judgment of adherent beauty about it could always be resolved if the latter would only abstract from the concept involved in his judgment of adherent beauty (*CPJ*, 5:231).[30] In his discussion of the ideal of beauty in the next section, however, Kant seems to imply the opposite when he argues that if one recognizes something as a work of art – for example, an archaeological artifact – then "the fact that [it is] regarded as a work of art is already enough to require one to admit that one relates [its] shape to some sort of intention and to a determinate purpose" (*CPJ*, §17, 5:236n), even if one does not actually know what that purpose is. This suggests that it is not always in one's power to abstract or divert one's attention from a concept that applies to an object.[31]

But maybe the solution lies in the *objects* of taste: that is, maybe some but not all objects are beautiful because some but not all objects make it particularly easy to grasp the unity or harmony of the manifolds they present independently of any concept that applies to them. As Malcolm Budd puts it, in the case of a beautiful object, its "structure will in reflection on its form both be a continuing stimulus to the imagination and make easy the task of the understanding . . . an object's form will be contemplated with disinterested pleasure when the manifold combined by the imagination is both rich enough to entertain the imagination in its combinatory activity and such as to facilitate the understanding's detection of regularity within it."[32] Once again, there is certainly textual evidence for ascribing such a view to Kant. I earlier quoted a sentence from the conclusion of §9, where Kant refers to the "*facilitated* (*erleichterten*) play of both powers of the mind" (5:219; emphasis added), and this reference to "facilitation" is not unique, but had in fact long been used by Kant: one of his earliest notes on aesthetics (found among his notes on the chapter on "empirical psychology" in Baumgarten's *Metaphysica*) states that "In everything that is to be approved in accordance with taste there must be something that facilitates [*erleichtert*] the differentiation of the manifold (delineation)" as well as "something that advances comprehensibility (relations, proportions), something that makes possible taking it all together

30 I return to the adherent beauty later in this section and in Section 9.

31 I have discussed this tension at greater length in *Kant and the Claims of Taste*, second edition, pp. 220–5.

32 Budd, "The Pure Judgment of Taste as an Aesthetic Reflective Judgment," p. 258.

[*Zusammennehmung*] (unity), and finally something that promotes the distinction from everything [else] possible (precision)."[33] So there is no doubt that the idea that some objects particularly facilitate our grasp of them in ways that others do not, and that this fact is intimately connected to their beauty, was a part of Kant's thought, and interpreters are hardly mistaken to observe this.

Nevertheless, there are philosophical difficulties with the idea that our response to beauty depends on some cognitive process that precedes our application of a determinate concept to an object or even upon the possibility of abstracting from such a concept. Before turning to these problems, however, I will discuss some problems with the multicognitive interpretation, which in the end must also contend with these deeper issues. First, there are two obvious textual difficulties with the multicognitive approach. One is that even if it were clear that the parenthetical phrase "*unbestimmt welches Begriffs*" (*sic; FI*, VII, 20:221) should be translated in a way that suggests that the mind ranges indeterminately among a multitude of determinate concepts, Kant only uses this sort of phrase, twice, in a single passage: in Section VII of the first Introduction, Kant's other use of a similar phrase comes three paragraphs prior to the passage cited from 20:221, when he says that "In our power of judgment we perceive purposiveness insofar as it merely reflects upon a given object . . . in order to bring the empirical intuition of that object under some concept (it is indeterminate which [*unbestimmt welchen*])" (20:220).[34] This usage is not repeated in Section VIII of the first Introduction, in the published Introduction to the third *Critique*, or in the body of the work. In all of these places, Kant typically says that the experience and judgment of beauty requires *no* concept, no *determinate* concept, or only the *faculty* of concepts without any concept. Thus he writes: "to discover beauty . . . requires nothing but mere reflection (without any concept)" (*FI*, VIII, 20:229) and that the "contemplation" leading to a judgment of taste "is not directed to concepts" (*CPJ*, §5, 5:209); that in the state of the free play of the powers of

[33] R 625 (1769? 1764–68?), 15:271; previously cited in *Kant and the Claims of Taste*, second edition, pp. 17–18.

[34] Here I omit the continuation of this sentence, in which Kant says that we may also perceive purposiveness in mere reflection upon an object "in order to bring the laws which the concept of experience itself contains under common principles," since this bears on the use of reflecting judgment to establish a system of empirical laws, which is a distinct form of reflecting judgment. For a full discussion of the different forms of reflecting judgment, see my "Kant's Principles of Reflecting Judgment," in Paul Guyer, ed., *Kant's Critique of the Power of Judgment: Critical Essays* (Lanham: Rowman & Littlefield, 2003), pp. 1–60.

cognition "no determinate concept restricts them to a particular rule of cognition" (*CPJ*, §9, 5:217); and that "the apprehension of forms in the imagination" that grounds the response to and judgment of beauty "can never take place without the reflecting power of judgment, even if unintentionally, at least comparing them to its faculty for relating intuitions to concepts" (*CPJ*, VII, 5:190; cf. also §35, 5:287). None of these phrases suggests that Kant supposes that aesthetic experience involves an *indeterminate* concept,[35] let alone an *indeterminate multitude* of concepts; they all suggest that the experience of beauty somehow involves our *faculty* of concepts without involving any particular concepts at all.

My second textual point is that none of Kant's *examples* of beautiful objects and our experience of them suggests that any indeterminate multitude of concepts or conceptual possibilities is necessarily involved in such experience. Kant's paradigmatic examples of free beauties of both nature and art, such things as hummingbirds and crustacea, designs *à la grecque* and musical fantasias, "do not represent anything, no object under a determinate concept" (*CPJ*, §16, 5:229);[36] instead, of course, Kant insists that the proper object of taste is pure spatial or temporal form, "**shape** or **play**," for example, design in a work of visual art or composition in a piece of music (*CPJ*, §14, 5:225). These examples do not sit well with the suggestion that the object of the experience of beauty is really a play of *concepts* or *conceptual possibilities*. And even when Kant first introduces a kind of beauty that clearly does involve a concept, namely, adherent beauty, such beauty involves only *one* concept, the concept of the intended end of the object with such beauty, with which the form of the adherently beautiful object must somehow be compatible. There is no suggestion that adherent beauty any more than free beauty involves a play among any indeterminate multitude of concepts.[37] Likewise, when

35 I should note here that although Kant does eventually argue that the resolution of the "antinomy of judgments of taste" does require the assumption that in some sense, judgments of taste rest on an "indeterminate and also indeterminable concept," namely, the idea of the supersensible substratum of humanity and of appearances generally (*CPJ*, §57, 5:339–40), it is questionable whether he needs such a claim to resolve the antinomy (see *Kant and the Claims of Taste*, chapter 10), and in any case is not part of this claim that any indeterminate concept or multitude of concepts is part of the experience of beauty itself, rather than an underlying ground for the universal subjective validity of this experience.

36 For a subtle discussion of the ambiguities of Kant's use of the term "represent" here, see Eva Schaper, "Free and Dependent Beauty," in her *Studies in Kant's Aesthetics* (Edinburgh: Edinburgh University Press, 1979), pp. 78–98.

37 In "Dependent Beauty as the Appreciation of Teleological Style," *Journal of Aesthetics and Art Criticism* 55 (1997): 387–400, Robert Wicks argues that we experience an object with dependent beauty as if it satisfied its end in an indeterminate multitude of ways, but he

Kant finally presents his theory of fine art, he suggests that a work of art typically has a content, an "aesthetic idea," which connotes a "rational idea," on the one hand, through a wealth of "attributes" or images, on the other, but he does not suggest that in the experience of a work of fine art the mind plays among a multitude of possible conceptualizations *of* the work of art itself (*CPJ*, §49, 5:314).

Textual evidence aside, the philosophical problem with the multicognitive approach is that it is not clear why an experience of flitting back and forth among an indeterminate multitude of concepts for a single object should be *pleasing*. To be sure, one can well imagine that *some* such experiences are pleasing, as reveries or daydreams sometimes are; but then again, the experience of ranging over an indeterminate multitude of possible concepts for an object without being able to settle on a determinate one for the object at hand is sometimes frustrating, indeed a nightmare – just imagine, or remember, going back and forth among several answers to an exam question, each of which seems plausible without one seeming conclusively correct. When Rush, for example, writes that "any beautiful thing will permit a seamless, effortless, and potentially endless series of unconscious 're-imaginings',"[38] that sounds as if it might sometimes be pleasant – the words "seamless" and "effortless" (reminiscent of Kant's term "*erleichtert*") are obviously meant to sound that way – but it is not clear why an endless series of "re-imaginings" might not also be frustrating – unless, that is, it satisfies some independent criterion for aesthetic satisfaction.

Now Rush's characterization of the free play of the faculties here does bring out one point that is not always clear in interpretations of Kant's idea, namely, that the contemplation of the beautiful should be understood as a state of mind that is sometimes *protracted* rather than instantaneous. This is indeed suggested by Kant when he maintains that the pleasure in the beautiful "has a causality in itself, namely that of **maintaining** the state of the representation of the mind and the occupation of the cognitive powers without a further aim," and thus that "We **linger** over the consideration of the beautiful because this consideration strengthens and reproduces itself" (*CPJ*, §12, 5:222). In fact, he needs to say this, because the only entirely general characterization of pleasure, whether

does not, like Rush or Allison, equate these with an indeterminate multitude of concepts or conceptual possibilities. So his approach is not a pure case of what I have called the multicognitive approach.

[38] Rush, "The Harmony of the Faculties," p. 58.

pleasure in mere sensation, in reflection, or in the determination of the will, that he thinks can be given is that "**Pleasure** is a **state** of the mind in which a representation is in agreement with itself, as a ground, either merely for preserving itself (for the state of the powers of the mind reciprocally promoting each other in a representation preserves itself), or for producing its object" (*FI*, VIII, 20:230–1). Pleasure is a state that we would rather prolong than end – that, in a way, is the only possible definition of pleasure. But the very generality of this characteristic means that we can hardly infer from it anything particular about the pleasure *in beauty* – for example, that it must be a temporally extended play among "conceptual possibilities." Rather, Kant seems to assume that states of pleasure are pleasurable from the outset, and do not depend upon their temporal duration or prolongation to become pleasurable, although precisely because they are pleasurable we are naturally disposed to prolong them.[39] This suggests that he does not understand the pleasure in beauty as something that could emerge only from a temporally extended play with conceptual possibilities, but rather as a state that is at least sometimes more instantaneously pleasurable – as the contemplation of a graphic design (but perhaps not a musical composition) might be – and that we would then like to prolong.

6. But the deeper philosophical problem for both the precognitive and the multicognitive approaches to the harmony of the faculties is that the very idea of a state of our cognitive powers that does not involve any determinate concepts is dubious. In fact, this idea is inconsistent both with an ordinary assumption about judgments of taste that Kant clearly shares with the rest of us and with the most fundamental claims of Kant's theory of knowledge.

The ordinary assumption about judgments of taste, which Kant clearly shares with the rest of us, is that the objects of such judgments must be identified by means of particular empirical concepts and that we must be cognizant of the application of such concepts to them in order to make such judgments, just as is the case with any other kinds of judgments about objects, in spite of whatever features are distinctive of aesthetic judgments. An aesthetic judgment does not have the form "This is beautiful," but rather "This *F* is beautiful": this hummingbird,

[39] Here one should no doubt add "other things being equal." Some pleasures are of course too intense for us really to want to prolong them very long or else accompanied with such negative consequences that we cannot on reflection want to prolong them very long.

this sunset, this painting, this symphony, this part of the garden (but not the other), this facade of the building (but not its other elevations), or the public spaces of this hotel (but not its guest rooms). And these objects or parts of objects cannot be individuated without concepts – as Wittgenstein taught us, pointing by itself won't do.[40] But we didn't have to wait for Wittgenstein to realize this: it was always evident in our practices of judgment (as Wittgenstein would have said, he was just assembling reminders). It is certainly evident in Kant's examples of aesthetic judgments: in spite of his insistence that these judgments are in some sense independent of determinate concepts, he always supposes that they are about particular objects, which can only be individuated by means of such concepts – for example, this hummingbird, this foliage border (but not the rest of the wall), this fantasia (but not another piece in the concert) (*CPJ*, §16, 5:229), this design or pattern in the painting (but not its colors), and for that matter, this painting (but not its frame) (*CPJ*, §14, 5:225–6). And presumably he did not think, any more than we would, that such concepts, or more precisely terms for them, are just used to tell others to what objects we are responding, to which they should also respond; for Kant, a particular concept, whether a concept such as *triangle* that is to be applied to objects in pure intuition or one such as *plate* or *dog* that is to be applied to objects in empirical intuition, is a rule for constructing (in the case of pure intuition) or recognizing (in the case of empirical intuition) an instance of the kind of object the concept names,[41] so we could not know what object we are responding to with a pleasurable feeling of beauty, or which object we should attend to in order to confirm for ourselves another's judgment of beauty (see *CPJ*, §32, 5:282), except by using a determinate concept to delimit some portion of our total visual or other experiential field, at or during some particular time, as the object of our attention, response, and aesthetic judgment. Thus, whereas Kant may well have thought that we can abstract from *some* concepts that we would ordinarily apply to possible objects of taste – in particular, concepts of their intended *use* or *end* (*CPJ*, §15, 5:226–7; §16, 5:229–31) – his own examples of paradigmatic judgments of taste suggest that he could not very well have thought that we could assess our aesthetic responses to objects or even respond to them at all without individuating them by

[40] Ludwig Wittgenstein, *Philosophical Investigations*, trans. G. E. M. Anscombe, second edition (New York: Macmillan, 1958), Part I, §§33–45.

[41] See *Critique of Pure Reason*, "On the schematism of the pure concepts of the understanding," A 137-42/B 176–81.

means of ordinary concepts such as *triangle* or *plate, hummingbird* or *painting.*

But we do not have to rely solely on Kant's examples for this conclusion. It is also implied by the most fundamental aspects of his theory of knowledge. This is hardly the place for a detailed discussion of the *Critique of Pure Reason,* but a brief outline of the central argument of the "Transcendental Analytic" should do for our present purposes. The first *Critique* argues that it is possible for me to attach the "I think" to any representation that I have, or to include any representation in the transcendental unity of my apperception (A 116; §16, B 131–2); that including any representation in the transcendental unity of my apperception requires the application of one or more of the categories or pure concepts of the understanding to it (A 119; §20, B 143); but that the pure concepts of the understanding are in fact nothing but the forms of determinate empirical concepts, just as the pure forms of intuition are nothing but the forms of empirical intuitions (A 111, 119, 125; §13, B 128–9; §22, B 146–7), so that the application of the *categories* to all the objects of my representation also requires the application of *determinate empirical concepts* to all of them (for example, the category of substance can only be applied to empirical intuition through the empirical concept of matter, and the concept of causation through the empirical concept of a rule-governed change in motion).[42] But these premises entail that we can never be conscious of a representation at all, *a fortiori* of a representation of an object, *a fortiori* of an object of actual or potential aesthetic response and judgment, without the application of some determinate empirical concept to it. Further, we may also consider the application of a concept to a manifold that is required for the transcendental unity of apperception as bringing the faculty of understanding into a certain kind of correspondence with a manifold of sensibility reproduced by the imagination, namely, that of the synthetic unity of the manifold required and/or constituted by the application of that concept to it (A 104; §17, B 137). This means not only that we cannot be conscious of an object at all without applying some determinate concept to it, but also that we cannot be conscious of it at all without the existence of some form of correspondence between understanding and imagination in the experience of that object.

This brief account of the argument of the first *Critique* should be enough to show that Kant cannot have thought that beautiful objects are

[42] These examples are of course drawn from Kant's 1786 *Metaphysical Foundations of Natural Science.*

those to which we apply the categories without applying any determinate concepts to them, since he clearly thought that the categories are only the forms of determinate concepts and can be applied to intuitions only through determinate concepts.[43] So how are we to understand the free yet harmonious play of imagination and understanding that is distinctive of the experience of beauty if we cannot understand it as involving the simple absence of ordinary determinate concepts of objects? The simplest answer to this would be to follow the lead of Kant's argument in §§15–16 and say that the kind of harmony of the faculties distinctive of the experience of beauty requires only the absence of any concept of the determinate intended *end* or *use* of the object of that experience. However, there are a number of difficulties with such a proposal. First, it is merely negative – it tells us nothing positive about the harmony of the faculties by means of which we might recognize the occurrence of that state. Second, it would provide too inclusive a criterion of the beautiful: surely there are many objects of our experience, if not indeed the majority of them, that either have no intended use or from whose intended use we can abstract without finding them in the least beautiful. I can find some stones beautiful, and others not, but I do not have to abstract from any intended use or purpose to find the former beautiful, nor is the absence of any intended use or purpose sufficient to make me find the latter beautiful.

Most importantly, however, although Kant surely does say repeatedly that the free play of the faculties has nothing to do with the satisfaction of any end, this statement is actually too broad for his own purposes. For in the Introduction to the third *Critique*, Kant suggests that pleasure *is* typically connected with the attainment of an aim (*Erreichung jeder Absicht*),[44] although such pleasure is most noticeable (*merklich*) when the aim is attained in an unexpected way (*CPJ*, VI, 5:187); and in the discussion of the "primacy of practical reason" Kant also suggests that every power of the mind has a characteristic aim, and thus a characteristic interest – "To

43 I earlier attributed this view to Rudolf Makkreel, although with the qualification expressed in note 16; Malcolm Budd may also suppose that the categories can be applied to objects independently of any determinate concepts at "The Pure Judgment of Taste," pp. 247–8.

44 Strictly speaking, Kant says that the attainment of every end is connected with pleasure, not that every pleasure is connected with the attainment of some end. But since he never offers any other general explanation of pleasure – his only other general statement about pleasure, as we have already seen (*FI*, VIII, 20:230–1 and *CPJ*, §12, 5:222), is about the *consequence* of pleasure, namely, that pleasure is a state that produces a desire for its own continuation – it seems reasonable to take him as making both assumptions.

every faculty of the mind one can attribute an *interest*, that is, a principle that contains the condition under which alone its exercise is promoted" – on the way to making his argument that the interest of practical reason (or our interest in the practical use of reason) requires us to believe in propositions that can be neither proved nor disproved by or for theoretical reason but are required for the rationality of moral conduct.[45] This means that the free play of the cognitive powers cannot be understood as a condition in which no ends or interests *of any kind* are involved at all, nor can it be understood simply as a condition in which no determinate interest other than that of one or more powers of the mind itself is involved, for that brings us back to a merely negative characterization of this state of mind. Instead, it must be understood as a condition in which some fundamental end or interest of the mind itself is satisfied, although in an unusual and therefore unexpected way that is still to be explained. Finally, to hold that genuine aesthetic response cannot involve any end at all would wreak havoc with Kant's recognition of the special cases of adherent beauty and artistic beauty, for the former is a kind of beauty that is somehow connected with the proper end of its object (*CPJ*, §16, 5:229–30), and the latter is clearly the product of intentional human action (*CPJ*, §43, 5:303–4), and must thus somehow involve an end. Since Kant does not assert that adherent beauty and artistic beauty are simply misnamed, thus spurious kinds of beauty, it would seem that any satisfactory interpretation of the free play of imagination and understanding in the case of free beauty should be able to be extended to those kinds of beauty as well without paradox.

7. So if the free play of imagination and understanding cannot be understood either as a state of mind that involves no determinate concepts at all or even as a state of mind that involves merely no concept of an end or interest, we still face the question, how is it to be understood? My proposal is that the only way we can understand Kant's concept consistently with our own and his assumptions about the determinacy of the objects of aesthetic judgment, as well as with his assumption about the judgmental and therefore object-referring structure of consciousness itself, is by replacing the precognitive and multicognitive approaches with what I will now call a "metacognitive" approach to the free play of the cognitive powers. On such an approach, the free and harmonious play of imagination and understanding should be understood as a state of mind

45 *Critique of Practical Reason*, 5:119–21.

in which the manifold of intuition induced by the perception of an object and presented by the imagination to the understanding is recognized to satisfy the rules for the organization of that manifold dictated by the determinate concept or concepts on which our recognition and identification of the object of this experience depends, yet as one in which it is *also* felt that – or as if – the understanding's underlying objective or interest in unity is being satisfied in a way that *goes beyond* anything required for or dictated by satisfaction of the determinate concept or concepts on which mere identification of the object depends. A beautiful object can always be recognized to be an object of some determinate kind, but our experience of it always has even more unity and coherence than is required for it to be a member of that kind, or has a kind of unity and coherence that is not merely a necessary condition for our classification of it. On such an approach, the free play of imagination and understanding is not a condition that must precede any ordinary cognition, nor must we forget or abstract away from our ordinary cognition of the object to take pleasure in its beauty; nor must the experience of beauty consist in a play among alternative cognitions or conceptualizations of the object. We can, indeed we must be able to, have ordinary cognition of the object, but we experience it as beautiful precisely because we experience it as inducing a degree or type of harmony between imagination and understanding – between the manifold it presents and our desire for unity – that goes beyond whatever is necessary for ordinary cognition. And this explains why we can ordinarily judge not only "This *F* is beautiful" – for example, "This Haydn sonata is beautiful" or "This Pollock is beautiful" – but also judge that "This *F* is beautiful but that one is not" – for example, "This Haydn sonata is beautiful but that one is not," or "This Pollock is beautiful but that one is not." We could not make such judgments, although we surely do, unless our aesthetic judgments were compatible with our ordinary classificatory judgments, and gave expression to the way in which some objects but not others occasion a free play of imagination and understanding that goes beyond the relation between them that is required for ordinary cognition.

Now I cannot claim that there are any passages in Kant that unequivocally imply the metacognitive rather than precognitive and paracognitive approaches; if there were, then presumably the latter approaches would not have seemed as plausible as they have. But there are certainly passages that are compatible with the metacognitive approach, and some that at least suggest it. Both kinds of passages may be found in Section VIII of the first Introduction, Kant's central discussion of aesthetic judgment in that text.[46] When Kant writes that "An aesthetic judgment in general can therefore be explicated as that judgment whose predicate can never be cognition (concept of an object) (although it may contain the subjective conditions for a cognition in general). In such a judgment the determining ground is sensation" (*FI*, VIII, 20:224), he does not actually say that an aesthetic judgment is incompatible with ordinary cognition of its object: the *predicate* of the judgment that can never be cognition or a concept of the object is, after all, the predicate "beautiful," and it is the application of *this* predicate that can have only sensation as its determining ground; and this at least leaves open the possibility that the *subject* of the aesthetic judgment can be identified only by means of an ordinary determinate concept. If that is so, then the occurrence of the sensation of pleasure that is the basis of the application of the predicate "beautiful" would have to be compatible with the recognition of the satisfaction of the determinate conditions necessary for the application of the subject-concept of the judgment – for example, *painting* or *sonata in three movments* – and the feeling of pleasure would thus naturally be understood as the feeling of a degree or type of harmony between the cognitive faculties that goes beyond whatever is necessary to satisfy the concept. We could say the same about Kant's subsequent statement that "since a merely subjective condition of a judgment does not permit a determinate concept of that judgment's determining ground, this can only be given in the feeling of pleasure, so that the aesthetic judgment is always a judgment of reflection" (*FI*, VIII, 20:225): this can be taken to say only that the determining ground for the *predicate* of the aesthetic judgment, namely, "beautiful," cannot be a determinate concept.

Perhaps one could also find more positive evidence for the metacognitive approach in the following passage from the preceding page in the first Introduction:

> By the designation "an aesthetic judgment about an object" it is therefore immediately indicated that a given representation is certainly related to an object but that what is understood in the judgment is not the determination of the object but of the subject and its feeling. For in the power of judgment understanding and imagination are considered in relation to each other, and this can, to be sure, first be considered objectively, as belonging to cognition (as happened in the transcendental schematism of the power of judgment); but one

[46] It should be recalled that the two locutions in the first Introduction in support of the multicognitive approach come in the preceding section (*FI*, VII, 20:220–1), prior to the main discussion.

can also consider this relation of two faculties of cognition merely subjectively, insofar as one helps or hinders the other in the very same representation and thereby affects the **state of mind**, and [is] therefore a relation which is **sensitive** (which is not the case in the separate [*abgesonderten*] use of any other faculty of cognition).

(*FI*, VIII, 20:223)

The first sentence of this passage clearly implies that an aesthetic judgment is made about a particular object, and must therefore be compatible with the recognition that the object satisfies the conditions for membership in some determinate kind, but that the *predicate* of the aesthetic judgment – "what is understood in the judgment" – cannot be based on this determinate concept, and must instead be based on a relation between the cognitive powers that in some way goes beyond it. In the second sentence, Kant says that the relation between imagination and understanding can *first* be considered "objectively" and then *also* considered subjectively, "insofar as one helps or hinders the other *in the very same representation*" (emphasis added): perhaps this is intended to indicate that in an aesthetic judgment we are conscious of both the object's satisfaction of the ordinary conditions for cognition and also of some way in which our experience of it goes beyond those conditions. And in the final clause I have quoted, Kant does not say that the aesthetic use of judgment is a use separate from every other faculty of cognition, but only that the sensitive relation that is the basis of the aesthetic judgment is not found in the separate use of any *other* faculty of cognition, that is, in any other kind of judgment. Thus he might be taken to say that the aesthetic response to the beauty of an object is not completely separate from the ordinary cognition of it, but rather in some sense additional to it.

Kant's initial description of the basis for aesthetic judgment in the published Introduction (VII, 5:189–90), as shown earlier, provides some of the best evidence for the precognitive approach to the harmony of the faculties. But even here Kant does follow his statement that the pleasure in the experience of beauty "is connected with the mere apprehension (*apprehensio*) of the form of an object of intuition without a relation of this to a concept for a determinate cognition" with the gloss that "Such a judgment is an aesthetic judgment on the purposiveness of the object, which is not grounded on any available concept of the object and does not furnish one" (5:190), and this at least suggests that there *are* concepts available for the object and that the experience of its beauty must be compatible with the availability of those concepts. Perhaps a more conclusive textual basis for the metacognitive approach could be found, however, in this passage from Kant's concluding comment on the "Analytic of the Beautiful" rather than anywhere in the introduction to the "Analytic":

> But if in the judgment of taste the imagination must be considered in its freedom, then it is in the first instance taken not as reproductive, as subjected to the laws of association, but as productive and self-active (as the authoress of voluntary forms of possible intuitions); and although in the apprehension of a given object of the senses it is of course bound to a determinate form of this object and to this extent has no free play (as in invention), nevertheless it is still quite conceivable that the object can provide it with a form that contains precisely such a composition of the manifold as the imagination would design in harmony with the **lawfulness of the understanding** in general if it were left free by itself.
>
> (*CPJ*, General Remark following §22, 5:241)

Here, Kant suggests that in the perception of a beautiful object, at least one that is already extant as opposed to first being invented, the imagination *is* bound to a determinate form for that object, presumably that required by the concept used to identify and classify it, but that *at the same time* the imagination feels as if it has had the freedom to invent forms going beyond this determinate form, but forms that at the same time still satisfy in some way the general requirement of lawfulness stemming from the understanding. A natural way to comprehend all this is precisely to understand a beautiful object as inducing a play among the cognitive powers that feels as if it satisfies the understanding's general requirement for unity and coherence in a way that goes beyond what is required to satisfy the conditions for the application of a determinate concept to the object.

Still, I think it must be conceded that the best argument for the metacognitive approach is not that some passage in Kant's text unequivocally and conclusively implies it, but that it is the only way to make sense of all of Kant's assumptions. Like anyone, Kant assumes that the object of an aesthetic judgment is always identified by means of a determinate concept, and furthermore his own theory of apperception requires that the object of any sort of judgment be picked out by a determinate concept. Kant also assumes that pleasure must be connected with the satisfaction of some underlying objective, and further that if judgments of taste are to be universally valid, the pleasure they express must be connected to the intersubjectively valid powers of cognition. So the pleasure expressed by a judgment of taste must be connected to the satisfaction of our underlying objective in cognition, namely, the unification of our manifolds of intuition. But if the pleasure in beauty is to be noticeable and the imagination is to be free, this satisfaction of the underlying objective of cognition must be in some way unexpected and not determined by any rule. The only way to put all these assumptions together is to suppose that in the experience of beauty in an object we recognize that the ordinary conditions for cognition of such an object are satisfied, yet also feel[47] that our experience of the manifold presented by the object satisfies our demand for unity in a way that goes beyond whatever is necessary for the satisfaction of those ordinary conditions.

8. Once we have accepted this conclusion, however, we can see that the precognitive and multicognitive approaches to the harmony of the faculty can in the end be taken to characterize specific ways in which our experiences of unity and coherence in the manifold presented to us by particular objects can go beyond the conditions necessary for ordinary cognition – although it should be implied precisely by the fact that the harmony of the faculties must be a free play that there can be no single, concrete description of this state, so that these approaches cannot be more than abstract descriptions of some ways in which objects might yield a metacognitive harmony. The grain of truth in the precognitive approach is simply that the most general way to describe the manner in which our experience of a beautiful object goes beyond the necessary conditions for ordinary cognition is by saying that in addition to satisfying those conditions, which consist in a manifold's display of the properties required by the predicates in a determinate concept (such as displaying three intersecting straight lines as required by the concept *triangle*, or being a slightly concave, more or less circular piece of fairly rigid and fairly non-absorbent material as required by the concept *plate*, or being an intentionally designed and colored array of pigment on a wood panel or canvas as required by the concept *painting*), the experience *also* seems to satisfy the understanding's general requirement of unity and coherence in some further way, which is not specified by such determinate concepts and is not manifest in the experience of every object that does satisfy such concepts. A beautiful plate satisfies the necessary conditions

[47] I say "feel" here both because it is Kant's theory that we recognize the existence of the harmony of the faculties precisely through the feeling of pleasure this state causes (see *CPJ*, §9, 5:219) and also because one presumably does not have to be aware of Kant's theoretical explanation of that pleasure to feel it or even to judge the object to be beautiful. But presumably one does have to recognize in at least some rough-and-ready way that the object satisfies the conditions for its subsumption under the determinate concept by means of which it is individuated and referred to – one does not just feel that a certain object is a hummingbird or a sonata.

for the application of the concept *plate* in the same way that an indifferent or downright ugly plate does, but the relations among the precise features of its shape, material, decoration and so on provide a further gratification for the understanding's interest in coherence that is not specified by any further determinate concept and cannot be captured by one. Ordinary or ugly plates do not provide this further gratification for the understanding apart from their satisfaction of the determinate concept *plate*. *Mutatis mutandis*, the same goes for beautiful and ordinary paintings.

The multicognitive interpretation, by contrast, can be seen as describing a particular way in which *some* beautiful objects go beyond satisfying the necessary conditions for subsumption under the determinate concepts by means of which they are individuated and recognized, namely, by prompting a free yet harmonious play among images and thoughts they may suggest, a free play that itself seems to satisfy the understanding's demand for coherence but that is not dictated by any determinate concepts of the objects and cannot generate any such determinate concept. For example, a successful novel may suggest a host of thoughts about character, virtues, vices, choice and chance, and so on, that are not required simply for the work to count as a novel, that are not dictated by any further particular rule, such as for novels of a particular period or genre, yet that nevertheless seem to stimulate the imagination in their variety and yet satisfy the understanding in their coherence. Obviously we enjoy freedom in a play of concepts that goes beyond the minimum organization required for classification of our object, and equally obviously we only enjoy such play when it does not degenerate into chaos; so we can describe what we enjoy as a play of concepts that nevertheless satisfies the understanding's general requirement of unity.

It is important to note here, however, that there is no need, arising either from Kant's theory of the harmony of the faculties or from our own experience, to suppose that *every* beautiful object must satisfy the requirement of an indeterminate but coherent play of imagination through an indeterminate but coherent play of *concepts* or "conceptual possibilities." Some types of art, such as various forms of literature, some representational painting and sculpture, some music with words, and so on, surely suggest a variety of ideas and thoughts to us, and what we enjoy in them will no doubt be an indeterminate yet coherent play among such thoughts. In other cases, however – for example, some forms of architecture, non-representational painting and sculpture, some music without words, and so on – it would seem most plausible to say that what we enjoy is a free yet coherent play not among concepts but among perceptual forms, between shape and color, between light and shade, among tones, between melody and harmony, and so on – or also between forms and concepts. It would be forced and misleading to identify all those with concepts or "conceptual possibilities." After all, Kant is thinking of a free play of the imagination that nevertheless satisfies the understanding's demand for lawfulness, and the Latinate word "imagination" as well as the German "*Einbildungskraft*" connote above all a play with *images* or *Bilder* – in Kantian terms, with intuitions rather than with concepts. It would seem to be a reasonable accommodation between Kant's theory and our experience to say that *sometimes* it is with more conceptual thoughts or ideas that the imagination plays, but an entirely unreasonable interpretation of Kant's theory as well as of our own aesthetic experience to insist that the imagination *always* plays with concepts rather than intuitions.

9. Finally, I would argue that only the metacognitive interpretation of the harmony of the faculties can make sense without paradox of Kant's recognition of adherent beauty and artistic beauty. Kant describes "free beauty" as that which is judged "according to mere form" and without a "concept of any end for which the manifold should serve the given object," while "adherent beauty," such as "the beauty of a human being (and in this species that of a man, a woman, or a child), the beauty of a horse, of a building (such as a church, a palace, an arsenal, or a garden-house) presuppose[s] a concept of the end that determines what the thing should be, hence a concept of its perfection" (*CPJ*, §16, 229–30). Yet he does not deny that adherent beauty is a kind of beauty at all, as he should say if all experience of beauty had to be independent of concepts altogether, nor does he say that we must ignore an object's actual or intended purpose in order to respond to its adherent beauty – we would have to abstract from an object's purpose, if we can, to judge it as a free beauty, but this is not to say that we have to abstract from its purpose to judge it as having any sort of beauty at all (5:231). But how can a response that presupposes a concept of the purpose that an object is supposed to serve, and therefore the conditions that it needs to satisfy in order to serve that purpose, be a response to beauty at all? On the metacognitive approach, this is not a puzzle: an object that we experience as having adherent beauty would be one that we experience as satisfying the conditions required by the determinate concept of its purpose, just as we recognize any beautiful object as satisfying some determinate concept, though not necessarily a concept of a purpose, but also as having a degree or kind of unity that goes beyond anything required by that concept of purpose, and thus as inducing a free play of imagination and understanding in addition to the satisfaction of the former conditions.

There are in fact several ways in which this could be the case, each of which is suggested by particular turns of phrase in Kant's discussion of adherent beauty. In some cases, the object's intended purpose may simply restrict permissible forms for it, and we may not take any especially noticeable pleasure in its suitability for this purpose, instead taking our pleasure primarily in ways in which it goes beyond what is necessary for that suitability, although were the object unsuitable for its purpose, our displeasure at that might block the possibility of any pleasure in it at all; in such cases, as Kant says, the imagination "would merely be restricted" by the purpose of the object, so that, for example, "One would be able to add much to a building that would be pleasing in the intuition of it if only it were not supposed to be a church." In other cases, we might take as it were independent pleasures in the object's suitability for its purpose and in the free play it nevertheless affords our cognitive powers, so that our complete response to it is as it were a sum of two pleasures. In such cases we would enjoy "the combination of the good . . . with beauty," and "the **entire faculty** of the powers of representation" would gain "if both states of mind are in agreement" (230–1). In yet other cases, we might enjoy what we take to be an unusual degree of coherence *between* the purpose of the object and aspects of its appearance not directly dictated by its purpose.[48] But in each of these cases we would clearly be enjoying some free play of imagination and understanding that goes beyond the object's satisfaction of the determinate conditions imposed by the concept of its purpose, whether that play is simply one that takes place *within* the bounds set by the purpose of the object or is a play *between* the purpose and the form of the object.

Kant also makes beauty in fine art seem paradoxical when he states that "In a product of art one must be aware that it is art, and not nature; yet the purposiveness of its form must still seem to be as free from all constraint by arbitrary rules as if it were a mere product of nature. . . . art can only be called beautifui if we are aware that it is art and yet it looks to us like nature" (*CPJ*, §45, 5:306). The chief difference between art and nature, as Kant has just maintained, is that art is "production through freedom, i.e., through a capacity for choice that grounds its actions in reason"

[48] I have discussed these possibilities and the textual basis for them more fully in "Free and Adherent Beauty: A Modest Proposal." *British Journal of Aesthetics* 42 (October, 2002) 357–66; in the present volume, Chapter 5.

(*CPJ*, §43, 5:303), thus something produced intentionally and with a purpose in mind. Kant then seems to be saying that we must recognize a work of art as a product of intention and yet be able to ignore or abstract the intended purpose of its production – to see it as if it were mere nature – in order to respond to its beauty. But there is no need for him to require us to perform any such mental gymnastics, for as he goes on to argue, a truly successful work of art is a product of genius, and genius is nothing but the "talent" or "natural gift" that allows the artist to *go beyond* the "rules that first lay the foundation by means of which a product that is to be called artistic is first represented as possible" (*CPJ*, §46, 5:307). In other words, a work of art is always produced with a variety of ends and rules in mind – the specific point the artist may have in producing that work, the rules that follow from the medium and genre within which he intends to work, perhaps the constraints that follow from the larger economic and political objectives he may have, and so on – but those rules are never *sufficient* to determine the character of a truly successful work, because its success depends precisely on our experience, prompted by the genius of the artist, of a free play of our cognitive cognitive powers, which must be compatible with but also go beyond the satisfaction of all such rules and constraints. Thus, while "if the object is given as a product of art, and is as such supposed to be declared to be beautiful, then, since art always presupposes an end in the cause (and its causality), a concept must *first* be the ground of what the thing is supposed to be" (*CPJ*, §48, 5:311; emphasis added), yet if it is in fact to be beautiful, *then* "the unsought and unintentional subjective purposiveness of the free correspondence of the imagination to the lawfulness of the understanding presupposes a proportion and disposition of this faculty that cannot be produced by any following of rules . . . but that only the nature of the subject can produce" (*CPJ*, §49, 5:317–18). The metacognitive approach to the harmony of the faculties allows us to reconcile these two requirements without difficulty: a beautiful work of art must first satisfy the conditions imposed by the various intentions embodied in it, but must also produce a free play of imagination and understanding going beyond the mere satisfaction of all those constraints.

Now Kant also proposes that artistic genius is always manifested in the "presentation of **aesthetic ideas**," where an "aesthetic idea is a representation of the imagination that occasions much thinking thought without it being possible for any determinate thought, that is, **concept**, to be adequate to it" (*CPJ*, §49, 5:314). An aesthetic idea seems to be a central conception for a work of art that connotes a "rational idea," that is, a central intellectual and in fact typically moral content, on the one hand, through an indeterminate wealth of "thoughts" or attributes, on the other.[49] The conception of aesthetic ideas could easily suggest the multicognitive approach to the harmony of the faculties. But two points should be clear. First, while Kant's conception no doubt captures something that is central to our experience of many works of art, he gives no reason to suppose that *every* work of art has a theme, let alone a moral theme, that is realized through a free play of further thoughts; his own earlier examples of art in the "Analytic of the Beautiful" clearly implied that in at least some cases of genuinely beautiful art we respond to form alone. (And he certainly gives no argument for his claim two sections later that *all* beauty, the beauty of nature as well as of art, involves the expression of aesthetic ideas [*CPJ*, §51, 5:320]). But second, and more important for my argument here, it should be clear that even where a work of art does give us the experience of beauty through an aesthetic idea, the analysis of art and genius that has preceded Kant's introduction of the concept of aesthetic ideas clearly entails that we must experience such a work of art as both satisfying a variety of determinate rules, necessary for it to be a product of intentional activity and to be the kind of object that it is, and *also* as generating a free play of imagination and understanding, in this case a play between the theme of the work and the variety of images and thoughts by which it is realized, that goes beyond anything dictated by all those rules. In other words, Kant's theory of aesthetic ideas, whether we take it, as he intended, as an account of all works of artistic genius or rather, as seems more reasonable, as an account of some, requires the metacognitive rather than the multicognitive approach to the harmony of the faculties.

10. In conclusion, then, I have argued that although there is certainly textual evidence for both the precognitive and multicognitive approaches to the interpretation of the harmony of the faculties, and indeed little unequivocal textual evidence for what I have called the metacognitive approach, only the latter approach is consistent with Kant's epistemology, with his and our assumptions about the grammatical form of aesthetic judgments, and with his own recognition of adherent beauty and artistic beauty as genuine and ultimately paradigmatic forms of beauty. Moreover, the germs of truth in the precognitive and multicognitive approaches

49 For a fuller account, see my "Kant's Conception of Fine Art," *Journal of Aesthetics and Art Criticism* **52** (1994): 175–85, reprinted as Chapter 12 in the second edition of *Kant and the Claims of Taste*.

can be incorporated into the metacognitive interpretation as characterizations of some of the ways in which the play of imagination in aesthetic experience can go beyond the satisfaction of the requirements of ordinary concepts, and thus of the ordinary conditions of cognition – but since the very concept of the harmony of the faculties as the explanation of our pleasure in beauty requires that our experience of beauty not be constrained by any determinate rules, such characterizations can never offer anything more than some examples of the ways in which our experience of beauty can go beyond the determinate requirements of cognition.

4

Beauty and Utility in Eighteenth-Century Aesthetics

There was considerable debate about the relationship between beauty and utility in eighteenth-century aesthetic theories from Shaftesbury to Kant. But nobody gave a plausible account of this relationship until Kant, and even he failed to give an extensive statement of the key premise on which his solution to this puzzle rests, or even an explicit statement of his solution, at least until many sections after he had first presented his solution. In this essay, I will try to make Kant's analysis of the relationship between beauty and utility clear and expose the philosophical assumption on which his solution rests.

The debate about beauty and utility began with the third Earl of Shaftesbury. In a well-known passage of *The Moralists*, Shaftesbury's spokesman Theocles argues that "the property or possession" of the object of a vista, such as a vale or an orchard, is not necessary for "the enjoyment of the prospect," and then continues to press his interlocutor Philocles:

> Suppose that, being charmed as you seem to be with the beauty of those trees under whose shade we rest, you should long for nothing so much as to taste some delicious fruit of theirs; and having obtained of Nature some certain relish by which these acorns or berries of the wood become as palatable as the figs or peaches of the garden, you should afterwards, as oft as you revisited these groves, seek hence the enjoyment of them by satiating yourself in these new delights.

Philocles replies that a "fancy of this kind" would be "sordidly luxurious" and "absurd." In other words, he agrees that the enjoyment of a beautiful prospect is not dependent upon the possibility of the consumption of anything in it and hence upon possession of it, on which the possibility of consumption might in turn depend.[1] This insistence upon the independence of the response to beauty from the possibility of possession of an object and any property of it, the enjoyment of which might depend upon its possession, such as its utility, is often thought to be the origin of the supposedly characteristic eighteenth-century doctrine that aesthetic response and its expression in a judgment of taste must be disinterested.

Now it is clear that Shaftesbury himself did not think that the independence of the response to beauty from the sordidly luxurious fancy of consumption implies that there is no relationship between beauty and utility. For in a passage in the *Characteristics*'s concluding "Miscellaneous Reflection" he states that the same sorts of shapes, proportions, symmetry, and order that make objects beautiful also make them well-adapted to activity, and thus that beauty and utility "are plainly joined":

> 'Tis impossible we can advance the least in any relish or taste of outward symmetry and order, without acknowledging that the proportionate and regular state is the truly prosperous and natural in every subject. The same features which make deformity create incommodiousness and disease. And the same shapes and proportions which make beauty afford advantage by adapting to activity and use. Even in the imitative or designing arts... the truth or beauty of every figure is measured from the perfection of Nature in the just adapting of every limb and proportion to the activity, strength, dexterity, life and vigour of the particular species or animal designed.

Thus beauty and truth are plainly joined with the notion of utility and convenience, even in the apprehension of every ingenious artist, the architect, the statuary, or the painter.[2] Shaftesbury's immediate interest, here, however, is in analogizing the inward beauty of the mind sought in morality to the external beauty of bodies sought in the arts, and in arguing that philosophy is necessary to achieve the former, just as artistry is necessary to achieve the latter. He does not therefore spend any time explaining precisely how beauty and utility are "plainly joined" and how, if at all, they also differ. The net result is that Shaftesbury persuaded everyone who followed that the response to the beauty of an object must

[1] Anthony Ashley Cooper, Third Earl of Shaftesbury, *Characteristics of Men, Manners, Opinions, Times*, ed. Lawrence E. Klein (Cambridge: Cambridge University Press, 1999), 319.

[2] Shaftesbury, *Characteristics*, 415. The editor, Lawrence Klein, cites a passage from Vitruvius, *On Architecture* 4.2.5–6, as a precedent for this passage. The heart of this passage is this: the ancients "adapted everything appropriately and by conventions truly derived from nature to the perfections of their works, and they approved things the explanations for which could have a justification in reality." This passage suggests an intimate connection between beauty in architecture to patterns existing "in reality," or possibly to truth, but does not so clearly link either those patterns in reality or their beauty to their utility.

be independent of the possibility of personal possession of it, but he left the door open to a wide variety of views on the relation between our pleasure in beauty and that in utility that might still satisfy this negative condition.

So Francis Hutcheson, who presented himself as a follower of Shaftesbury in his first major work, which was also the first professional treatise on aesthetics in Great Britain,[3] took our response to beauty to be an immediate sensory response, although a response of our "internal sense" rather than of any of our external senses, to an object – a response that, precisely because it is immediate, is necessarily independent of any thought of the utility of the object:

This superior Power of Perception is justly called *a Sense*, because of its Affinity to the other Senses in this, that the Pleasure is different from any *Knowledge* of Principles, Proportions, Causes, or of the Usefulness of the Object: we are struck at the first with the Beauty: nor does the most accurate *Knowledge* increase this Pleasure of Beauty, however it may superadd a distinct rational Pleasure from Prospects of *Advantage*, or may bring along that peculiar kind of Pleasure, which attends the Increase of Knowledge.[4]

On Hutcheson's account, the sensory character of the response to beauty itself precludes any connection between this response and the recognition of utility generally, thus utility for anyone, not just for oneself. Moreover, although Hutcheson proceeds to specify a property of objects that characteristically causes this response – he argues that it can be empirically shown that this response is typically induced by the perception of "uniformity amidst variety" (*Inquiry*, 17) in objects – he does not suggest that there is any special connection between uniformity amidst variety and the utility of objects, so that the response to the beauty of an object might be a response to what makes it useful, even if it is not the same as a recognition of its utility. He does eventually allow that uniformity amidst

3 Hutcheson's work clearly deserves the title of the first systematic treatise on aesthetics in English, even though it preceded by ten years Alexander Baumgarten's coinage of the term itself; indeed, Hutcheson's work was a more general treatise on aesthetics than either Baumgarten's master's thesis *Meditationes philosophicae de nonnullis ad poema pertinentibus* ("Philosophical mediations on some matters pertaining to poetry") of 1735 (for the definition of the term "aesthetics," see its §cxvi) or his much larger but incomplete *Aesthetica* of 1750–58 (see its §1). In spite of the vast outpouring of works on aesthetics in eighteenth-century Britain, the term "aesthetics" itself seems to have been used in English as the term for the philosophical discussion of beauty and art only beginning in several reference works published in 1830.

4 Francis Hutcheson, *An Inquiry into the Original of our Ideas of Beauty and Virtue*, 4th ed. (London: D. Midwinter *et. al.*, 1738), 11; hereafter, *Inquiry*.

variety is the basis for cognition and that it is a sign of God's benevolence that he has constituted us so that we enjoy the pleasure of beauty in what is also valuable for our knowledge (*Inquiry*, 93–103), but Hutcheson does not equate knowledge in general with the recognition of utility, so he maintains the difference between beauty and utility throughout his treatise.

Hutcheson's position was not widely accepted, however; on the contrary, it met with incredulity. George Berkeley objected to it vigorously in his *Alciphron*, published in 1732, seven years after the first edition of Hutcheson's *Inquiry*. There he asks a series of questions, to which, like Socrates, he expects immediate assent:

> And, to make the proportions just, must not those mutual relations of size and shape in the parts be such as shall make the whole complete and perfect in its kind? . . .
>
> Is not a thing said to be perfect in its kind when it answers the ends for which it was made? . . .
>
> The parts, therefore, in true proportions must be so related, and adjusted to one another, as that they may best conspire to the use and operation of the whole? . . .
>
> But the comparing parts with one another, the considering them as belonging to one whole, and the referring this whole to its use or end, should seem the work of reason: should it not? . . .
>
> Proportions, therefore, are not, strictly speaking, perceived by the sense of sight, but only by reason by means of sight. . . .
>
> Consequently beauty is . . . an object, not of the eye, but of the mind.[5]

Berkeley does not simply identify the response to beauty with knowledge of the utility of an object, rather leaving place for some element of sensory response with his statement that beautiful proportions are perceived "by reason by means of sight"; but he obviously thinks that the feeling of beauty is dependent upon and very closely connected with the recognition of the utility of an object.

Hutcheson, however, was not moved by this criticism, and in the fourth edition of his *Inquiry*, published in 1738, he rebutted the "ingenious Author of *Alciphron*" by arguing that objects with irregular and displeasing shapes could perform their appointed functions as well as objects with regular ones, thus that the beauty of objects was not a necessary condition for their utility, and he therefore maintained unshaken his confidence that there is no direct connection between the utility and the beauty

5 George Berkeley, *Alciphron, or the Minute Philosopher*, in *The Works of George Berkeley, Bishop of Cloyne*, eds. A. A. Luce and T. E. Jessop (London: Nelson, 1950), 3: 124.

of objects or between our responses to these entirely distinct properties. Hutcheson argues against Berkeley by counterexample: against the claim "that all Beauty observed is solely some *Use* perceived or imagined," he takes the example of ordinary things such as "Chairs, Doors, Tables, and some other Things of obvious Use," and argues

> that in these very Things *Similitude* of Parts is regarded, where unlike Parts would be equally useful: Thus the Feet of a Chair would be of the same Use, tho' unlike, were they equally long; tho' one were strait, and the other bended; or one bended outwards, and the other inwards: A Coffin-shape for a Door would bear a more manifest Aptitude to the human Shape, than that which Artists require.
>
> (*Inquiry*, Additions and Corrections, following 304)

A chair with mismatched legs would be just as useful as one with well-matched legs, as long as they are equal in length, but it would obviously be ugly rather than beautiful; and the preferred rectangular shape for doors is more beautiful than a coffin shape, wider at the shoulders than at the feet, although no more useful. According to Hutcheson, what makes an object beautiful – namely, uniformity amidst variety, which in this case lies in the shape of its several parts – is simply different from what makes it useful.

Two decades later, yet another Irishman, Edmund Burke, although critical of Hutcheson's postulation of a special internal sense for the perception of beauty, took his side in the debate with Berkeley about the relation between beauty and utility. Where Hutcheson appealed to artifacts for his counterexamples to Berkeley, Burke appealed to nature to argue against the "opinion" that "the idea of utility, or of a part's being adapted to answer its end, is the cause of beauty." In "framing this theory," he scornfully observes, "experience was not sufficiently consulted":

> For on that principle, the wedgelike snout of a swine, with its tough cartilage at the end, the little sunk eyes, and the whole make of the head, so well adapted to its offices of digging, and rooting, would be extremely beautiful. The great bag hanging to the bill of a pelican, a thing highly useful to this animal, would be likewise as beautiful in our eyes. The hedgehog, so well secured against all assaults by his prickly hide, and the porcupine with his missile quills, would be then considered as creatures of no small elegance.[6]

Many attributes of creatures that are highly useful, at least to their possessors, are not beautiful or are downright ugly or even ridiculous, so,

[6] Edmund Burke, *A Philosophical Enquiry into the Origin of our Ideas of the Sublime and Beautiful*, 2nd ed., ed. J. T. Boulton (London: Routledge & Kegan Paul, 1958), 105; hereafter, *Enquiry*.

Burke implies, utility could hardly be a sufficient condition for beauty. Burke is willing to admit that the adaptation of the features of organisms to their ends can cause us to "look up to the Maker with admiration and praise," but he insists that this attitude can "produce approbation, the acquiescence of the understanding, but not love, or any passion of that species," that is, the kind of response we are looking for in the case of beauty (*Enquiry*, 108). It must be said, however, that Burke does not consider whether his own account of beauty really escapes his objection to any connection between beauty and utility. His own account is basically that we find beautiful what is either identical with, or reminiscent of, what we find sexually attractive, such as "the smoothness; the softness; the easy and insensible swell; the variety of the surface . . . ; the deceitful maze, through which the unsteady eye slides giddily," which we find in "that part of a beautiful woman where she is perhaps the most beautiful, about the neck and breasts" (*Enquiry*, 115). Of course, it is easy to object that a swine might find the neck and breasts of a human woman just as indifferent or even as ugly as we find its snout, or even that human females might find the attributes that Burke finds so beautiful in them ridiculous in human males. All of this suggests that locating beauty in utility certainly exposes judgments of beauty to the charge of relativism across species or even across genders (and undoubtedly other distinctions) within a single species, but in the absence of a convincing argument for the necessary universality of judgments of beauty both across and within species, this fact by itself provides no argument against the connection.

Meanwhile, rather than taking one side or the other in this debate, David Hume had already tried to resolve it by accepting both sides, that is, by recognizing two varieties of beauty, one of which depends upon the appearance of utility and the other of which is unrelated to that. In *A Treatise of Human Nature*, the first part of which was published just one year after Hutcheson's reply to Berkeley in the fourth edition of his *Inquiry* and the second of which appeared the following year, Hume maintained that all cases of beauty are marked by the occurrence of a common and distinctive kind of feeling but that this distinctive feeling can be produced in two different ways, one of which depends upon utility or its appearance, while the other does not: "*Beauty* of all kinds gives us a peculiar delight and satisfaction; as *deformity* produces pain, upon whatever subject it may be plac'd, and whether survey'd in an animate or inanimate object," Hume writes, and indeed claims that "Pleasure and pain . . . are not only necessary attendants of beauty and deformity, but constitute their very essence."[7] Although joined by their common effect (the special feeling of pleasure that is apparently distinctive of all cases of beauty), those cases may be divided into two classes on the basis of their distinct causes: "Thus the beauty of all visible objects causes a pleasure pretty much the same, tho' it be sometimes deriv'd from the mere *species* and appearance of the objects; sometimes from sympathy, and an idea of their utility" (*Treatise*, 393). In principle, then, Hume divides the difference between Hutcheson and Berkeley. In practice, however, he shades the argument in favor of Berkeley, for while distinguishing between the two varieties of beauty, he also maintains that the majority of the cases of beauty are actually cases of the beauty of utility rather than the beauty of mere "*species* or appearance": "Most of the works of art are esteem'd beautiful, in proportion to their fitness for the use of man, and even many of the productions of nature derive their beauty from that source. Handsome and beautiful, on most occasions, is not an absolute but a relative quality, and pleases us by nothing but its tendency to produce an end that is agreeable" (*Treatise*, 368–9). The beauty of "tables, chairs, scritoires, chimneys, coaches, saddles, ploughs," convenient and well-appointed houses and swift-sailing ships, and hills "cover'd with vines or olive-trees," constitute the numerical majority of cases of beauty (*Treatise*, 235).

About the beauty of "*species* or appearance," or "absolute" rather than "relative" beauty, Hume believes that there is very little that can be said: "Some of these qualities produce satisfaction in [us] by particular *original* qualities of human nature, which cannot be accounted for" (*Treatise*, 377). He shows no inclination to accept Hutcheson's empirical induction that all cases of absolute beauty are responses to the perception of uniformity amidst variety, let alone to attribute any explanatory force to this induction. About the beauty of utility, however, or relative beauty, Hume has quite a bit to say. The chief problem with explaining beauty by utility, as we have already seen from Burke's extreme cross-species cases, is that to do so threatens the possibility of intersubjectively valid judgments of beauty: if the utility of an object is the reason for being pleased with it, then it would seem that it should please only those sorts of creatures to whom it is in fact useful, or even more exclusively those individuals who can actually use it – that is, in the case of things like desks, houses, ships, and fields, the owners of those objects or those few others whom

[7] David Hume, *A Treatise of Human Nature*, ed. David Fate Norton and Mary J. Norton (Oxford: Clarendon Press, 2000), 195; hereafter, *Treatise*.

the owners might favor with the use or benefit of their possessions. But in fact any human who can perceive it properly, not just its owner, seems to take pleasure in the sight of a beautiful house or ship.

Hume proposes to explain away this apparent paradox by appeal to the operations of sympathy and imagination; indeed, it is in order to illustrate the workings of sympathy and the imagination, primarily in the context of moral judgment, that Hume discusses aesthetic phenomena in the *Treatise* at all. His explanation includes three cases. First, in the case of a well-designed artifact or well-endowed piece of nature that is useful but can in fact be used only by a particular proprietor, the rest of us enjoy it because of our sympathy with the pleasure of that proprietor: a beautiful house, for example, "must delight us merely by communication, and by our sympathizing with the proprietor of the lodging. We enter into his interest by the force of the imagination, and feel the same satisfaction, that the objects naturally occasion in him" (*Treatise*, 235). Second, in the case of an object that is beautiful because it is otherwise well adapted to serve an end that, however, it cannot actually serve because some particular condition necessary to that end is missing, we nevertheless enjoy its beauty because our imagination fills in the missing condition: "A man, whose limbs and shape promise strength and activity, is esteem'd handsome, tho' condemned to perpetual punishment," because our imagination frees him from his bonds (*Treatise*, 373). And finally, in the case of objects that are not genuinely useful at all but have the appearance of those that are, imagination produces the pleasure of beauty or pain of deformity through the mechanism of the association of ideas in addition to that of sympathy. This is typical, of course, of representational or mimetic art:

> There is no rule in painting more reasonable than that of ballancing the figures, and placing them with the greatest exactness on their proper centers of gravity. A figure, which is not justly ballanc'd, is disagreeable, and that because it conveys the ideas of its fall, of harm, and of pain: Which ideas are painful, when by sympathy they acquire any degree of force and vivacity.
>
> (*Treatise*, 235)

In other words, the appearance of disutility produces the characteristic pain of deformity or ugliness through the association of ideas and sympathy, and the appearance of utility produces the characteristic pleasure of beauty through those same mechanisms.

Hume's confidence that he can subsume both absolute and relative beauty, that is, both the Hutchesonian and Berkeleian accounts of beauty, under a single rubric depends upon his conviction that there is a single feeling of pleasure distinctive of all and only these objects, a conviction that he asserts but makes no effort to defend. That is certainly one point at which his account could be attacked. A more specific objection would be that he does not in fact respond to Hutcheson's riposte to Berkeley that a chair with mismatched legs would be just as useful as one with matched legs but obviously not as beautiful. In other words, Hume does not show that utility, even when supplemented by the mechanisms of sympathy and the association of ideas, is a sufficient condition for beauty. He leaves himself open to the objection that in all his cases of beautiful houses, coaches, and ships we are responding to some feature, such as symmetry, that is independent of their utility or perhaps even itself the basis of their utility, rather than responding directly to their utility. Thus Hume still leaves the exact relationship between beauty and utility obscure.

While this debate was going on in Great Britain, what was happening on the continent? In Germany, aesthetic theory developed within the framework established by Leibniz and Wolff, and the key to this framework was the idea that the perception of beauty is a sensory or intuitive – which is to say, clear but confused rather than clear but distinct – perception of the perfection of its object: the "intuitive cognition of perfection" as Wolff put it,[8] or, as his follower Johann Christoph Gottsched asserted, "The metaphorical as well as common taste have to do only with clear, but not entirely distinct, concepts of things."[9] For these writers, perfection was a general ontological category, which included far more than utility; in fact, they thought that each of the arts had its own particular end and thus its own perfection, so that the achievement of mimesis could be the perfection of painting or literature and that of symmetry the perfection of architecture. But their conception of perfection certainly had room for utility as a kind of perfection, and to the extent that we can take pleasure in the clear but confused perception of utility that would be as good a case of beauty as any other. So the continental aestheticians saw no special reason to distinguish our pleasure in beauty from our pleasure in utility.

Now where does Kant stand in this debate? It certainly seems as if he simply takes the side of Hutcheson. Kant of course begins his "Analytic of the Beautiful" with the proposition that "the satisfaction that determines

[8] Christian Wolff, *Vernünftige Gedancken von Gott, der Welt and der Seele des Menschen* (1720), new ed. (Halle: Renger, 1751), §404.

[9] Johann Christoph Gottsched, *Versuch einer critischen Dichtkunst vor die Deutschen*, in Gottsched, *Schriften zur Literatur*, ed. Horst Steinmetz (Stuttgart: Reclam, 1972), 62.

the judgment of taste is without any interest,"[10] and he defines the beautiful as the object of such a satisfaction independent of any interest (5: 211). In the third moment of the "Analytic," arguing that the judgment of taste is grounded on the "form of purposiveness" in an object rather than any actual purpose it may be judged to have (5: 221), Kant explicitly asserts that the judgment of beauty must be independent from any judgment of utility:

> Objective purposiveness can be cognized only by means of the relation of the manifold to a determinate end, thus only through a concept. From this alone it is already clear that the beautiful, the judging of which has as its ground a merely formal purposiveness, i.e., a purposiveness without an end, is entirely independent of the representation of the good, since the latter presupposes an objective purposiveness, i.e., the relation of the object to a determinate end.
>
> Objective purposiveness is either external, i.e., the utility of the object, or internal, i.e., its perfection. That the satisfaction in an object on account of which we call it beautiful could not rest on the representation of its utility is sufficiently obvious from the two preceding main sections, since in that case it would not be an immediate satisfaction in the object...
>
> (5: 226)

So Kant certainly does not identify the beauty of an object with its utility, perceived confusedly or otherwise, and thus far his position seems to be a straightforward reversion to that of Hutcheson.

Yet just as in his theoretical and practical philosophy, Kant's general approach in aesthetics is also to try to resolve the differences between competing positions, while preserving the truth in each. It would therefore be surprising if in one of the great debates of the aesthetic theory of his time he simply took one side against the other rather and did not try find some common ground between them. And indeed, in the section immediately following the one just cited, Kant does recognize a form of beauty that is connected to utility or even dependent upon it. This is what he calls "adherent beauty." Here Kant now calls the pure case of beauty he has been analyzing up to this point – that which "presupposes no concept of what the object ought to be" – "free beauty," but he contrasts it to a second kind of beauty that "does presuppose such a concept and the perfection of the object in accordance with it," namely, adherent beauty, which, "as adhering to a concept (conditioned beauty) [is] ascribed to

[10] Immanuel Kant, *Critique of the Power of Judgment*, ed. Paul Guyer, trans. Paul Guyer and Eric Matthews (Cambridge: Cambridge University Press, 2000), 5: 204 (the pagination from the Akademie edition is provided in the margins of the Cambridge edition).

objects that stand under the concept of a particular end" (5: 229). And in many cases of adherent beauty, the concept of the end or what the thing ought to be that is presupposed by the judgment of its beauty is clearly a concept of its intended use and of the features necessary for it to serve that intended use. Thus, Kant illustrates the concept with these examples:

> But the beauty of a human being (and in this species that of a man, a woman, or a child), the beauty of a horse, of a building (such as a church, a palace, an arsenal, or a garden-house) presuppose a concept of the end that determines what the thing should be, hence a concept of its perfection, and is thus merely adherent beauty.
>
> (5: 230)

Perhaps it would be strange, indeed morally inappropriate, to say that the end of a human being is its intended use, and it might even seem strange to say that the beauty of an animal like a horse is dependent upon an end that is a use, although when we think of the differences between what we find beautiful in a draft horse and what we find beautiful in a race horse we might pause over this. But certainly the different ends on which the different beauties of a palace, arsenal, or garden-house depend are nothing but their different intended uses, and in depending upon their ends, the beauties of such things depend on nothing other than their utility. The use of a palace is to provide luxurious accommodations for rulers and impressive rooms for the receptions of their guests and emissaries, so a beautiful palace must be useful for those purposes; the use of an arsenal is to provide secure storage for arms and munitions, and that of a garden-house to provide refreshing refuge from summer heat, so the design of those buildings must be compatible with those purposes, and so on. What many, if not most, cases of adherent beauty depend upon is nothing other than their utility, although any case of adherent beauty must also involve more than mere utility, since, to be sure, not every secure arsenal or breezy gazebo is beautiful. An object that possesses adherent beauty must be one that is well-adapted to its intended use but also goes beyond this condition in an aesthetically satisfying way.

Now, one might think that Kant would introduce the case of adherent beauty, the examples for which seems so reminiscent of Hume's examples of the beauty of utility, only to dismiss it as a case of pseudo-beauty, that is, not a genuine case of beauty at all. But Kant does not do that. Failing that, one might think that Kant would have to analyze our pleasure in adherent beauty as a compound pleasure, a combination of the pleasure of agreeableness occasioned by the utility of an object with the entirely independent pleasure of beauty occasioned by its mere form, a compound experience of pleasure that might be entitled to be called a pleasure in beauty because one of its parts is genuine pleasure in beauty – but a part each of whose parts is brought about independently of the other. Some of Kant's language suggests such an analysis, as in the following passage:

> To be sure, taste gains by this combination of aesthetic satisfaction with the intellectual in that it becomes fixed and, though not universal, can have rules prescribed to it in regard to certain purposively determined objects.... Strictly speaking, however, perfection does not gain by beauty, nor does beauty gain by perfection; rather, since in comparing the representation by which an object is given to us with the object (with regard to what it ought to be) we cannot avoid at the same time holding it together with the subject, the entire faculty of the powers of representation gains if both states of mind are in agreement.
>
> (5: 230–1)

Here Kant explicitly talks of two separate states of mind, which can combine to the benefit of one's state of satisfaction overall: one that flows from the comparison of the object with a concept of what the object ought to be, which in most cases is to say with a concept of its utility, and the other that flows from the comparison of the representation of the object with the subject's powers of representation themselves, which may induce a harmony among these faculties and thus pleasure in beauty proper.

On such an analysis, the two pleasures ought to be additive: that is, one ought to be able to experience either without the other, although one's pleasure will be greater if both are experienced rather than one without the other. In particular, if the pleasure of free beauty in the mere form of an object is completely independent from the pleasure of adherent beauty in its utility, then one ought to be able to experience the former even in the case of an object which is obviously ill-suited to its intended end and thus does not afford the latter. But that is precisely the case that Kant does not allow. Instead, he refers to adherent beauty as "conditioned beauty" and claims that we can take any pleasure in the form of an object that obviously has an end only if its form is compatible with or suitable for that end. This is what Kant expresses by the use of the words "if only" (*wenn... nur*) in the following illustration of his idea.

> One would be able to add much to a building that would be pleasing in the intuition of it if only it were not supposed to be a church; a figure could be beautified with all sorts of curlicues and light but regular lines, as the New Zealanders do with their tattooing, if only it were not a human being; and the latter could have

much finer features and a more pleasing, softer outline to its facial structure if only it were not supposed to represent a man, or even a warrior.

(5: 230)

Forms that we would find freely beautiful if they were present in objects that do not have obvious purposes or uses cannot be found so if they would contradict the purpose or use of the object. In other words, the suitability of an object's appearance to its intended use is a necessary condition for our finding the object beautiful, even if finding it beautiful is not reducible to finding its form suitable to its use. Beauty is not identical to utility, but where an object should have utility, then its utility is a necessary condition for its beauty.

In a later passage – the concern of which is the distinction between nature and art – Kant reiterates his solution that adaptation to use should be understood as a necessary although not sufficient condition for beauty in any object that has a use, even though this means that its beauty is not "pure" and the judgment upon it is not a "mere judgment of taste":

To be sure, in the judging especially of living objects in nature, e.g., a human being or horse, objective purposiveness is also commonly taken into account for judging its beauty; but in that case the judgment is also no longer purely aesthetic, i.e., a mere judgment of taste. Nature is no longer judged as it appears as art, but to the extent that it really is art (albeit superhuman); and the teleological judgment serves as the foundation for the aesthetic and as a condition of which the latter must take account.

(5: 311–12)

The central claim in this passage is that when we judge an object to have a purpose, then its being well-adapted to that purpose is a necessary condition for our taking any further and purely aesthetic pleasure in it. This holds in the case of natural objects, where we may be forced to think of their being well-suited to their purposes as a product of superhuman artistry, but would presumably hold equally well in the case of artifacts such as arsenals and gazebos, where their utility as well as any purely aesthetic properties they may have can be attributed to ordinary human artistry.

This is the solution to the question of the proper relation between beauty and utility suggested by Kant's careful repetition of the language of necessary conditions. It seems to be on the right track. We know from Hutcheson's example of the chair with mismatched legs that utility is not a sufficient condition for beauty: that chair may be just as stable and sturdy as another, but it will clearly not be beautiful. Thus, Hume is wrong to suggest that we will find a house beautiful just because it is convenient and commodious: it might be so, but it also may be a pastiche of styles – a little Arts and Crafts here and Bauhaus there – that we can only find grating. But it does seem right that we cannot find something such as a chair or a house that does have an obvious use beautiful if it cannot but strike us as ill-suited to its function: we cannot really take pleasure in a chair that looks like it would collapse as soon as anyone sat on it, no matter how elegant its design, nor in a house that would quickly be discovered to be awkward and inconvenient no matter how striking its initial appearance. Beauty seems to require something more than mere utility, be it elegance in design, harmony in materials and colors, and who knows what else, but also seems to be incompatible with obvious disutility, and in that sense utility seems to be a necessary condition of beauty. This relationship would seem to accommodate the intuition of Berkeley and Hume that, in the words of the latter, "a great part of the beauty, which we admire either in animals or in other objects, is deriv'd from the idea of convenience and utility" (*Treatise*, 195), while being compatible with Hutcheson's and Burke's examples of artifacts and organisms, mismatched chairs and swine and pelicans, that are useful (to others or themselves) without being beautiful.

It might seem as if we ought to be able simply to ignore or abstract from the intended purpose or use of an object in order to enjoy the beauty of its form, indeed that we ought to be able to do so not only when that form might be ill-suited to the intended use of the object but even when it might be well-suited to a use of which we heartily disapprove, as when we admire the elegant design of a lethal weapon. Kant seems to presuppose that we are capable of such abstraction when he states that "A judgment of taste in regard to an object with a determinate internal end would thus be pure only if the person making the judgment either had no concept of this end or abstracted from it in his judgment" (5: 231). Perhaps Kant does think that when it is a question of the internal end of an object rather than its external end. But in fact he recognizes that it is not at all easy for us to abstract from the intended use of an object in any case in which we recognize that the object must have or have had an intended use; indeed he maintains that in such a case we will think about the intended use of the object even when we do not know what that might be or have been:

There are things in which one can see a purposive form without cognizing an end in them, e.g., the stone utensils often excavated from ancient burial mounds, which are equipped with a hole, as if for a handle, which, although they clearly betray by their shape a purposiveness the end of which one does not know, are nevertheless not declared to be beautiful on that account. Yet the fact that they are regarded as a work of art is already enough to require one to admit that one relates their shape to some sort of intention and to a determinate purpose.

(5: 236n)

The main point of this comment is obviously to emphasize that relating the form of an object to its intended purpose is not a sufficient condition for finding it beautiful. Yet the passage also suggests that if we recognize an object to have a purpose at all, which we must do in the case of every human artifact, we cannot but think of what its purpose might have been, even if we lack knowledge of that point. Thus the idea that we could make a pure judgment about the free beauty of an object simply by abstracting from its end or utility seems to be in trouble. Instead, it seems as if we should admit that the utility of an object that we judge should have utility is a necessary but not a sufficient condition of its beauty. We should then say that what Kant calls adherent beauty is a genuine case of beauty, not a pseudo-case, and also that the adherent beauty of an object is not simply added to its free beauty, but is rather what the beauty of an object is called when it is, in Kant's word, "conditioned" by the requirements for the utility of the object. In other words, beauty is beauty, always produced by the harmonious play of imagination and understanding induced by the form of an object,[11] but when that play is constrained by our requirement that the form first be suitable to the use of the object, then such beauty is called adherent beauty.

Nevertheless, it may seem too simple to say that the perception of the utility of any particular object judged to be of a kind that ought to have utility is merely a necessary condition of its being felt to be beautiful. Surely the recognition of the utility of an object enhances the pleasure of our response to its beauty, just as our recognition of its beauty enhances our pleasure in its utility, so the relation between beauty and utility seems additive after all. If that is so, then shouldn't the relation between apparent disutility and pleasure be subtractive, so that the perceived disutility of an object detracts from our pleasure in its beauty without necessarily blocking it? Perhaps what should be said here is that the relation between utility and beauty is additive, so that our pleasure in the one can enhance our pleasure in the other, and that, in principle, the relation between disutility and beauty is correspondingly subtractive – but that in fact our distress at the appearance of disutility in an object is so great that it is

[11] See Kant, *Critique of the Power of Judgment*, 5: 189–90; 5: 217–18; 5: 281, and elsewhere.

always sufficient to reduce the pleasure that we might take in what would otherwise be the beauty of the object to nothing. That would indeed *explain* why the appearance of utility in an object expected to have utility functions as a necessary condition for its beauty: its disutility would simply wipe out any other pleasure we might take in it.

Now, why should this be so? Why cannot we simply ignore the intended use of an object and judge whether its form is beautiful in complete independence from its utility? And why should our distress at disutility be so great as to block any other pleasure we might take in an object? The answer to this question, at least for Kant and most other eighteenth-century thinkers, is simply that the human mind is inherently teleological – that is, it is natural for us to seek purposes and to find them wherever we can, and to be frustrated when we cannot find them where we think we should be able to do so but to be gratified when we do, and all the more gratified when we succeed in finding purposes where we would have thought we couldn't. In fact, we are particularly frustrated when we fail to find purposiveness where we expect to, although not noticeably pleased when we do find it where we expect to, while when we find it where we do not expect to, we are noticeably pleased, although when we do not find it where we do not expect to find it, we are not noticeably displeased. This set of assumptions would explain the relationship that we find between the perception of utility and of beauty: where we judge that an object is ill-adapted to its intended use, our frustration at that is so great as to block other potential pleasures in the object, such as pleasure in the beauty of its form; but where an object is well-adapted to its intended use or other purpose, we pretty much take that for granted, and need an additional element such as beauty of form to take an especially noticeable pleasure in it.

It is clear that Kant's aesthetic theory is based upon the assumption that pleasure, or at least pleasure beyond purely physiological sensory stimulation, is caused by the recognition of the attainment of an end. In the Introduction to the third *Critique*, he states that "The attainment of every aim is combined with the feeling of pleasure" (5: 187), although what he actually assumes is the inverse, namely, that every feeling of pleasure is combined with the attainment of an end, for what he next does is to search for the end that is attained in the case of a free judgment of beauty in spite of its obvious disinterestedness and independence of ordinary ends: the free play between imagination and understanding is introduced precisely because it is a state that we regard as the attainment of our general end in cognition, although apart from its ordinary condition, namely, the subsumption of an object under a determinate concept.[12] What I am suggesting now is that Kant also assumes the converse of this principle, namely, that every evident failure to attain an end is accompanied with frustration or displeasure, although just as the attainment of an end is particularly remarkable and the pleasure in it therefore especially prominent when it is unexpected, so is the failure to attain an end particularly evident only when its attainment would naturally be expected. So we are not noticeably displeased at the absence of beauty when we have no right to expect it – which is perhaps most of the time – but we are noticeably frustrated when an end we expect is not met – as when a chair or a house that should be well-adapted to its intended use is not. And our frustration at the latter will be sufficiently intense to block any pleasure we might have found in some unexpected feature of an object that would otherwise strike us as beautiful.

But his assumption of the essentially teleological character of the human mind is not evident just in Kant's aesthetics; it is apparent throughout his philosophy. The "Critique of Teleological Judgment" that accompanies the "Critique of Aesthetic Judgment" is a complex analysis of our tendency to seek purposiveness and utility throughout nature: Kant argues that we naturally look at everything in nature as if it were designed for a purpose, that this attitude is by itself theoretically unjustified, but that certain things in nature–namely, organisms–force the thought of design upon us, and then that since we can conceive of design only in terms of our own intentional production, and that is always aimed at some end or goal, we have to find a goal for things in nature after all, although if that is assumed to be something of intrinsic value, then it can ultimately be only our own moral development.[13] But the assumption goes beyond the third *Critique:* Kant's argument in the *Groundwork for the Metaphysics of Morals* also begins with the assumption that it is natural for us to assume that everything in nature has a purpose to which it is well-adapted, which serves as the premise for his argument that the purpose of reason must be

[12] For the details of this interpretation, see my *Kant and the Claims of Taste,* 2nd ed. (Cambridge: Cambridge University Press, 1997), esp. 70–88, and Chapter 3 of the present work.

[13] This is the argument that extends from §61 to §84 of the "Critique of Teleological Judgment." I have offered interpretations of it in a number of places; see especially "The Unity of Nature and Freedom: Kant's Conception of the System of Philosophy," in *The Reception of Kant's Critical Philosophy,* ed. Sally Sedgwick (Cambridge: Cambridge University Press, 2000), 19–53, and "From Nature to Morality: Kant's New Argument in the 'Critique of Teleological Judgment,'" in *Architektonik und System in der Philosophie Kants,* eds. Hans Friedrich Fulda and Jürgen Stolzenberg (Hamburg: Meiner, 2001), 375–404.

to produce a good will rather than happiness, since it does not seem very well-adapted to produce the latter.[14] In the *Critique of Pure Reason* too, Kant reveals his view that we all assume that "Everything that nature itself arranges is good for some aim," here in the context of explaining that even the existence of the dialectical conflicts to which pure reason is exposed in its theoretical use turns out to have the beneficial effect of revealing its proper practical vocation.[15] Of course, Kant's argument throughout his work is that this assumption is a regulative rather than constitutive principle which permits of dogmatic use in practical but not theoretical reasoning – but that is entirely compatible with the assumption that as a matter of psychological fact we will experience great frustration at the failure to find purposiveness where we expect to and great pleasure when we find it where we do not expect to.

Further, it is not just Kant who assumes the fundamentally teleological character of the human mind. Obviously, the Leibnizian world-view, dominant in Germany throughout the eighteenth century, equates an explanation of anything with a sufficient reason for it in the mind of an intelligence – that is, it imposes the model of our own intentional production upon reality at large. Yet even the hard-headed empiricist Hume allows his spokesman Philo to begin the conclusion of the *Dialogues Concerning Natural Religion* with these words:

> A Purpose, an Intention, a Design strikes every where the most careless, the most stupid Thinker; and no man can be so harden'd in absurd Systems, as at all times to reject it. *That Nature does nothing in vain,* is a Maxim establish'd in all the Schools, merely from the Contemplation of the Works of Nature, without any religious Purpose . . . [16]

And true to his approach throughout his work, Hume does not waste his effort arguing against what he takes to be a native disposition of the human mind, but rather only carefully delimits the significance we should ascribe to such a disposition, in this case cautioning against trying to draw too precise an analogy between human intentional production and the purposive production of the world as a whole.

[14] See Kant, *Groundwork of the Metaphysics of Morals,* 4:395.

[15] Kant, *Critique of Pure Reason,* ed. and trans. Paul Guyer and Allen W. Wood (Cambridge: Cambridge University Press, 1998), 645 (= A 743/B 771).

[16] David Hume, *Dialogues Concerning Natural Religion,* reprinted in Hume, *The Natural History of Religion and Dialogues Concerning Natural Religion,* eds. A. Wayne Colver and John Valdimir Price (Oxford: Clarendon Press, 1976), 245.

I have argued that we should understand Kant as resolving the eighteenth-century debate over the relationship between beauty and utility with the thesis that utility is a necessary although not sufficient condition for beauty in those sorts of objects where we would expect utility, a condition that can be explained by the inherent tendency of the human mind to seek purposiveness and to be frustrated when it does not find it where it expects to – the case of utility – and to be particularly pleased when it finds it where it does not expect to – the case of beauty. It should be clear that on this account Kant's solution depends upon a thesis in empirical psychology, as my last remark, that Kant's general conception of the teleological character of human thought is not so different from Hume's model of mind, would also suggest. But as I have long argued that the very foundation of Kant's aesthetic theory, the thesis that our pleasure in beauty is produced by a harmony between imagination and understanding, is also a claim in empirical psychology,[17] I will not take this result as an objection to the present analysis.[18]

[17] See my *Kant and the Claims of Taste*, chapter 9, esp. 287–8.

[18] An earlier version of this essay was presented at the annual meeting of the American Society for Aesthetics in October 2001. I would like to thank Daniel Dahlstrom and John Brown for their very helpful comments on that occasion.

5

Free and Adherent Beauty

A Modest Proposal

There have been three different approaches to the interpretation of Kant's concept of adherent beauty. In one, an object's satisfaction of constraints imposed on its form by its intended function is just a necessary condition for our pleasure in its beauty, but makes no direct contribution to our pleasure in it. In the second, our pleasures in an object's function and in its form are thought to be separate pleasures that combine into a compound pleasure greater than either of its parts. In the third, our pleasure in adherent beauty is thought to be a special pleasure in the interaction between an object's function and its form. I argue that each of these interpretations has a basis in Kant's statements, and properly so, because they represent three different ways in which form and function can actually relate in our experience and appreciation of objects that do have intended functions.

Kant opens §16 of the "Analytic of the Beautiful" in the *Critique of the Power of Judgment*[1] with his famous distinction between "free" and

[1] Immanuel Kant, *Critique of the Power of Judgment*, ed. Paul Guyer, trans. Paul Guyer and Eric Matthews (Cambridge: Cambridge University Press, 2000). Hereafter *CPJ*; citations will be identified by section number and volume and page number of the German text of the Academy edition, *Kant's gesammelte Schriften*, edited by the Royal Prussian (subsequently German and then Berlin-Brandenburg) Academy of Sciences (Berlin: Georg Reimer, subsequently Walter de Gruyter: 1900–). The text of the *Kritik der Urtheilskraft* is in vol. 5, and was edited by Wilhelm Windelband. The best current German edition, Immanuel Kant, *Kritik der Urteilskraft*, edited with introduction and bibliography by Heiner Klemme and notes by Pietro Giordanetti (Hamburg: Felix Meiner, 2001), provides the Academy pagination, as does the Cambridge translation, and also provides the pagination of Kant's own second edition of the third *Critique*, the preferred text.

"adherent" beauty:

> There are two kinds of beauty: free beauty (*pulchritudo vaga*) or merely adherent beauty (*pulchritudo adhaerens*).[2] The first presupposes no concept of what the object ought to be; the second does presuppose a concept and the perfection of the object in accordance with it. The first are called (self-subsisting) beauties of this or that thing; the latter, as adhering to a concept (conditioned beauty), are ascribed to objects that stand under the concept of a particular end.
>
> (*CPJ*, §16, 5:229)

Since Kant has been arguing from the outset of the "Analytic" that a judgment of taste is based on the feeling of pleasure produced by an object independently of its subsumption under any concepts, an argument that has just culminated in the previous §15 with the insistence against the rationalist aesthetics of Leibniz, Wolff, Baumgarten, and Meier that a judgment of beauty is not a confused judgment about the perfection or "objective purposiveness" of an object precisely because "to judge objective purposiveness we always require the concept of an end" (*CPJ*, §15, 5:227), this distinction raises an obvious question. If adherent beauty presupposes a concept of the object, how can it be a kind of beauty at all? Why isn't it just an obscure perfection of the object, or – to switch from talking about properties to talking about judgments[3] – why isn't a judgment of adherent beauty a confused judgment about some objective perfection of the object?

I raised this question in 1979 in *Kant and the Claims of Taste*.[4] Eva Schaper also raised it that year in the chapter on "Free and Dependent

[2] Kant here uses the adjective *anhängende*, and subsequently uses the alternative *adhärierende* (230). In his 1911 translation, J. C. Meredith translated both as "dependent." This would be a natural translation of *abhängende*, which Kant does not use as an adjective directly modifying "beauty" (*Schönheit*), although at one point in the section he does write that the judgment of taste is no longer a "pure and free" judgment if it is "dependent" (*abhängig*) on a purpose and thus based on a judgment of reason (230). His term *anhängende* connotes not the idea of one thing hanging from something else, that is, depending on it, but rather of one thing being attached to something else, that is, adhering to it. Since he both equates *anhängende* with the Latin *adhaerens* and uses the German *adhärierende* interchangeably with it, Matthews and I preferred the translation "adherent" to Meredith's "dependent" for both of Kant's German terms. But as will shortly become evident, the mere choice of a translation for Kant's terms will not by itself resolve the philosophical puzzles about the meaning of his distinction.

[3] As was recommended by Donald W. Crawford in *Kant's Aesthetic Theory* (Madison: University of Wisconsin Press, 1974), p. 56.

[4] Paul Guyer, *Kant and the Claims of Taste*, 2nd ed. (Cambridge: Cambridge University Press, 1997), p. 218.

Beauty" in her *Studies in Kant's Aesthetics.*[5] In *Kant and the Claims of Taste,* I offered a simple solution to this problem.[6] In the case of adherent beauty, the concept of the object that is presupposed by the judgment *constrains* or *restricts* what forms we can find beautiful in an object of a certain sort by considerations deriving from its intended function, but such constraints are not sufficient to determine what forms we will find beautiful in such an object. For that, we must still experience a free play of imagination and understanding with the form of the object (or, as I would add, its other sensible and representational properties), and thus we still have a genuine response to beauty and can make a genuine judgment of taste, although within the constraints imposed by the intended purpose of the object. So, for example, that an edifice is intended as a cathedral means that it must have a cruciform floor plan, but of course not every edifice with a cruciform floor plan is beautiful; a beautiful cathedral must satisfy that constraint but also, within the limits imposed by that constraint, induce a free play of imagination and understanding in us. Thus, as I said then, in the case of adherent beauty "the relation between purpose and dependent beauty is a negative one."[7]

In Chapter 4 of the present volume, I have refined this approach to take account of the fact that Kant suggests that the requirement of satisfying its intended purpose does not merely constrain what we can find beautiful in an object that we take to have a purpose, but functions as a *necessary condition* for it: that is, he suggests that unless the form of the object is at least compatible with its purpose, we cannot take any pleasure in what would otherwise be its beauty at all. As Kant says, "a figure could be beautified with all sorts of curlicues and light but regular lines, as the New Zealanders do with their tattooing, if only it were not a human being" (*CPJ*, §16, 5:230). In this case, patterns that we might find beautiful in some other sort of object are assumed (to be sure, without explanation) to be incompatible with the moral end of human beings, and our pleasure in them as beautiful is supposed to be blocked for that reason. I have

5 Eva Schaper, *Studies in Kant's Aesthetics* (Edinburgh: Edinburgh University Press, 1979), pp. 80–81. This chapter had previously been published in *Akten des IV. Internationalen Kant-Kongresses,* Teil 1 (Berlin: Walter de Gruyter: 1974), pp. 247–262.

6 But not as simple a solution as that proposed by Crawford, who said that Kant's designation of dependent beauty, or, as he prefers, the dependent judgment of beauty, was simply a concession to common ways of talking, and that in Kant's view this judgment is in fact just a disguised judgment of perfection and not a genuine aesthetic judgment at all. See his *Kant's Aesthetic Theory,* p. 56.

7 Guyer, *Kant and the Claims of Taste,* p. 219.

suggested that this can be understood on my "negative" model of adherent beauty by simply supposing that our *dis*pleasure at *dys*functionality, the violation of an end whether of utility or morality, is so great that it always outweighs any purely aesthetic pleasure we might otherwise take in the form of an object, thereby reducing it to nothing.[8] But this remains a "negative" solution: when the requirement of functionality, whether pragmatic or moral, is satisfied, then the judgment of adherent beauty is genuinely aesthetic because the form of the object allows for a free play of our cognitive faculties within the limits set by its purpose.

This approach has been criticized. Wicks has held that my "negative" or what he calls 'external' model does not do justice to Kant's initial statement that adherent beauty *presupposes* a concept of what the object ought to be; that requires, he argues, some more intimate connection between the intended purpose of the object, that is, what it ought to be, and its form.[9] He goes on to propose that in the case of dependent beauty, the requirement of free play, which must be met if dependent beauty is to be a genuine case of beauty at all, is met by the way "we run through many determinate images" suggested by an object "in view of their suitability for realizing an object's given purpose." This is a case of free play because "Each image is determinate, but there is a free play within the imagination insofar as none of these images (at this stage) is selected as a concrete way to realize the object's purpose."[10] It is the supposition that the mind plays with different images of how an object might realize its purpose that leads Wicks to call dependent beauty "teleological style." I have criticized this solution elsewhere,[11] and do not mean to repeat my criticisms here; I only wish to register Wicks's call for a more "positive" or "internal" account of the relation between intended end and aesthetic character, between function and form, in the case of adherent beauty.

Likewise, Budd has also proposed, in his case not as an interpretation but as a criticism of Kant, that the judgment of adherent beauty should be understood as a "non-compound" judgment, not a mere "combination of the judgment that O is a good specimen of kind K and the judgment

[8] Paul Guyer, "Beauty and Utility in Eighteenth-century Aesthetics," *Eighteenth-Century Studies*, vol. 35 (2002), pp. 439–453; Chapter 4 of the present volume.

[9] Robert Wicks, "Dependent Beauty as the Appreciation of Teleological Style," *Journal of Aesthetics and Art Criticism*, vol. 55 (1997), pp. 387–400, at p. 398.

[10] *Ibid.*, p. 393.

[11] Paul Guyer, "Dependent Beauty Revisited: A Reply to Wicks", *Journal of Aesthetics and Art Criticism*, vol. 57 (1999), pp. 357–361.

that the sensory manifold of O has a beautiful form,"[12] but rather as a "non-compound aesthetic judgment about a natural being *as being an instance of kind K*."[13] But although he does not think, as does Wicks, that Kant himself clearly recognized this form of aesthetic judgment, his account of what Kant should have thought is much like Wicks's account of what Kant did think: a judgment of adherent beauty, as Kant should have understood it, "will depend on the character of the natural functions of a certain natural kind and the ways in which they are realized in the appearance of something of that kind" – the sort of thing displayed in "the gracefulness of a gazelle's leaping motion, or the manifest suitability of the bodily parts to the creature's ability to flourish in its natural environment, as with the wings of an eagle or a hummingbird."[14] One might object that this model of a judgment of adherent beauty satisfies Kant's requirements for an aesthetic judgment insofar as it focuses on the sensible appearance of the object, but that does not make adequate room for Kant's requirement of a free play between imagination and understanding. One might also observe that Budd's definition would obviously have to be modified to make room for the judgment of adherent beauty in works of art rather than nature, since Kant clearly supposes that at least some works of art possess adherent beauty.[15] But again, I do not want to develop a criticism of Budd's proposal, but just to acknowledge his sense that in the case of adherent beauty there ought to be a response to a more intimate connection between the function of an object and its form than a "negative" or "external" approach to the concept allows.

Allison, on the contrary, has recently argued for a more purely conjunctive or additive model of adherent beauty than I proposed, indeed for precisely the kind of "compound" conception of the judgment that Budd rejects. On his account, Kant's aim in proposing this concept is not, as Allison interprets me to claim, to attempt "(unsuccessfully) to impose constraints on the pure judgment of taste beyond those derivable from the harmony of faculties alone,"[16] but rather to indicate "how taste can

[12] Malcom Budd, "Delight in the Natural World: Kant on the Aesthetic Appreciation of Nature. Part I: Natural Beauty," *British Journal of Aesthetics*, vol. 38 (1998), pp. 1–18, at p. 10.

[13] *Ibid.*, p. 13.

[14] *Ibid.*, pp. 14–15.

[15] See, for example, *CPJ*, §48, 5:311. Henry Allison has recently argued that Kant does not intend all artistic beauty to be regarded as adherent beauty; see his *Kant's Theory of Taste: A Reading of the Critique of Aesthetic Judgment* (Cambridge: Cambridge University Press, 2001), pp. 290–298. This claim can be debated, but I will not do so here.

[16] My account does not actually focus on constraints for the judgment of taste, as if the point of Kant's introduction of adherent beauty was to make judgments of taste more

enter into more complex forms of evaluation in which it plays a subordinate role without compromising its inherent purity."[17] He does not, as he continues, reject completely the idea that the intended function of an object places some constraints on its form; rather, what he goes on to argue is that in such a case the object's satisfaction of its function, while it does impose some constraint on what could count as beautiful in its form, is also the ground of an *additional* pleasure in the object, which combines with the purely aesthetic pleasure in the object's form to constitute a more complex response and a more complex evaluation, which is "no longer *purely* a judgment of taste, but [which] does not undermine the *purity* of the taste component itself."[18] Thus, the "proper contrast" between free and adherent beauty "is between two ways in which the beauty of an object (which as such is always the object of a pure judgment of taste) is to be considered: either solely in its own terms, or as an ingredient in a larger whole."[19] An obvious question about this proposal is whether it does justice to Kant's suggestion, stressed by my approach, that in the case of adherent beauty the conditions for an object's functionality operate as some sort of *necessary condition* on our pleasure in its beauty. One might also ask whether Allison's proposal that in the case of adherent beauty our pleasure in an object's form is part of a larger whole differs in any way from the thought that our pleasure in its perfection is merely combined with our pleasure in its form. This is why I refer to Allison's account as essentially additive, although he might not be happy with that description. But again, instead of pressing these objections, I merely want to register Allison's recognition that our response to adherent beauty in some way involves a combination of pleasures, not a single pleasure.

What I now want to propose is that these three approaches to adherent beauty – the external or negative model of an object's purpose as restricting permissible forms for its beauty, the internal model of the adherently beautiful as an especially pleasing instance of a certain kind, and the additive or conjunctive model of separate pleasures in beauty and in perfection – should not be understood as three competing and mutually

rule-bound (although Kant does in fact suggest that, in the passage from 5:231 to be quoted later); my suggestion was rather that in the case of adherent beauty, the concept of the object's purpose functions as a constraint on the free play of our imagination and understanding itself, or our response to beauty, although not in a way that completely eliminates the room for such play.

[17] Allison, *Kant's Theory of Taste*, p. 140.

[18] *Ibid.*, p. 141.

[19] *Ibid.*, p. 142.

exclusive interpretations of Kant's conception, but rather should be seen as reflecting three different ways in which function can actually relate to form in our experience, *all* of which are suggested if not clearly distinguished in Kant's all too brief but actually quite rich account. In fact, Kant makes three key statements about the character of adherent beauty, and each of these statements reflects one of the ways in which function can relate to form in cases of adherent beauty, that is, the beauty of objects that we do recognize as having intended ends or functions.

(i) First, as I noted at the outset, Kant begins his discussion by stating that adherent beauty *presupposes* a concept of "what the object ought to be" and "the perfection of the object in accordance with it" (*CPJ*, §16, 5:229).

(ii) But he also immediately continues to characterize adherent beauty as "conditioned beauty," and two paragraphs later says that the concept which is presupposed in the case of adherent beauty is one "by which the imagination, which is as it were at play in the observation of the shape [*Gestalt*], would merely be restricted" (5:230). And this restriction, it turns out, functions as a necessary condition: Kant apparently supposes that the incompatibility of an object's form with its intended function blocks the possibility of *any* pleasure in features of it that might otherwise seem beautiful. This leads to a whole paragraph implying that in the case of objects that have certain ends or functions, their functionality is a necessary condition of their beauty, one line of which I already quoted:

> One would be able to add much to a building that would be pleasing in the intuition of it if only it were not supposed to be a church; a figure could be beautified with all sorts of curlicues and light but regular lines, as the New Zealanders do with their tattooing, if only it were not a human being; and the latter could have much finer features and a more pleasing, softer outline to its facial structure if only it were not supposed to represent a man, or even a warrior.
>
> (*CPJ*, §16, 5:230)

And finally, (iii) Kant suggests that in the case of adherent beauty, there is a combination of two independent pleasures, a pleasure in the pure beauty of the object on the one hand and on the other a pleasure in its goodness or perfection in accordance with some end. First he notes, in a negative tone, that "the combination of the good (that is, the way in which the manifold is good for the thing itself, in accordance with its end) with beauty does damage to its purity" (5:230). But then he makes it clear that this accusation of impurity is not a negative value judgment,[20] and that

[20] Schaper stressed this point; see "Free and Dependent Beauty," pp. 79, 97–98.

in fact the combination of pleasure in the pure beauty of form with that in the perfection of an object relative to an end may constitute a greater good overall than that of either pleasure on its own. In the paragraph following the last one quoted, Kant repeats his formulation that in the case of a judgment of adherent beauty the judgment is "restricted" by the concept of the end attributed to the object, and thus the judgment "is no longer a free and pure judgment of taste," and then he continues:

> To be sure, taste gains by this combination of aesthetic satisfaction with the intellectual in that it becomes fixed and, though not universal, can have rules prescribed to it in regard to certain purposively determined objects. But in this case these are also not rules of taste, but merely rules for the unification of taste with reason, i.e., of the beautiful with the good, through which the former becomes usable as an instrument of the intention with regard to the latter, so that the determination of the mind that sustains itself and is of subjective universal validity can underlie that which can only be sustained through strenuous resolve but is objectively universally valid. Strictly speaking, however, perfection does not gain by beauty, nor does beauty gain by perfection; rather, since in comparing the representation by which an object is given to us with the object (with regard to what it ought to be) we cannot avoid at the same time holding it together with the subject, the *entire faculty* of the powers of representation gains if both states of mind are in agreement.
>
> (*CPJ*, §16, 5:230–1)

There are at least three things going on in this fascinating paragraph. First, Kant seems to be suggesting that we are so interested in finding something approximating determinate rules for making judgments of taste that we are willing to sacrifice at least a little of the free play of imagination in pure aesthetic response for some gain in determinacy of judgment. This could point the way to the discussion of the "ideal of beauty" in the next section (§17), where Kant makes it clear that it is actually in behalf of reason's interest in a maximum rather than taste's interest in universal subjective validity that we seek an "archetype" of taste (*CPJ*, §17, 5:232). Second, Kant alludes to the way in which the cultivation of taste may, without completely sacrificing the freedom of the imagination in aesthetic experience, actually support our resolve to act as morality requires, a point he will develop further in the "General Remark" following the analytics of the beautiful and sublime (see 5:266–272) and to which he will return in the "Doctrine of Virtue" of the *Metaphysics of Morals* seven years later (see especially its §17, 6:643). And finally, Kant observes that even though beauty and perfection remain distinct, and neither is directly augmented by the other, *we* gain by combining them.

He speaks of a gain to our "entire faculty of the powers of representation," and it is, to say the least, far from clear exactly what that is supposed to mean or how much it is supposed to include; but at the very least it suggests that our total state of pleasure is increased by the combination of pleasure in beauty with pleasure at goodness.

Now I suggest that these three statements, each of which has been taken as the basis for an alternative interpretation of Kant's conception of adherent beauty, should simply be taken conjointly to describe three different possible relations between beauty and functionality that we encounter in our experience. (i) First, Kant's suggestion that in the case of adherent beauty the compatibility of an object's form with its intended purpose is a restriction on its beauty or a necessary condition of our finding it beautiful can be taken to indicate that our interest in functionality is so great that the appearance of *dysfunctionality* will always block any other pleasure we might take in an object, *a fortiori* will block pleasure in what would otherwise be its beauty. This negative relation between function and beauty would be satisfied even in a case in which a beautiful object's non-dysfunctionality makes no positive contribution to our pleasure in it, and thus the sum total of our pleasure in it must be due to the free play of imagination and understanding that takes place within the limits on the object's form imposed by the requirements of its end or function. For example, imagine a lamp whose design is not only pleasing but also does not interfere with its function as a light source, but where there is nothing exceptional in the way that it serves its function as a light source and we do not take any special pleasure in its fulfilment of that function. It should be noted here, by the way, that our interest in what I have been calling functionality or what Kant would call perfection is quite general: an object's failure to satisfy either our moral expectations or some other practical but non-moral expectations will be sufficient to block any pleasure in its beauty. This should be evident from Kant's examples: in addition to instancing limits on the "beauty of a human being," where the restrictions on permissible forms of beauty presumably derive from the requirements of respecting human beings as ends in themselves, Kant also mentions "the beauty of a horse," a creature that has no moral standing of its own,[21] as well as the beauty of buildings, "such as a church, a palace, an arsenal,

[21] Kant does argue that we have an indirect duty *to ourselves* to treat beautiful objects in non-human nature humanely (as we would say), a duty arising from the fact that because of our general obligation to try to be moral we should do everything in our power to do so and therefore should not damage "a natural predisposition" that, "though not of itself moral . . . greatly promotes morality or at least prepares the way for it"; this is the basis of

or a garden-house" (5:230), at least some of which certainly have practical but not moral purposes. Thus any suggestion that it is only moral ends that restrict permissible forms in the case of adherent beauty is incorrect.[22]

(ii) But that is just one possible relation between purpose and beauty. Another possibility would be that suggested by Kant's statement that in the *combination* of beauty and perfection, although neither gains by the other, there is a total gain to our own "entire faculty" of representation. This would cover the case in which we are not merely not aware of any evident dysfunctionality in an object, but are aware of and take pleasure in its functionality – again, whether moral or practical in some other sense – and are also aware of and take pleasure in the beauty of the object, but do not directly link the two; thus we have, as it were, two separate pleasures that are independent of each other but which each contribute to our total state of pleasure. To continue with our previous example, imagine here a beautiful Ming vase successfully altered to make a very good lamp: it might strike us both as lighting our room particularly well, which pleases us, and as a very beautiful object, which also pleases us, but we need not perceive any direct connection between its being a good light source and a beautiful *objet d'art*.

(iii) Finally, there would be the case, suggested to at least some interpreters by Kant's statement that adherent beauty *presupposes* a concept of what the object ought to be, in which we perceive an "internal" connection between an object's purpose and its form, or in which we perceive an object as an especially beautiful instance of its kind, and take a special pleasure in that relationship. This would be the case, idealized by twentieth-century theorists of architecture and design, in which we feel that there is a real interaction between an object's form and its function – for example, a case in which we feel that the object's form is not just compatible with its function but expresses it beautifully, so that its function is clarified and its form enhanced for us. Our example here might be some contemporary lamp, no doubt Italian, where we have not just an elegant combination of geometrical forms and gleaming materials, but also where so many extraneous elements have been eliminated and the

Kant's argument, alluded to earlier, in §17 of the "Docrine of Virtue" of the *Metaphysics of Morals* (6:443).

[22] Such a view was proposed by Geoffrey Scarré in "Kant on Free and Dependent Beauty," *British Journal of Aesthetics*, vol. 21 (1981), pp. 351–362. It was criticized in Paul Crowther, "The Claims of Perfection: A Revisionary Defence of Kant's Theory of Dependent Beauty," *International Philosophical Quarterly*, vol. 26 (1986), pp. 61–74.

design is so clever that the beauty of the object strikes one as lying in the lamp simply as a pure source of light. Here we might think that the interaction between the object's form and its function is so pleasurable to us that our pleasure in the object is greater than our pleasures in its form and its functionality considered apart could possibly be. Thus the "internal" connection between form and function suggested by Kant's "presupposition" language would be a third way in which form and function can relate in a beautiful object recognized by us as having an intended purpose.

It would be a mistake, I think, though one made throughout the twentieth century, to suppose that this last, "internal" relation between form and function should always be the ideal for designers. Rather, it would seem to be an empirical question whether the pleasure that would be induced by an ideally complete interaction between form and function in an object is always greater than the combination of separate pleasures in beauty and in functionality on some alternative design for that object might be, or even greater than the pleasure in the beauty that simply falls within the permissible design-constraints for some object where the object's satisfaction of those constraints is not the source of any noticeable pleasure at all. One can certainly imagine a well-functioning lamp made out of a Ming vase so beautiful that, even though we do not see any special suitability of this form to its function, our total pleasure in it is still greater than our pleasure in some other lamp where we are conscious of a specially pleasing interaction between form and function.

Thus I conclude that we should regard Kant's three different explications of the concept of adherent beauty not as the basis for three competing interpretations of his concept, but as theoretically consistent characterizations of three different possibilities for relations between form and function that we can encounter in our interaction with the world of nature and artifact around us: the case in which the requirements for avoiding dysfunctionality place some constraints on what we can find beautiful in an object, but where our pleasure in the object is really just a pleasure in the free play of our cognitive faculties that its form can induce within these constraints; the case in which we take separate pleasures in an object's functionality and its beauty, and can, as it were, simply combine these two separate pleasures; and the case where we take a distinct pleasure in our sense of the interaction or free play between form and function in an object. As the previous paragraph suggests, we should not assume that this list of possibilities necessarily represents a scale of increasing pleasure and therefore increasing value; it will in fact be an empirical question whether our pleasure in any particular case falling under one of these possibilities is lesser or greater than our pleasure in some particular case falling under one of the others. For that reason, it may be a good thing that Kant's own allusions to the three different possibilities I have analysed do not in fact occur in the order in which I have presented them.

6

Kant on the Purity of the Ugly

Kant opens the "Analytic of the Beautiful" in the "Critique of the Aesthetic Power of Judgment" with the statement that "In order to decide whether or not something is beautiful, we do not relate the representation by means of understanding to the object for cognition, but rather relate it by means of the imagination (perhaps combined with the understanding) to the subject and its feeling of pleasure or displeasure" (*CPJ*, §1, 5:203).[1] Kant then argues that only a pleasure in objects that is independent from their merely sensory agreeableness or their prudential or moral goodness is the ground for an affirmative judgment of their beauty, so it seems plausible to suppose that he also means to assert that there is a distinctive displeasure, free of any displeasure in an object's sensory disagreeableness or prudential or moral badness, on which a negative but still purely aesthetic judgment that such an object is ugly rather than beautiful must be based.

It might therefore seem that Kant's aesthetic theory must include an account of a purely aesthetic experience and judgment of ugliness as well as beauty.[2] However, Kant does not explicitly identify the judgment that

[1] All citations to the *Critique of the Power of Judgment* will be drawn from Immanuel Kant, *Critique of the Power of Judgment*, edited by Paul Guyer, translated by Paul Guyer and Eric Matthews (Cambridge: Cambridge University Press, 2000). Citations will be identified by the abbreviation "*CPJ*" followed by Kant's section number and the volume and page number of the passage in *Kant's gesammelte Schriften*, edited by the Royal Prussian (later German and then Berlin-Brandenburg) Academy of Sciences (Berlin: Georg Reimer, later Walter de Gruyter, 1900 –). Citations to other passages in Kant will be located by volume and page number in this edition.

[2] So, for example, Hud Hudson has argued that it must be possible to reconstruct an "Analytic of the Ugly" to accompany the "Analytic of the Beautiful," in which judgments

an object is not beautiful with the judgment that it is ugly, or give any explicit account of a purely aesthetic experience of displeasure on which a judgment of ugliness could be based; indeed, he does not discuss any form of ugliness at all in the "Analytic of the Beautiful," mentioning ugliness only much later, in his discussion of fine art, when he maintains that there can be beautiful artistic representations of "things that in nature would be ugly or displeasing," such as "the furies, diseases, devastations of war, and the like" (*CPJ*, §48, 5:312). This fact has led some authors to argue that Kant does not hold judgments of ugliness to be pure aesthetic judgments,[3] and has even led one author to imply, at least by his title, that "Kant finds nothing ugly."[4] The last thought certainly goes too far: of

of ugliness, like judgments of beauty, can be shown to be disinterested and yet universally and necessarily valid (Hud Hudson, "The Significance of an Analytic of the Ugly in Kant's Deduction of Pure Judgments of Taste," in Ralf Meerbote, ed., and Hud Hudson, associate ed., *Kant's Aesthetics, North American Kant Society Studies in Philosophy*, vol. 1 (Atascadero: Ridgeview Publishing Co., 1991), pp. 87–103), and Henry Allison has gone so far as to assert that the "inclusion of space" for "negative judgments of taste" is "criterial for the adequacy of an interpretation of Kant's theory of taste," because "negative judgments must have the same status (as judgments of taste) and the same claim to validity as their positive counterparts" (Henry E. Allison, *Kant's Theory of Taste: A Reading of the Critique of Aesthetic Judgment* (Cambridge: Cambridge University Press, 2001), pp. 54, 71. The arguments of Allison and Hudson were preceded by Christian Strube, "Das Häßliche und die 'Kritik der ästhetischen Urteilskraft': Überlegungen zu einer systematischen Lücke," *Kant-Studien* 80 (1989): 416–46).

3 See Reinhard Brandt, "Die Schönheit der Kristallen und das Spiel der Erkenntniskräfte. Zum Gegenstand und zur Logik des ästhetischen Urteils bei Kant," in Reinhard Brandt and Werner Stark, eds., *Autographen, Dokumente und Berichte: Zu Edition, Amtsgeschäften und Werk Immanuel Kants, Kant-Forschungen*, vol. 5 (Hamburg: Felix Meiner Verlag, 1994), pp. 19–57, and Miles Rind, "Can Kant's Deduction of Judgments of Taste Be Saved?" *Archiv für Geschichte der Philosophie* 84 (2001): 20–45. Brandt emphasizes the fact that Kant, in spite of his references to the "feeling of pleasure and displeasure," never actually discusses the case of the ugly or the feeling of displeasure as a distinct case of feeling, so it is better to understand his conjunctive references as references to our capacity to feel pleasure or displeasure, which, however, feels only pleasure in its purely aesthetic use. This is no doubt right, but does not address the fundamental issue of why Kant cannot allow a purely aesthetic experience of the ugly. Rind recognizes, as I will also argue, that Kant's basic theory of the harmony of the faculties excludes the possibility that the experience of ugliness is a purely aesthetic response, and therefore that our experience of displeasure in the case of ugliness necessarily "arises from some other source" (p. 29). But Rind also thinks that the free play of the faculties is present in the experience of every object, thus that every object is beautiful to some degree, though of course some are more so than others, and that ugly objects are ones in which the displeasure from "some other source" drowns out whatever degree of beauty the object happens to have. This fails to recognize the possibility of aesthetic indifference that, as we will see in the next section, Kant clearly held.

4 David Shier, "Why Kant Finds Nothing Ugly," *British Journal of Aesthetics* 38 (1998): 412–18.

course Kant finds some things ugly – for example, the furies, diseases, and the devastations of war. But I agree with the interpretation that for Kant the judgment that an object is ugly is not a pure aesthetic judgment, as indeed these examples of things that are ugly because they are disagreeable or morally offensive strongly suggest. In this essay, I will explain why Kant cannot hold that judgments of ugliness are pure aesthetic judgments, and argue that he must instead understand the undeniable experience of ugliness as an impure aesthetic experience – indeed, an experience that reveals that while pure aesthetic judgments must be independent of moral judgments, our aesthetic experience as a whole is intimately connected with our moral judgments.

I. Aesthetic Trivalence

On Kant's account, we do not need any feeling of displeasure and judgment of ugliness at all in order to judge that something is not beautiful. This is because Kant holds that pleasure and pain (or positive displeasure) are extremes between which lies the neutral state of feeling neither pleasure nor pain, and he correspondingly holds, although he does not mention this in the third *Critique*, that beauty and ugliness are extremes between which lies the aesthetically indifferent. Kant's view is that while the predicate "beautiful" may be *asserted* of an object only on the basis of a feeling of pleasure induced by that object, it can be *withheld* from an object *either* when that object fails to produce a feeling of either pleasure or displeasure *or* when it produces an actual feeling of displeasure. Thus an object may fail to be beautiful when it is aesthetically indifferent as well as when it is actually painful and ugly. Kant makes this explicit in a variety of places. In several of his early notes on aesthetics, he observes that there are three aesthetic categories, not two: one note characterizes pleasure (*Lust*) as "A," indifference (*Gleichgültigkeit*) as "non A," and displeasure (*Unlust*) as " –A," and then presents the "beautiful, the ordinary, and the ugly" (*schön, alltägig, häßlich*) as a trichotomy expressing these three possibilities, along with similar trichotomies such as "good, valueless, evil" and "esteem, disregard, contempt" (*Achtung, Gringschätzung, Verachtung*) (*R* 669, 15:196–7). Another note simply lists "beautiful +, not-beautiful (dry) 0; ugly –" as three alternative aesthetic predicates.[5] These trichotomies mean that objects can be denied to be beautiful when

[5] These passages are cited by Wenzel, "Kant Finds Nothing Beautiful?" p. 418, as well as Strube, "Das Häßliche," p. 421.

they are "ordinary" or "indifferent" and produce no feeling of pleasure or displeasure at all, as well as when they are actually ugly and produce a feeling of real displeasure. Thus we do not need a feeling of displeasure, let alone a purely aesthetic feeling of displeasure, in order to make the negative judgment that something is not beautiful – which is the only form of negative aesthetic judgment that Kant actually mentions in the opening statement of the "Analytic of the Beautiful." Kant also notes that a judgment of ugliness is not the only alternative in his lectures on logic and metaphysics. Thus, although he states in the 1772 *Logik Philippi* that "Ugliness is . . . something positive, not a mere lack of beauty, rather the existence of something contrary to beauty" (24:364),[6] he also states in the 1789 *Logik Pölitz* that "To distinguish the beautiful from that which is not beautiful (not from that which is ugly, because that which is not beautiful is not always ugly) is taste" (24:514).[7] Similarly, in the late (1794–95) *Metaphysik Vigilantius*, he holds that "That which pleases through mere intuition is *beautiful*, that which leaves me indifferent in intuition, although it can please or displease, is *non-beautiful*; that which displeases me in intuition is ugly. Now on this pleasure rests the *concept of taste*" (29:1010).[8] Thus, although whatever feeling of displeasure it is that leads us to call something ugly will certainly require us to refrain from judging it to be beautiful, we do not need such a positive feeling of aversion in order to refrain from a judgment of beauty; mere indifference will suffice for that. Kant's theory of taste therefore does not require a purely aesthetic feeling of ugliness in order to explain the possibility of negative judgments of taste, that is, verdicts of "not beautiful." Indeed, the passage from the *Metaphysik Vigilantius* states that the concept of taste is founded only on "this pleasure," leaving open the possibility that the aesthetic judgment of whether something is beautiful or not can be founded simply on the presence or absence of a single purely aesthetic feeling, namely, the pleasure in beauty.

However, to say just that is to be too short with this interesting passage, which suggests two further points. First, the passage suggests that we can judge something to be not beautiful when the *mere intuition* of it leaves us indifferent, even if we have *other reasons* to be pleased or displeased with it. This need not mean that there is a special form of purely aesthetic

[6] Cited by Wenzel, "Kant Finds Nothing Beautiful?" p. 418.

[7] Cited by Strube, "Das Häßliche," p. 417.

[8] Translation from Immanuel Kant, *Lectures on Metaphysics*, tr. Karl Ameriks and Steve Naragon (Cambridge: Cambridge University Press, 1997), p. 480. This passage is partially cited by Allison, *Kant's Theory of Taste*, p. 72.

indifference in mere intuition, but could mean that we can recognize the absence of the distinctively aesthetic pleasure that we would take in the mere intuition of a beautiful object even in the case where we have some other reason for being either pleased or displeased with an object. But, second, when Kant goes on to state that what displeases *in intuition* is ugly, there he might seem to suggest after all that there must be a purely aesthetic form of displeasure on which judgments of ugliness are based. If that were so, then, even though not all negative judgments of taste need to be based on such a distinctive form of displeasure, because some or perhaps even most are based on mere indifference, nevertheless some negative judgments, namely judgments of ugliness, would have to be based on a distinctively aesthetic displeasure. Kant's trichotomy would then appear to imply that judgments of beauty are based on a positive purely aesthetic response, judgments of indifference or ordinariness on the absence of any aesthetic response whatever, and judgments of ugliness on a negative but also purely aesthetic response.[9]

II. The Harmony of the Faculties and the Possibility of Ugliness

However, Kant's account of the basis of a purely positive aesthetic response – that is, his explanation of our pleasure in beauty – leaves no room for a negative but purely aesthetic response to ugliness. Kant's account of our pleasure in beauty is, of course, that such pleasure is the result of a "mutual subjective correspondence" or "play" (*CPJ*, §9, 5:218) between the cognitive powers of imagination and understanding that occurs in response to the representation of an object but "is not grounded on any available concept of the object and does not furnish one" (*CPJ*, Introduction VII, 5:190). It is, in other words, a harmony between imagination and understanding achieved without appeal to any concept of the object. There would then seem to be two alternatives to such a state of mind: the representation of an object might lead to a harmony between imagination and understanding, but only with the assistance of a determinate concept of the object; or engagement with the representation of an object might not lead to any harmony between imagination and understanding at all, but only to a disharmony between them. The first of these alternatives would seem to be what takes place in the vast number

9 This must be how Allison understands Kant's trichotomy, since he cites it in support of his view that Kant does countenance a purely aesthetic response to ugliness (*Kant's Theory of Taste*, p. 72).

of cases of ordinary cognition of aesthetically indifferent objects, where the manifolds of our representations of such objects are unified by determinate concepts of those objects without any noticeable free play of our faculties and therefore without any particular pleasure. The second alternative, however, might be thought to be what occurs in the experience of something ugly, where the engagement of our cognitive powers with the object does not lead to any harmony at all, with or without the benefit of a concept of the object.[10] However, this possibility is blocked by the entire epistemology of the *Critique of Pure Reason*. The first *Critique* argues that it is possible for me to attach the "I think" to any representation that I have, or to include any representation in the transcendental unity of my apperception; that including any representation in the transcendental unity of my apperception requires the application of one or more of the categories or pure concepts of the understanding to it; but that the pure concepts of the understanding are in fact nothing but the forms of determinate empirical concepts, just as the pure forms of intuition are nothing but the forms of empirical intuitions, so that the application of the categories to all the objects of my representation also requires the application of determinate empirical concepts to all of them. For example, the category of substance can only be applied to empirical intuition through the empirical concept of matter, and the concept of causation through the empirical concept of a rule-governed change in motion. But these premises entail that we can never be conscious of a representation at all, *a fortiori* of a representation of an object, without the application of some determinate empirical concept to it. And if the application of a concept to a manifold brings the faculty of understanding into harmony with a manifold of sensibility reproduced by the imagination, this means we cannot be conscious of an object without some form of harmony between understanding and imagination, although such a harmony will in this case not be a free play of the faculties. This in turn is to say that for Kant there are really only two possible relations between imagination

[10] Precisely in order to make room for this last possibility, Allison insists that the concept of the free play of the cognitive faculties must not be regarded as identical to the concept of their harmony: only if these concepts are separated will the idea of a free play that ends in disharmony rather than harmony make sense (*Kant's Theory of Taste*, pp. 116–17). What Allison fails to consider, however, is that even if the concepts of free play and harmony are distinguished, so that it is not analytically true that all free play must result in harmony and therefore that the only pure aesthetic response to objects must be our pleasure in their beauty, this conceptual point does not suffice to establish the real possibility that any engagement of the cognitive faculties with an object could result in an insuperable disharmony between imagination and understanding.

and understanding in the experience of any object: a state of free play between them that results in harmony without dependence upon any of the determinate empirical concepts that apply to the object of this state, although surely there are such concepts; or a harmony between them that does depend upon such concepts. A state of sheer disharmony between them is not consistent with the transcendental unity of apperception.

So harmony without a concept or harmony with a concept, but no simple absence of harmony: this, in a nutshell, is why Kant cannot allow a purely aesthetic origin for ugliness. This simple statement naturally raises as many questions as it answers. One question, of course, is: if it is so obvious that there cannot be a purely aesthetic response of disharmony to ugliness, why have so many interpreters of Kant failed to see this? A second question is: if our experience of any object always involves the subsumption of an empirical manifold of intuition under a determinate empirical concept formed in accordance with a pure concept of the understanding, how can there ever be any free play of imagination and understanding *without* a concept, that is, any experience of beauty? And finally, while Kant's epistemology of ordinary cognition and of aesthetic experience may preclude any purely aesthetic experience of ugliness, surely there is such a thing as ugliness, so how does Kant understand our experience of ugliness?

The answer to my first two questions requires a fuller discussion of Kant's central idea of the free play of imagination and understanding than I have given thus far. This idea is notoriously slippery, and there are a number of different interpretations of it in the literature. We might classify these interpretations as "precognitive," "multicognitive," and "metacognitive." On the precognitive interpretation, the harmony of the faculties occurs when our experience of an object feels as if it satisfies our underlying demand for cognition even when it also feels as if it satisfies only the conditions for cognition short of the application of a concept to the object but not that last condition. Kant certainly suggests this sort of approach when he writes, in the "First Introduction" to the *Critique of the Power of Judgment*, that

> In the power of judgment understanding and imagination are considered in relation to each other, and this can, to be sure, first be considered objectively, as belonging to cognition (as happened in the transcendental schematism of the power of judgment); but one can also consider this relation of two faculties of cognition merely subjectively, insofar as one helps or hinders the other in the very same representation and thereby affects the **state of mind**,

and then continues:

> A merely **reflecting** judgment about a given object . . . **can be aesthetic** if (before its comparison with others is seen), the power of judgment, which has no concept ready for the given intuition, holds the imagination (merely in the apprehension of the object) together with the understanding (in the presentation of a concept in general) and perceives a relation of the two faculties of cognition which constitutes the subjective, merely sensitive condition of the objective use of the power of judgment in general (namely, the agreement of those two faculties with each other).
>
> (*FI*, 20:223–4)

Such passages suggest that the harmony of the faculties takes place when all the subjective conditions of cognition are satisfied but the objective condition of cognition – namely, the subsumption of the representation of an object under a determinate concept of that object – is not.

By a "multicognitive" interpretation of the harmony of the faculties, I mean one that understands it as a condition in which it seems to us as if we are simultaneously cognizing the object under a number of different concepts, any of which seems to provide a sense of unity to our manifold of representation although none of which seems to apply to it definitely and conclusively.[11] The central thought here is that the free play of the faculties is like cognition insofar as the understanding entertains a variety of concepts under which its object might be subsumed, but unlike cognition in that it never commits itself to the subsumption of the object under a single one of these concepts. Kant also seems to suggest this sort of approach in at least one passage in which he writes as if the harmony of the faculties involves the subsumption of the manifold of representation afforded by the beautiful object under *some* concept but where it is indeterminate *which* concept that is:

> If, then, the form of a given object in empirical intuition is so constituted that the **apprehension** of its manifold in the imagination agrees with the **presentation** of a concept of the understanding (though which concept be undetermined), then in the mere reflection understanding and imagination mutually agree for the advancement of their business, and the object will be perceived as purposive merely for the power of judgment . . .
>
> (*FI*, VII, 20:220–1).

[11] Allison promotes such an interpretation when he writes that the "basic idea" of the "reciprocal quickening" of imagination and understanding "is presumably that the imagination in its free play stimulates the understanding by occasioning it to entertain fresh conceptual possibilities, while, conversely, the imagination, under the general direction of the understanding, strives to conceive new patterns of order" (*Kant's Theory of Taste*, p. 171).

Such a passage seems to allow for the possibility that free play consists in playing with multiple concepts for comprehending the object without commitment to any single one of them.

Finally, by a "metacognitive" interpretation of the harmonious and free play of the faculties, I mean one that recognizes that for Kant all consciousness of an object must involve its subsumption under some determinate concept, so that the felt harmony of the manifold of representation afforded by an object with the understanding's general requirement of unity must be a feeling that it is unified in some way that goes *beyond* the unity that is dictated by whatever determinate concept the object is subsumed under – as it were, an *excess* of felt unity or harmony. It is not easy to lift from its context any single statement that clearly suggests such an approach, but every one of Kant's *examples* of an object that we judge to be beautiful makes it clear that he assumes that we typically know perfectly well what sort of object the thing is, thus subsume it under some determinate concept, and indeed have to do so in order to be able to refer our experience to a particular object and to make a particular judgment of taste at all, but at the same time experience it as having a degree of unity or inducing a harmony between our imagination and understanding that cannot be traced to that concept, or is not determined by it. Thus, for example, we recognize that a beautiful object is a bird, indeed a parrot, a hummingbird, or a bird of paradise, and must do so in order to say "That's a beautiful bird, or parrot ... ", although *what* we find beautiful in the object must be some sort of unity that goes beyond whatever is necessary to classify it as a bird or even as one of these particular species of bird. If we did not subsume the objects we find beautiful under some determinate concepts, we could not even make particular aesthetic judgments about them: we could not say that it is this parrot rather than that hummingbird that we find beautiful.

Now, this last point is crucial, for it makes it clear that we cannot take either of the turns of phrase that are the basis of the first two proposed interpretations of the free play of the faculties as the complete characterization of our state of mind when experiencing this aesthetic response. Thus, while we might be tempted to think that we could experience the satisfaction of the subjective conditions of cognition prior to the satisfaction of any objective condition for cognition of an object – that is, the predication of some determinate empirical concept of it – we must realize that in that case we could not be making any judgment of beauty about a particular object at all; in order to do that, we must subsume the object under some determinate concept, yet *also* feel that there is some way in which it satisfies the subjective requirement of harmony in our manifolds of representation that cannot be traced back to that concept. Likewise, while we might be tempted to think that we could experience a free play among possible concepts for an object without determinately subsuming it under any one of them, we must in fact be subsuming the object under some determinate concept in order to recognize it as the object of our experience at all, but then experiencing a free yet harmonious and therefore enjoyable play among *further* concepts that the object suggests to us without determinately instantiating them. In other words, if we are to maintain both our own and Kant's assumption that particular judgments of taste are made about particular objects, then the first two proposed interpretations of the free play of the faculties, the precognitive and multicognitive approaches, must be understood only as ways to cash out the third: that is, the idea of a felt satisfaction of the general requirement of unity or of a free play among possible concepts for an object must be taken as descriptions of the way in which we can feel a unity in our experience of an object that goes beyond the unity associated with any of the determinate concepts under which we subsume it in our ordinary cognition of it.

This conclusion then provides the basis for answers to the first two of the three questions that I posed. First, while it might have seemed that we could have a state of purely aesthetic reflection or free play that does not result in any harmony between imagination and understanding at all, or that does not result in a free play among several possible "fresh conceptual possibilities" for the object, and could thus result in a state that would constitute a purely reflective aesthetic basis for a judgment of ugliness, we can now see that this is not really possible within Kant's epistemology: for Kant, we can always recognize a particular object of our experience, and any time we can recognize such an object there must be that degree of unity between imagination and understanding that is necessary for the subsumption of our manifold of representations of the object under a determinate concept, even if that *further* degree of unity that might lead us to experience the object as beautiful is lacking. But this is just to say that our experience of an object must always involve a harmony between imagination and understanding with a concept, even if it does not involve a harmony between these two powers that is free of any concept, and thus that while many objects will certainly be aesthetically indifferent, they cannot be felt to be ugly simply on the basis of any complete absence of harmony in our experience of them. And, second, we can now see how the experience of beauty is possible even though every object of our experience is subsumed under one or in fact many determinate concepts: we are capable of experiencing kinds of unity in an object or free play in our representation of it that go beyond those particular unities in virtue of which it satisfies the determinate concepts that we apply to it. That is why we can experience some but by no means all of the objects of our cognition as beautiful.

III. The Sources of Ugliness

But now it might seem as if Kant has excluded the possibility of ugliness altogether. Yet like any reasonable person, he clearly does find some things ugly – remember the furies, disease, and the devastations of war. How can he find such things ugly if even they must involve some harmony between imagination and understanding, namely that which allows these very concepts to be applied to them? These very examples suggest the answer to this question: judgments of ugliness are not purely reflective aesthetic judgments at all, but are dependent upon sensory or else practical judgments – that is, they involve expressions of our feelings of displeasure at things that are disagreeable in some physiological or psychological way or bad or evil in the light of our prudential or moral practical reason. In Kant's terms, these instances of ugliness contrast with the agreeable or the good, not with the purely aesthetic response to beauty (*CPJ*, §5, 2:209–10). Diseases and injuries produce pain and disfigurement, which we find profoundly disagreeable when we suffer them ourselves, when we fear catching them from others, and when we see others suffering them even if we do not fear infection or similar injuries ourselves. Finding disease and injury disagreeable and their effects ugly is not a purely aesthetic response. The devastations of war produce injuries and disfigurements to persons and their surroundings which are not only disagreeable to our senses but also offensive to our practical judgments and moral sensibilities. Our displeasure at these devastations is not purely aesthetic, but involves response to the disagreeable, the bad, and the evil. As these are the only examples of the ugly that Kant gives, we may at least conjecture that he assumes that all cases of ugliness are to be analyzed as violations of our standards for the agreeable and/or the good, not as objects of a negative yet purely aesthetic response. The absence of a purely aesthetic response to beauty, then, leads to the negative aesthetic judgment of ordinariness or indifference, but the negative judgment of ugliness is not based on a purely reflective aesthetic response at all, but on feelings of displeasure at the disagreeable, the imprudent, and the immoral.

How could such an account be reconciled with Kant's statement in the *Metaphysik Vigiliantius* (29:1010) that the ugly is that which displeases *in intuition*? The answer should be as obvious as the question: our response to the ugly is based on our *perception* of the (sufficiently) disagreeable and immoral, and ugliness is the *perceivable expression* of the disagreeable and the immoral (just as the beautiful is, at least sometimes if not always, the expression of aesthetic ideas; see *CPJ*, §51, 5:320). When Kant states that the ugly displeases in intuition, after all, he does not say that the ugly displeases in intuition in a purely free and reflective manner. So that statement does not contradict the explanation of ugliness I have ascribed to Kant, but only claims that the perception of the disagreeable or immoral, as opposed to the mere thought of it, is a necessary condition of the experience of ugliness. The fact that judgments of ugliness are responses to *perception* would suffice to make them aesthetic for Kant, but they would not be *pure* aesthetic judgments, involving only the free play of the cognitive powers.

To be sure, Kant apparently does not himself offer a general account of ugliness at all. He offers his examples of ugliness only in illustration of his (by no means idiosyncratic or original) thesis that "Beautiful art displays its excellence precisely by describing beautifully things that in nature would be ugly or displeasing" (*CPJ*, §48, 5:312). However, the analysis of ugliness that I have just ascribed to him offers a good explanation of this possibility: if our response to the ugliness of the described or depicted content of a work of art were a negative but purely aesthetic response then, one would think, it would simply cancel out a positive purely aesthetic response to the form or other aesthetically enjoyable properties of the artistic depiction or description, leading to a state of aesthetic neutrality, just as the speed of a ship in one direction combined with an equal speed of the current in the other will leave the ship stuck in the same place. But if our responses to the beauty of the depiction on the one hand and the ugliness of what is depicted on the other have fundamentally different sources, then we can understand how we can experience both responses without an inescapable conflict between them.

Of course, that these responses have fundamentally different sources and do not *necessarily* conflict with each other does not mean that they cannot *in fact* conflict with each other, a point that Kant assumes when he continues that "only one kind of ugliness cannot be represented in a way adequate to nature without destroying all aesthetic satisfaction, hence beauty in art, namely, that which arouses **loathing** [*Ekel*]" (*loc. cit.*). Kant does not define this feeling here, nor does he give any examples of what would produce it. It would be natural for us to think that he means simply that some things produce such a degree of physical or moral revulsion that we cannot possibly enjoy any aesthetic qualities and artistic merits in the depiction of them, enjoyable as the latter might have been in connection with some other content – our disgust would psychologically block any appreciation of such aspects of the objects. That is also a perfectly reasonable thing to believe, and would have been so for Kant. As David Hume wrote, in a work that Kant knew well, the "finer emotions of the mind are of a very tender and delicate nature, and require the concurrence of many favourable circumstances to make them play with facility and exactness, according to their general and established principles,"[12] and Kant could certainly have believed that the conditions for the occurrence of the free play of imagination and understanding "are of a very delicate and tender nature," easily disturbed by intense emotions from other sources, even if in his view there are no "general and established principles" for the occurrence of the response to beauty. But Kant seems to have in mind something more complex than this general point, for although he does not define what he means by "loathing," he does say this:

> For since in this strange sensation, resting on sheer imagination, the object is represented as if it were imposing the enjoyment which we are nevertheless forcibly resisting, the artistic representation of the object is no longer distinguished in our sensation itself from the nature of the object itself, and it then becomes impossible for the former to be taken as beautiful.
>
> (*CPJ* §48, 5:312)

This suggests that we do not feel loathing simply when our revulsion at the content of a work of art overwhelms our potential pleasure in its aesthetic merits, but rather that we feel loathing when we feel manipulated *by the artistic representation*, when we feel that the representation – and therefore of course the artist who makes it or other agency of the art-world that may push it on us – is attempting to *impose* pleasure upon us when we would prefer to remain with our feelings of disagreeableness or moral disapproval rather than indulge in the enjoyment of beauty. In other words,

[12] David Hume, "Of the Standard of Taste," in *Essays Moral, Political and Literary* (Oxford: Oxford University Press, 1963), pp. 231–55, at p. 237. Kant was of course familiar with this essay, which appeared in Hume's *Four Dissertations* in 1757 and was almost immediately translated into German in *Vier Abhandlungen von David Hume* (translated by Friedrich Gabriel Resewitz) (Quedlingburg und Leipzig: Andreas Franz Biesterfeld, 1759), modern reprint, with an introduction by Heiner F. Klemme (Bristol: Thoemmes Press, 2001).

loathing, at least as Kant treats it here, may itself be a moral response to an attempt to abridge our freedom through the beautification of that which we feel should not be beautified, rather than a simple aversion, which may but need not be moral in origin, to the ugliness of a content that outstrips the beauty of its depiction. Since the freedom of the imagination is essential to the experience of beauty, indeed so essential that it is in virtue of this freedom that the beautiful can serve as a symbol of the freedom of choice and action that is the central value of morality itself (*CPJ*, §59, 5:353–4), an abridgement of our freedom of response to an object can of course block the free play of imagination that is necessary for the experience of beauty. But this should not be taken to mean that the feeling of loathing is any more a pure aesthetic response than the response to ordinary ugliness is; it seems rather to be a moral response to an attempt to impose an aesthetic response upon us instead of allowing us the free play of imagination and understanding that is essential to successful aesthetic response.[13]

How convincing is what I have alleged to be Kant's analysis of ugliness, suggested by both his epistemological explanation of our response to beauty and his examples of ugliness, namely, that our displeasure in ugliness cannot be a pure aesthetic response, but must instead be our response to that which is disagreeable or immoral? In many cases we surely use the term "ugly" just as Kant suggests, to express our revulsion at that which we find, especially although not exclusively in our fellow humans, unhealthy or sickening, sexually unattractive, or offensive to our moral standards. Thus we find ugly those who are disfigured by disease or injury, those with whom we cannot imagine being intimate, or those whose physical appearance suggests attitudes towards themselves or others that we find morally contemptible – for instance, if we share Kant's attitude towards tattooing (*CPJ*, §16, 5:230), we may find those who have chosen to cover their bodies with tattoos ugly even if we would find the patterns

[13] Strube appears to suggest that "loathing" is a purely aesthetic response when he writes that "'Ekel' bezeichnet dann eine Art von Geschmacksunlust in einer ästhetischen Beurteilung" ("Das Häßliche," pp. 420–1), although he subsequently argues that there is at least one type of the "ekelhaft" which is not purely aesthetic, and so must be based on some other form of disapprobation (pp. 439–45). This is representative of his basic strategy, which is to reconcile the obviously non-aesthetic character of the examples of the ugly and the loathsome that Kant provides with his own insistence that there must be such a thing as the purely aesthetic ugly and even the purely aesthetic loathsome by distinguishing sub-categories of the ugly and the loathsome, namely, the purely aesthetic and the not purely aesthetic. This seems to me to be an invention without any basis in Kant's texts.

with which they have chosen to cover themselves beautiful in some other context, indeed even in the tattoo artist's pattern-book. As this last example suggests, the physical standards of disagreeableness and moral standards of offensiveness on which our judgments of ugliness are based may be either "natural" or "conventional," and thus our judgments of ugliness may find either widespread or limited acceptance – notably, Kant does not argue that the predicate "ugly," like the predicate "beauty," should be used only when we have a well-founded claim to subjective universal validity.[14]

But aren't there cases of ugliness that do not really reflect responses to disagreeableness or immorality? In the visual arts, for example in some abstract paintings, don't we find some combinations of color downright ugly, just as we might find others quite beautiful: in paintings that consist of little but different regions of color, such as works by Josef Albers or Mark Rothko, can't we find some of their combinations beautiful but others ugly? Kant's response to this counterexample, of course, would be that our response to color as such is never a purely reflective aesthetic response, but is always a merely physiological response of agreeableness or disagreeableness (*CPJ*, §14, 5:225), so his answer could be that our displeasure in a painting whose combination of colors we find jarring is no more a purely aesthetic response than is our pleasure in one whose combination of colors we like.

But what about cases where ugliness seems to lie in one of the more formal dimensions that Kant insists is always the only proper object of taste: for example, an irregular shape in a visual object where, we should have thought, only a regular shape could be beautiful, or a note or sequence in a musical composition that is violently discordant with the rest?[15] These cases may seem harder to discount. Sometimes, of course, they might just be cases in which our expectations for certain *types* – genres, styles, periods, and so on – of works are disappointed or violated: an asymmetry that we might find beautiful in an Art Nouveau home could strike us as hideous in a Renaissance church, or a sequence of notes that we might accept in an atonal piece by Schönberg might be jarring in a sonata by Hayden. But if it is just our preconceived notion of how a certain type of object should look or sound that is being violated, we may

[14] Some of the discussion in the literature on Kant on ugliness revolves around the question of whether judgments of ugliness have subjective universal validity; see Hudson, "Analytic of the Ugly," pp. 90–1; Strube, "Das Häßliche," pp. 432–5; Brandt, "Die Schönheit der Kristalle," p. 34; and Shier, "Why Kant Finds Nothing Ugly," pp. 414–15. But Kant nowhere says that judgments of ugliness are universally subjectively valid.

[15] Strube equates the ugly with the "unformed"; "Das Häßliche," p. 420.

not have a pure aesthetic response and judgment at all: at least for Kant, a genuinely aesthetic response must always be a free response to an individual object, and a generalization about what is beautiful in a certain class of objects is not a genuinely aesthetic judgment (*CPJ*, §8, 5:215–16), so our disappointment and displeasure in a particular work's violation of such a generalization would also not be a purely aesthetic response. And no doubt in many cases our judgment that a work is ugly *is* really an expression of our discomfort at its failure to satisfy our expectations for objects in a certain group rather than the result of a free engagement with that object itself unhampered by preconceptions as to how it ought to be. Here the thought that a judgment of ugliness might not be a pure and therefore free judgment of taste might be a valuable corrective to our no doubt natural and frequent tendency to like best that which is most like what we have enjoyed before, and freeing ourselves from our preconceptions may well allow us to appreciate the new kind of beauty that the object does have to offer.

But perhaps there are forms of design or composition which we all dislike apart from any preconceptions about how objects of a certain type or genre should look or sound, even if they violate none of our sensory standards of agreeableness or moral standards of goodness, and even if they can be brought under some concept or other which allows for the unification of the manifold of our experience of them, thereby satisfying Kant's general requirement for the unity of apperception. If there are such cases, then we might have to say that our displeasure in such objects cannot be connected to their resistance to our power of cognition or to our faculty of desire, and so could only be grounded in a purely aesthetic failure of reflective judgment. But for Kant, of course, there are no objects that are literally unformed – our power to impose the pure forms of intuition on all our experience is enough by itself to guarantee that – and I do not think that those who insist that our displeasure in ugliness must be a pure aesthetic response have produced convincing examples of such cases. Until we have an example of ugliness that can be conclusively demonstrated not to displease us merely by being physically disagreeable or morally offensive or failing to meet our expectations for objects in a certain class, Kant's approach to ugliness remains at least plausible.

IV. Displeasure and the Sublime

So it looks as if the alternatives to the purely aesthetic pleasure in a free harmony of imagination and understanding that is the basis for judgments of beauty are either indifference, the absence of pleasure that characterizes the conceptually-determined correspondence between imagination and understanding which is the foundation of ordinary cognition, or the displeasure that leads us to call something ugly but which is based in sensory disagreeableness or moral disapprobation rather than in any purely aesthetic disposition of reflective judgment. Does this leave any room at all for purely aesthetic displeasure in Kant's theory? The natural place to look for such room would be in Kant's account of the experience of the sublime, which Kant explicitly describes as including an element of displeasure as well as an element of pleasure, and as thus on balance a "negative pleasure" akin to the mixed moral feeling of respect rather than a purely positive pleasure. Thus Kant opens his discussion of the sublime by writing that "Since the mind is not merely attracted by the object, but is also always reciprocally repelled by it, the satisfaction in the sublime does not so much contain positive pleasure as it does admiration or respect, i.e., it deserves to be called negative pleasure" (*CPJ*, §5:245), and he concludes his discussion of the first form of the sublime, the mathematical sublime, by stating that this "feeling of the sublime is thus a feeling of displeasure from the inadequacy of the imagination in the aesthetic estimation of magnitude for the estimation by means of reason, and a pleasure that is thereby aroused at the same time from the correspondence of this very judgment of the inadequacy of the greatest sensible faculty in comparison with ideas of reason, insofar as striving for them is nevertheless a law for us" (*CPJ*, §27, 5:247). On a casual reading, it may seem as if what Kant is claiming is this: that our attempt to grasp the magnitude of anything very vast by our ordinary method of reiterating some determinate unit of measurement a determinate number of times inevitably fails, because we cannot complete an infinite synthesis, and this fact is unpleasant to us; but the very fact that we even attempt to grasp the infinite by this means reveals to us that we have a faculty of pure reason that imposes this task upon us, and this realization is pleasing, so pleasing that the experience on the whole is pleasing, although in that bittersweet way that Kant attempts to capture by calling it a negative pleasure and comparing it to the feeling of respect. On such an account, the moment of displeasure might seem to be purely aesthetic in nature, arising from a disharmony between the ambition of the imagination and the power of the understanding, even if the pleasure that follows might seem to depend too directly on our conception of the demand of our own faculty of reason to be considered independent of any concept, and thus purely aesthetic.

Such an interpretation of the experience of the mathematical sublime might seem to threaten the premise of my argument against a purely aesthetic experience of ugliness, because it countenances the possibility of a failure of harmony between the imagination and the understanding, although one that is then compensated for by a certain sort of harmony between imagination and reason – and if there could be a straightforward failure of harmony between imagination and understanding in the case of the sublime, why couldn't there also be a pure disharmony between those two faculties in the case of the ugly? But a more careful interpretation of Kant's theory of the mathematical sublime would show that it does not posit any disharmony between imagination and understanding at all. For Kant does not argue that there is any problem in estimating any magnitude by our ordinary means of iterating determinate units. No matter how vast or formless what we perceive may *seem*, nothing that we perceive is actually perceived as infinite (this is of course the premise of Kant's resolution of the first two antinomies of pure reason in the first *Critique*); so we can assign a determinate magnitude to anything that we perceive, in a harmonious exercise of both imagination and understanding, by choosing a unit of appropriate size that will allow us to measure the whole in a manageable number of iterations. There is no threat to ordinary cognition in the mathematical sublime. Rather, the moment of displeasure in this experience arises from the attempt at what Kant calls the *aesthetic* "comprehension" of the vast and formless, the attempt to grasp it in something like a *single image* that captures the parts and the whole at the same time, like a single view of one of the great pyramids that would contain a clear differentiation of all its visible parts and yet a clear image of the whole at one and the same time (*CPJ*, §26, 5:252). *This* is something that we may indeed be able to pull off in the case of a pyramid, by standing at the right distance from it,[16] but that we cannot pull off in the case of the vast heavens above or even a vast mountain range such as the Alps or Sierras, and thus the attempt to grasp such an image is bound to fail and hence cause displeasure. But such an attempt is not an effort to measure the magnitude of its object through the cooperation of imagination and understanding; it is rather more like an attempt to grasp this magnitude by the imagination *alone* – that is what it means to

[16] Kant appeals to the experience of the pyramids at Giza and of St. Peter's in Rome (neither of which he himself had ever seen) in order to make this point about the experience of the sublime, but does not actually say that the pyramids or St. Peter's *are* sublime; his view seems to be that any works of human art, even ones of such grand scale as these, are too obviously finite to induce a genuine experience of the sublime.

call it an attempt at *aesthetic* comprehension. In Kant's words,

> Nature is thus sublime in those of its appearances the intuition of which brings with them the idea of its infinity. Now the latter cannot happen except through the inadequacy of even the greatest effort of our imagination in the estimation of the magnitude of an object. Now, however, the imagination is adequate for the mathematical estimation of every object, that is, for giving an adequate measure for it, because the numerical concepts of the understanding, by means of progression, can make any measure adequate for any given magnitude. Thus it must be the **aesthetic** estimation of the magnitude in which is felt the effort at comprehension which exceeds the capacity of the imagination to comprehend the progressive apprehension in one whole of intuition, and in which is at the same time perceived the inadequacy of this faculty...
>
> (*CPJ*, §26, 5:255)

What redeems this experience from being one of sheer displeasure is then the realization that although the imagination has attempted to *execute* this project of aesthetic comprehension on its own, it did not *undertake* this project on its own, but was rather attempting to do the bidding of reason: "now the mind hears in itself the voice of reason, which requires totality for all given magnitudes, even for those that can never be entirely apprehended although they are (in the sensible representation) judged as entirely given, hence comprehension in **one** intuition" (*CPJ*, §26, 5:254). The idea that the imagination should attempt to grasp something truly vast "in one intuition," in other words, was not *understanding*'s idea, but *reason*'s idea. Kant's suggestion then seems to be that once we get over our initial disappointment that imagination cannot carry out the bidding of reason all by itself, we will take pleasure in the very fact that we have a faculty of reason capable of coming up with such a project in the first place. "Thus the inner perception of the inadequacy of any sensible standard for the estimation of magnitude by reason" – not by understanding, mind you – "corresponds with reason's laws, and is a displeasure that arouses the feeling of our supersensible vocation in us, in accordance with which it is purposive and thus a pleasure to find every standard of sensibility inadequate for the ideas of reason" (*CPJ*, §27, 5:258).[17]

Kant's analysis of the experience of the mathematical sublime is probably even more subtle than thus far suggested, because he concludes it by describing this experience as "a feeling that we have pure self-sufficient reason" (*CPJ*, §27, 5:258), "a feeling of displeasure concerning the

[17] The first edition of the third *Critique* has "of reason" (*der Vernunft*), as translated here; the second edition has "of understanding" (*des Verstandes*). Given the argument of the preceding section §26, this change in the second edition seems like a mistake.

aesthetic faculty of judging an object that is yet at the same time represented as purposive, which is possible because the subject's own incapacity reveals the consciousness of an unlimited capacity of the very same subject, and the mind can aesthetically judge the latter only through the former" (5:259). That we have a *feeling* of reason's self-sufficiency and can *aesthetically judge* its capacity through imagination may suggest that we do not simply suffer a failure of imagination which leads us to the purely conceptual or propositional recognition that imagination is failing at a task set for it by reason, but that we actually have some sort of imaginative representation of the power of reason, or that in this experience we are in a complex imaginative state, which somehow seems to fail to grasp the infinite and yet to grasp it at the same time. Indeed, one could argue that Kant has presupposed this from the outset of his discussion of the sublime: since the vast aspects of nature that trigger this experience are not *actually* endless or would be recognized by the understanding as such – certainly the Alps are not actually endless – the very sense that we are seeing something endless or infinite that cannot be comprehended by the imagination must itself be a product of the imagination. Be that as it may, we can stop our analysis of the sublime here: however it plays out, it should be clear by now that the experience of the (mathematical) sublime is not an experience of disharmony between the imagination and understanding, and should not give rise to the thought that there can be such a disharmony in the case of the ugly.

Further, it is far from clear that the experience of the sublime is a *pure* aesthetic experience, a product of reflective judgment alone, at all. The experience of the mathematical sublime seems to depend upon the recognition that we have a faculty of reason; even if we somehow feel this fact, we must also interpret our feeling, connect it to this recognition. This seems even more evident in the case of the dynamical sublime, where the displeasing sense that the forces of nature could cause our physical destruction subsequently leads to pleasure because these forces "allow us to discover within ourselves a capacity for resistance of quite another kind, which gives us the courage to measure ourselves against the apparent all-powerfulness of nature" (*CPJ* §28, 5:261). The experience of the might of nature triggers a recognition of our own powers, but a recognition that has to be put into concepts. To be sure, in both cases Kant supposes that we have some sort of *feeling* of our powers, so the experience is aesthetic on that score; and of course he also insists that the ideas of reason – the ideas created by the faculty of reason, but perhaps also the idea of the faculty of reason itself – are indeterminate rather than determinate, because they can never be fully instantiated in experience. So the experience of the sublime in both of its forms clearly involves feelings that are not connected to the subsumption of objects under determinate concepts, and can therefore be counted as genuinely aesthetic. Yet they so centrally involve intellectual content that it seems hard to call them *purely* aesthetic. In at least one place, Kant does suggest that the "sublime in nature" is the object of a "pure aesthetic judgment" (*CPJ*, §30, 5:279); but he also writes that "a far greater culture, not merely of the aesthetic power of judgment, but also of the cognitive faculties on which that is based, seems to be requisite in order to make a judgment about" the sublime rather than the beautiful, and that "The disposition of the mind to the feeling of the sublime requires its receptivity to ideas" (*CPJ*, §29, 5:264–5). Thus, while Kant himself seems to be ambivalent about it, his own analysis suggests that we should not take the experience of the sublime as a model for a pure aesthetic experience.

V. Is Even the Experience of Beauty Impure?

I conclude, then, that while Kant obviously recognizes the existence of ugliness, he does not hold that our experience of ugliness is a pure aesthetic experience. The ugly is what we find physically disagreeable or morally offensive, and although the latter experiences place limits on the freedom of our imagination in its play with the understanding, they are not themselves pure aesthetic experiences. Further, while there might seem to be a place for a purely aesthetic displeasure in the experience of the sublime, this experience does not, as might be thought, involve any disharmony between imagination and understanding that could be an alternative to the harmony between these two faculties that is the core of the experience of beauty, and it is in any case by no means clear that the experience of the sublime in either of its forms is a pure rather than mixed aesthetic experience. So on Kant's theory, only the experience of beauty can be a pure aesthetic experience; the experience of the ordinary or indifferent is the simple absence of aesthetic experience, and the experiences of the sublime and the ugly are at best mixed aesthetic experiences.

Does the purity of the experience of beauty and the impurity of the experiences of the ugly and the sublime introduce an intolerable discontinuity into Kant's aesthetic theory? I suggest that the conclusion that the experiences of the ugly and the sublime are not purely free and reflective aesthetic experiences is not only consistent with everything Kant suggests about those experiences themselves, but also consistent with what he has to say about beauty, for the simple reason that on Kant's account by no means all experiences of beauty are pure aesthetic experiences or experiences of free beauty either – many experiences of beauty, after all, are experiences of adherent beauty connected to a determinate concept of the beautiful object's function (*CPJ*, §16) or of artistic beauty connected to the determinate intention of the artist, although in the case of a work of genius in some way going beyond his intention (*CPJ*, §49). These cases of beauty are *genuine* cases of beauty, because they involve the free play of imagination *with* concepts or *within* the limits set by concepts, but they are not cases of *free* beauty. Indeed, when Kant concludes that "Beauty (whether it be beauty of nature or of art) can in general be called the **expression** of aesthetic ideas" (*CPJ*, §51, 5:320), he may even be suggesting that there is no such thing as the free experience of beauty at all. Perhaps we come *closest* to having an experience that is just a harmonious free play of imagination and understanding in the experience of isolated objects of nature such as hummingbirds, crustacea, and crystals, and from such cases we can extrapolate to the idea of a simple harmony between imagination and understanding as a necessary condition of any purely aesthetic experience; but in the end, all of our experiences of such harmony are also associated with ideas of reason through the intermediary of aesthetic ideas, and thus our experiences of beauty, just like those of the ugly and the sublime, are impure rather than pure. This might be due to our own subjective tendency to read moral signficance into every experience that we can, a tendency that certainly underlies Kant's entire argument in the "Critique of Teleological Judgment"; but this would be no objection to Kant's conclusion, for the ability to experience a free play between imagination and understanding is itself a distinctively human tendency that we cannot automatically attribute to any other rational being (should there be such).

To argue that in Kant's view all our experiences of beauty are really mixed rather than pure would hardly be implausible – it would, after all, bring Kant's theory into closer alignment with his great predecessor, Moses Mendelssohn,[18] among others, and make his theory less of an anomaly among eighteenth-century aesthetic theories. But it certainly would be the task of another essay. If my reflections on Kant's treatment of the ugly and the sublime have even pointed us in this direction, that will be enough for now.

[18] See Mendelssohn's important paper of 1757, "On the main principles of the fine arts and sciences," translated in Moses Mendelssohn, *Philosophical Writings*, edited by Daniel O. Dahlstrom (Cambridge: Cambridge University Press, 1997), pp. 169–91.

7

Beauty, Freedom, and Morality

Kant's Lectures on Anthropology and the Development of His Aesthetic Theory

I

A "critique of taste" was one of Kant's long-standing philosophical ambitions. Indeed, his first announcement in 1771 to his student Marcus Herz of what was to become the *Critique of Pure Reason* included the theory of taste in the scope of the projected work: "I am currently occupied with a work which under the title *The Bounds of Sensibility and of Reason* is to work out in some detail the relationship of the fundamental concepts and laws destined for the sensible world together with the outline of that which the theory of taste, metaphysics, and morals should contain."[1] But as it turned out, the *Critique of Pure Reason* that Kant finally published in 1781 contained only a dismissive reference to Baumgarten's "failed hope" for a science of "aesthetics" that would comprise "what others call the critique of taste,"[2] and the second edition of the *Critique* was only minimally more encouraging on this score.[3] Meanwhile, Kant's first two major works on morals, the *Groundwork for the Metaphysics of Morals* published in 1785 and the *Critique of Practical Reason*, begun as part of Kant's revisions for the second edition of the first *Critique* in 1787 but released as a separate work at Easter 1788, made no mention of the project of a critique of taste at

[1] Letter 67, to Marcus Herz, June 7, 1771; 10: 123. All citations to Kant will be located by volume and page number in Kant's *Gesammelte Schriften*, edited by the Royal Prussian (later German) Academy of Sciences (Berlin: Georg Reimer [later Walter de Gruyter & Co.], 1900 –). Unless otherwise noted, translations are my own.

[2] *Critique of Pure Reason*, A 21 n; translation from Immanuel Kant, *Critique of Pure Reason*, edited and translated by Paul Guyer and Allen W. Wood (Cambridge: Cambridge University Press, 1998), p. 156.

[3] *Critique of Pure Reason*, B 35–6 n; Guyer and Wood, p. 173.

all. Yet in December 1787, when the printing of the *Critique of Practical Reason* had barely been completed, Kant suddenly announced, this time to his new disciple Karl Leonhard Reinhold, that he had returned to the old project of "the critique of taste," and indeed that he expected to finish a book on it by the following Easter.[4] (In fact, it would take him two more years, until the end of January 1790, to finish the newly announced book.) Was there anything other than the obvious fact of having finished his exhausting work on the critiques of metaphysics and morality that suddenly allowed Kant to resume this old project?

The extensive evidence for the development of Kant's aesthetic theory that is now available in his recently published lectures on anthropology from 1772–73 to 1788–89, lectures in which Kant dealt with issues in aesthetics far more extensively than he did in his lectures on logic and metaphysics, puts us in a new position to interpret the letter to Reinhold and to answer this question. The letter is initially confusing, for it suggests two different things as the key to Kant's new project. First, Kant suggests that by reflecting on a tripartite division of the mind into the "faculty of cognition, the feeling of pleasure and displeasure, and the faculty of desire," he has been enabled to find an *a priori* principle for the feeling of pleasure and displeasure just as he had previously found *a priori* principles for the faculties of cognition and desire.[5] Not only do the lectures on anthropology as well as those on logic and metaphysics make it clear that there was nothing new in Kant's tripartite division of the powers of the human mind, but the lectures on anthropology make it clear as no other sources do that Kant had in fact long considered the possibility and sometimes even asserted that there are *a priori* principles for the feeling of pleasure and displeasure, in the form of principles of taste.[6] But Kant suggests a different point when he continues that "he now recognizes three parts of philosophy, each of which has its *a priori* principles which one can enumerate and in such a way determine the scope of possible knowledge – theoretical philosophy, teleology, and practical philosophy. . . . "[7] By itself, the idea that teleology might be a central part of philosophy is not new for Kant – in spite of his rejection of its traditional theological foundation in the argument from design, he had clearly been looking for a way to include teleology within his philosophy since his early work on

[4] Letter 313, to Karl Leonhard Reinhold, December 28 and 31, 1787, 10: 513–16.
[5] Ibid., 10: 514.
[6] For example, *Anthropologie Collins* (1772–3), 25: 179; *Anthropologie Parow* (1772–3), 25: 376.
[7] Letter to Reinhold, 10: 514–15.

The Only Possible Basis for a Demonstration of the Existence of God (1763). What is unprecedented in Kant's work, however, is the suggestion in the letter to Reinhold that there is an intimate connection between aesthetics and teleology. We can now see that it must be precisely this connection that finally enabled Kant to write the third *Critique*, for what the lectures on anthropology show is that what the *Critique of Judgment* adds to all the elements of his aesthetic theory that were already in place by the mid-1780s is all and only those elements of the theory that reveal the teleological significance of the experience of beauty and of the existence of both natural and artistic beauty. In other words, what we can now see is that everything in Kant's account of the aesthetic was in place before the end of 1787 except for his understanding of its fundamental significance. Only once the project of the "critique of taste" was transformed into a "Critique of Aesthetic Judgment" that would be paired with a "Critique of Teleological Judgment," I propose, did it finally become worth Kant's while to write it.

This claim, of course, depends upon a particular interpretation of Kant's mature teleology. As I understand it, the point of Kant's mature teleology is to unify the system of nature that Kant established in the first *Critique* with the system of freedom that he developed in his writings on moral philosophy by showing that we must and how we can conceive of nature as a realm fit for the realization of the objectives set for us by morality. The teleology of the third *Critique* is a complement to the argument from the highest good to the postulate of the rational authorship of nature that Kant had been making since the first *Critique*. In that argument, Kant argued that morality sets us not merely the single goal of perfecting the virtuousness of our intentions, but also the goal of realizing a systematic form of human happiness, a condition that can be realized only in nature, and in nature only if the laws of nature have been authored to be compatible with the moral law. In the "Critique of Teleological Judgment," Kant then adds that the task of understanding nature itself leads us to the same vision of the unity of the laws of nature and of freedom. Kant argues that we can only understand a particular kind of thing in nature, namely, organisms, as purposive systems; that once we are forced to understand organisms as purposive systems it becomes natural for us to look at nature as a whole as a purposive system; but that we can do this only if we can conceive of some single and determinate ultimate end for nature, which we can do in turn only if we conceive of the only thing that is an end in itself, namely, the cultivation of human morality, as the final end of nature. Thus both morality and science drive us to the vision of nature as a realm fit by its own laws for the realization of the objective set by the moral law – a vision, to be sure, that is a regulative ideal produced by reflective judgment, not a speculative assertion demonstrated by theoretical reason, but which is nevertheless the ultimate and driving vision of Kant's philosophical career.[8]

Against this background, we can now see that the real novelty of Kant's mature aesthetic theory lies in those of its elements that interpret aesthetic experience as evidence of the existence and character of human freedom and the existence of both natural and artistic beauty as evidence of nature's hospitality to human freedom. The lectures on anthropology show that Kant had long understood many of the distinctive features of aesthetic experience and judgment just as he would analyze them in the *Critique of the Power of Judgment*, but what is missing from them is precisely his mature understanding of how to preserve the distinctive character of the aesthetic even while showing how it fits into his larger moral and teleological vision.

The lectures on anthropology, for which Kant used as his text the chapter on empirical psychology in Baumgarten's *Metaphysics*, which was also touched upon in Kant's metaphysics lectures but is here treated far more extensively, allow us to discern the following pattern in the development of Kant's aesthetic theory. At the beginning of the 1770s, Kant had already arrived at the idea that a judgment of taste is based on an immediate yet universally and necessarily valid feeling of pleasure in an object, a response that in some sense could even ground an *a priori* judgment. At that point, however, he understood such a universally valid pleasure to arise solely from the harmony between the form of a beautiful object and the universally valid laws of human sensibility, as contrasted to human understanding and reason. However, in the middle of the 1770s – the period that was also decisive for the evolution of the *Critique of Pure Reason* – Kant developed the theory that we usually take to be characteristic only of the later *Critique of the Power of Judgment*, the theory, namely, that our pleasure in beauty is the product of a harmonious interaction between sensibility or imagination on the one hand and understanding

[8] I have argued for this interpretation of Kant's mature teleology in a number of papers, including "The Unity of Nature and Freedom: Kant's Conception of the System of Philosophy," in Sally S. Sedgwick, ed., *The Reception of Kant's Critical Philosophy* (Cambridge: Cambridge University Press, 2000), pp. 19–53, and "From Nature to Morality: Kant's New Argument in the 'Critique of Teleological Judgment,'" in Hans Friedrich Fulda and Jürgen Stolzenberg, eds., *Architektonik und System in der Philosophie Kants* (Hamburg: Felix Meiner Verlag, 2001), pp. 375–404, both reprinted in my *Kant's System of Nature and Freedom* (Oxford: Clarendon Press, 2005).

on the other that is induced in us by a beautiful object. From that insight, Kant was able to begin to develop some of the characteristic features of his later aesthetic theory, particularly his theory of art, including his account of art as the product of genius understood as an exceptional harmony between imagination and understanding and a classification of the arts organized around the different ways in which sensible form and intellectual content can be related. Yet the one thing that is missing throughout all of Kant's expositions of these ideas throughout the 1770s is any but the most conventional comments on the connection between aesthetic experience and morality. Only in Kant's lectures on anthropology from 1788–9 do we suddenly find him prominently characterizing the harmony between imagination and understanding that is central to both aesthetic experience and artistic creativity as a form of freedom; and only after that happens can the most novel parts of the aesthetic theory of the *Critique of Judgment* emerge, particularly the interpretations of the dynamical sublime and of the experience of beauty as the symbol of the morally good as evidence of the freedom of the human agent and the interpretations of the intellectual interest in natural beauty and genius as the source of artistic beauty as evidence of nature's hospitality to human freedom. This development, in which the freedom of the imagination that is distinctive of aesthetic experience and artistic production turns out to be evidence of the fit between freedom and nature, is what finally allows the integration of Kant's aesthetic theory into his teleological vision and the emergence of a unified *Critique of the Power of Judgment.* In what follows, I shall simply trace the course of this development in a little more detail.

II

Kant's basic theory of judgments of taste is built upon two distinct elements: first, a logico-linguistic analysis of the claims of an aesthetic judgment, according to which a person who claims that an object is beautiful is claiming that the pleasure that she takes in the object is one that can reasonably be expected to occur in any other properly situated observer of the object; and, second, a psychological explanation of the causes of such a pleasure, which explains why such an expectation is reasonable.[9] This structure is already present in Kant's earliest lectures on anthropology,

9 See Paul Guyer, *Kant and the Claims of Taste* (Cambridge: Harvard University Press, 1979; 2nd ed., Cambridge: Cambridge University Press, 1997), ch. 3; in 2nd ed., p. 60.

the transcriptions *Collins* and *Parow* from 1772–3, where it is indeed presented in a way that helps to explain the order of exposition in the "Analytic of the Beautiful" of the later *Critique of the Power of Judgment.* Kant begins in a way that makes the influence of Francis Hutcheson more obvious than it is in the later book: the first of the "conditions of taste" that he lists is that "Beauty pleases immediately," from which he infers that "pure beauty, which exists solely for taste and affords a certain pure enjoyment, is empty of all utility."[10] From this Kant infers that "taste is a sensible judgment, although not a power of judgment of the senses and of sensation, but rather of intuition and comparison, for obtaining pleasure and displeasure through intuition."[11] Here Kant is clearly following Hutcheson, who had argued that the capacity to detect and respond to beauty "is justly called *a Sense,* because of its Affinity to the other Senses in this, that the pleasure is different from any *Knowledge* of Principles, Proportions, Cause, or of the Usefulness of the Object; we are struck at first with the Beauty," and that it follows from this that no "Resolution of our own, nor any *Prospect* of Advantage or Disadvantage, [can] vary the Beauty or Deformity of an Object."[12] Kant does not use the term "disinterested" here, but he is obviously following Hutcheson in taking immediacy to be the most salient feature of aesthetic response and apparently aesthetic judgment – that is, the judgment about an object that we make on the basis of our response to it – as well, and in inferring disinterestedness, in the sense of the irrelevance of the use or other practical value of an object to the aesthetic response to and judgment on it, from this fact. Kant preserves this starting point in the first moment of the "Analytic of the Beautiful,"[13] although there he simply begins with the assertion of the disinterestedness of judgments of taste rather than inferring that feature from the immediacy of aesthetic response, thus obscuring what should perhaps be regarded as the ultimately psychological starting point of his whole analysis.[14]

Kant next introduces his second "condition of taste," the claim that an object which is to ground a judgment of taste must please universally,

10 *Collins,* 25: 176; cf. *Parow,* 25: 374.

11 *Collins,* 25: 177; cf. *Parow,* 25: 375.

12 Francis Hutcheson, *An Inquiry into the Original of our Ideas of Beauty and Virtue,* 4th ed. (London: Midwinter, Bettesworth, et al., 1738), treatise I, sec. I, §§xii–xiii, p. 11.

13 See *Critique of the Power of Judgment,* §2, 5: 204–5.

14 Kant's framework analysis of what is claimed by the judgment of taste recurs throughout the lectures on anthropology. For a particularly clear version and detailed exposition from ten years after the initial *Collins* and *Parow* lectures, see *Menschenkunde,* 25: 1095–1108.

that is, please everyone who is in a proper position to respond to the object in question. As he is recorded to have said in one set of the 1772–3 transcriptions, "That which is to be in accordance with taste must please universally, i.e., the judgment of taste is not to be made in accordance with the private disposition [*Beschaffenheit*] of my subject to be affected with pleasure by an object, but in accordance with the rules of universal satisfaction";[15] in the other set of notes from this year, the statement reveals even more clearly the structure of his emerging theory: "That which is to please in taste must be universal, the judgment that is to be made through it must not be a private but a universal judgment, or a universal ground of satisfaction."[16] This second formulation suggests more clearly than the first that for a judgment such as the judgment of taste to be universally valid it will have to be based on a universal ground, so that in this case the pleasure in a beautiful object that is the subject of such a judgment and which by it is to be imputed to others will have to be shown to be something that can itself reasonably be expected to be universally felt, at least under appropriate conditions. Kant brings out this last point, that a judgment of taste is concerned with what all would feel under appropriate conditions rather than with what everyone might feel under actual conditions, by characterizing the judgment of taste as "ideal" and "*a priori*": "With regard to actual taste I must make the judgment about what pleases universally on the basis of experience, but in regard to ideal taste one can make it *a priori*."[17] The early Kant often seems to suppose that all judgments of taste are merely empirical observations about what happens to please people, as indeed his criticism of Baumgarten in the "Transcendental Aesthetic" of the first *Critique* implies.[18] The present passage shows that matters are not quite that simple, that Kant recognized at least as early as 1772–3 that there is at least some sense in which judgments of taste are *a priori*, and that the innovation of the *Critique of the Power of Judgment* cannot lie simply in this assertion, as a hasty reading of the letter to Reinhold might suggest.

I call the thesis that judgments of taste claim universal validity the heart of the "logico-linguistic" aspect of Kant's theory of taste because in the later "Analytic of the Beautiful" he will present this claim by appeal to the logical concept of the "quantity" of the judgment of taste and will support

[15] *Collins*, 25: 179.
[16] *Parow*, 25: 376.
[17] *Collins*, 25: 179; cf. *Parow*, 25: 376.
[18] See note 2.

it by an appeal to how we actually talk about beauty, specifically by the observation that although it sounds right to us to defuse any suggestion of universal validity when we report our own pleasure in something we consider merely agreeable by explicitly restricting our judgment to our own case – as when I say something like "Canary Islands wine is agreeable to me" – it does not sound right to us to add such a restriction to our judgments of beauty.[19] In the lectures on anthropology, Kant does not actually try to support this analytical claim, but instead proceeds more directly to what I consider the psychological aspect of his theory, that is, his characterization of our response to beauty itself, which is necessary in order to show how it can be reasonable for us to claim universal validity for our judgments of taste, at least ideally and *a priori*. Here is where we find the crucial difference between Kant's earlier and later accounts of taste: while after the mid-1770s Kant will argue that our pleasure in a beautiful object is caused by the harmonious play between imagination and understanding that it induces, a state that he will argue can reasonably be expected to be induced in any properly situated observer, in the lectures from 1772–3 he argues that our pleasure in beauty is occasioned by the harmony between object and the laws of our sensibility alone. An object is beautiful simply if it agrees with the laws of human sensibility and by so doing facilitates its own intuition: "What facilitates the sensible intuition pleases and is beautiful, it is in accordance with the subjective laws of sensibility, and it promotes the inner life, since it sets the cognitive powers into activity."[20] The restriction of the explanation to the agreement of an object with the laws of human sensibility is by no means a careless omission; on the contrary, it mirrors precisely what we find in Kant's lectures on logic from this period and in his lectures on metaphysics from this period and for quite a while longer. Thus, in his lectures on logic in the early 1770s, Kant says that "An aesthetic perfection is a perfection according to laws of sensibility,"[21] and in logic lectures from the early 1780s, although his discussion of aesthetics is by then considerably more refined, Kant still insists that aesthetic perfection has nothing to do with

[19] See *Critique of the Power of Judgment*, §7, 5: 212.

[20] *Collins*, 25: 181; cf. *Parow*, 25: 379. The last clause of the sentence cited in the text refers to the general theory of pleasure that Kant maintains in these lectures, namely, that pleasure is the consciousness of the promotion of life, which in turn consists in activity, while pain is consciousness of the hindrance of life, or of obstacles to activity; see, for example, *Collins*, 25: 167–9.

[21] *Logik Blomberg*, 24: 24; translation from Immanuel Kant, *Lectures on Logic*, translated and edited by J. Michael Young (Cambridge: Cambridge University Press, 1992), p. 32.

the understanding and its concern, namely, truth, but only with the laws of sensibility; truth, he says, may be the "*conditio sine qua non*" of aesthetic perfection but is at most its "foremost negative condition, since here it is not its principle end"; the principle end in the case of beauty is still just "pleasantness and agreement of sensibility."[22] Likewise, Kant maintains the same view in his lectures on metaphysics from the mid-1770s: "What is an object of intuition or of the sensible power of judgment, that *pleases*, and the object is beautiful.... Taste is thus the power of judgment of the senses, through which it is cognized what agrees with the senses of others.... The universal agreement of sensibility is what constitutes the ground of satisfaction through taste."[23]

Before Kant even explains what he means by the agreement of a beautiful object with the laws of sensibility, he wants to make it clear that such an explanation of our experience of beauty will be adequate to fulfill the claim raised by the universal validity of a judgment of taste. He does not dignify such an argument, as he later will, with the title of a "deduction of judgments of taste";[24] indeed, it would have been surprising if he had, since as far as we can tell by 1772–3 Kant had not yet introduced the idea of a "deduction" of any form of judgments into his emerging theoretical philosophy. But the basic strategy of his later deduction of aesthetic judgments was already present, namely, that of showing that judgments of taste rest on a foundation that is just as universal as that of ordinary cognitive judgments; only at this point his view is not yet that judgments of taste are grounded in the subjective satisfaction of the conditions for judgment in general that is constituted by harmony between imagination and understanding,[25] but simply that the laws of sensibility are just as universal as the laws of understanding, so an object that pleases in virtue of its agreement with the laws of sensibility gives rise to a judgment that is just as objective as a judgment about an object of the understanding made on the basis of concepts of the understanding. In Kant's words,

Judgments about beauty and ugliness are objective, but not in accordance with rules of the understanding, rather in accordance with those of sensibility. Sensibility has its rules as well as the understanding does. Certain principles

[22] *Wiener Logik*, 24: 811; Young, p. 270.

[23] *Metaphysik* L_1, 28: 250–1; translation from Immanuel Kant, *Lectures on Metaphysics*, translated and edited by Karl Ameriks and Steve Naragon (Cambridge: Cambridge University Press, 1997), p. 66.

[24] See *Critique of the Power of Judgment*, §38, 5: 289–90.

[25] See above all the First Introduction to the *Critique of Judgment*, §VIII, 20: 223–5.

of taste must be universal and hold universally. Thus there are certain rules of aesthetics.[26]

The details of Kant's later deduction of aesthetic judgments must of course change as the details of his explanation of aesthetic response change; but the idea of the possibility of such a deduction is not in fact one of the major innovations of the *Critique of Judgment.*

That said, we can now ask what Kant means by the agreement of an object with the laws of sensibility and the facilitation of intuition by such agreement. What he has in mind is simply that such properties of the form of an object as proportion and symmetry make it easier to take in, grasp, and remember the object as a whole than would otherwise be the case. Dividing beautiful objects into those that are spatially extended and those that are temporally extended – a distinction that could have been suggested by Gotthold Ephraim Lessing's recently published *Laokoön* (1766), but which of course would also have been suggested by Kant's own analysis of the fundamental forms of sensibility in his inaugural dissertation, *On the Forms and Principles of the Sensible and Intellectual World* of 1770 – Kant argues that beautiful objects are ones the spatial or temporal forms of which make it easy for us to grasp them as wholes. In his words,

The facilitation takes place through space and time. Alteration in space is figure, in time it is merely play. The play of alteration is facilitated through proportion in the parts. Symmetry facilitates comprehensibility and is the relation of sensibility. In the case of a disproportionate house I can represent the whole only with difficulty, while in the case of a well-constructed house, by contrast, I see equality in the two sides. Equality of parts promotes my sensible representation, facilitates the intuition, increases the life of activity and favors it, hence the whole must please me, and for the same reason likewise everything [that is beautiful], for this rule is the basis in all such cases.[27]

In the case of objects with temporal rather than spatial extension, such as a piece of music (or musical performance), analogous properties such as symmetry and proportion in the rhythm and harmony also "facilitate sensible comprehension."[28] Kant goes on to suggest other sorts of objects, such as dances and gardens, in which it is also the facilitation of the grasp of the whole by the regularity of the relevant parts that is the basis of our pleasure, a pleasure that is universal because "All human

[26] *Collins*, 25: 181.
[27] Ibid., 25: 181.
[28] Ibid., 25: 182.

beings have conditions under which they can represent a great manifold."[29] These conditions are what Kant means by the laws of sensibility: formal properties such as proportion and equality allow objects to agree with the laws of our sensibility. "Since proportion and equality of division much facilitate our intuitions, they thus accord with the subjective laws of our sensibility, and that holds for everything which makes the representation of the whole easy for us, and which promotes the extension of our cognitions."[30]

Such formal properties of spatial and temporal structure will hardly disappear from Kant's mature theory of beauty; on the contrary, they seem to be precisely what he will continue to consider to be the most important properties of proper objects of pure judgments of taste. Surely it is such properties that Kant has in mind when he argues in the *Critique of the Power of Judgment* that "All form of the objects of the senses . . . is either **shape** or **play**," and thus that while "The **charm** of colors or of the agreeable tones of instruments can be added," nevertheless "**drawing**" in the case of the plastic arts and "composition" in the case of music "constitute the proper object of the pure judgment of taste."[31] Nevertheless, when Kant transforms his basic explanation of our pleasure in beauty from the agreement of an object with the laws of sensibility alone to the harmony between imagination and understanding that an object induces in us, the possible range of objects of taste will be vastly expanded, even if at the cost of the "purity" of judgments of taste; and it is on this expansion of the range and significance of objects of taste that Kant's eventual inclusion of the aesthetic into his teleological vision of the unity of the systems of nature and freedom will depend. So let us now see how Kant begins this transformation of his aesthetic theory.

III

Kant's lectures on anthropology from the third quarter of the 1770s are represented by two more sets of lectures, *Friedländer* from 1775–76 and *Pillau* from 1777–78. A fundamental change in Kant's thought is immediately evident: while the overall structure of Kant's aesthetic theory, already apparent in the lectures of 1772–3, remains unchanged, these lectures document Kant's change in the crucial explanation of our response to

29 Ibid., 25: 182.
30 *Parow*, 25: 379.
31 *Critique of the Power of Judgment*, §14, 5: 225.

beauty from his initial theory that our pleasure in beauty is the result of the harmony between an object and the laws of our sensibility alone to the theory that he would henceforth hold, namely, that this pleasure is due to the fact that a beautiful object induces a harmonious play between multiple cognitive faculties, namely, sensibility and understanding. In the *Friedländer* lectures, this new idea appears twice. First, it is presented under "The concept of the poet [*Dichter*] and the art of poetry [*Dichtkunst*]," a subdivision of the section on "The faculty for invention" (*Dichten*) that is included in the description of the faculties of cognition, which, in these as in all the anthropology lectures, is the first of the three main divisions of the subject, the latter two concerning pleasure and displeasure and then the faculty of desire. Kant simply begins this section by stating that a poem involves a harmonious play between what must be regarded as aspects of objects that appeal to sensibility on the one hand and to understanding on the other: he says that "The harmonious play of thoughts and sensations is the poem."[32] He then reinvokes his earlier language of laws, but in a way that makes clear the new thought that aesthetic response involves a harmonious relationship between multiple faculties within the subject as well as between the subject and the object:

> The play of thoughts and sensations is the correspondence [*Uebereinstimmung*] of subjective laws; if the thoughts correspond with my subject then that is a play of them. Secondly, it is to be observed about these thoughts that they stand in relation to the object, and then the thoughts must be true, and that the course of the thoughts corresponds with the nature of the mental powers, thus with the subject, and therefore the succession of thoughts corresponds with the powers of the mind. This harmonious play of thoughts and sensations is the poem.[33]

This account is not yet a completely general account of beauty and our response to it. Since the "thoughts" involved in a poem are, as we would say, propositional, we can respond to them as truths, and this may not be true for other kinds of art, let alone for natural beauties. Further, Kant here refers to the sensory aspect of the poem as "sensations," whereas in most other passages, both earlier and later, he typically downplays the significance of sensations in contrast to that of the pure forms of intuition in our response to beauty. What will generalize from this account, however, is the suggestion that the relationship between a beautiful object and our response to it is complex, inducing a harmonious relationship between different faculties of the mind itself. This will ultimately open

[32] *Friedländer*, 25: 525.
[33] Ibid., 25: 525–6.

the way to a far more extensive account of the possible range of beautiful objects than Kant has thus far given as well to the complex account of the importance of aesthetic objects and our experience of them that will eventually be offered in the *Critique of the Power of Judgment.*

Kant begins to generalize this account of a poem and our response to it later in the same lectures, in the section on pleasure where his chief discussion of aesthetic theory typically occurs. Here Kant divides pleasure into "sensual, ideal and intellectual," with the second of these terms standing for the aesthetic.[34] He then says that "ideal enjoyment . . . rests on the feeling of the free play of the mental faculties." This free play involves the impression of an object upon the senses, but is not a passive response to that; rather, the impression of the object upon the senses evokes an active response in which the mind brings its powers of thought to bear upon a sensory impression:

> The senses are the receptivity of impressions, which promote our sensible enjoyment, but we cannot bring our mental powers into agitation through objects just insofar as they make an impression on us, but rather insofar as we think them, and that is the ideal enjoyments, which are, to be sure, sensible, but not enjoyments of sense. A poem, a novel, a comedy are capable of affording us ideal enjoyments, they arise from the way in which the mind makes cognitions for itself out of all sorts of representations of the senses. Now if the mind is sensitive of a free play of its powers, that which creates this free play is an ideal enjoyment.[35]

Clumsy as it sounds, this passage indicates remarkable progress in Kant's thought. Instead of conceiving of a beautiful object as simply agreeing with laws of sensibility, laws according to which we can more readily grasp something symmetrical than we can something asymmetrical, Kant is now clearly conceiving of aesthetic response as more complex and more active: sensibility provides us with a variety of materials, and then the mind sees what it can make of them. Further, Kant suggests that there are different ways in which the mind can make something of its objects for ideal enjoyment: a poem, a novel, a comedy are different genres, and the suggestion seems to be that the mind responds to them differently, more complexly than just detecting symmetry or proportion. This suggestion is strengthened when Kant continues the passage by mentioning tragedy, and suggesting that in this case the mind can even transform pain into pleasure. This can only be done if the mind is thought of as active rather than passive in its aesthetic response.

34 Ibid., 25: 559.
35 Ibid., 25: 560.

This passage is also the first in which Kant characterizes the harmonious play of the mind in aesthetic response as a *free* play. This is clearly important to him, since he explains our pleasure in life itself as pleasure in the free exercise of our capacities, and thus explains the pleasurableness of aesthetic response by the fact that it is a form of the free exercise of our mental powers. At this stage, however, Kant immediately *distinguishes* the free play of the mental powers that is the basis of ideal enjoyment from the "use of freedom in accordance with rules" that is the basis of intellectual enjoyment, or the foundation of morality. Kant does not yet see that he can use the characterization of aesthetic response as a form of free play to *connect* aesthetic response to moral judgment even while preserving the distinctness of aesthetic response. That is the key move that is made only in the *Critique of the Power of Judgment.*

The generalization of this new account is also evident in a number of ways in the *Pillau* lectures, given one year later than the *Friedländer* lectures. First, in the section on the faculty for invention, where *Friedländer* had offered its definition of a poem, *Pillau* now makes a more general statement about beauty in the language that Kant will henceforth use: "We can call the harmonious play of the understanding and of sensibility the beauty of the spirit. A beautiful spirit thinks in such a way that there is understanding, but in harmony with sensibility."[36] Second, Kant begins to use the possibilities afforded by his newly complex characterization of aesthetic response to develop what will become central features of his mature theory of the fine arts, the account of genius as the source of fine art, on the one hand, and the classification of the fine arts, on the other, on the basis of the particular relationship between sensibility and understanding that is paradigmatic for each medium of fine art.

Although Kant treats genius prior to the classification of the arts in the *Critique of the Power of Judgment,* in the anthropology lectures he treats the arts and their differences first. The key to Kant's approach is his recognition that since aesthetic response involves understanding as well as sensibility, the several fine arts can be distinguished from each other by the particular ways in which sensibility and understanding are related in our response to them. Kant first illustrates this with a distinction that will be repeated in all the subsequent lectures on anthropology and preserved in the *Critique of the Power of Judgment,*[37] namely, the distinction between "oratory" (*Beredsamkeit*) and "poetic art" (*Dichtkunst*) as two species of the

[36] *Pillau,* 25: 761.
[37] See §51, 5: 321.

"*humaniora*" or "arts which decorate a beautiful spirit." Kant argues that "oratory" is "the art of enlivening ideas of the understanding through sensibility," where the pleasure in the sensible form of the oration has to be subordinated to the orator's underlying intent to convince his audience of the truth of the ideas he is attempting to enliven, while "poetry" is "the art of giving the play of sensibility unity through the understanding," where it is the pleasure that will be produced and not the business of conviction that is the "primary purpose" (*Haupt-Zweck*) of the enterprise.[38] This distinction could not be drawn unless each form of art involved both sensibility and understanding. Next, Kant expands his earlier classification of the arts to reflect the fact that the materials of art are not merely spatial and temporal forms of sensibility, but include intellectual elements as well, so that different forms of art differ precisely in the various ways in which they paradigmatically relate sensible and intellectual elements and thereby induce different varieties of free play between our sensibility and understanding. Kant had previously distinguished simply between arts that employ spatial and temporal manifolds, but he now subsumes that distinction under a broader distinction between "material" and "spiritual" arts. The "material" arts are those in which sensible forms predominate, whether these be spatial forms as in the case of "painting, sculpture, architecture and the art of pleasure-gardening," or temporal forms, as in the case of "music proper and dance music"; the "spiritual arts" are "oratory" and "poesy" (now *Poësie*).[39] All of these forms of art are seen as pleasing us immediately because all of them "harmoniously move the powers of the mind,"[40] but they differ in which materials of sensibility they employ and in which of the two main faculties, sensibility or understanding, as it were, takes the lead in the harmonious dance between them.

The possibilities for such distinctions afforded by Kant's new conception of aesthetic response are even further exploited in the more extensive discussion of the arts in the *Menschenkunde* lectures from 1781–82, which were originally edited by F. C. Starke and published in 1831.[41]

38 *Pillau*, 25: 760.
39 Ibid., 25: 760.
40 Ibid., 25: 761.
41 *Immanuel Kant's Menschenkunde oder philosophische Anthropologie. Nach handschriftlichen Vorlesungen herausgegeben von Fr. Ch. Starke* (Leipzig, 1831), edited in the *Akademie* edition under the title "*Menschenkunde*" (25: 849–1203). The new edition of *Menschenkunde*, however, supplements its text with additions from a manuscript from the same semester known as *St. Petersburg*. This does not add noticeably to Kant's discussions of poetry, genius, and taste, but adds a major section on freedom (25: 1142–54) that will be of great interest for the interpretation of Kant's moral philosophy.

This discussion is interesting not just for its wealth of detail, but also because it introduces yet another vector for the distinction and classification of forms of art, namely, a distinction between "illusion" (*Schein*) or "appearance" (*Apparenz*) on the one hand and "reality" on the other. Kant discusses painting and sculpture as art forms that play with the tension between illusion and reality: painting creates the illusion of three-dimensional space and objects in two dimensions, while sculpture can create the illusion of a living corporeal figure out of a nonliving corporeal object.[42] But it is the sense of a playful tension between illusion and reality that is essential to our pleasure: as we move from sculpture to waxworks, Kant observes, we begin to lose our sense of illusion, "rather the object itself seems to be there," and we begin to react with distaste rather than pleasure.[43] What is crucial for aesthetic response is not just that both sensibility and understanding be involved, but that a sense of play between them, and thus room for the exercise of imagination, be preserved.

This discussion is important, for it suggests that Kant's concept of harmonious and free play between the faculties of cognition can be a more interesting basis for aesthetic theory than it is often taken to be. But since my main concern is to trace the path by which Kant was ultimately able to integrate his aesthetic theory into his teleology rather than to pursue the merits of his aesthetic theory for its own sake, I must leave this discussion aside and return to the second main development in Kant's aesthetic theory in the mid-1770s, his concept of genius.

The *Pillau* lectures were the first to be given after the publication of a German translation of Alexander Gerard's *An Essay on Genius* in 1776.[44] Gerard's work may well have accounted for Kant's emphasis on the concept of genius from this time on, but it should also be noted that Kant could not have understood this concept in the way that he did without his new conception of aesthetic response. Kant equates genius (*Genie*) with spirit (*Geist*), and characterizes the latter first simply as the "spontaneity" to invent or produce something.[45] But then he goes further and states that "Spirit is no particular faculty but that which gives all faculties unity. Understanding and sensibility or now better imagination are the faculties of the human being: now to give these two unity, that is spirit. It is

[42] Ibid., 25: 1000.
[43] Ibid., 25: 1001.
[44] Gerard, Alexander. *Versuch über das Genie.* Translated by Christian Garve (Leipzig, 1776).
[45] *Pillau*, 25: 781.

thus the general unity of the human mind, or also the harmony between them."[46] As the response to beauty has been reinterpreted to consist in a harmony between sensibility – or, as Kant now says, imagination, that is, the ability not just to derive sensible content from current experience but also the capacity to recall and foresee such content – and understanding, so must the capacity to create beauty through human art be understood as depending upon a special degree of harmony and unity between the capacities of mind.[47]

The *Pillau* lectures add a second element to Kant's characterization of genius that also implies a corresponding addition to his concept of art. Kant continues what we have just quoted by stating that "Spirit is also the enlivening of sensibility through the idea [*Idee*]." Such an idea, he says, is not a mere concept, which is just an abstraction, but rather "concerns the unity of the manifold as a whole; it thus contains the principle of the manifold as a whole."[48] He continues to try to explain what he means in terms that we might think of as a definition of an "ideal" rather than an "idea": it takes genius to come up with the idea that can be enlivened in a work of art, he argues, because an idea, say an idea of a human being as represented in a painting, can go beyond any particular human being who actually exists, and must therefore "be invented out of the head" of the genius. The point seems to be that genius manifests itself both in the invention of content for art and in the invention of sensible forms by means of which to present and enliven such content. Again, this is a development that is possible only once the underlying conception of aesthetic response has been changed from that of agreement of an object with laws of sensibility alone to the idea of a free play between sensible and intellectual and active rather than merely passive faculties.

Only in the *Critique of the Power of Judgment* will Kant proceed beyond this abstract characterization by showing how the contents of art and the paradigmatic products of genius can be *rational* and *moral* ideas that yet still leave room for the free play of imagination that is indispensable for our pleasure in beauty. The last course on anthropology that Kant gave before the publication of the third *Critique*, however, the *Busolt* lectures of 1788–9, show that at this point, just after the publication of the second *Critique* and when he was already composing the third, Kant was far bolder than ever before in his use of the language of *freedom* in the presentation of

46 Ibid., 25: 782.
47 For a very similar passage, see also the transcription by *Mrongovius* (1784–5), 25: 1313.
48 *Pillau*, 25: 782.

the key concepts of his aesthetics. This is evident above all in his treatment of genius. Here Kant states that "genius is the originality of imagination," and that "In the case of the genius the imagination and its disposition must be extraordinarily great and masterly." Then he goes on to say, in words that he does not seem to have used before, that:

> The freedom of the imagination must also be a chief ingredient. In the other powers of the mind, one seeks rules. But the imagination will be independent. It is bold, it is creative, and it is always doing violence to the rules of the understanding, which would as it were clip its wings. However, the imagination must also be under laws. If it subjects itself to laws, where its greatest freedom takes place, where the happiest agreement with the greatest possible determinacy of the understanding and reason exists, then does it have the disposition which is required for a genius.[49]

In this remarkable passage, the imagination of the genius is described in terms that make it sound like an exemplar for the objective of morality, namely, the realization of the greatest possible individual freedom within the limits of the rule of reason – which rules only to ensure that a like degree of freedom is extended to all. For the first time, here on the verge of the completion of the *Critique of the Power of Judgment*, does Kant suggest that the essence of aesthetic creativity and the response it can arouse may not lie in its contrast to morality but in its affinity to it.

IV

This striking characterization of genius is just a hint of what is to come, however. With the hindsight afforded to us by the new documentation of the development of Kant's aesthetic theory prior to the *Critique of the Power of Judgment* that we have just considered, we can see that what is most innovative in the published work of 1790 is Kant's systematic elaboration of the connections between the aesthetic and the moral, connections that do not undermine the uniqueness of the aesthetic but do allow the aesthetic to assume its proper place in Kant's teleological vision of the unity of the systems of nature and freedom. These connections are made possible by what have been identified as the two key innovations in Kant's aesthetic theory over the course of its development, namely, the explanation of aesthetic response as the harmonious play between our sensible and intellectual capacities and the interpretation of this play in turn as a form of freedom.

49 *Busolt*, 25: 1493–4.

To be sure, Kant had not completely neglected links between the aesthetic and the ethical in his lectures on anthropology; given his conception of the importance of these lectures for the moral education of his students – a conception reflected in the title of the handbook that he finally published only once he had ceased lecturing, that is, the *Anthropology from a Pragmatic Point of View* of 1798 – it would have been surprising if he had. But the connections that he drew throughout the lectures remained conventional. At the very first mention of the fine arts in the lectures, he acknowledges that art can present moral truths in an accessible and powerful way: "The entire use of the beautiful arts is that they present moral propositions of reason in their full glory and powerfully support them."[50] Later in the first series of lectures, he argues that the cultivation of taste refines us and makes us sociable, in a way that is "somewhat analogical to morality," by teaching us to take pleasure not merely in things that contribute to our own well-being but also in things that can be shared: "By means of taste my enjoyment can be shared. Taste arranges all the enjoyments of people in such a way that it contributes something to the enjoyments of others. A [piece of] music can be listened to with enjoyment by many hundreds of people."[51] Conversely, Kant also argues, taste depends upon the existence of society and the need for sociability, because a person who lived in solitude – on a desert island, as Kant often says, with the image of Robinson Crusoe in mind – would have no need to distinguish between merely private pleasures and those that can be shared with others, nor would he have any incentive to adorn himself or anything else in a way that could be pleasing to others.[52] But none of these comments can prepare the way for the elaborate framework of connections between the aesthetic and the moral that structures so much of the "Critique of Aesthetic Judgment" and may

[50] *Collins*, 25: 33.

[51] Ibid., 25: 187.

[52] For example, *Menschenkunde*, 25: 1096–7. The anthropology lectures afford rich material for a discussion of whether Kant adequately distinguishes between the question of whether one could make a judgment of taste entirely on one's own, without empirical evidence about the judgments of others by which to form one's own taste, and whether one would have any incentive to make such judgments and preserve or create objects of beauty apart from the society of others. The anthropology lectures thus noticeably augment the materials for a discussion of these issues found in Kant's logic notes and lectures, on which my earlier discussion of this issue was based; see Paul Guyer, "Pleasure and Society in Kant's Theory of Taste," in Ted Cohen and Paul Guyer, eds., *Essays in Kant's Aesthetics* (Chicago: University of Chicago Press, 1982), pp. 21–54. These materials will have to be examined more closely on another occasion.

well be, if my interpretation of Kant's letter to Reinhold is correct, its very *raison d'etre.*

I have discussed many of these connections before,[53] so here I will merely offer an overview that will identify the innovations in Kant's mature aesthetic theory and show how these innovations allowed Kant to make his aesthetics part of his moral teleology without undermining his account of the uniqueness of aesthetic experience. Kant begins his exposition in the "Critique of Aesthetic Judgment," just as he always did in the anthropology lectures, with the distinction between the agreeable, the beautiful, and the good.[54] This division allows him to distinguish aesthetic judgment from a masked or confused judgment of moral perfection,[55] and leads him to the characterization of pure aesthetic judgment as a response to the form of sensible objects alone, independent of any conception of the representational content and significance of those objects.[56] But Kant's conception of the restricted focus of a pure judgment of taste is not, as it turns out, intended to restrict the subject matter of fine art or even, as we ultimately see, the interpretation of the significance of the beauty and sublimity of nature. Rather, the concept of a pure judgment of taste functions heuristically, allowing us to identify the free play of our cognitive faculties as the foundation of all aesthetic response and judgment. As soon as that identification has been completed, in §16 of the "Analytic of the Beautiful," Kant begins to build upon the underlying notion of the harmony of the faculties, expanding his initial restriction of the object of such free play to sensible form alone and even his initial restriction of the faculties involved to mere sensibility or imagination and understanding. The larger argument of the "Critique of Aesthetic Judgment" is nothing less than that the imagination can be in free harmony with reason as well as with understanding, and that this harmony can involve content as well as form. Thus Kant can assign moral and teleological significance to aesthetic response without denying the pleasure of free play that is its hallmark; rather, this significance depends on the characterization of aesthetic response as a form of freedom.

53 See my *Kant and the Experience of Freedom* (Cambridge: Cambridge University Press, 1993), and "The Symbols of Freedom in Kant's Aesthetics," in Herman Parret, ed., *Kant's Asthetik – Kant's Aesthetics – L'esthétique de Kant* (Berlin: Walter de Gruyter, 1998), pp. 338–55, reprinted as Chapter 9 in the present volume.

54 *Critique of the Power of Judgment*, §§2–5, 5: 204–11.

55 Ibid., §15, 5: 226–9.

56 Ibid., §4, 5: 207 and §16, 5: 229–30.

For my present purposes, Kant's new insights into the relations between the aesthetic and the moral can be organized into three groups, which I will list in the order in which they are introduced into the text of the "Critique of Aesthetic Judgment." First, Kant recognizes that art may have content, and indeed explicitly moral content, without sacrificing the freedom of play between the imagination on the one hand and understanding and/or reason on the other. Second, Kant argues that aesthetic experience can reveal something about our own capacities of morality to us without sacrificing what makes it distinctively aesthetic. Finally, Kant suggests that the experience of beauty in both nature and art can be understood as evidence of the fit between nature and our own objectives that is the fundamental regulative principle of his teleology.

That art can have morally significant content without thereby undermining the possibility of a distinctively aesthetic response to it is the first point that Kant makes after acknowledging that our response to an object can remain aesthetic even when it goes beyond a focus upon pure form as long as there is still room for free play between the imagination and understanding. I take that recognition to be the point of Kant's distinction between two kinds (*Arten*) of beauty, free and dependent, in §16;[57] after all, if Kant had meant to deny that we can have a properly aesthetic response to anything other than mere form, he would not have maintained that dependent beauty is a kind (*Art*) of beauty at all, but could have maintained only that it is a kind of pseudo-beauty, which he pointedly does not. So a judgment of dependent beauty cannot be merely a masked judgment of perfection, but must rather be based on our experience and enjoyment of the room for play between a concept and its constraints on the one hand and the form of an object on the other. In §17, then, under the rubric of the "Ideal of Beauty," Kant considers the problem of how there can be a unique or maximal archetype of beauty – a problem that is not set by the logic of taste at all, which requires only that anything that properly seems beautiful to anyone seem beautiful to everyone, not that there be any one thing that seems maximally beautiful to all – but rather "rests upon reason's indeterminate idea of a maximum."[58] His argument is then that this archetype can be found only in the representation of the human figure as the expression of human morality, because human morality is the only thing that is an end in itself and that can thus even pick out a unique candidate for the status

[57] Ibid., 5: 229–30.
[58] Ibid., §17, 5: 232.

of archetype, but also because the human beauty that is used as an expression of human morality cannot itself be conceived to be discovered by any mechanical process, such as averaging the features of whatever humans any individual has actually encountered, but must be seen as a product of the human imagination.[59] To make moral ideas "visible in bodily manifestation" therefore requires pure ideas of reason and great force of imagination united in anyone who would merely judge them, let alone anyone who would present them[60] – in other words, a harmony between the idea of reason and the free play of imagination.

Kant can be seen as expanding this conception when he more fully develops his theory of fine art later in the *Critique.* The heart of this theory is the claim that paradigmatic works of artistic genius are characteristically organized around an "aesthetic idea," a representation of the imagination that makes a rational or moral idea on the one side palpable through a sensible form and a wealth of imagery on the other.[61] The key to Kant's thought here is not just that works of art can present moral ideas in their full glory, as he had held from the outset of his anthropology lectures, but that they do this precisely by affording a sense of free play between the rational or moral idea on the one hand and both sensible form and a wealth of imagery on the other. As he puts it:

> In a word, the aesthetic idea is a representation of the imagination, associated with a given concept, which is combined with such a manifold of partial representations in the free use of the imagination that no expression designating a determinate concept can be found for it, which therefore allows the addition to a concept of much that is unnameable, the feeling of which animates the cognitive faculties and combines spirit with the mere letter of language.[62]

Kant's point here is simply that great art must both deal with serious content and yet retain a sense of play and freedom of the imagination.

These doctrines might be thought of as a refinement of views expressed in Kant's anthropology lectures but not as radical departures. He clearly breaks new ground, however, with his next idea, the idea that we can have genuinely aesthetic experiences that nevertheless give us an intimation of our own moral capacities. This theme is touched upon in Kant's treatment

59 Ibid., 5: 233–4.
60 Ibid., §17, 5: 235.
61 For a full account of this interpretation of an aesthetic idea, see my "Kant's Conception of Fine Art," *Journal of Aesthetic and Art Criticism* 51 (1994): 175–85, reprinted as ch. 12 in the 2nd ed. of *Kant and the Claims of Taste.*
62 *Critique of the Power of Judgment*, §29, 5: 316.

of the sublime and in his thesis that the beautiful is a symbol of the morally good.

Kant's treatment of the sublime is another innovation in the *Critique of the Power of Judgment.* Although the sublime had already been well-established as a fundamental aesthetic concept by writers from Addison to Burke, Kant mentions it only rarely in the anthropology lectures, and then only in a limited way that suggests that even without proportion and symmetry the sheer magnitude of natural objects can affect the magnitude of our own feeling.[63] This might appear to anticipate his later conception of the "mathematical sublime," but the distinction between the "mathematical" and the "dynamical" sublime, the view that each involves a complex disharmony between imagination and understanding but also a satisfying harmony between imagination and reason, and above all the view that in the experience of the dynamical sublime imagination gives us an intimation of the power of our own practical reason, all appear to be new to the *Critique*, further evidence of Kant's newfound confidence that the aesthetic can in fact be connected to the moral without loss of its own freedom. In particular, Kant's view about the experience of the dynamical sublime appears to be that it is a genuine aesthetic experience because in it the independence and power of what is morally important in our own existence is made palpable by a feeling and not just by an abstract concept of how that which is most important in us cannot be threatened by even the most destructive forces of mere physical nature. "Nature is here called sublime merely because it raises the imagination to the point of presenting those cases in which the mind can make palpable to itself the sublimity of its own vocation even over nature."[64] It might perhaps seem a stretch to describe this experience as one of free play, but the essential idea remains that the imagination can present a fundamental idea of reason while manifesting its own special character as well.

While the sublime makes the independence of practical reason from mere nature palpable, the beautiful can serve as a symbol of the morally good because the freedom of imagination that is the essence of the experience of beauty can serve as a symbol of the freedom of the will that is the basis of morality, even though the latter must be a form of freedom governed by law while the former only gives a sense of satisfying the understanding's basic desire for unity without being determined by any

63 *Collins*, 25: 198.
64 *Critique of the Power of Judgment*, §28, 5: 262.

concept functioning as a rule. The heart of Kant's analogy is the claim that "The **freedom** of the imagination (thus of the sensibility of our faculty) is represented in the judging of the beautiful as in accord with the lawfulness of the understanding (in the moral judgment the freedom of the will is conceived as the agreement of the latter with itself in accordance with universal laws of nature)."[65] Only once Kant had transformed his initial conception of beauty as the agreement of an object with the laws of our sensibility to that of the object's stimulation of free play between imagination and our higher cognitive faculties did such a conception of the symbolic value of beauty even become possible.

The greatest innovation of the *Critique of the Power of Judgment*, however, is its unification of aesthetics into Kant's overarching vision of teleology. Kant is cautious about connecting aesthetics and teleology too soon, before the reader has fully understood aesthetic experience in its own terms; and thus, for example, in introducing the deduction of aesthetic judgment he makes it quite clear that the task of such a deduction is not to offer a teleological explanation of the existence of natural beauty but only to provide a guarantee for the universal validity of our judgments about beauty through their foundation in fundamental facts about our shared cognitive constitution.[66] However, Kant also argues that once the teleological viewpoint has been forced upon us in our attempt to explain the special nature of organisms anyway, it is only natural for us to take a teleological viewpoint both of nature as a whole and of the beauty that we find in nature:

> Even beauty in nature, i.e., its agreement with the free play of our cognitive faculties in the apprehension and judging of its appearance, can be considered in this way as an objective purposiveness of nature in its entirety, as a system of which the human being is a member, once the teleological judging of nature by means of natural ends which have been provided to us by organized beings has justified us in the idea of a great system of nature. We may consider it as a favor that nature has done for us that in addition to usefulness it has so richly distributed beauty and charms, and we can love it on that account, just as we regard it with respect because of its immeasurability . . .[67]

The argument of Kant's teleology, as I suggested at the outset, is that the thought that the world is the product of intelligent design may be suggested to us or even forced upon us by our experience of organic

[65] Ibid., §59, 5: 354.
[66] Ibid., §§30–1, 5: 279–81.
[67] Ibid., §67, 5: 380.

nature, but that the only use we can make of this thought is for the regulative conception of the natural world as designed to be a fit arena within which we can reasonably strive to fulfill our moral vocation. It is into this conception of a world in which we can and must posit that the systems of nature and freedom can be united that the "Critique of Teleological Judgment" now invites us to incorporate our understanding of our aesthetic experience. Once Kant allows us this hindsight, however, we can see that he has already laid the foundation for the incorporation of aesthetic experience into moral teleology in two crucial moments in the "Critique of Aesthetic Judgment."

The first of these moments is Kant's account of the "intellectual interest in the beautiful" (§42). Kant presents this interest, which he limits to natural beauty, as a superior alternative to an interest in artistic beauty, which he dismisses – in what seems to be a rejection of an argument running throughout the anthropology lectures – as at best serving an empirical, not deeply moral interest in sociability, and as at worst serving only the purpose of self-aggrandizement.[68] In the intellectual interest in nature, by contrast, we add to our immediate satisfaction in the experience of a naturally beautiful object – a pleasure that is to be explained strictly in terms of the free play of our cognitive faculties – a further satisfaction in the fact "that nature should at least show some trace or give a sign that it contains in itself some sort of ground for assuming a lawful correspondence of its products with our satisfaction that is independent of all interests."[69] Our deepest interest, of course, is that nature contain a ground for assuming its correspondence with the satisfaction of our moral interest, which is independent of all empirical interests but not of the interest of practical reason itself; but we can interpret nature's creation of beauty as evidence of its hospitality to our unselfish interest in morality as well. This conception of the intellectual interest in beauty does not depend upon an innovation in Kant's aesthetic theory itself, but rather in his development of the new moral teleology that is the deepest innovation of the *Critique of the Power of Judgment.*[70]

The second key step in Kant's integration of the aesthetic into his new moral teleology is implicit in his treatment of artistic genius. As we saw, Kant had long included the topic of genius in his lectures on

[68] Ibid., §41, 5: 296–8.

[69] Ibid., §42, 5: 300.

[70] See my "From Nature to Morality: Kant's New Argument in the 'Critique of Teleological Judgment'" (see note 8).

anthropology, and once he transformed his conception of aesthetic response into the idea of the harmony between cognitive faculties he correspondingly transformed his conception of genius into that of someone possessing a special degree of harmony among his cognitive faculties and able to express that in ways communicable to others. What he never seems to have done prior to writing the *Critique of the Power of Judgment,* however, is to characterize this special degree of harmony and the capacity to communicate it to others as a *gift of nature,* although the equation of this "talent" with a "natural gift" is the very first feature of the third *Critique*'s account of genius.[71] By characterizing genius as a gift of nature, however, Kant implies that the existence of artistic as well as of natural beauty is evidence of the harmonious fit between nature and human objectives: just as the existence of natural beauty, that is, the beauty of nature outside of our own minds and dispositions, such as the beauty of flowers and birds and perhaps even of our own bodies, is evidence or at least a suggestion of nature's fitness as an arena in which to realize our moral objectives, so nature's production of a special human disposition, the special talent needed to produce beautiful art, can serve as evidence or at least a suggestion of the receptiveness of our own dispositions to the requirements of morality, that is, the possibility that we can successfully harmonize our own inclinations and reason in the way necessary to formulate morally requisite intentions in the first place. If "nature in the subject (and by means of the disposition of its faculties) must give the rule to art,"[72] surely that must give us some confidence that by means of the proper disposition of its faculties the subject can generally give the rule to nature in itself.

Such an interpretation of Kant's concept of genius might seem to mean that we must see him as retracting his dismissive attitude to artistic beauty, expressed only a few sections previously.[73] In fact, we do not have to see him as retracting his previous view, but only as refining it by means of a new perspective that has been introduced in the meantime: as long as we think merely of the immediate pleasure to be gained from art, we may be tempted to use it for base purposes such as mere self-aggrandizement; but once we reflect upon the real character of the genius that is needed to produce fine art, we can begin to see the very existence of fine art as one more bit of evidence for the ultimate harmony between our rational

71 *Critique of the Power of Judgment,* §46, 5: 307.

72 Ibid., §26, 5: 307.

73 That is, in the attack upon the "empirical interest in beauty" in §41.

objectives and our natural ones that is the heart of Kant's teleological vision. Perhaps the remarkable progress of Kant's argument within the *Critique of the Power of Judgment* itself, in which what has just been set aside is constantly being reintroduced in a subtler way, recapitulates the broader progress of Kant's aesthetic thought as a whole, in which so many of the elements simply described within the framework of his anthropology are suddenly transformed by the driving vision of his teleology.

8

The Ethical Value of the Aesthetic

Kant, Alison, and Santayana

Western philosophy effectively begins with Plato's ban of most poetry from his ideal republic because of its immoral influence on the education of his guardians. Recently, there has been renewed debate about the relation between aesthetics and morality, with its focus on such questions as whether criticism of the moral attitudes expressed by a work of art is a proper part of aesthetic criticism of the work, whether works of art should be free of censorship or even eligible for public support regardless of the moral attitudes they may express,[1] and whether the experience of art plays an indispensable role in the development of the capacity for moral reasoning and judgment.[2] This debate has been revived after a long period of quiescence, at least in Anglo-American "analytical" aesthetics, where a rigid barrier had been maintained between aesthetics and ethics under the aegis of such slogans as the "autonomy of art"[3] and "art for art's sake."[4]

[1] This debate of the 1980s and 1990s may be moot as I write; the *New York Times* of February 20, 2003, reports that many states are considering eliminating funding for the arts altogether because of their current budget crises.

[2] For several surveys of the recent debates, see Berys Gaut, "Art and Ethics," in Berys Gaut and Dominic McIver Lopes, eds., *The Routledge Companion to Aesthetics* (London: Routledge, 2001), pp. 341–52, and Nöel Carroll, "Art and Ethical Criticism: An Overview of Recent Directions of Research," *Ethics* 110 (2000): 350–87.

[3] See the entry on "Autonomy" in Michael Kelly, ed., *Encyclopedia of Aesthetics* (New York and Oxford: Oxford University Press, 1998), vol. I, pp. 170–84, especially the sub-entries "Historical Overview" (pp. 170–5) by Casey Haskins and "Critique of Autonomy" (pp. 175–8) by Peter Bürger.

[4] See Crispin Sartwell, "Art for Art's Sake," in Kelly, *Encyclopedia of Aesthetics*, vol. I, pp. 118–21.

This separation of the aesthetic and the ethical is usually thought to have been introduced into modern philosophy in the eighteenth century by such thinkers as the Third Earl of Shaftesbury and Francis Hutcheson,[5] but above all by Immanuel Kant, whose "Analytic of the Beautiful" in his third great critique, the *Critique of the Power of Judgment* of 1790, opens with the claim that the "satisfaction that determines the judgment of taste is without any interest,"[6] thus that the satisfaction "of the taste for the beautiful is a disinterested and **free** satisfaction; for no interest, neither that of the senses nor that of reason, extorts approval" (*CPJ*, §5, 5:210). However, Kant's assertion of the disinterestedness of judgments of taste is only the beginning of a complex analysis of aesthetic experience, aesthetic judgment, and the nature of art, which ends up by drawing a large number of beneficial connections between aesthetic experience and moral conduct. Kant thus undermines the idea that there can or should be a rigid barrier between the aesthetic and the ethical even before it gets off the ground, and indeed introduces some connections between them which have yet to be taken up in the current debate. The first objective of this essay will be to present Kant's complex account of the ethical value of the aesthetic.

In spite of the many connections between the aesthetic and the ethical that Kant makes, it may still be felt that a crucial element is missing from his account, namely, a recognition that our moral sensibilities are often immediately engaged in our experience of nature and art itself. To point up this hole in the heart of Kant's account, I will expound the very different view of aesthetic experience that was offered by another work published in the very same year as Kant's third *Critique*, namely, the *Essays on the Nature and Principles of Taste* by Archibald Alison.[7] But Alison's reduction of all aspects of aesthetic experience to emotional and typically moral associations may swing too far in the opposite direction from Kant,

5 Hutcheson clearly intended such a view; it is much less clear whether Shaftesbury did. For discussion, see my *Kant and the Experience of Freedom: Essays on Aesthetics and Morality* (Cambridge: Cambridge University Press, 1993), chapter 2, "The Dialectic of Disinterestedness," especially pp. 50–61, and Chapter 1 of the present volume.

6 Immanuel Kant, *Critique of the Power of Judgment*, edited by Paul Guyer, translated by Paul Guyer and Eric Matthews (Cambridge: Cambridge University Press, 2000), §2, 5:204. This work will be abbreviated "*CPJ*"; the pagination given refers to the pagination of the standard edition of Kant's works, *Kant's gesammelte Schriften*, edited by the Royal Prussian (later German, then Berlin-Brandenburg) Academy of Sciences [(Berlin: Georg Reimer (later Walter de Gruyter)], 1900 –). Citations from other works of Kant will also be located with their volume and page number in this edition.

7 I will cite Archibald Alison, *Essays on the Nature and Principles of Taste*, second edition (Edinburgh: Bell & Bradfute and Archibald Constable and Co., 1811).

and it could well be thought that an adequate account of our aesthetic experience and its moral significance requires some sort of synthesis between Kant's disinterestedness and Alison's emotionalism. I will suggest that such a synthesis was offered almost exactly a century after the works of those two by George Santayana, in his first book, *The Sense of Beauty.*[8] Santayana is particularly striking because he rejects an assumption common to Kant, Alison, and many participants in the contemporary debate: while they all assume that the ultimate justification of the aesthetic must be its ethical value, Santayana provocatively argues that ethics is only the means for putting us in a position to enjoy the positive and intrinsic value of the aesthetic.

I. Kant

Following the canonical model introduced into eighteenth-century aesthetics by Edmund Burke,[9] Kant divides the "Critique of the Aesthetic Power of Judgment" (the first half of the *Critique of the Power of Judgment*) into two main books, the "Analytic of the Beautiful" and the "Analytic of the Sublime." But Kant actually analyzes three main forms of aesthetic experience – the experience of beauty, paradigmatically natural beauty; the experience of the sublime, again paradigmatically of sublimity in nature; and the experience of fine art – and each of these forms of aesthetic experience has distinctive connections to morality.

As noted, Kant begins his analysis of the judgment of taste, that is, our claim that a particular object is beautiful, from the premise that our pleasure in a beautiful object occurs independently of any interest in the existence of the object as physiologically agreeable (*CPJ*, §3, 5:205–7) or as good for some purpose expressed by a determinate concept of utility or morality (*CPJ*, §4, 5:207–9). Yet, he insists, a judgment of taste does not express a merely idiosyncratic association of pleasure with an object: to call an object beautiful is to speak with a "universal voice," to assert that the pleasure one takes in the object is one that should be felt by anyone who responds to the object, at least under ideal or optimal circumstances, even though "there can also be no rule in accordance with which someone could be compelled to acknowledge something as beautiful"

[8] George Santayana, *The Sense of Beauty: Being the Outline of Aesthetic Theory* (New York: Scribner's, 1896; republished New York: Dover, 1955); henceforth "*SB*."

[9] See Edmund Burke, *A Philosophical Enquiry into the Origin of our Ideas of the Sublime and Beautiful*, ed., J. T. Boulton (London: Routledge & Kegan Paul, 1958).

(*CPJ*, §8, 5:216). How can one's pleasure in an object be independent of its subsumption under any determinate concept and its satisfaction of any determinate interest and yet be valid for all who properly respond to the object? Kant's answer is that although our pleasure in a beautiful object is not a response to its subsumption under a determinate concept, it is an expression of the free play of the cognitive faculties of imagination and understanding that such an object induces, and that those cognitive faculties must in fact work the same way in everyone. "If pleasure is connected with the mere apprehension of the form of an object without a relation of this to a concept for a determinate cognition, then the representation is thereby related not to the object, but solely to the subject, and the pleasure can express nothing but its suitability to the cognitive faculties that are in play in the reflecting power of judgment, insofar as they are in play" (*CPJ*, Introduction VII, 5:189–90). One of the clearest of his attempts to explain this idea is the statement that we experience a beautiful object as having a form "that contains precisely such a composition of the manifold" of its perceived properties and aspects "as the imagination would design in harmony with the **lawfulness of the understanding** in general if it were left free by itself" (*CPJ*, General Remark following §22, 5:240–1). That is, we experience a beautiful object as having the kind of unity that we ordinarily find in objects by subsuming them under a determinate concept but independently of any such subsumption,[10] and because finding such unity is our ultimate cognitive aim, we take pleasure in this discovery, especially since the unity we find must appear contingent – as it were, unexpected – if it is not linked to any determinate concept (see *CPJ*, Introduction VI, 5:186–7).

In this account, Kant makes two striking assumptions. First, he asserts that in "pure" judgments of taste our pleasure in beauty is a response only to the perceptible *form* of an object, not to any matter or content it may have – for example, in pictorial arts, "the **drawing** is what is essential," while the "colors that illuminate the outline . . . can . . . enliven the object in itself for sensation, but cannot make it . . . beautiful" (*CPJ*, §14, 5:225). Second, he assumes that the cognitive faculties of all human beings really do work the same way, that is, respond to particular objects in the same way, even when they are in "free play" rather than at serious work. The

[10] This is not to say that we do not subsume an object we find beautiful under any determinate concepts at all; we must if we are even to identify the object of our pleasure and judgment of taste in any determinate way. Kant's theory must rather be that when we find an object beautiful we experience it as having a degree of unity that cannot be explained by any of the determinate concepts under which we do subsume it.

second of these claims seems indefensible,[11] but Kant never backs off from it. The first of these claims also seems unjustifiable,[12] but this time Kant modifies his claim almost as soon as he makes it. While he continues to maintain that in pure judgments of taste our pleasure is in the unity or harmony of the form of the object alone, he quickly recognizes that there is a variety of *impure* forms of beauty – of no lesser value than pure beauty – where what we respond to with the free play of our imagination and understanding is harmony *between* an object's perceptible form and its matter, its content, or even its purpose. Thus, two sections after the assertion of formalism just cited, Kant introduces the category of "adherent beauty," which is the kind of harmony between an object's form and its intended function that pleases us in a beautiful summer-house or racehorse;[13] and he subsequently assumes that successful works of fine art normally have intellectual content and please us in virtue of the harmony among their content, form, and material.

Kant interposes his analysis of the experience of the sublime between his initial analysis of pure beauty and his later analysis of fine art. Kant recognizes two forms of the sublime, the "mathematical" and the "dynamical." In both cases, he holds that our experience is a mixture of pain and pleasure, a moment of pain due to an initial appearance of disharmony between the limits of imagination and the extraordinary demands of our faculty of reason, followed by pleasure that it is our own reason that is stretching our imagination. The mathematical sublime involves the relationship between imagination and theoretical reason, which is the source of our idea of the infinite; our experience of this form of the sublime is triggered by the observation of natural vistas so vast that they painfully defy our attempts to comprehend them, not (as is often thought) by the ordinary mechanism of reiterating a determinate unit of measurement a determinate number of times, rather in a single grasp of "aesthetic comprehension," but which then pleases us because this very effort reminds us that we have a power of reason capable of formulating even the aesthetic task of comprehending the infinite (*CPJ*, §26, 5:254–5). Further, Kant holds that in this experience we do not just infer that we have such a

[11] For my full account of the problems with this assumption, see my *Kant and the Claims of Taste* (Cambridge, Mass.: Harvard University Press, 1979; second edition, Cambridge: Cambridge University Press, 1997), chapters 7–9.

[12] See *Kant and the Claims of Taste*, chapter 6.

[13] This characterization of adherent beauty is a simplification; for a fuller account, see my "Free and Adherent Beauty: A Modest Proposal," *British Journal of Aesthetics*, October 2002; chapter 5 in the present volume.

faculty, but actually experience "a feeling that we have pure self-sufficient reason" (*CPJ*, §27, 5:258) – somehow, in seeing a vast mountain range or the "starry skies above" it *feels* to us as if we are directly grasping the infinite, even though in the cool light of understanding we know that we are not. In the case of the dynamical sublime, what we experience is ultimately a harmony between our imagination and practical reason. This experience is induced by natural objects that seem not just vast, but overwhelmingly powerful and threatening – volcanoes, raging seas, and the like (*CPJ*, §28, 5:261). Here we experience an element of fear and pain at the thought of our own physical injury or destruction followed by the satisfying feeling that we have "within ourselves a capacity for resistance of quite another kind, which gives us the courage to measure ourselves against the apparent all-powerfulness of nature," namely, "our power (which is not part of nature) to regard those things about which we are concerned (goods, health and life) as trivial, and hence to regard its power (to which, to be sure, we are subjected in regard to these things) as not the sort of dominion over ourselves and our authority to which we would have to bow if it came down to our highest principles and their affirmation or abandonment" (*CPJ*, §28, 5:262). In other words, the experience of the dynamical sublime is a *feeling* of our freedom to adhere to our fundamental moral principles no matter what threats, or for that matter blandishments, nature puts in our way.

Now we can turn to Kant's analysis of fine art and our experience of it. For Kant, all art is intentional human production that requires skill or talent, not "that which one **can** do as soon as one **knows** what should be done" (*CPJ*, §43, 5:303). Yet fine art is produced with the intention of promoting the free play of the cognitive powers. That a work of fine art must be the product of intention and yet produce the free play of the mental powers in response to it seems like a paradox, the paradox that "beautiful art, although it is certainly intentional, must nevertheless not seem intentional" (*CPJ*, §45, 5:306–7). Further, Kant also assumes that although our pleasure in beauty should be a response to the form of an object alone, fine art is paradigmatically mimetic, that is, has representational or semantic content: "A beauty of nature is a **beautiful thing**; the beauty of art is a **beautiful representation** of a thing" (*CPJ*, §48, 5:311) (although not necessarily of a beautiful thing). This too seems like a paradox. Kant aims to resolve both of these apparent paradoxes through his theory that successful works of fine art are products of genius, a natural gift that gives the rule to art (*CPJ*, §46, 5:307). A work of genius must have "spirit," which it gets through its content, typically, as Kant assumes without argument, a rational idea, indeed an idea relevant to morality, such as the idea of "the kingdom of the blessed, the kingdom of hell . . . death, envy, and all sorts of vices, as well as love, fame, etc." But in order to be beautiful, a work of art must leave room for the freedom of the imagination, and cannot present such ideas to us directly and mechanically (indeed, such ideas *cannot* be directly and adequately presented in sensible form). Instead, a work of art succeeds when it presents an "aesthetic idea," a representation of the imagination that "at least strive[s] toward something lying beyond the bounds of experience, and thus seek[s] to approximate a presentation of the concepts of reason," but also "stimulates so much thinking," such a wealth of particular "attributes" or images and incidents, "that it can never be grasped in a determinate concept, hence which aesthetically enlarges the concept itself in an unbounded way" (*CPJ*, §49, 5:314–15) – thereby stimulating a pleasurable feeling of free play among the imagination, understanding, and reason while at the same time satisfying the demand that a work of art have both a purpose and a content.

We can now turn to the specific links that Kant draws between aesthetics and ethics. I will enumerate six such links. (1) First, Kant evidently holds that objects of aesthetic experience can present morally significant ideas to us. This is obvious in the theory of aesthetic ideas, where Kant indeed assumes that works of art always have some morally relevant content. But this view takes other forms as well. In fact, Kant maintains that all forms of beauty, natural as well as artistic, can be regarded as expressions of aesthetic ideas: natural objects can suggest moral ideas to us even if such suggestion is not the product of any intentional human activity (*CPJ*, §51, 5:319). In the section entitled "The Ideal of Beauty," Kant also maintains that beauty in the human figure can be taken as "the visible expression of moral ideas, which inwardly govern human beings." Here he wants to argue that only human beauty can be taken as a unique archetype or standard for beauty, because it is the only form of beauty that expresses something absolutely and unconditionally valuable, namely, the moral autonomy of which humans alone are capable, but at the same time that there is no determinate way in which this unique value can be expressed in the human form, thus that there is always something free and therefore aesthetic in the outward expression in the human figure of the inner moral value of the human character (*CPJ*, §17, 5:235–6).

(2) The second connection I have in mind is Kant's claim that the experience of the dynamical sublime is nothing other than a feeling of the power of our own practical reason to accept the pure principle of morality

and to act in accordance with it in spite of all the threats or inducements to do otherwise that nature might place in our way. Because the experience of the dynamical sublime so centrally involves an intimation of our own capacity to be moral, Kant actually insists that "the sublime in nature is only improperly so called, and should properly be ascribed only to the manner of thinking, or rather its foundation in human nature" (*CPJ*, §30, 5:280). And while he does not want to claim that this experience is identical to explicit moral reasoning, but only a "disposition of the mind that is similar to the moral disposition" (*CPJ*, General Remark following §29, 5:268), he does argue in at least one place that the complex character of the experience of the sublime makes it the best representation in our experience of our moral situation itself:

> The object of a pure and unconditioned intellectual satisfaction is the moral law in all its power . . . and, since this power actually makes itself aesthetically knowable only through sacrifices (which is a deprivation, although in behalf of inner freedom . . .), the satisfaction on the aesthetic side (in relation to sensibility) is negative . . . but considered from the intellectual side it is positive . . . From this it follows that the intellectual, intrinsically purposive (moral good), judged aesthetically, must not be represented so much as beautiful but rather as sublime, so that it arouses more the feeling of respect (which scorns charm) than that of love and intimate affection, since human nature does not agree with that good of its own accord, but only through the dominion that reason exercises over sensibility.
>
> (*CPJ*, General Remark following §29, 5:271)

In spite of this emphatic statement, however, Kant elsewhere argues (3) that there are crucial aspects of our moral condition that are symbolized by the beautiful rather than the sublime. Here I refer to his claim that the beautiful is the symbol of the morally good because there are significant parallels between our experience of beauty and the structure of morality, and indeed that it is only insofar as the beautiful is the symbol of the morally good that we have any right not merely to predict that under ideal circumstances others should agree with our appraisals of beauty but actually to demand that they do so (*CPJ*, §59, 5:353). Kant adduces "several aspects of this analogy, while not leaving unnoticed its differences":

> 1) The beautiful pleases **immediately** (but only in reflecting intuition, not, like morality, in the concept). 2) It pleases **without any interest** (the morally good is of course necessarily connected with an interest, but not with one that precedes the judgment on the satisfaction, but rather with one that is thereby first produced). 3) The **freedom** of the imagination (thus of the sensibility of our faculty) is represented in the judging of the beautiful as in accord with the lawfulness of the understanding (in the moral judgment the freedom of the will is conceived as the

agreement of the latter with itself in accordance with universal laws of reason). 4) The subjective principle of the judging of the beautiful is represented as **universal**, i.e., valid for everyone . . . (the objective principle of morality is also declared to be universal . . .)

(*CPJ*, §59, 5:354)

The most striking of Kant's claims here is that because the experience of beauty is an experience of the freedom of the imagination in its play with the understanding, it can be taken as a palpable symbol of the freedom of the will to determine itself by moral laws that is necessary for morality but that is not itself something that can be directly experienced.[14] In other words, it is the very independence of aesthetic response from direct determination by concepts, including moral concepts, thus its disinterestedness, that makes the experience of beauty an experience of freedom that can in turn symbolize moral freedom. Presumably this can be reconciled with Kant's earlier claim that the sublime is the most appropriate symbol of morality by observing that while the experience of beauty makes the freedom of the will palpable to us, it is only the mixed experience of the sublime that brings home to feeling that this freedom must often be exercised in the face of resistance offered by our own merely natural inclinations.[15] But however this tension is to be handled, Kant's claim that the experience of beauty is a feeling of freedom can be separated from his claim that particular judgments of beauty are universally valid: the experience of beauty could symbolize the freedom of our wills even if we do not all derive this experience from the same particular objects; and if it is important to us that we have this feeling, it might suffice that we each get this experience from some object or other that strikes us as beautiful, and be unnecessary that we all get this experience from the very same objects.[16]

(4) Kant's fourth connection between the aesthetic and the ethical lies in his theory of the "intellectual interest" in the beautiful. Here Kant

[14] See *Critique of Practical Reason*, 5:29.

[15] See my "The Symbols of Freedom in Kant's Aesthetics," in Hermann Parret, ed., *Kant's Ästhetik – Kant's Aesthetics – L'esthétique de Kant* (Berlin and New York: Walter de Gruyter, 1998), pp. 338–55; chapter 9 in the present volume.

[16] Anthony Savile has attempted to block this criticism on the basis of Kant's theory of aesthetic ideas, arguing that some works of art may so uniquely exemplify specific and indispensable moral ideas that we have a right to demand that everybody experience and appreciate those specific objects (see his *Aesthetic Reconstructions: The Seminal Writings of Lessing, Kant, and Schiller* (Oxford: Basil Blackwell, 1987), p. 171). The idea that any indispensable moral idea could be aesthetically realized only in one particular work of art seems implausible.

argues that although our basic pleasure in a beautiful object must be independent of any antecedent interest in its existence, we may add a further layer of pleasure to that basic experience if the existence of beautiful objects suggests some more generally pleasing fact about our situation in the world. What Kant then argues is that since in the case of morality

> it also interests reason that the ideas (for which it produces an immediate interest in the moral feeling) also have objective reality, i.e., that nature should at least show some trace or give a sign that it contains in itself some sort of ground for assuming a lawful correspondence of its products with our satisfaction . . . reason must take an interest in every manifestation in nature of a correspondence similar to this; consequently the mind cannot reflect on the beauty of **nature** without finding itself at the same time to be interested in it.
>
> (*CPJ*, §42, 5:300)

Kant's claim is that it is of interest to practical reason that nature be hospitable to its objectives, so we take pleasure in *any* evidence that nature is amenable to our objectives, even when those are not specifically moral; and the natural existence of beauty is such evidence, because the experience of beauty is itself an unexpected fulfillment of our most basic cognitive objective.

(5) Kant's fifth claim is that aesthetic experience is conducive to proper moral conduct itself. In the third *Critique* he states that "The beautiful prepares us to love something, even nature, without interest; the sublime, to esteem it, even contrary to our (sensible) interest" (*CPJ*, General Remark following §29, 5:267), where being able to love without any personal interest and to esteem even contrary to our own interest are necessary preconditions of proper moral conduct. Kant makes a similar point in his later *Metaphysics of Morals* (1797) when he argues that "a propensity to wanton destruction of what is *beautiful* in inanimate nature," even though we do not owe any moral duties directly to anything other than ourselves and other human beings, nevertheless "weakens or uproots that feeling in [us] which, though not of itself moral, is still a disposition of sensibility that greatly promotes morality or at least prepares the way for it: the disposition, namely, to love something (e.g., beautiful crystal formations, the indescribable beauty of plants) even apart from any intention to use it."[17] As in the case of the intellectual interest in beauty, these claims that aesthetic experience can be conducive to proper moral conduct would

[17] *Metaphysics of Morals*, Doctrine of Virtue §17, 6:643; translation from Mary J. Gregor, *Immanuel Kant, Practical Philosophy*, (Cambridge: Cambridge University Press, 1996), p. 564.

seem to be problematic for Kant if interpreted to mean that aesthetic experience can substitute for or even strengthen pure respect for the moral law as our fundamental motivation to be moral. If Kant is to be consistent, he needs to argue that aesthetic experiences can prepare us for successful moral *conduct* without substituting for pure moral *motivation*. How he might do this is a question I shall take up in the sequel.

(6) Finally, in the last section of the "Critique of the Aesthetic Power of Judgment," its brief "Appendix on the methodology of taste," Kant suggests that the cultivation or realization of common standards of taste in a society can be conducive to the discovery of the more general "art of the reciprocal communication of the ideas of the most educated part" of a society "with the cruder, the coordination of the breadth and refinement of the former with the natural simplicity and originality of the latter" (*CPJ*, §60, 5:356), where this art is apparently necessary to the realization of the goal of "**lawful** sociability," or the establishment of a stable polity on the basis of principles of justice rather than sheer force. Thus Kant suggests that aesthetic experience can be conducive to the development of sound politics as well as personal ethics, although the two are of course not unconnected, since Kant is a political moralist who believes that we have a moral duty to establish a just state, not merely a prudential interest in doing so.[18]

So in spite of the disinterestedness of aesthetic response, indeed on the basis of it, Kant recognized a variety of ways in which aesthetic experience is conducive to moral conduct. How can we make this catalogue theoretically perspicuous, and how can we reconcile it with the purity of moral motivation demanded by Kantian ethics? Kant himself does not explicitly address these questions. Indeed, although he begins the third *Critique* by insisting that we must be able to "throw a bridge" across the "great chasm" that separates the "theoretical cognition of nature" from the "laws of freedom," and that this will somehow be accomplished by aesthetic (and teleological) judgment (*CPJ*, Introduction IX, 5:195), it is not clear what chasm he has in mind. The *Critique of Practical Reason* had argued that although we cannot have theoretical knowledge of the freedom of our will to choose whatever morality requires of it, we can confidently infer the reality of this freedom from our immediate awareness of our obligation under the moral law combined with the principle that

[18] See my "Kant's Deductions of the Principles of Right," in Mark Timmons, ed., *Kant's Metaphysics of Morals: Interpretative Essays* (Oxford: Oxford University Press, 2002), pp. 23–64.

if we ought to do something then we must be able to do it;[19] and the second *Critique* had also argued that since morality imposes an end upon us, namely, that of realizing the highest good, the greatest happiness consistent with the greatest virtue, we must believe this to be possible, and thus must postulate "a supreme cause of nature having a causality in keeping with the moral disposition."[20] If Kant has already established that on the basis of our awareness of our obligations under the moral law we can be confident that we have free will and that all of the laws of nature are at least consistent with our realization of the ends commanded by the moral law, just what more needs to be done in order to throw a bridge between the theoretical cognition of nature and the laws of freedom?

Let me answer this question by way of a contrast. Henry Allison has recently suggested that Kant wants the moral significance of the aesthetic to provide a solution to the problem of radical evil.[21] The problem of radical evil, which Kant described only in *Religion within the Boundaries of Mere Reason* three years after the third *Critique*, is that although we all know what morality requires of us, we often choose to do something immoral anyway. Allison assumes that this is because we are unsure of the possibility of succeeding in doing what morality requires of us, and the assurance that beauty provides us that nature is amenable to our moral objectives will remove this uncertainty. This seems to be both too narrow an account of Kant's links between aesthetics and morality and too optimistic an account. It is too optimistic, because for Kant the freedom to choose evil is one and the same with the freedom to choose good, and the fact that we sometimes use this freedom to choose evil can be neither explained nor remedied. Since we can only be good freely, nothing, thus no amount of aesthetic experience or education, can force us to be good. And this is surely a realistic restriction on any account of the ethical value of the aesthetic. Second, Allison's account is too narrow because it overlooks the variety of ways in which Kant thinks that the aesthetic can support our efforts to be moral without forcing us to use our freedom to be good rather than evil.

I propose the following, broader approach. Kant clearly recognizes that in order to act morally, we need to (i) understand the moral law and what it requires of us; (ii) believe that we are in fact free to choose to

[19] See *Critique of Practical Reason*, §6, 5:30, and *Religion within the Boundaries of Mere Reason* (1793), 6:62, 66–7.

[20] *Critique of Practical Reason*, Dialectic, 5:125; translation from Gregor, p. 240.

[21] See Henry E. Allison, *Kant's Theory of Taste: A Reading of the Critique of Aesthetic Judgment* (Cambridge: Cambridge University Press, 2001), pp. 230–5.

do what it requires of us rather than to do what all our other motives, which can be subsumed under the rubric of self-love,[22] might suggest to us; (iii) believe that the objectives or ends that morality imposes upon us can actually be achieved, and (iv) have an adequate motivation for our attempt to do what morality requires of us in lieu of the mere desirability of particular goals it might happen to license or even impose in particular circumstances. All of these together constitute the conditions of the possibility of morality. Kant also thinks that at one level all these conditions are satisfied by pure practical reason itself: (i) the very form of pure practical reason gives us the moral law;[23] (ii) this first "fact" of pure practical reason implies the reality of our freedom to be moral by means of the principle that we must be able to do what we know we ought to do;[24] (iii) we can postulate by pure practical reason alone that the laws of nature are compatible with the demands of morality because both laws ultimately have a common author;[25] and finally (iv) pure respect for the moral law itself can be a sufficient motivation for us to attempt to carry it out (and attempts to do so have "moral worth" only when that is our motivation).[26] But Kant also recognizes that we are sensuous as well as rational creatures, and need sensuous as well as rational presentation and confirmation of the conditions of the possibility of morality. He explicitly acknowledges this three years after the *Critique of the Power of Judgment*, when in *Religion within the Boundaries of Mere Reason* he asserts "the natural need of all human beings to demand for even the highest concepts and grounds of reason something that *the senses can hold on to*, some confirmation from experience or the like."[27] The third *Critique* and the *Religion* should in fact be seen as part of a common project to show how the morality of pure reason can be represented in our actual experience. In the *Religion*, Kant argues that it is necessary for human beings to represent the "invisible church" required for realization of the kingdom of ends by means of an historical "ecclesiastical faith"; in the third *Critique*, the six links between aesthetics and morality that we have found provide

[22] See *Critique of Practical Reason*, Theorem II, 5:22; Gregor, p. 155.
[23] See, for example, *Critique of Practical Reason*, Theorem III, 5:27; Gregor, p. 160.
[24] See *Critique of Practical Reason*, Problem II, Remark, 5:30; Gregor, pp. 163–4.
[25] See *Critique of Pracitcal Reason*, Dialectic, Section V: "The Existence of God as a Postulate of Pure Practical Reason," 5:124–32; Gregor, pp. 239–46.
[26] See *Groundwork for the Metaphysics of Morals*, Section I, especially 400–1; Gregor, pp. 55–6.
[27] Immanuel Kant, *Religion within the Boundaries of Mere Reason*, 6:109; in Kant, *Religion and Rational Theology*, edited and translated by Allen W. Wood and George Di Giovanni (Cambridge: Cambridge University Press, 1996), p. 142.

sensuous representation of what we also know in a purely intellectual way through pure practical reason.

(i) First, the sensuous presentation of moral ideas, above all through aesthetic ideas in the case of works of artistic genius, but perhaps also through the image of a maximally coherent moral character that is expressed by the beautiful human figure as the "ideal of beauty," offer us a sensuous presentation of the moral law itself – which is ultimately the requirement of rational consistency among our own exercises of free choice and between our own acts of free choice and those of others[28] – as well as of other thoughts connected with the very idea of morality, such as the blessedness that comes from fulfilling the demands of morality, the contempt that is deserved by their rejection, and the like – for so might we interpret various of the specific examples of rational ideas expressed through aesthetic ideas that Kant gives (see *CPJ*, §49, 5:314).

(ii) Second, the feeling of our freedom to choose to live up to the demands of morality in spite of all the threats of nature that we experience in the dynamical sublime, as well as the tendency to interpret the beautiful as a symbol of the morally good, are ways in which the freedom of will that we can intellectually infer from our consciousness of the moral law becomes palpable to us as sensory creatures. In the latter case, Kant explicitly argues that "to demonstrate the reality of our concepts, intuitions are always required," and that even ideas of pure reason that go beyond the limits of our sensibility need at least a symbolic "hypotyposis" or presentation that can make them sensible (*CPJ*, §59, 5:351). It is our nature, in other words, to seek sensible symbols even of that which is too abstract to be fully grasped by the senses, and just as we may use the image of a handmill to represent the despotism of absolute monarchy, so we may use the sensuous experience of the freedom of the imagination to represent the indubitable but intangible fact of the freedom of our will (*ibid.*, p. 354).

(iii) Third, the hint from the experience of beauty that nature is amenable to the realization of our objectives is sensible evidence for that which is otherwise only a postulate of pure practical reason, namely, the consistency of the laws of nature and the law of freedom. Kant calls the pleasure that we take in such sensory evidence the basis of an "intellectual interest" in beauty, presumably because the fact that beauty confirms

[28] See especially Kant, *Moral Philosophy from the lecture notes of George Ludwig Collins* (Winter Semester, 1784–5), 27:345–7; in Immanuel Kant, *Lectures on Ethics*, eds., Peter Heath and J. B. Schneewind (Cambridge: Cambridge University Press, 1997), pp. 126–8.

for us is of interest to us as agents with pure practical reason, and does not interest us in the merely empirical way that the possibility for self-aggrandizement or harmless socializing through the possession of valuable works of art does. Nevertheless, the evidence for the amenability of nature to our objectives that the existence of beauty offers us is evidence for our senses, and thus supplements the postulate of pure practical reason. This thought, while not, as Allison thinks, Kant's only link between aesthetic experience and morality, is certainly important to him. It is indeed the central thesis of the "Critique of the Teleological Power of Judgment" that the experience of the internal systematicity of organisms inevitably leads us to view the whole world as a moral system, but a moral system that we must create by the exercise of our own freedom (see especially *CPJ*, §§82–84, 5:425–36); thus what ties the two halves of the third *Critique* together is precisely the idea that the experience of natural beauty on the one hand and of the purposiveness of organisms on the other hand both offer us what we experience as evidence rather than a mere postulate of pure practical reason that the system of morality can be realized in nature.[29]

(iv) Finally, when Kant suggests that the experience of beauty prepares us to love disinterestedly and that of the sublime to esteem even contrary to our own interest, and that aesthetic experience may help bridge the gaps between the different classes and interest-groups that inevitably arise in any complex polity, he is suggesting that aesthetic experience can actually help us to act as morality requires.

Two objections seem obvious here. First, it may seem strange that Kant should require any evidence at all of the realizability of objectives in morality itself, since he so famously makes moral worth a matter of the purity of our motivation rather than the realization of desirable consequences through our action.[30] The reply is that this is just a restriction on morally praiseworthy *motivation:* what Kant holds is that we deserve esteem insofar as we are *motivated* to act by our respect for the moral law

[29] I have interpreted the argument of the "Critique of the Teleological Power of Judgment" along these lines in a number of places; see especially "From Nature to Morality: Kant's New Argument in the 'Critique of Teleological Judgment'," in Hans Friedrich Fulda and Jürgen Stolzenberg, eds., *Architektonik und System in der Philosophie Kants* (Hamburg: Felix Meiner Verlag, 2001), pp. 375–404, and "Purpose in Nature: What is Living and What is Dead in Kant's Teleology?" in Dietmar Heidemann and Kristina Engelhard, eds., *Warum Kant heute? Systematische Bedeutung und Rezeption seiner Philosophie in der Gegenwart* (Berlin: Walter de Gruyter, 2003), pp. 383–413.

[30] See *Groundwork for the Metaphysics of Morals* (1785), Section I, 4:401.

itself, but that what the moral law commands us actually *to do* is to treat every person as an unconditionally valuable end, and in the name of that goal to further the *realization* of their freely and lawfully chosen particular ends. Then he naturally supposes that it is rational for us to attempt to do this only if we believe it to be at least possible that we shall succeed in doing so; and in the absence of some grounds for this belief the irrationality of attempting to do what morality requires of us would necessarily undercut our motivation to be moral even though that motivation is not itself an immediate desire for the consequences of our actions.[31] That nature is amenable to the realization of our objectives, something of which the existence of natural beauty gives us at least a hint, is thus a condition of the rationality of morality itself.[32]

The more difficult problem is that Kant seems to suggest that aesthetic experience can lead to the formation of feelings that can serve as *motivations* to do what morality requires us to do in various particular circumstances. How could such a suggestion be reconciled with Kant's premise that respect for the idea of duty itself is a sufficient motivation to be moral, and the only motivation that can make us morally worthy (the premise that we have just seen is compatible with the thesis that morality requires us to attempt to realize the highest good)?

There are two approaches to this problem. First, one can argue that Kant adduces the purity of motivation from all mere inclination that

[31] I have analyzed this argument, and criticized it on the ground that rationality may require only the *absence* of any evidence for the *impossibility* of achieving the intended goal, in several places, including "From a Practical Point of View: Kant's Conception of a Postulate of Pure Practical Reason," chapter 10 of my *Kant on Freedom, Law, and Happiness* (Cambridge: Cambridge University Press, 2000), and "Ends of Reason and Ends of Nature: The Place of Teleology in Kant's Ethics," *Journal of Value Inquiry* 36 (2002): 161–86. For a similar criticism, see also J. D. McFarland, *Kant's Concept of Teleology* (Edinburgh: Edinburgh University Press, 1970), p. 122.

[32] Kant's restriction of this evidentiary role to natural beauty seems unnecessary. Since he argues that artistic beauty is a product of genius, and genius is a gift of nature, he should recognize that artistic as well as natural beauty is evidence of nature's amenability to our own objectives, although in this case nature, as it were, working within our own skins rather than outside them. Kant seems to have been worried that art can be put to morally perverse rather than beneficial use – we can all too easily take the possession of beautiful art as a basis for pride and self-aggrandizement (see *CPJ*, §42, 5:298), and because art is to some degree the product of intention, there is always the danger that the audience for art can be manipulated by the intentions of the artists or of others working through the artist. Nevertheless, these are dangers that can be avoided, and when our pleasure in a work of artistic genius is free and pure, then it does seem as if we should take the existence of artistic genius itself as a sign of nature's amenability to our own objectives, and thus as a ground for pleasure.

is required for moral worth just in order to determine the character of the moral law – it must be a law that someone actually free of all inclination could act upon, thus a merely formal law.[33] But once that law and particular obligations that follow from it have been identified, it is surely our duty always to comply with it, thereby avoiding moral condemnation, out of whatever motivation to do so is actually available to us, even if the kind of motivation that is available to us will not win us any special moral praise. Thus we would have a duty to develop morally useful feelings from aesthetic experience even if fulfilling our moral obligations by using those feelings as motivations will only spare us moral contempt but not earn us moral esteem. This must be at least partly right, since it is certainly our duty always to observe the moral law, even when the pure motivation of respect for the law is not available to us and we cannot earn any special esteem by doing so.

But instead of looking at aesthetically induced feelings just as second-best motives for fulfilling our duty, we can also look at the motivation of respect for duty as a *higher-order* motivation, which grounds our commitment to do what the moral law requires of us in any and all particular circumstances and therefore gives us a motive to develop whatever *particular* feelings and dispositions will enable us to perform the morally requisite actions in those particular circumstances, including aesthetically induced feelings if they turn out to be effective for this purpose. Kant suggests such a model when he discusses feelings of benevolence and sympathy in the "Doctrine of Virtue" of the *Metaphysics of Morals*. There he suggests that nature has "implanted in human beings receptivity" to "sympathetic" feelings as *means* by which we can accomplish the moral end of beneficence to others, and thus that we have a "particular, although only conditional, duty" to use such feelings "as a means to promote active and rational benevolence,"[34] or to use them "as so many means to sympathy based on moral principles."[35] There are two thoughts here. First, although the general motivation of respect for duty is what must lead us to make the fulfillment of the moral law our overarching objective, and commits us to particular duties such as beneficence, we are moved to act in particular circumstances by more concrete feelings, and thus must develop feelings, and especially develop dispositions to feeling that are natural to us – dispositions to sympathy, but also dispositions

[33] See *Groundwork for the Metaphysics of Morals*, 4:402; Gregor, pp. 56–7.
[34] *Metaphysics of Morals*, "Doctrine of Virtue" §34, 6:456; Gregor, p. 575.
[35] *Metaphysics of Morals*, "Doctrine of Virtue" §35, 6:457; Gregor, p. 575.

to admire natural beauty – that can serve as such means. But second, this duty is always "conditional" – that is, our sympathy must be "based on moral principles" – for it always remains for reason to check whether what our feelings, even our most benevolent and beneficial feelings, prompt us to do in any particular situation is in fact morally appropriate. The idea would be that we cannot act without feelings, but that we cannot act on feelings alone, because feelings, no matter how well-cultivated, may not always be fully responsive to the moral situation at hand, and need the guidance of moral principles for their proper exercise. We should not act on our benevolent feelings, whether developed through aesthetic experience or otherwise, in cases where our so doing might, for example, help another to violate his own moral duty.[36] Natural feelings, including those prompted by or developed out of aesthetic experience, may be necessary conditions for performing particular actions required by morality, but can never be sufficient conditions – they always require the guidance of moral principles.

But Kant never argues that any feelings stimulated by aesthetic experience are a *necessary* condition for the fulfillment of our moral obligations – indeed, given the parallel project of the *Religion*, he could not very well think this. And although he does insist that we always need some form of sensible presentation for even the most abstract ideas of reason, and that our feeling of the freedom of the imagination in the experience of beauty can serve as such a symbol for the intangible freedom of the will postulated by morality, he never says that it is the only possible sensible symbol of that freedom – his reinterpretation of the central symbol of Christianity precludes this,[37] and the later discussion of sympathetic feeling to which we have just appealed to show how feelings might be morally appropriate means to the accomplishment of ends enjoined upon us by the pure motivation of respect for duty itself assumes that there are sympathetic feelings that are directly "implanted" in us by nature rather than produced through aesthetic experience and education. Thus, although Kant clearly supposes that dispositions flowing from aesthetic experience *can* be morally beneficial and should be preserved and cultivated

[36] In Barbara Herman's famous example, we should not let ourselves act on our benevolent feelings toward something struggling with a heavy burden when that person is actually a thief attempting to remove a valuable object from a museum. See Barbara Herman, "On the Value of Acting from the Motive of Duty," in her *The Practice of Moral Judgment* (Cambridge, Mass.: Harvard University Press, 1993), pp. 1–22, at pp. 4–5.

[37] See especially *Religion*, 6:60–2, 82; Wood and Di Giovanni, pp. 103–5, 121.

for that reason,[38] he could not mean to argue that such feelings are the *only* morally beneficial feelings, or even necessary, let alone sufficient conditions for the fulfillment of our moral obligations. These will both be points to keep in mind as we turn to the contemporaneous work of Archibald Alison.

II. Alison

Archibald Alison, a clergyman rather than a professor, first published his *Essays on the Nature and Principles of Taste* in the same year as Kant's *Critique of the Power of Judgment*, and did not know of Kant's book, or apparently of any German aesthetic theory, either while he was writing his own, or twenty-one years later, when he was preparing it for a second edition. Nevertheless, it is fruitful to compare his work to Kant's, because his views are so precisely opposed to Kant's. While Kant attempted to find an *a priori* principle for judgments of taste, Alison self-consciously attempted to use a strictly empiricist method of argument; while Kant insisted that "charm and emotion" were not any part of the basis for a pure judgment of taste, Alison argued that "simple" emotions such as love and awe are at the heart of every aesthetic experience, and indeed every aspect of every aesthetic experience; and while Kant held that aesthetic experience could be conducive to moral development, but only indirectly and only when constrained by independently held moral principles, Alison held that the aesthetic experience of emotions is directly beneficial to moral development without the need of any independent moral principles. In what follows, I leave aside methodological issues and focus on the latter two contrasts.

Alison holds that at the heart of every aesthetic experience, whether of a natural object or a work of art, there is some particular emotion, such as cheerfulness, gladness, tenderness, pity, melancholy, admiration, and feelings of power, majesty, and terror.[39] Following Burke (in this regard like Kant) he assumes that these particular emotions fall into the two groups of emotions of beauty and of sublimity, beautiful objects being those that produce such feelings as cheerfulness and gladness while sublime objects produce such feelings as melancholy, admiration, or terror: "Thus, when we feel either the beauty or sublimity of natural scenery," for

[38] See, again, *Metaphysics of Morals*, "Doctrine of Virtue" §17, 6:443; Gregor, p. 564.
[39] Archibald Alison, *Essays on the Nature and Principles of Taste* (second edition) (Edinburgh: Bell & Bradfute, 1811), Vol. I, p. 75. This work will be abbreviated "*ENPT*."

example, "Trains of pleasing or of solemn thought arise spontaneously within our minds" (*ENPT*, Vol. I, p. 5). Alison argues that such emotions are not produced by their objects immediately, but only by trains of associations:

> When any object, either of sublimity or beauty, is presented to the mind, I believe every man is conscious of a train of thought being immediately awakened in his imagination.... The simple perception of the object, we frequently find, is insufficient to excite these emotions, unless it is accompanied with this operation of mind, unless, according to common expression, our imagination is seized, and our fancy busied in the pursuit of all those trains of thought, which are allied to this character or expression.
>
> (*ENPT*, Vol. I, pp. 4–5)

Why the emotion should be connected with its object by a train of associations is complicated. Alison begins with the assumption that the immediately perceptible properties of objects do not directly arouse our emotions, but that our emotions are instead aroused only by more abstract properties that what is immediately perceived may in some way signify: delicate or vigorous colors, for example, are not intrinsically pleasing, but please us because we associate them with youth or health. So the mind needs to traverse at least one link of association – recall some experience of an association of a perceptible property that is not obviously freighted with emotion with some other property that is – before it can experience the object now before it with an emotion. But Alison also assumes that the chains of association intervening between the present object and the felt emotion will be considerably longer than one link. There appear to be at least two reasons for this. First, Alison holds that multiple associations with the perceived object multiply or strengthen its emotional impact: thus, experiences like the "view of the house where one was born" or of "the school were one was educated" "recall so many images of past happiness and past affections, they are connected with so many strong or valued emotions, and lead altogether to so long a train of feelings and recollections, that there is hardly any scene which one ever beholds with so much rapture" (*ENPT*, Vol. I, pp. 23–4). But further, Alison also suggests that we enjoy the activity of association, the play of imagination itself, so that the pleasure we take in the play of associations intensifies the core emotion in any particular aesthetic experience:

> That there is a pleasure also annexed, by the constitution of our nature, to the exercise of imagination, is a proposition which seems to require very little illustration. In common opinion, the employment of the imagination is always

supposed to communicate delight; when we yield to its power, we are considered as indulging in a secret pleasure, and every superiority in the strength or sensibility of this faculty is believed to be attended with a similar increase in the happiness of human life.

(*ENPT*, Vol. I, pp. 163–4)

That Alison ascribes this view of the pleasure of imagination to "common opinion" might suggest that he himself is about to reject it, but he does not; instead, he appeals to the authority of no less than Jean-Jacques Rousseau to confirm it, quoting lengthy extracts from the *Reveries of a Solitary Walker* in which Rousseau describes the pleasure of letting the mind wander freed at least temporarily from its ordinary troubles and passions.[40] Alison argues that this pleasure in the play of the imagination is both a necessary condition for the aesthetic experience of emotion and that it intensifies it: "when this exercise of the imagination is not produced, the Emotions of Taste are unfelt, and . . . when it is increased, these Emotions are increased with it" (*ENPT*, Vol. I, p. 169). Alison concludes that "The pleasure, therefore, which accompanies the Emotions of Taste, may be considered not as a simple, but as a complex pleasure; and as arising not from any separate and peculiar Sense, but from the union of the pleasure of SIMPLE EMOTION, with that which is annexed, by the constitution of the human mind, to the Exercise of IMAGINATION" (*ENPT*, Vol. I, pp. 169–70).

Alison's recognition of our pleasure in the exercise of the imagination seems to parallel Kant's explanation of our pleasure in beauty as due to the free play of imagination and understanding. However, Alison not only regards this pleasure primarily as intensifying our pleasure in the arousal of emotions through association, which Kant does not regard as any part of properly aesthetic experience at all, but also, unlike Kant, does not regard this pleasure as ever being occasioned by any purely cognitive play with the formal properties of objects. He devotes a great deal of his treatise to the beauty and sublimity of forms,[41] and what he argues

[40] *ENPT*, Vol. I, pp. 165–9; Alison's extracts are from the *Reveries of the Solitary Walker*, Fifth and Seventh Walks; in *The Collected Writings of Rousseau*, eds. Roger D. Masters and Chirstopher Kelly, Vol. 8 (Hanover and London: University Press of New England, 2000), pp. 41–8, 57–68. A characteristic passage from Rousseau is this: "I delighted in this ocular recreation which in misfortune relaxes, amuses, distracts the mind, and suspends the troubled feeling. . . . Fragrant odors, intense colors, the most elegant shapes seem to vie with each other for the right of capturing our attention. To give oneself up to such delicious sensations, it is necessary only to love pleasure" (p. 59).

[41] *ENPT*, Essay II, "Of the Sublimity and Beauty of the Material World," Chapter IV, "Of Forms," Vol. I, pp. 314–76 and Vol. II, pp. 3–205.

here is precisely that even the pleasure we take in features of the form of objects is based on our emotional associations with those forms. For example, we experience tender and affectionate feelings toward gentle curves not because of our affection for these geometrical forms as such, but because we associate them with infancy and youth in organisms of all kinds, which we love, perhaps further because of our love of infancy and youth in our own kind (see *ENPT*, Vol. I, pp. 331–3). We also take pleasure in such forms because they make us think of ease rather than difficulty (*ENPT*, Vol. I, p. 334). Conversely, "forms which distinguish bodies that are connected in our minds with ideas of danger or power . . . great duration . . . splendor or magnificence . . . awe or solemnity, are in general sublime" (*ENPT*, Vol. I, pp. 321–3). Alison's model is thus something like this: we take pleasure in objects that have certain emotional associations for us, and even in features of the form of such objects that themselves have emotional associations for us. For us to experience these pleasures, the imagination needs to be able to play freely, so that the chains of association necessary to experience these emotions can be played out and also because the pleasure that we take in the play of the imagination itself can intensify our pleasure in these emotional associations. But it is the emotional associations themselves that are the basis of our aesthetic experience.

The centrality of emotion in aesthetic experience is evident in another aspect of Alison's theory that might also initially seem reminiscent of Kant. Early in his exposition, Alison claims that there are two distinctive features of the chains of association that produce our pleasures in the beautiful and sublime: first, that "the ideas or conceptions of which they are composed are ideas of emotion," but second, "that there is always some general principle of connection which pervades the whole, and gives them some certain and definite character" (*ENPT*, Vol. I, p. 77). The trains of thought "which take place in the mind, upon the prospect of objects of sublimity and beauty," differ from ordinary trains of thought, "1 *st*, In respect of the Nature of the ideas of which [they are] composed, by their being ideas productive of Emotion; and, 2 *dly*, In respect of their Succession, by their being distinguished by some general principle of connection, which subsists through the whole extent of the train" (*ENPT*, Vol. I, p. 78). Here Alison might appear to be arguing that we take pleasure in the unity of the train of association itself, a pleasure in form that would be distinct from our pleasure in experiencing particular emotions. But he is not; rather, what he argues is that our pleasure in the emotions aroused by our train of associations in the experience of a particular object must have an *emotional* consistency, or that the whole train of associations must arouse a *single* emotion. This is the point of the examples that he offers, passages from the works of even the greatest poets such as Homer, Virgil, Horace, and Milton, which suffer the "defect" of a bit, often a concluding line, that strikes a different emotional tone than all that has gone before (*ENPT*, Vol. I, pp. 135–47). The only exception to his rule that Alison countenances is the case in which "the Emotion is violent and demands relief, or faint and requires support, or long-continued and requires repose" (*ENPT*, Vol. I, p. 149). Alison does not explain why we ordinarily require emotional consistency in an aesthetic experience, but the exceptions he allows would be consistent with an essentially quantitative explanation, that is, that he takes us to be interested in maximizing the intensity and duration of our emotional experience, which we can ordinarily do best by maintaining emotional consistency but which might sometimes require an element of variation. He seems to have no thought that we might enjoy a play among contrasting emotions for its own sake, that even within a single work variety might be the spice of life.

So much for Alison's analysis of aesthetic experience; I now turn to his much briefer account of the ethical significance of such experience, about which I will make two points. (1) First, Alison's theory that our responses to beautiful and sublime objects depend upon our emotional associations with those objects implies that our responses to and judgments of such objects will not be universal, for surely we do not all have the same emotional associations with objects. Alison recognizes this implication, and observes that emotional associations range from those that are widely shared among all human beings, or "strongly marked in every period of the history of human thought," to those that depend upon circumstances of "education" or "fortune" that may be shared among groups of humans but not among all of us at any one time or throughout history, to those that are thoroughly "*individual*," and which give to "material qualities or appearances a character of interest which is solely the result of our own memory and affections" (*ENPT*, Vol. II, pp. 421–2). But where many thinkers of the period, Kant foremost among them, would have seen such variation in our emotional associations as a threat to the universal validity of our judgments of taste, Alison embraces it. For he recognizes that human emotional associations vary because human circumstances vary, and the fact that different people can take aesthetic pleasure in different objects is therefore nothing less than "the means of diffusing happiness (in so far as it depends upon the pleasures of taste), with a very impartial equality among mankind." If our "pleasures of taste" in objects were *not* grounded in emotional associations formed by our particular circumstances, then these pleasures would not be available to many of us much of the time. "If the Beauty or Sublimity of the objects of the material world arose from any original and determinate law of our nature, by which *certain* colours, or sounds, or forms, &c. were necessarily and solely beautiful, then there must of necessity have followed a great disproportion between the happiness of mankind, by the very constitution of their nature" (*ENPT*, Vol. II, p. 425). Alison also argues that the variety in aesthetic responses that ensues from its dependence upon emotional associations that are themselves variable is a "great source of the progress and improvement of human ART in every department, whether mechanical or liberal" (*ENPT*, Vol. II, p. 430). If there were fixed standards of taste, then "the common artist would hardly dare to deviate from them, even when he felt the propriety of it" (*ENPT*, Vol. II, p. 431); but the absence of such fixed standards is a challenge to human invention, which constantly lead to the development of new, sometimes successful, and sometimes even widely enjoyed works of art. Now Alison does not suggest that this variation in the pleasures of taste itself in any way contributes to the development of morality. But we might say that it has moral value: since the variability of tastes and the possibility of ever new invention in the arts increase rather than diminish the availability of the pleasures of taste, we could argue that any attempt to impose uniformity upon tastes and a restrictive canon upon the arts would be an unnecessary and even immoral restriction of the availability of the pleasures of taste.

(2) What Alison does explicitly maintain – and this is my second point – is that aesthetic experience directly produces moral emotions, and even that these moral emotions are sufficient to develop moral character. He asserts that the beauties and sublimities of the natural world, the beautiful and the sublime in the fine arts, and the beauties of the human countenance and form all have this effect. First, "While the objects of the material world are made to attract our infant eyes, there are latent ties by which they reach our hearts; and wherever they afford us delight, they are always the signs or expressions of higher qualities, by which our moral sensibilities are called forth.... There is not one of those features of scenery which is not fitted to awaken us to moral emotion" (*ENPT*, Vol. II, pp. 436–7). Then he claims about works of art that if they affect us by "being expressive of fineness, delicacy, gentleness, majesty, solemnity, &c. they then awaken corresponding emotions in our bosoms, and give exercise to some of the most virtuous feelings of our nature" (*ENPT*, Vol. II, p. 438). And finally, when we respond to expressions of the human

countenance or postures of the human form that "can awaken admiration or excite sensibility," then "we share in some measure in those high dispositions, the expressions of which we contemplate," and "our own bosoms glow with kindred sentiments" (*ENPT*, Vol. II, pp. 339–40). For all these reasons, Alison insists that "It is on this account that it is of so much consequence in the education of the Young, to encourage their instinctive taste for the Beauty and Sublimity of Nature," which will be the foundation for their appreciation of beauty and sublimity in the fine arts and in their fellow men: "amid the hours of curiosity and delight," their taste for beauty and sublimity will "awaken those latent feelings of benevolence and of sympathy, from which all the moral or intellectual greatness of man finally arises" (*ENPT*, Vol. II, pp. 446–7).

It is easy to raise objections against Alison's confident assertions. We can all readily imagine individuals with highly developed aesthetic sensibilities who are morally indifferent or even callous toward their fellow human beings. Kant seemed to fear that "virtuosi of taste . . . are not only often but even usually vain, obstinate, and given to corrupting passions" (*CPJ*, §42, 5:298); and we do not have to go that far, but can easily imagine – or recall – refined fanciers of the arts who are willing to rob a museum, or pillage whole cities, to enrich their own collections. Even if the experience of natural or artistic beauty and sublimity sometimes or often produces beneficial moral sentiments, it does not seem always to do so. There are also more specific objections to Alison's position. First, although Plato's fear that the artistic depiction of moral weakness would weaken rather than strengthen the character of his guardians of the state and Aristotle's question about why we take pleasure in the depiction of unpleasant things were widely debated in the eighteenth-century, often in the form of the "problem of tragedy,"[42] Alison does not even raise these qualms; he seems to assume without argument that aesthetic experiences will always produce morally beneficial and never morally deleterious emotions. Second, there seems to be a danger of circularity in Alison's theory: while Alison concludes that aesthetic experiences can engender moral emotions, he has argued throughout his work that aesthetic experience depends upon antecedent emotional associations; and won't these associations often, if not always, already involve moral sentiments? He has claimed, for example, that sublime objects may please us because they suggest power or majesty; but won't we take pleasure in the suggestion of

[42] See, for example, Hume's essay "Of Tragedy," in David Hume, *Essays Moral, Political and Literary* (Oxford: Oxford University Press, 1963), pp. 221–30.

power or majesty because we have favorable associations with the thought that power and majesty may be put to morally good use? Finally, it is the conclusion of Alison's entire work, as we have seen, that aesthetic experience awakens "those latent feelings of benevolence and sympathy from which all the moral or intellectual greatness of man finally arises," and thus lays "the foundation of an early and a manly piety." While this statement does not assume that aesthetic experience is the only way to awaken those moral sentiments, it does assume that aesthetic experience always does so. That, as we have already observed, is problematic; but what is even more problematic is Alison's assumption here that the feelings of benevolence and sympathy are sufficient to produce *all* the moral or intellectual greatness of man, that is, that moral success needs only moral sentiments and no independent moral principles. Alison's position rests firmly on the moral sense theory of eighteenth-century Britain, and must stand or fall with that moral philosophy itself.

III. Santayana

George Santayana published *The Sense of Beauty* in 1896, just over a century after the works of Kant and Alison. The book eschews almost all historical references, but was based on a course on aesthetics that Santayana gave at Harvard from 1892 to 1895, and is in fact clearly intended to take a stance on many of the great issues of modern aesthetics. Without naming names, Santayana dismisses the grand aesthetic theories of such nineteenth-century metaphysicians as Schelling, Hegel, and Schopenhauer with the remark that "Such value as belongs to metaphysical derivations of the nature of the beautiful, comes to them not because they explain our primary feelings, which they cannot do, but because they express, and in fact constitute, some of our later appreciations" (*SB*, p. 7) – in other words, if you already look at the world through the lense of some metaphysical theory, then you can incorporate aesthetic experience into it, but aesthetic experience itself will never compel you to adopt any such metaphysical theory.[43] Instead, Santayana adopts a position that is much closer to that of eighteenth-century thought. While his theory is often reduced to the slogan that "Beauty is pleasure regarded as the quality

43 For a contemporary critique of the metaphysical or "speculative" tradition in the philosophy of art, see Jean-Marie Schaeffer, *Art of the Modern Age: Philosophy of Art from Kant to Heidegger*, translated by Steven Rendell (Princeton: Princeton University Press, 2000). Schaeffer has friendly things to say about more recent American anti-metaphysicians such as Nelson Goodman, but unfortunately does not discuss Santayana.

of a thing" (*SB*, p. 31) – a remark that clearly echoes Kant's claim that even though our judgment of an object's beauty is based entirely on the pleasure that we feel in that object, because we take that pleasure to be universally valid we can speak "as if beauty were a property of the object" (*CPJ*, §6, 5:211) – this is shorthand for a fuller analysis. This fuller analysis is that beauty is "value positive, intrinsic, and objectified" (*SB*, p. 31). That beauty is a value means that "it is not a perception of a matter of fact or of a relation; it is an emotion, an affection of our volitional and appreciative nature" (*loc. cit.*). That it is positive means that it does not consist in relief at the removal of something unpleasant or evil, but that it is entirely pleasant, and "That we are endowed with the sense of beauty is a pure gain which brings no evil with it" (*loc. cit.*). That it is intrinsic means that this entirely positive pleasure is not instrumental, that is, not dependent on some further good such as utility to which it is merely a means, but lies in the "immediate perception" of the object (*SB*, p. 32). Finally, that beauty is value that is objectified means that although as a value beauty "cannot be conceived as an independent existence which affects our senses and which we consequently perceive" (*SB*, p. 29), and is an "emotional element, a pleasure of ours," we nevertheless "regard it as a quality of things" (*SB*, p. 30) because in our consciousness of this pleasure we do not focus on our own sensory organs and our feelings of them, as we may do in the pleasures of eating or sex,[44] but focus entirely on the object and thus locate even our own pleasure in the object.

Santayana offers insightful arguments in behalf of these criteria, but here I will emphasize only two aspects of Santayana's larger theory. Although Santayana's definition of beauty might seem to be the kind of essentialist definition of aesthetic that "analytical" aestheticians rejected in the wake of Wittgenstein,[45] Santayana in fact anticipates many

44 However, Santayana is no prude, and will have none of the neo-Platonic insistence that there is no connection between the pleasures of sex and aesthetic pleasure. Instead, here firmly in the camp of Burke, he writes that "The capacity to love gives our contemplation that glow without which it might often fail to manifest beauty; and the whole sentimental side of our aesthetic sensibility – without which it would be perceptive and mathematical rather than aesthetic – is due to our sexual organization remotely stirred" (*SB*, p. 38). For an attack upon the neo-Platonic barrier between sexual and properly aesthetic attraction which is written under the aegis of Nietzsche and completely omits reference to Santayana, see Ekbert Faas, *The Genealogy of Aesthetics* (Cambridge: Cambridge University Press, 2002).

45 For the seminal articles in this tradition, see Morris Weitz, "The Role of Theory in Aesthetics," *Journal of Aesthetics and Art Criticism* 32 (1956): 27–35, and Maurice Mandelbaum, "Family Resemblances and Generalizations Concerning the Arts," *American Philosophical Quarterly* 2 (1965): 219–28.

mid-twentieth century theorists[46] in insisting that his definition places no *a priori* restrictions on what sorts of objects and their properties may be found to produce positive, intrinisic, and objectified pleasure. Instead, he maintains that "All human functions may contribute to the sense of beauty... whenever they are inextricably associated with the objectifying activity of the understanding. Whenever the golden thread of pleasure enters that web of things which our understanding is always busily spinning, it lends to the visible world that mysterious and subtle charm which we call beauty" (*SB*, p. 35). This is the basis for Santayana's synthesis of Kant and Alison, for he illustrates this claim precisely by showing how both formal aspects of objects and their emotional associations, and indeed qualities of their very matter itself, can yield pleasure that is positive, intrinsic, and objectified.

Using an empirical method more akin to Alison's rather than a putatively *a priori* method like Kant's, Santayana enumerates matter, form, and expression as the aspects of objects that turn out to yield aesthetic pleasure. His description of matter may seem eccentric where it includes both sexual and social passions aroused by an object (*SB*, pp. 37–42), which Alison would have treated as emotional associations. His account is less surprising when he lists properties of objects accessible to the "lower senses," then sound and color as aspects of objects that may produce pleasure satisfying his criteria for the aesthetic (*SB*, pp. 42–8). The only claim that sounds *a priori* in this part of the book is the little argument that "Form cannot be the form of nothing. If, then, in finding or creating beauty, we ignore the material of things, and attend only to their form, we miss an ever-present opportunity to heighten our effects. For whatever delight the form may bring, the material might have given delight already, and so much would have been gained toward the value of the total result" (*SB*, p. 49). This seems hard to deny, and to be a valuable corrective to both Kant and Alison. It might be thought that Kant has allowed for the aesthetic effect of the material aspects of objects when he allows that "The **charm** of colors or of the agreeable tones of instruments can be added" to the properly aesthetic objects of design in works of visual art and composition in works of music (*CPJ*, §14, 5:225), but Kant does not seem to recognize as Santayana does that the perception of matter is a necessary condition of the perception of form, and his concession seems needlessly grudging.

46 See especially William E. Kennick, "Does Traditional Aesthetics Rest on a Mistake?" *Mind* 67 (1958): 317–34.

Santayana thinks it clear that the aesthetic effects of form cannot be reduced to those of matter, since although the latter, as we have just seen, are sometimes pleasing in themselves, it is also possible that "sensible elements, by themselves indifferent, are so united as to please in combination" (*SB*, p. 53). He also, unlike Alison, thinks it evident that the aesthetic effects of form "cannot be reduced to expression without denying the existence of immediate aesthetic values altogether" – that "would be like explaining sea-sickness as the fear of shipwreck" (*SB*, p. 54). He does not think that there is any single explanation of our positive, intrinsic, and objectified pleasure in formal aspects of objects; instead, he enumerates both physiological and intellectual reasons why we take such pleasure in such properties as symmetry, unity, multiplicity in uniformity, typicality, idealization and in the right circumstances even in indeterminacy (for the last, see *SB*, pp. 82–90). Here Santayana is clearly acknowledging the significance and even centrality of the features that Kant and so many before him, back to the Renaissance and before, had made central to their theories of beauty, although with three crucial qualifications: (i) as is already clear, he does not believe that form is the only aesthetically significant property of objects; (ii) he does not believe that any *a priori* definition or delimitation of aesthetically significant form is possible, only an open-ended list to suggest the kinds of things we may find formally pleasing; and (iii), most clearly anti-Kantian, he sees no point in insisting upon a contrast between a merely physiological and some more purely intellectual appreciation of form. So Santayana's account of the role of form in the experience of beauty has both Kantian and anti-Kantian aspects.

Finally, Santayana adds expression as a quality of objects that can also yield positive, intrinsic, and objectified pleasure, and defines expression in terms that could have been quoted from Alison:

> We not only construct visible unities and recognizable types, but remain aware of their affinities to what is not at the time perceived; that is, we find in them a certain tendency and quality, not original to them, a meaning and a tone, which upon investigation we shall see to have been the proper characteristics of other objects and feelings, associated with them once in our experience.... The quality thus acquired by objects through association is what we call their expression.
>
> (*SB*, p. 119)

As in the case of form, Santayana adds that "Expression may... make beautiful by suggestion things in themselves indifferent, or it may come to heighten the beauty which they already possess" (*SB*, p. 120). By this he makes it clear that beauty may be found in both of the sources only separately recognized by Kant and Alison, as well as in the material aspects of objects where neither of them found it; and in the case of any given object it may be found in one, two, or all three of these dimensions. He does not, however, argue that any object is necessarily more beautiful the more of these dimensions of beauty it has; again, that would be an *a priori* claim alien to his empiricist spirit. How beautiful any particular object is and what the sources of its beauty are can only be determined by experience.

Perhaps the characterization of the sources of beauty as matter, form, and expression will still seem too restrictive to contemporary aestheticians, although Santayana's description of each of these categories is sufficiently general that it is far from clear what they might leave out. In any case, his tripartite approach seems to be both a synthesis of and improvement on the reductive views of Kant and Alison. Particularly when it comes to the relation between aesthetic and ethical value, Santayana sees no reason to exclude ethical associations from the immediate object of pure taste and settle for an entirely indirect connection, as Kant does, nor to attempt to reduce all pleasure in beauty to ethical associations, as Alison does. In this regard he again seems to improve upon both. But what is most striking is Santayana's inversion of the most fundamental assumption about the relation of aesthetic and ethical value that both Kant and Alison clearly share. This is a point that Santayana argues in his analysis of the positive character of aesthetic pleasure.

In a tacit reference to Kant, Santayana argues that requirement of the "disinterestedness of aesthetic delights" is overstated: while "Appreciation of a picture is not identical with the desire to buy it," he says, "it is, or ought to be, closely related and preliminary to that desire." Instead, he proposes, the traditional concept of disinterestedness is a clumsy expression of the fact that aesthetic pleasure is positive, that is, pleasurable in its own right, not as a mere means to some other end nor as a mere removal of an ill: "The truth which the theory is trying to state seems rather to be that when we seek aesthetic pleasures we have no further pleasure in mind; that we do not mix up the satisfactions of vanity and proprietorship with the delight of contemplation" (*SB*, p. 25). He then defines the ethical in negative terms: "moral judgments are mainly and fundamentally negative, or perceptions of evil," and the task of morality is basically to remove evils: "The sad business of life is . . . to escape certain dreadful evils to which our nature exposes us" (*SB*, pp. 16–17). He concludes from this that were morality to be successful, and the evils of life actually removed, "then we shall find little but aesthetic pleasures remaining to constitute unalloyed happiness." That might seem like an overstatement – after all, there would seem to be plenty of positive pleasures that do not satisfy all the criteria of the aesthetic – but Santayana tries to forestall that objection by adding that even "The satisfaction of the passions and appetites, in which we chiefly place earthly happiness, themselves take on an aesthetic tinge when we remove ideally the possibility of loss or variation" (*SB*, pp. 19–20). We need not follow Santayana in this last step to appreciate his point that if ethics is concerned with the removal of evils from life, and if it were ever to be successful, then we would need positive values to give a point to life, and that aesthetic pleasures could certainly number among these. On such an account, we should not always look at aesthetics as if it must be the handmaiden of morality, but can think of morality as in fact the handmaiden of aesthetics.

Of course Santayana is not so naïve as to think that we ever will be finished with the sad business of morality, and find ourselves in some sort of contra-Platonic ideal state where we can do nothing but devote ourselves to the positive pleasure of the enjoyment of natural and artistic beauty. As he puts it, "The appreciation of beauty and its embodiment in the arts are activities which belong to our holiday life, when we are redeemed for the moment from the shadow of evil and the slavery to fear, and are following the bent of our nature where it chooses to lead us" (*SB*, p. 17). We are never redeemed from the shadow of evil for more than a moment, so the positive pleasure of beauty can never be more than a holiday. Nevertheless, it seems right that morality's effort to remove the evils from life would be incoherent unless we recognized some positive values that give life a point, and also that even while the work of morality remains unfinished we may still need some vacations to enjoy the positive values of life. Santayana's thesis that aesthetic values are among those things that directly give life a point seems like an important thing to keep in mind as we consider eighteenth-century or contemporary accounts of how aesthetic experience can also support the efforts of morality. Santayana ends *The Sense of Beauty* with a sentence that sounds very much like Kant: "Beauty is a pledge of the possible conformity between the soul and nature, and consequently a ground of faith in the supremacy of the good" (*SB*, p. 164). But for him the enjoyment of beauty must be part of the good, not just a symbol for and pledge of the possibility of a purely moral good.

To sum up: In spite of, or even by means of, his concept of the disinterestedness of aesthetic experience, Kant shows us a number of ways in which the aesthetic can support the effort to be moral without substituting for or even being indispensable to that effort. But while he is right to stress that aesthetic experience offers only indirect support for the effort to be moral, his initial account of that experience itself seems to keep the engagement of our emotional sensibilities too far from it. Alison corrects for Kant's exclusion of emotional sensibility from our immediate aesthetic experience, but at the cost of reducing every aspect of aesthetic enjoyment to emotional association, and overstates the role of the aesthetic in ethical development. Santayana shows how to strike a more judicious balance between the engagement of our emotions and the engagement of our more purely perceptual and intellectual capacities in the experience of beauty, and also reminds us that we should think about how morality can facilitate the enjoyment of the aesthetic as well as about how the aesthetic can facilitate the achievement of morality.

9

The Symbols of Freedom in Kant's Aesthetics

Kant's *Critique of Judgment* is a work full of puzzles.[1] Here is one. Summing up his discussion of the sublime, Kant says that

> The intellectual (morally-) good, purposive in itself, must not be represented as beautiful, but rather as sublime, so that it arouses more the feeling of respect (which scorns charm), rather than that of love and familiar inclination; for human nature does not accord with that good of itself, but only through the violence that reason does to sensibility.
>
> (*CPJ*, §29 GR, 271)[2]

[1] Many of these puzzles are explored in my earlier book, *Kant and the Claims of Taste* (Cambridge, Mass.: Harvard University Press, 1979), and my more recent *Kant and the Experience of Freedom: Essays on Aesthetics and Morality* (Cambridge: Cambridge University Press, 1993). The present chapter was conceived of in part as an introduction to some of the themes of the latter work for the audience at the colloquium on Kant's aesthetics at Cerisy-La-Salle, although it also goes beyond that book in several ways, including the contrast between the beautiful and the sublime and the analysis of the thesis that beauty is the symbol of the morally good to be given later.

[2] Citations to Kant's works will be given by an abbreviation of the title, a section number where Kant supplied one (in this case, "GR" indicates the General Remark following the numbered section), and the volume and page number of the text printed in Kant's *Gesammelte Schriften*, edited by the Königlichen Preußischen (later Deutschen) Akademie der Wissenschaften (Berlin: Walter de Gruyter and predecessors, 1900 –), except in the case of the *Critique of the Power of Judgment*, where the volume (number 5) will be omitted. Abbreviations to be used include: *CPJ* for *Critique of the Power of Judgment*, *CPrR* for *Critique of Practical Reason*, *G* for *Groundwork of the Metaphysics of Morals*, and *DV* for *Doctrine of Virtue*, Part II of the *Metaphysics of Morals*. Translations from Kant are my own. The *Akademie* edition page numbers are reproduced in the margins of the translation by James Creed Meredith (Oxford, 1911 and 1928), as well as in *The Critique of the Power of Judgment*, edited by Paul Guyer, translated by Paul Guyer and Eric Matthews (Cambridge: Cambridge University Press, 2000).

This naturally suggests that if any form of aesthetic experience is to furnish a symbol of the central concept of morality, it would be the experience of the sublime and not that of the beautiful. Eighty pages later, however, bringing both the "Dialectic" and the entire "Critique of Aesthetic Judgment" to its conclusion, Kant seems to assert the opposite:

> Now I say: the *beautiful* is the symbol of the morally-good;[3] and also only in this regard (that of a relation that is natural to everyone, and which everyone also imputes to others as a duty) does it please with a claim to the agreement of everyone else, whereby the mind at the same time is conscious of a certain ennoblement and elevation above the mere receptivity for a pleasure through sensory impressions . . .
>
> (*CPJ*, §59, 353)

Here Kant emphatically asserts that it is the beautiful which is the primary aesthetic symbol of morality, and then goes on to suggest that it is only in virtue of this at least symbolic connection to morality that the beautiful can actually sustain the claim to the agreement of all that his original analysis of judgments of taste had shown to be essential to them (see *CPJ*, §§7–8).

Several questions about this contrast leap to mind. First, do these statements contradict each other? If so, has Kant simply forgotten the first by the time he writes the second, or does he mean to express a change of mind without admitting as much? Second, how could Kant possibly claim that the beautiful is the paradigmatic symbol of the morally good and can fulfill its claim to the agreement of all only in that role when he had initially defined the beautiful precisely by the disinterestedness of our judgment on it, or by the fundamental difference between the beautiful on the one hand and both the sensually agreeable and the good, including the morally good, on the other (see especially *CPJ*, §5, 209–10)? Or to put this question into other words, how can Kant maintain what is assumed to be the autonomy of aesthetic experience and judgment and yet maintain that the judgment on the beautiful, or for that matter on any object of taste, depends on any connection to moral autonomy? Isn't the subservience of the aesthetic to moral autonomy incompatible with its own autonomy?

[3] It should be noted that in the first passage Kant had used the expression *Moralisch-Gut*, while here he uses the expression *Sittlich-Gut*; in my view, however, Kant's alternation between these latinate and germanic terms does not by itself here indicate any conceptual distinction.

This essay will suggest some answers to these questions. I will argue that the two statements with which I began do not literally contradict each other, because Kant means the sublime and the beautiful to represent different aspects of his overall conception of morality. I will also show that there is not an outright contradiction between Kant's conception of the autonomy of the aesthetic and the idea of using aesthetic experience as a symbol of morality, but rather that the very possibility of using the aesthetic as a symbol of the moral depends on the freedom of the imagination which is essential to Kant's conception of the aesthetic. In conclusion, however, I shall argue that Kant's conception of the autonomy of the aesthetic by no means suggests that in the realm of taste, unlike anywhere else, we can enjoy total liberty from the constraints of morality; although perhaps later and indeed contemporary aesthetes may fancy such an idea, that is not a view we could reasonably expect to find in a philosopher whose deepest conviction is the primacy of practical reason.

1. The Sensible Representation of the Moral

Let us begin with a word about the very idea of any need for and indeed any possibility for an aesthetic representation of morality at all. In the *Critique of Practical Reason,* Kant had asserted, in his doctrine of the "fact of reason," that every human agent necessarily becomes conscious of the moral law in any attempt to reason about a course of action, just as every human being necessarily becomes conscious of the *a priori* laws of mathematics in any attempt to construct a figure or a sum at all, and that from this immediate consciousness of our obligation under the moral law we can also infer without either any experience or any further premise our freedom to comply with the requirements of this law regardless of all of our previous history and inclinations. Moreover, Kant had also asserted that neither the moral law nor the fact of our freedom *could* be learned from experience: not the moral law, because "as a law it is commanded unconditionally, without borrowing anything from experience or the will of any other" (i.e., a divine will) (*CPrR,* §7, 5:31), and not freedom, "for experience gives us only the law of appearances, thus the mechanism of nature" (*CPrR,* §6, 5:29). On this account, then, it seems that nothing but pure reason is needed to know the law by which we ought to govern our freedom and the freedom to govern ourselves by that law, and that experience or feeling could not in any way supply us with that knowledge.

So what could have set Kant upon a search for any aesthetic symbols of morality in a work published only two years after this bold assertion of the fact of freedom? To put it bluntly, I think the answer can only be that the rationalism of the *Critique of Practical Reason* was too austere even for Kant himself, and that he quickly came to see that although he could never allow the *content* of the moral law and our obligation to adhere to it to be contingent upon our feelings, nevertheless the very fact that makes that law appear to us in the form of an imperative, the fact that we are not purely rational wills but are finite, embodied creatures, also makes it necessary that not just the constraints but also the attractions of morality be accessible to our senses as well as our intellect. Throughout the *Critique of the Power of Judgment*, Kant is concerned to bridge the gulf between the realm of nature and the realm of freedom, and one of the forms this effort takes is that of finding ways in which morality, based in freedom, can be made accessible to feeling as well as reason. Aesthetic experience then becomes vital because it can contribute to the development of moral feeling:

> The spontaneity in the play of the cognitive faculties, whose accord contains the ground of [aesthetic] pleasure, makes the concept [of finality] into an intermediary the consequences of which are serviceable for the connection of the territory of the concept of nature with the concept of freedom, in that this accord at the same time advances the receptivity of the mind for moral feeling.
>
> (*CPJ*, §IX, 197)

Instead of disdaining the cultivation of moral feeling, Kant now clearly believes that every means for cultivating moral feeling and thus narrowing the gap between our sensible and our intellectual being must be seized. Thus he later says that although we cannot simply presuppose that other persons will in fact pay attention to every opportunity for the aesthetic enhancement of their moral feeling, "nevertheless . . . attention ought to be paid to these moral dispositions on every suitable occasion" (*CPJ*, §39, 293). Kant never quite puts it this way, but I think we may reasonably impute to him the recognition that precisely because we are finite and embodied rather than pure and holy wills, we cannot let any means for bringing our sensible nature into harmony with the demands of reason escape us, and if the realm of the aesthetic, with its natural hold upon our feelings, offers us any opportunities for the strengthening of our moral feeling, then we must take advantage of those opportunities.

The premise of what is perhaps Kant's most radical new argument in the third *Critique* is, then, that the aesthetic can provide sensory representations of moral ideas in ways that can increase their grasp upon our feelings, and that taste can be demanded of every human being for precisely that reason.[4] There are a number of different ways in which the aesthetic can make the moral accessible to our senses. First, although ordinary experience of the "mechanism of nature" can give evidence neither of our freedom nor of our obligation under the unconditional law of morality, aesthetic experience can provide at least symbolic representation of both the fact of our freedom and its universal law, and thus increase the hold of the rational ideas of these upon our feelings. These are the special roles of the sublime and the beautiful as symbols of the morally good. But further, both the aesthetic experience of the suitability of the forms of individual natural objects for our cognitive faculties as well as the teleological judgment of the suitability of the system of nature as a whole for those faculties can provide us with sensible representation of the receptivity of nature to our practical reason as well, and thus evidence for the possibility of the realization of our moral intentions, or of the highest good. As Kant puts it:

> The power of judgment provides the mediating concept between the concepts of nature and the concept of freedom, which makes possible the transition from the purely theoretical to the purely practical, from the lawfulness in accord with the former to the final end in accord with the latter, in the concept of a *purposiveness* of nature; for thereby is known the possibility of the final end, which can only become actual in nature and in harmony with its laws.
>
> (*CPJ*, §IX, 196)

As Kant's conception of morality increasingly recognizes the intrinsic connection between rationality and the realization of ends, the concept of the highest good becomes increasingly central to it. As Kant likewise increasingly recognizes the importance of the representation of morality in a sensibly accessible form, he turns to aesthetics for sensory evidence of the possibility of the realization of the ends of morality as well as for symbolization of its conditions and demands.

In what follows, I will show how these two lines of thought appear in Kant's text. Let us begin by returning to our opening contrast between the beautiful and the sublime.

[4] This claim is to be distinguished from that originally advanced by Crawford 1974, and several subsequent authors, including Rogerson 1986, that the link to morality is necessary to complete the *deduction* of pure judgments of taste about particular objects. For further discussion, see the Introduction to my 1993, especially 12–19.

2. The Sublime and the Negative Conception of Freedom

At the most general level, the symbolic roles of the beautiful and sublime can be distinguished yet related by thinking of the sublime as the aesthetic representation or palpable experience of the negative conception of freedom and the beautiful as that of the positive conception of freedom. This distinction between two conceptions of reason is stated at the opening of the final chapter of the *Groundwork of the Metaphysics of Morals.* There Kant calls the description of freedom as "that property of [the] causality [of the will] by which it can be effective independently of foreign causes *determining* it" a "*negative*" definition or explanation (*Erklärung*), in contrast to the "*positive* concept" of it, which is "all the more rich and fruitful," as the "concept of a causality which brings *laws* along with it," or the fact that "freedom, although it is to be sure not a property of the will in accordance with laws of nature, is not at all on that account lawless, but must rather be a causality in accordance with immutable laws, but of a special sort." This positive concept of a special sort of causality is then called "autonomy, i.e., the property of the will of being a law to itself" (*G*, 4: 446–7). The negative conception of freedom is simply the concept of the independence of the determination of the human will from the ordinary mechanisms of nature, without any further specification of the means by which this independence is achieved, while the positive conception of freedom or autonomy specifies that such independence is achieved by conformity to an alternative law the will gives to itself, a law shortly to be identified, of course, with the principle of morality given by pure reason. The experience of the sublime, then, as an aesthetic experience of our independence from complete domination by natural forces, is a symbol of our freedom merely negatively conceived, and the experience of the beautiful offers a more complex symbolization of the autonomous law of pure practical reason and of the relationship between this law and the morally determined will as well as moral feeling.

Kant's treatment of the sublime is divided into two parts, the mathematical and the dynamical sublime. Under the first rubric, Kant describes how our feeling of frustration at our inability to grasp an infinite magnitude is replaced by pleasure in our realization that we nevertheless possess a faculty of pure reason capable of conceiving of such a magnitude (*CPJ*, §26, 254; §27, 257, 259). In other words, the experience of the mathematical sublime gives pleasurable evidence of our possession of pure reason in a paradigmatically theoretical application. That certainly makes it tempting immediately to assume that the experience of the dynamical sublime is a pleasurable experience of our possession of pure practical reason.[5] Close reading of Kant's analysis of the second form of the sublime, however, reveals that what he offers is a description of our independence from domination by natural forces without any positive characterization of the faculty by means of which we achieve such independence – in other words, an experience of freedom only in its negative sense. The key section on the dynamical sublime describes it four times, and not once does Kant actually mention the faculty of reason or practical reason. First he says that "Nature, considered in the aesthetic judgment as might [*Macht*] that has no force [*Gewalt*] over us, is *dynamically-sublime*" (*CPJ*, §28, 260). Next he says that we call threatening rocks, thunder clouds, volcanoes, and the boundless ocean "sublime, because they elevate the strengths of the soul above their common average and let us discover a power to resist within us of quite another sort, which gives us the courage to measure ourselves against the apparent omnipotence [*Allgewalt*] of nature" (261). Then he says that "the irresistibility of [the] power [of nature] gives us knowledge of our physical impotence, considered as natural beings, but at the same time reveals a capacity to estimate ourselves as independent of it, and a superiority over nature, on which is founded a self-preservation of quite another sort than that which can be threatened and endangered by nature outside us" (261–2). Finally, he says that "sublimity is not contained in any thing of nature, but only in our mind, insofar as we can be conscious of being superior to nature in us and thereby also to nature outside us (so far as it influences us)" (264). In each of these passages, the experience of the sublime is described as an experience of our independence from domination by the forces of nature, but in none of them is there any explicit assertion that the faculty by means of which we possess this independence is pure reason, let alone pure practical reason. For this reason, the experience of the sublime is not itself a complete symbol of morality.

Perhaps this explains what would otherwise be inexplicable about the next step of Kant's argument, his claim that the possibility of the experience of the sublime *presupposes* considerable development of moral ideas rather than contributing to it. As he puts it, "In fact, without the development of moral ideas, that which we, prepared through culture, call sublime, would strike raw mankind merely as terrifying" (*CPJ*, §29, 265). If the experience of the sublime directly revealed our faculty of pure practical reason, it is hard to see how it could ever be terrifying, for it

[5] See, e.g., Crowther 1989, 111, and Makkreel 1990, 83.

would instead always be immediately uplifting. However, if it is supposed to make palpable only our independence from nature, yet that independence cannot itself be understood except by means of a prior recognition of our pure practical reason – as the argument of the *Critique of Practical Reason* would imply – then it may be understood why the experience of the sublime presupposes the development of moral ideas. Of course, then it may be hard to explain what the experience of the sublime *adds* to the cultivation of moral feelings. At most, it would seem as if the capacity to experience the sublime would be *evidence* of the development of moral feeling, and something we expect in ourselves and others precisely as evidence of the development of moral feeling that we demand. And this indeed seems to be how Kant conceives of our expectation of sensitivity to the sublime (see *CPJ*, §29, 266).

Nevertheless, the fact that the experience of the sublime is essentially an experience of freedom conceived in a negative and therefore incomplete way hardly means it is an insignificant experience. On the contrary, Kant often characterizes the constraint of duty itself primarily in terms of its requirement of independence from the ordinary incentives of natural inclination, and thus the experience of the sublime can seem virtually identical with the fundamental moral feeling of respect for duty itself. This is perhaps most evident in Kant's paean to duty in the second *Critique*'s chapter on incentives, where he calls duty a "sublime, great name," which suggests nothing "beloved" and "ingratiating" but rather a law before which "all inclinations are dumb," and which "proudly strikes down every connection to inclinations" (5:86). To be sure, here Kant does go on to make explicit that "*personality*, i.e., the freedom and independence from the mechanisms of the whole of nature" does ultimately have its root in the pure practical laws of our reason (87), but the key point remains that duty is characterized as sublime because the experience of it is first and foremost the experience of a power of resistance against natural inclinations; and the aesthetic experience of the sublime, triggered by natural objects without rather than within us, seems to be an experience only of such a power of resistance conceived negatively and thus without any positive presentation of its origin.

The fact that Kant characterizes the feeling of duty itself as sublime may suggest an answer to the question left dangling a moment ago, namely, why do we need the aesthetic experience of the dynamical sublime if it apparently presupposes the cultivation of moral feeling rather than contributing to it? From the outset of his discussion of duty in the *Groundwork*, Kant holds that the demands of duty and the merits of a good will may be most clearly perceived in cases where there is a conflict between inclination and duty – the man who is by nature selfish but acts generously out of the motive of duty, the man who would by nature sacrifice future comfort to present gratification but out of respect for the duty of his own long-term happiness does not, and so on (*G*, 4:397–9). Although Kant has often been read to be asserting that dutiful conduct is meritorious *only* when performed in the face of such contrary inclinations, and that such conflicts are therefore *desirable*, that does not seem to be his view.[6] Rather, he seems to be making primarily the heuristic point that the distinctive demands of duty and its merits can be most clearly perceived through such examples, and hardly suggesting that we seek to engender conflict between our duty and our inclinations in order to earn moral merit. But that may also mean that the sublime feeling of moral resistance to inclination may not be readily available to us, even in cases of compliance with the demands of duty, for the occurrence of this feeling may require actual conflict. As Kant puts it, "in aesthetic estimation (without a concept), the superiority over hindrances can be estimated only in accordance with the magnitude of the resistance" (*CPJ*, §28, 260). Instead, resistance of the necessary magnitude may be encountered more frequently in our aesthetic experience than in our moral conduct. Indeed, cases of genuine conflict between duty and inclination may really be quite rare: most of us, most of the time, at least in normal times, especially having been brought up within a moral culture, do not experience a fundamental conflict between duty and our deepest inclinations, although we may feel a bit constrained by morality around the edges. Yet that would mean that it might be quite unusual for most of us ever actually to experience the sublimity of resistance to inclination from the motive of duty in our conduct. We may then be more likely to experience the sublimity of negative freedom in an aesthetic than in a directly moral context. Thus the aesthetic experience of the sublime may be our primary window onto the sublimity of the feeling of respect for duty after all.

Developing such an argument in any detail would certainly go beyond the letter of Kant's text. At this point, we may have gleaned all that we should from the analysis of the feeling of the dynamical sublime as a palpable presentation of freedom in its negative sense. So let us now turn to beauty as the palpable presentation of freedom or autonomy positively conceived.

6 For defense of this claim, see Herman 1993, especially chapters 1 and 2.

3. The Beautiful and the Positive Conception of Freedom

Kant begins his discussion of "Beauty as the Symbol of Morality"[7] (*CPJ*, §59) by asserting that the exhibition of the reality of our concepts always requires intuitions. In the case of ideas, for which "suitable" (*angemessen*) intuitions cannot be given, this confirmation of reality cannot be direct. However, Kant does not drop the general assumption that some sort of confirmation of the reality of our concepts is always needed, but instead suggests that in the case of ideas of reason this confirmation will have to be indirect or "symbolic" (*CPJ*, §59, 351). In symbolism, there need be no resemblance manifest in intuition between any properties of two objects, one of which is the symbol of the other, and the resemblance can lie instead in the "procedure of the faculty of judgment" or the "form of" or "rules for" reflection on the two objects (351, 352). In other words, there need be no sense-perceptible similarity between a symbol and what it symbolizes, thus the latter need not be an object of perception at all, but there is a similarity in the structure of our thought or judgment about the two things, in virtue of which the one that can be experienced can serve as a symbol of the one that cannot. Kant's claim is then that beauty, or perhaps more literally beautiful objects, which can be experienced, can serve as the symbol of morality, which cannot be directly experienced, because of parallels between the structure of our experience and judgment of beauty and that of morality.

In his initial statement of the analogy, Kant adduces two separate features of our experience of beauty in virtue of which it is fit to serve as a symbol of morality. First, he says that "In this faculty," namely, taste,

> The faculty of judgment does not see itself as subjected to a heteronomy of laws of experience, as is otherwise the case in empirical judgment: in regard to the objects of such a pure delight it gives itself the law, just as reason does in regard to the faculty of desire.

Second, he says that in the case of taste, judgment

> Also sees itself as related, on account of its inner possibility in the subject as well as on account of the external possibility of a nature that harmonizes with it, to something in the subject and outside of it, which is neither nature nor freedom

7 Kant's word here is *Sittlichkeit*. Caygill 1989, 364, has recently translated this by the Anglo-Hegelian term "ethical life." I see no justification for this anachronism, nor any need to mark a distinction here between *Sittlichkeit* and *Moralität*, which Kant generally uses interchangeably with *Sittlichkeit* and clearly does so in the case of its two occurrences in the *Critique of the Power of Judgment*, one of which is in the present section and will be cited later.

but is connected to the ground of the latter, namely the supersensible (§59, 353).

In other words, he claims that there is an analogy between the autonomy of aesthetic judgment and the autonomy of pure practical reason, but also an analogy between the relation between aesthetic judgment and its external object, here taken to be the beautiful in nature, and that between practical reason and the realm in which it must be realized, also to be understood as nature. In the further explication of the analogy in the next paragraph, Kant emphasizes only the first of these two points; and most commentary, including my own, has consequently offered only a partial interpretation of the connections Kant has in mind. Here, however, I will explicate both parts of Kant's analogy.

In expanding upon the first part of the analogy, Kant makes what appear to be four separate points:

> 1) The beautiful pleases *immediately* (but only in reflecting intuition, not like morality [*Sittlichkeit*] in concepts). 2) It pleases *without any interest* (the morally good is to be sure necessarily connected with an interest, although not with one which precedes the judgment on the delight, but rather with one which is first produced by that). 3) The *freedom* of the imagination... is represented as harmonious with the lawfulness of the understanding in the estimation of the beautiful (in moral judgment the freedom of the will is conceived of as the agreement of the latter with itself according to universal laws of reason). 4) The subjective principle of the estimation of the beautiful is represented as *universal*, i.e., as valid for everyone, but not as cognizable through any universal concept (the objective principle of morality [*Moralität*][8] is also expounded as universal for everyone, i.e., for all subjects and also for all actions of the same subject, [but] thereby also as cognizable through a universal concept).
>
> (*CPJ*, §59, 353–4)

For present purposes, however, we may treat Kant as bringing out two main ways in which the reflective experience of beauty furnishes a palpable symbol of his positive conception of freedom or autonomy rather than the merely negative conception of moral independence from domination by nature that was symbolized by the experience of the sublime. Reversing the order of Kant's exposition, we may see him as saying, first, that the relationship between the freedom of the imagination and the lawfulness of the understanding which is the essence of the experience

[8] I have marked Kant's use of the two different terms *Sittlichkeit* and *Moralität* in such close proximity only to show that there does not appear to be any significant difference in meaning between them.

of beauty symbolizes the preservation and maximization of freedom both intra- and inter-personally by means of governance by universal law which is the positive essence of morality, and, second, that the naturally gratifying effect of the harmony between imagination and understanding on sensibility which is the explanation of the pleasure of aesthetic response symbolizes the ideal of achieving a harmony between reason and inclination which is, perhaps contrary to appearances and even contrary to his own account of the sublime, an essential component of his conception of a fully realized moral disposition. I will briefly comment on each of these points in turn.

First, the foundation of the entire analogy is Kant's idea that the experience of beauty is an experience of the free accord of the imagination with the lawfulness (although not any specific law) of the understanding, and that the essence of morality is the preservation and promotion of freedom by the self-legislation of universal law, although in this case freedom is not an object of experience. The interpretation of the experience of beauty as an experience of freedom is stressed in the "General Remark" summing up the "Analytic of the Beautiful." Here Kant amplifies the image of the free play between imagination and understanding, which he has earlier introduced (e.g. §9), by describing the form of a beautiful object as one "which the imagination, if left free, would have projected in harmony with the *lawfulness of the understanding* in general" (*CPJ*, §22 GR, 241). However, if the form of a manifold of intuition were seen as completely determined by a specific law of the understanding, there would be nothing particularly pleasurable about it (*CPJ*, §VI, 187), so the experience of beauty cannot simply presuppose that "the *imagination* be both *free* and yet *lawful in itself*, i.e., carry an autonomy with it"; it must instead be understood as "a lawfulness without a law and a subjective agreement of the imagination with the understanding without an objective one" (*CPJ*, §22 GR, 241). Nevertheless, what it is supposed to symbolize is precisely autonomy, or freedom in its positive sense, which is nothing less than the harmony between freedom and conformity to law as the condition under which freedom is maximally preserved and promoted, the condition under which "freedom of the will" is "in harmony with itself according to universal laws of reason."

This is hardly the place to attempt to show that Kant's various formulations of the fundamental principle of morality can be reduced to a conception of the law by means of which both intra- and inter-personal freedom of the will is maximally preserved and promoted;[9] a few of Kant's pithiest remarks will have to suffice here. In his best-known series of lectures on ethics, as given around 1780, he puts it thus:

> The inherent value of the world, the *summum bonum*, is freedom in accordance with a will which is not necessitated to action. Freedom is thus the inner value of the world ... But freedom can only be in harmony with itself under certain conditions; otherwise it comes into collision with itself;

and the moral law is simply the statement of those conditions necessary for the avoidance of the self-destruction of freedom.[10] Or as he puts it in another set of lectures, delivered in the fall of 1784 and thus within weeks of the composition of the *Groundwork of the Metaphysics of Morals*,

> The inner worth of man depends on his freedom, that he has his own will ... The freedom of man is the condition, under which man himself can be an end ... Right is the restriction of freedom, in accordance with which it can consist with the freedom of everyone else in accordance with a universal rule.[11]

The first of these passages occurs in a discussion of duties to oneself, and is the foundation of an argument that morality requires self-governance for the maximization of one's own freedom in all of one's self-regarding behavior; the second occurs in a discussion of external right, and argues that morality requires the regulation of freedom for the sake of its own maximization in the behavior of any community of humans. Together, they thus argue that morality consists in the regulation of freedom, as the ultimate source of value, by universal law precisely for the sake of its own maximization. The free conformity of the imagination to the lawfulness of the understanding in the experience of beauty then symbolizes the harmony in the use of freedom itself, achieved by harmony between freedom and universal law, which is the foundation of morality.

The first two of Kant's four claims, to which I now return, point to a further aspect of his moral ideal. Here he states that both the beautiful and the morally good please immediately, and that at least the latter also

9 I have made a start on this task in my "Kant's Morality of Law and Morality of Freedom," in my *Kant on Freedom, Law, and Happiness* (Cambridge: Cambridge University Press, 2000), chapter 4.

10 Kant, 1930, 122–3; cf. *Moralphilosophie Collins*, 27: 344, 346, or *Moral Mrongovius*, 27: 1482, 1484.

11 *Naturrecht Feyerabend*, 27: 1319–20.

creates an interest in its object.[12] Kant could be taken to be alluding to the fact that the determination of the will by the moral law, just like the harmony of imagination and understanding in the experience of beauty, is not without an effect on feeling; on the contrary, it has a direct effect on feeling in the form of the feeling of respect, which although it is partly a negative feeling of the constraint of self-conceit is also in part a positive and pleasurable feeling at our power to exercise such constraint (see *CPrR*, 5: 79–80). Taking Kant to mean just this, however, could collapse the distinction between the symbolic functions of the beautiful and the sublime we have established, so we should take him to be saying more than this. In particular, we should take Kant's initial suggestion that both the beautiful and the morally good *please immediately* to be intimating Kant's moral ideal, which is that although of course the requirements of duty can always conflict with inclination in principle, at least sometimes do so in fact, and can most readily be illustrated in those cases in which they do, in fact the true ideal of a virtuous human being includes the aim of *harmony* between duty and inclination, so that what duty requires in fact *should* also immediately please.

Again, this is hardly the place for a detailed exposition of a central although controversial claim of Kant's moral philosophy, and a few references will have to suffice. One of these would certainly be Kant's response to Friedrich Schiller in *Religion within the Limits of Reason Alone*, where he suggests that the "aesthetic character" of virtue is not "anxiously bowed down and repressed" but "courageous" and "joyful," and that the presence of an enduring conflict between duty and inclination is a sign of incomplete commitment to the moral law (6: 23–4 n.). Another would be his suggestion in the *Metaphysics of Morals* that although the duty of benevolence to others cannot assume the presence of an antecedent natural love to all others who have a claim to one's benevolence, in fact compliance with this duty out of principle will produce such natural love in practice:

> The saying "you ought to *love* your neighbor as yourself" does not mean that you ought immediately (first) to love him and (afterwards) by means of this love do good to him. It means rather *do good* to your fellow man, and your beneficence will produce love of man in you . . .
>
> (*DV*, Introduction §XII, 6: 402)

[12] Actually, although Kant does not acknowledge this, there is no reason why the experience of beauty should not also create an interest in its object even though it does not presuppose one; see my 1978.

Thus Kant assumes that a true commitment to duty not only should but will have an effect on feeling, indeed not just that of producing a moral feeling *alongside* of one's other, natural inclinations, consonant with morality or not as they may be, but also that of ultimately producing a joyful harmony *between* the demands of morality and one's natural feelings.[13] The immediacy of pleasure without antecedent interest in the experience of beauty symbolizes this part of the moral ideal as well as the more purely formal harmony between freedom and universal law in autonomy.

Here a question will naturally occur. Although one might see Kant's point that neither freedom itself not its universal law can themselves be presented in experience, and thus need aesthetic symbolization, would not the harmony between duty and inclination itself have a direct effect on feeling, thus obviating the need for symbolization? Kant's explication of his analogy is too brief to provide an answer to this question; we might just remember that the ideal of such harmony is indeed an ideal, rarely if ever achieved, and thus that although the moral ideal itself ideally includes an effect on feeling in practice it still needs representation by a more common effect on feeling, the experience of beauty.

So much for Kant's explication of the first main point of his analogy. Kant's initial statement of the analogy, however, included a second point, namely, that the beautiful can symbolize not just the harmony within our wills that morality demands, but also a harmony between the inner possibility of morality in the subject and its external possibility in nature. What does he mean by this?

Here Kant can only be alluding back to his earlier treatment of the "intellectual interest" in the existence of beautiful objects produced by nature rather than by art. Although Kant had earlier held that it is no part of the task of a deduction of pure aesthetic judgments to prove that objects gratifying our taste must exist in nature (*CPJ*, §31, 281–2), and our pleasure in beautiful objects cannot depend upon the assumption that we have some specific need which naturally existing objects fulfill, under this title he nevertheless explains that it is pleasing to us that beautiful objects exist in nature independently of our own intentional actions in producing art. This pleasure that we take in the existence of beautiful objects is distinct from our pleasure in their beauty itself. What is the

[13] For further discussion of these points, see my 1993, chapter 10, "Duty and Inclination," 335–93.

source of this additional pleasure? Kant's explanation is that

> Reason is also interested in the ideas (for which in the moral feeling it effects an immediate interest) also having objective reality, i.e., in nature at least showing a trace or giving a hint that it contains in itself some sort of ground for assuming a lawful accord of its products with our delight independent of all interest . . . thus reason must take an interest in every expression in nature of a harmony similar to this one.
>
> (*CPJ*, §42, 300)

In other words, it is a general interest of reason that its ideas be able to enjoy objective reality, or that nature be such as to allow for the realization of its intentions, and evidence that nature is receptive to our underlying cognitive aim in aesthetic experience is also a pleasing hint that nature will grant objective reality to the ideas of pure practical reason, that is, permit the realization of our moral intentions.

Taken to its logical conclusion, Kant's idea of intellectual interest would imply that the natural existence of beauty at least suggests the possibility of the realization in nature of the highest good, the complete realization of all morally acceptable intentions producing perfect happiness in proportion to perfect virtue, which so occupies him in the second half of the *Critique of the Power of Judgment*; a unifying theme of the two halves of the book would then be that both aesthetic and teleological judgment are connected to the highest good, beauty pointing to its possibility, which is precisely what is presupposed in any teleological judgment of nature as a whole as a system (see *CPJ*, §84, 435). Here then is a second way in which beauty as a symbol of morality goes beyond the sublime as a symbol of the merely negative freedom to avoid domination by nature: just as the experience of beauty symbolizes the positive harmony between freedom and law in the moral goal of autonomy and the harmony between duty and inclination in the ideal moral disposition, so the natural existence of beauty symbolizes the possibility of the natural fulfillment of the rational intentions of morality, or the highest good.

Again, a full exposition of this symbol would require a detailed analysis of Kant's ethics. Here I can only note that, contrary to the ordinary assumption that Kant means the morally good to be without any reference to the realization of ends at all (e.g. *G*, 4:394), *a fortiori* to the possibility of the realization of ends, when he comes to the most fundamental level of his argument he always makes it clear that a rational will never wills without an end (in his words, if "there are free actions there must also be ends to which, as their objects, these actions are directed" [*DV*, Introduction §III, 6:385]); thus if a rational will is to be constrained by a necessary law, that law must be linked to a necessary end (e.g. *G*, 4:428), and thus that a rational will can never be indifferent to the possibility of the realization of its ends. As he puts it in the *Religion*:

> For without all relation to an end no determination of the will can take place in humans, since it cannot be without all effect, the representation of which, if not as a ground of determination of the faculty of choice [*Willkür*] and an end determining its intention antecedently, yet as the consequence of its determination through the law to an end, must be able to be assumed... It cannot therefore be indifferent to morality [*der Moral*] whether it forms the concept of a final end of all things... or not: for thereby alone can the connection between purposiveness from freedom and the purposiveness of nature, with which we cannot at all dispense, be given objective practical reality.
>
> (*Religion*, 6:4–5)

In this passage, just as in his account of the intellectual interest in the beautiful, Kant asserts that reason has an interest in the "objective reality" or actual existence of its own purposes. In other words, while we may well have to see the good will as a valuable jewel even when it does not realize its end (again, *G*, 4:394), we cannot comprehend the good will in the first place except as a will to bring about a certain end, and we cannot conceive of rational indifference to the realization of this end.[14] On the contrary, although we necessarily admire the existence of a good will apart from its efficacy, we equally necessarily take pleasure in its efficacy; and in the existence of natural beauty we have a pleasing symbol of that pleasing possibility of the efficacy of the morally good will.

We thus see that what initially looked like a contradiction in Kant's account of the aesthetic symbolism of morality is in fact only a sign of its complexity, a complexity required by the complexity of Kantian morality itself. Far from being a simple image of the domination of natural instinct by rational law, which might be captured by the single symbol of the sublime, Kant's conception of morality involves a negative conception

[14] There is no doubt that Kant's treatment of the highest good in the 1790s, beginning with the *Critique of the Power of Judgment*, increasingly recognizes its central role in his ethics; but I would disagree with the suggestion of Paul Crowther that the highest good becomes important to Kant only when he tries to make our moral vocatiön the final end of nature itself in the "Critique of Teleological Judgment" (Crowther 1989, 43); on the contrary, the necessity of the highest good as the end of moral action is implicit in Kant's conception of rational willing from the outset, even though Kant himself does not always recognize this. For further discussion, see my 1994.

of freedom, a positive conception of autonomy, an ideal of harmony between moral disposition and aesthetic character, and the concept of the highest good as an end to which a rational will cannot be indifferent, all of which can be made palpable to human sensibility through the symbolic significance of both the beautiful and the sublime.

4. The Autonomy of the Aesthetic

This is the heart of my argument, but before concluding I will comment on what I take to be Kant's still instructive conception of the connection between autonomy in his ordinary sense, that is, morality, and what we now think of as the autonomy of the aesthetic, and especially the autonomy of art.

On the interpretation I have been advancing,[15] Kant's conception of the beautiful as the symbol of morality – and in considering the autonomy of art, we can confine ourselves to the case of the beautiful, since Kant thinks of the sublime as only a natural and not an artistic phenomenon (*CPJ*, §23, 245) – is essentially non-didactic. By that I mean that the experience of beauty is a symbol of morality precisely because it is an experience of the freedom of the imagination from any constraint by concepts, including the concepts of the morally right and good themselves (see above all *CPJ*, §4, 207–8). To the extent that the form of any object would appear to be constrained by an antecedent interest in intentionally illustrating a concept, including a concept of morality, neither it nor the experience of it could be a symbol of morality;[16] so even where art *does* have a moral concept as its content, it is not compatible with the beauty of art, and thus the possibility of its symbolizing morality, for this moral content to appear to dictate the form of the work of art. That is why rational ideas do not appear in works of artistic genius in their own form, but in the guise of *aesthetic* ideas, that is, unifying themes or images which suggest an idea of reason on the one hand and an inexhaustible and pleasing harmony of sensible forms and images on the other without being reducible to either by any rule (*CPJ*, §49, 316).[17] Even when art has

[15] See also my 1993, especially chapter 3, 94–130.

[16] I have argued that in the letters *On the Aesthetic Education of Mankind*, Schiller built on precisely this paradoxical feature of Kant's aesthetic theory, and thus offers confirmation of my interpretation; see my 1993, 116–17.

[17] For further elaboration of this interpretation of aesthetic ideas, see my 1994. For a different approach to the issue of aesthetic ideas and the independence of aesthetic experience from constraint by moral ideas, see Savile 1987, 174–9. His view seems to

moral content, then, Kant supposes that the freedom of the imagination must remain manifest in the experience of it in order for that experience to be both pleasurable and a symbol of morality.

But this by no means entails that the production of art is autonomous in the sense of being immune from moral constraints altogether. On the contrary, Kant assumes that although the form of any successful work of art must not appear to be dictated by any moral concept, the production of works of art, like any other human practice, is always subject to the most general constraint of compatibility with the fundamental demands of morality. Kant does not assert this thesis explicitly; perhaps he thought it too obvious for that to be necessary. But he does intimate his commitment to it on at least three different occasions. First, in his discussion of the intellectual interest in the beautiful, Kant twice mentions that this interest will not be felt if one discovers that one has been *tricked* or *deceived* into taking an artistic simulacrum of a natural beauty for the real thing (*CPJ*, §42, 299, 302). In both cases, what Kant explicitly says is that the object cannot produce an intellectual interest *unless* it deceives us into thinking it is natural, or it is the thought that unintentional nature is receptive to our intentional ends which is of interest to us; but it is not farfetched to think that Kant is also responding to the fact of deceit itself, and assuming that nothing that is itself immoral, in the way that a deception always is, could positively engage any moral interest. Second, in discussing the artistic representation of content, Kant mentions that fine art can successfully represent all sorts of things that are not naturally beautiful, but that there is nevertheless one domain of objects, namely, those which excite "*disgust*," where our pleasure in the aesthetic merits of the means of representation cannot possibly outweigh our displeasure at what is represented (*CPJ*, §48, 312).[18] It is perhaps not completely clear whether by the disgusting Kant means the physiologically or the morally upsetting (e.g. the flayed body of Marsyas or the flaying of Marsyas), but to the extent that he can be taken to mean the latter then he can be taken to be saying that at least as a matter of fact if not also as a matter of principle

be that there is an outright contradiction between the possibility of the freedom of the imagination in its response to a work of art and the supposition that the work illustrates a moral idea, which can be avoided only by postulating an independent pleasure in the exploration of specific moral ideas (176). I do not see the necessity of this way out if the difference between rational and aesthetic ideas is understood as turning on the freedom of the imagination in the latter, as I suggest.

[18] The significance of this passing remark has been blown out of all proportion in Derrida 1971.

the aesthetic cannot be expected to be free of the constraints of our fundamental moral principles and their affective consequences. Finally, discussing the combination of several media of fine art in a single work, Kant notes that "If the fine arts are not brought into a near or distant connection with moral ideas, which alone carry with them a self-sufficient delight," then "they serve merely for diversion," and in the course of time will make "the spirit dull" and "the mind . . . dissatisfied with itself and moody" (*CPJ*, §52, 326). There is no argument here that aesthetic pleasure itself depends on a connection to moral ideas, which would undermine the original conception of the freedom of the imagination. Instead, the assumption must be that any form of human occupation which cannot be seen as contributing to the advancement of morality, at least in the long run, must ultimately become distasteful to us, and that the freedom from moralistic constraint which is essential to the experience of aesthetic pleasure does not exempt the aesthetic from this underlying principle of human moral psychology. In all of these examples, then, Kant's assumption is that the freedom of the experience of beauty from direct constraint by moral ideas does not mean that the practice of art either can or should be immune from the general principles of morality.

Of course, aside from general recommendations such as avoiding outright deceit or the portrayal of the truly disgusting, Kant does not offer us any mechanical rules for striking the balance between the freedom of the imagination from constraint by moral ideas, which is necessary for the beautiful to be a symbol of morality, and the subjection of art to the general constraints of morality, which is an immediate consequence of the fact that art is a human practice. But that is how it should be: if a mechanical rule could be given, then there would be at least one aspect of the production of art that would no longer require genius.[19]

[19] For a more contemporary discussion of this point, for which the present comments could provide some historical foundation, see Devereaux 1993.

10

Exemplary Originality

Genius, Universality, and Individuality

At the outset of the eighteenth century, genius was characterized simply as exceptional facility in perception and representation, where the latter is the object of artistic production and the former its precondition. As the century progressed, and as long into the nineteenth century as genius remained a lively topic, it came to be characterized as a gift for invention, leading to originality in artistic representation. But only by a few, whom we might for this reason call philosophical geniuses, were the implications of the new conception of genius fully embraced. Immanuel Kant was the first to recognize that genius, as exemplary originality, would be a stimulus and provocation to continuing revolution in the history of art; and John Stuart Mill, inspired by Wilhelm von Humboldt, was the first to argue that the expression of individuality in such a form is good in and of itself. What led Kant to his position was a distinctive conception of aesthetic experience and thus of the aims of art; what led Mill to his was a distinctive conception of the human good in general. In what follows, I will bring out what is distinctive in their conceptions of genius by contrasting them with those of other apostles of genius, such as Alexander Gerard, Samuel Taylor Coleridge, and Ralph Waldo Emerson, whose conceptions of genius were not in fact as radical as those of Kant and Mill. My purpose is primarily historical, although it is of course motivated by the belief that Kant and Mill jointly provide an analysis of both the costs and the benefits of genuine artistic innovation and individuality that is worth remembering in an age of perpetual revolution in the arts.

1. Facility

A conception of genius typical for the early eighteenth century may be found in the widely read *Critical Reflections on Poetry, Painting and Music* by Jean-Baptiste Du Bos, which had already enjoyed five French editions beginning in 1719 before being translated into English in 1748.[1] Du Bos begins his second volume by recapitulating the argument of the first that we turn to art to have our emotions aroused and moved, so that formal and stylistic merits may be a necessary condition but are never a sufficient condition for our enjoyment of art. "The sublimity of poetry and painting consists in moving and pleasing," he writes, and " 'Tis impossible for either a poem, or picture, to produce this effect, unless they have some other merit besides that of regularity and elegance of execution. . . . In order to render a work affecting, the elegance of design and the truth of coloring, if a picture; and the richness of versification, if a poem, ought to be employed in displaying such objects as are naturally capable of moving and pleasing."[2] He then characterizes genius as the ability, innate as it will turn out, to discover moving and pleasing ideas for the content of such works, rather than the ability to represent such ideas correctly, which in his view can readily be acquired with due application:

> The resemblance therefore between the ideas, which the poet draws from his own genius, and those which men are supposed to have in the situation in which he represents his personages, the pathetic [*sic*] likewise of the images he has formed before he took either pen or pencil in hand, constitute the chief merit of poems and pictures. 'Tis by the design and invention of ideas and images, proper for moving us, and employed in the executive part, that we distinguish the great artist from the plain workman, who frequently excels the former in execution. The best versifiers are not the greatest poets, as the most regular designers are far from the greatest painters.[3]

The use of "invention" in the second sentence of this paragraph might make it sound as if the genius is distinguished by his originality or expression of individuality, his creation of an idea that no one else has had before, but such an interpretation is belied by the first sentence, which characterizes genius precisely as the ability to conceive of the response which everyone ought to have in a represented situation. This ability may

[1] L'Abbé Du Bos, *Critical Reflections on Poetry and Painting*, trans. Thomas Nugent (London: John Nourse, 1748).

[2] Ibid., 2:1–2.

[3] Ibid., p. 3.

be rare, but there is nothing original or individual about what it discovers. This becomes even clearer a few pages later, when Du Bos offers his official definition of genius as "an aptitude, which man has received from nature to perform well and easily that which others can do but indifferently, and with a great deal of pains"; that the ability may be rare, but that what it is an ability to discover is not in any significant sense individual is precisely what is implied when Du Bos continues, "We learn to execute things for which we have a genius, with as much facility as we speak our own mother-tongue."[4] Mother tongues are nothing if not common to entire populations. The assumption that genius is a rare ability but not an ability to do something rare is also evident in Du Bos's subsequent illustrations: generalizing from the ability to lead troops in war to "all other professions," Du Bos writes that

> Nature has thought fit to make a distribution of her talents amongst men, in order to render them necessary to one another; the wants of men being the very first link of society. She has therefore pitched upon particular persons to give them an aptitude to perform rightly some things, which she has rendered impossible to others; and the latter have a facility granted them for other things, which facility has been refused the former.[5]

Some people are born with an innate aptitude that will develop, under favorable circumstances, into the ability to lead troops; others, with a genius for the "administration of great concerns, the art of putting people to those employments for which they are naturally formed, the study of physic, and even gaming itself";[6] and some, as it turns out, with an aptitude for hitting upon ideas and images that can move and engage others. But just as there is nothing individualistic or idiosyncratic in what constitutes success in military leadership or civic administration, so – rare as his ability is – there is nothing individualistic in the moving ideas of the artistic genius as conceived by Du Bos.

This way of conceiving of genius would seem to have been quickly rejected in the second half of the century, but a change was not in fact immediate. The Scot Alexander Gerard, professor of moral philosophy and then divinity in Aberdeen and author of the prize-winning *Essay on Taste* of 1759,[7] published a lengthy *An Essay on Genius* fifteen years later.[8]

4 Ibid., p. 5.
5 Ibid., pp. 7–8.
6 Ibid., p. 7.
7 Alexander Gerard, *An Essay on Taste* (London: A. Millar, 1759).
8 Alexander Gerard, *An Essay on Genius* (London: W. Strahan, 1774); facsimile reprint with modern introduction edited by Bernhard Fabian (Munich: Wilhelm Fink Verlag, 1966).

The work starts with a definition of genius and then devotes most of its length, first, to an analysis of the various faculties that comprise genius – in particular, the relation between genius and judgment – and, second, to a contrast between the ways in which genius is manifested in natural science on the one hand and the fine arts on the other.[9] Gerard introduces his definition of genius by distinguishing it from a mere capacity for learning, which he says "is very general among mankind": "Mere capacity, in most subjects, implies nothing beyond a little judgment, a tolerable memory, and considerable industry. But true genius is very different, and much less frequent."[10] Instead, he states, "Genius is properly the faculty of *invention*; by means of which a man is qualified for making new discoveries in science, or for producing original works in art."[11]

The definition of genius as a faculty of invention, and in particular the contrast between making new discoveries in science and producing original works in art, might suggest that artistic genius is not only rare but also individualistic, that is, a capacity for the expression of unique ideas and points of view that might not immediately or indeed ever find wide acceptance, for any of a variety of reasons. However, the continuation of Gerard's argument makes it clear that he, like Du Bos, assumed genius to be a rare talent, but a talent for the production of works that would readily find wide acceptance. To be sure, genius not constrained by judgment runs the risk of idiosyncrasy: "Often, however, the bye-roads of association, as we may term them, lead to rich and unexpected regions, give occasion to noble sallies of imagination, and proclaim an uncommon force of genius, able to penetrate through unfrequented ways to lofty or beautiful conceptions. . . . The truest genius is in hazard of sometimes running into superfluities."[12] But this is only the occasion for genius "to prune the luxuriance, and rectify the disorder of its first conceptions. . . . Thus to render genius complete, fertility and regularity of imagination must be united."[13] And by "regularity of imagination," Gerard means precisely the ability of genius to limit its productions to those which can be understood and appreciated by the great majority even of those who do not themselves have

9 Kant's insistence that genius is manifest only in fine art, not natural science, is clearly intended as a reply to Gerard's thesis that genius is manifest in both; see Kant, *Critique of the Power of Judgment*, §57. However, this issue will not be central to the points I shall make about Kant later.

10 Gerard, *Essay on Genius*, pp. 7–8.

11 Ibid., p. 8.

12 Ibid., p. 54.

13 Loc. cit.

the "fertility" of imagination to produce them. This is made clear a few pages later when Gerard writes: "In studying a work of true genius, when we attend to the multitude and variety of the materials, we wonder how the author could have found them all; and when we reflect how proper and apposite every part is, we are apt to think that it must have occurred to almost any person. Such is the effect of copiousness and regularity of imagination, united and harmoniously exerted."[14] The contrast that structures these sentences clearly reveals Gerard's assumptions: the fertility of imagination that constitutes genius is rare, but it is a rare talent to invent conceptions which, once invented, "we are apt to think . . . must have occurred to almost any person," that is, conceptions that can be counted on readily to find wide acceptance, free of any taint of idiosyncrasy that might reduce their appeal to an audience limited by time, place, interest, or its own talent.

What accounts for Gerard's confidence that genius is a rare talent to produce widely and readily accepted inventions? The answer to this question must lie in an objective conception of the merits of works of art, and this is precisely what we find in Gerard in the form of the assumptions that works of art are essentially adorned imitations or decorated representations where the principles or mechanisms of both imitation and adornment are natural rather than conventional, and thus readily and widely shared. This conception of art emerges in the course of Gerard's contrast between the manifestations of genius in art and natural science. In the sciences, the end of genius is "the discovery of *truth*," and in art, "the production of *beauty*."[15] Scientific genius is characterized above all by "penetration . . . a force of imagination as leads to the comprehension and explication of a subject,"[16] in particular, an ability to discover causal connections that are not immediately apparent to all but that can be made apparent to all. By contrast, artistic genius is characterized by "brightness of imagination," which "fits a man for adorning a subject."[17] Gerard characterizes brightness of imagination in terms that foreshadow Kant's later description of the manifestation of genius in the production of aesthetic ideas: it is "such a strength of imagination as makes every present object suggest a multitude of ideas, and hurries the mind quickly from one thing, to others not very strictly connected with it."[18] This might

[14] Ibid., pp. 56–7.
[15] Ibid., p. 318.
[16] Ibid., p. 323.
[17] Loc. cit.
[18] Ibid., p. 325.

suggest an inherent risk, or opportunity, for idiosyncrasy in works of artistic genius, but Gerard is not worried about such a risk because he believes that the principles of both representation and its adornment are naturally widely shared. He claims that "The fine arts are commonly called imitative"; some are "purely and totally" or "strictly imitative," such as painting; others, such as poetry, are less strictly imitative, "But even in cases where the arts are least imitative, it will appear on attention that this principle is predominant."[19] He then assumes that we all naturally respond to imitations and their adornments in common ways:

> In genius for the arts, resemblance, the predominant principle of association, continually operates along with all the other principles, and, by uniting its force to theirs, causes them [to] suggest only, and suggest quickly, such ideas as are conducive to the imitation or representation which the artist has in view. The attributes, qualities, and circumstances of any subject, are connected with it by coexistence, and are naturally suggested to the imagination by this relation: the predominance of resemblance as an associating principle in the poet or painter, will make these to be suggested, whenever they are necessary for marking distinctly the object which he describes or represents; and it will make those of them to occur most readily which are properest for this purpose, even though they themselves be remote.[20]

Artistic genius consists in the ability to discover representations and the associations among them which are naturally proper for their purpose. Thus, just as scientific genius consists in the unusual ability to penetrate to causal connections which, once seen, will be accepted by all, so artistic genius consists in the unusual ability to create representations which, once created, will be accepted and appreciated by all. Either form of genius is rare, but its effects are assumed to be universal.

For all the emphasis upon the individuality of genius in the half-century or so after Gerard's essay – that is to say, in the Romantic period – the underlying assumption that genius is a rare talent to create works whose appeal can safely be assumed to be universal remains constant. We may see this in two representative figures from the height of the Romantic period, Samuel Taylor Coleridge and Ralph Waldo Emerson. Coleridge in fact does not characterize genius in terms of invention at all, but rather as a talent to make what is timeless seem as if it is new and original. In his words, "the character and privilege of genius, and one of the marks which distinguish genius from talents," is the ability "To find no contradiction

[19] Ibid., pp. 33–4.
[20] Ibid., pp. 349–50.

in the union of old and new; to contemplate the ANCIENT of days and all his works with feelings as fresh, as if all had then sprang forth at the first creative fiat. . . . To carry on the feelings of childhood into the powers of manhood; to combine the child's sense of wonder and novelty with the appearances, which every day for perhaps forty years had rendered familiar."[21] Genius is not a gift for discovery or invention so much as for rediscovery of what, in some sense, has been felt all along. And Coleridge assumes that what the genius in this sense rediscovers has been felt not only all along but also by all, so that the rediscoveries of the genius can readily be communicated to all: "And therefore is it the prime merit of genius and its most unequivocal mode of manifestation, so to represent familiar objects as to awaken in the minds of others a kindred feeling concerning them which is the constant accompaniment of mental, no less than of bodily, convalescence."[22] And even more clearly than in the case of Gerard, Coleridge's confidence in the universal validity of the discoveries of genius seems to be grounded in an objectivist conception of beauty itself. For Coleridge, basing his conception of artistic genius on the model of William Wordsworth, art does not seem to be representation so much as a transparent medium through which the beauty of the natural world itself is directly communicated to the audience for art, and he certainly assumes that the sense for natural beauty is innate and universal:

> And what then is the beautiful? What is beauty? It is, in the abstract, the unity of the manifold, the coalescence of the diverse; in the concrete, it is the union of the shapely (*formosum*) with the vital . . . it is not different to different individuals and nations, as has been said, nor is it connected with the ideas of the good, or the fit, or the useful. The sense of beauty is intuitive, and beauty itself is all that inspires pleasure without, and aloof from, and even contrarily, to interest. . . . Believe me, you must master the essence, the *natura naturans*, which presupposes a bond between nature in the higher sense and the soul of man.[23]

What the genius possesses is the talent for using art to make the beauty of nature as fresh as it was for us all as children, where what appears beautiful to us as children and once again through art is necessarily the same.

Ralph Waldo Emerson reaches a similar conclusion by emphasizing the universality of the subject rather than the object, that is, by insisting

[21] Samuel Taylor Coleridge, *Biographia Literaria, with his Aesthetical Essays*, ed. J. Shawcross (Oxford: Oxford University Press, 1907; corrected edition, 1954), 1:59.

[22] Ibid., pp. 59–60.

[23] Coleridge, "On Poesy or Art," in *Biographia Literaria*, 2:256–7.

on what he calls the "Over-soul" or common human capacity for experience and thought rather than by characterizing the appeal of the object in the experience of beauty. In his famous essay "Self-Reliance," first published in 1841, Emerson seems to be the spokesman for individuality and self-expression understood as nonconformity, thus suggesting that there can be no guarantee that works of genius, as products of self-reliance, will be received with universal approbation, indeed perhaps even that genius implies the impossibility of universal approbation, or even the necessity of disagreement: "Whoso would be a man must be a nonconformist. . . . Nothing is at last sacred but the integrity of your own mind."[24] However, Emerson's explicit definitions of genius stress precisely the confidence that the genius can have in the universal acceptability of his ideas. Thus, Emerson begins the same essay by stating that "To believe your own thought, to believe that what is true for you in your private heart is true for all men, – that is genius. Speak your latent conviction, and it shall be the universal sense; for the inmost in due time becomes the outmost."[25] And, in a later essay, Emerson states his view of genius more fully by stating that genius consists of two abilities of equal importance: the ability to discover what seem to be new ideas and the ability to communicate those discoveries with complete success to others:

In the intellect constructive, which we popularly designate by the word Genius, we observe the same balance of two elements as in intellect receptive. The constructive intellect produces thoughts, sentences, poems, plans, designs, systems. It is the generation of the mind, the marriage of thought with nature. To genius must always go two gifts, the thought and the publication. The first is revelation, which is always a miracle. . . . It is the advent of truth into the world, a form of thought now, for the first time, bursting into the universe, a child of the old eternal soul, a piece of genuine and immeasurable greatness. . . . But to make it available, it needs a vehicle or art by which it is conveyed to men. To be communicable, it must become picture or sensible object. The most wonderful inspirations die with their subject, if he has no hand to paint them to the senses. . . . The rich, inventive genius of the painter must be smothered and lost for want of the power of drawing, and in our happy hours we should be inexhaustible poets, if once we could break through the silence into adequate rhyme. As all men have some access to primary truth, so all have some art or power of communication in their head, but only in the artist does it descend into the hand.[26]

[24] Ralph Waldo Emerson, "Self-Reliance," in *Essays: First Series* (1841), in Emerson, *Essays and Lectures*, ed. Joel Porte (New York: The Library of America, 1983), p. 261.

[25] Emerson, "Self-Reliance," *Essays and Lectures*, p. 259.

[26] Emerson, "Intellect," *Essays and Lectures*, pp. 422–3.

But Emerson is confident that the power of invention which is one-half of genius is rooted in the common human mentality that he calls the Over-soul, and thus is necessarily accompanied by the power for communication that is the other half of genius. He has faith that the experience and minds of individuals share a common essence:

> We live in succession, in division, in parts, in particles. Meantime, within man is the soul of the whole; the wise silence, the universal beauty, to which every part and particle is equally related; the eternal ONE. And this deep power in which we exist, and whose beatitude is all accessible to us, is not only self-sufficing and perfect in every hour, but the act of seeing and the thing seen, the seer and the spectacle, the subject and the object, are one.[27]

And the genius in particular is characterized by his access to this Over-soul: "The same Omniscience flows into the intellect, and makes what we call genius. . . . It is a larger imbibing of the common heart. It is not anomalous, but more like, and not less like other men. There is, in all great poets, a wisdom of humanity which is superior to any talents they exercise."[28] The genius can be self-reliant and nonconformist in the pursuit of his ideas because he also enjoys a degree of access to the Over-soul that guarantees that in due course what he discovers or invents in this way will be accepted by others whose access to the Over-soul may not be as ready as his but who are, in the end, part and parcel of the same Over-soul or have the same access to it. As with others in the tradition of genius going back to Du Bos, Emerson really treats genius as a facility of access to ideas that is rare but which accesses ideas that are universally valid. There is no idea that with the benefit of genius also come the costs, at the very least, of working without any guarantee of universal acceptance and, at the worst, of actual discord and upheaval in the history of the works of the imagination.

2. Originality

But Kant's account of genius recognizes precisely these risks; indeed, it portrays them as inevitable accompaniments of genius. While Kant characterizes aesthetic judgment in general as a claim to the universal subjective validity of our response to the genuinely beautiful or sublime, he at the same time acknowledges that this universal subjective validity is an "idea" rather than an empirical reality; likewise, although he characterizes

[27] Emerson, "The Over-soul," *Essays and Lectures*, p. 386.
[28] Emerson, "The Over-soul," *Essays and Lectures*, p. 396.

genius as "exemplary originality," he understands the sense in which the originality of genius is "exemplary" precisely as both a provocation to and a model for the originality of others, thereby guaranteeing that the works of genius will not constitute a stable canon but a locus of constant upheaval.

Kant defines genius as "the talent (natural gift)" or "inborn productive faculty" "that gives the rule to art," or more precisely "**through which** nature gives the rule to art."[29] Kant immediately provides what might seem to be a misleading explanation of why genius must be conceived of as faculty for giving a rule to art. "Every art presupposes rules which first lay the foundation by means of which a product that is to be called artistic is first represented as possible," he says, but

> The concept of beautiful art does not allow the judgment concerning the beauty of its product to be derived from any sort of rule that has a **concept** for its determining ground, and thus has as its ground a concept of how it is possible. Thus beautiful art cannot itself think up the rule in accordance with which it is to bring its product into being. Yet since without a preceding rule a product can never be called art, nature in the subject (and by means of the disposition of its faculties) must give the rule to art, i.e., beautiful art is possible only as a product of genius.[30]

One might think, like Du Bos, that the rules in art concern only the techniques that must be mastered by any competent practitioner of a particular medium of art, whether genius or journeyman, and that genius should consist just in that gift of talent and inspiration by which the truly successful artist goes beyond the mechanical or technical rules of his medium – rules should be a necessary but not sufficient condition for artistic success, and genius should be that by which the artist breaks free of rules instead of being bound by them. But such a response to Kant's statement would misunderstand his position on several counts. First, since Kant treats art as a species of intentional and rational human production,[31] there must be some sense in which the whole of an artist's productive activity is guided by a conception of its desired outcome and the steps to be taken in order to achieve that outcome; a model on which part of the artist's work was guided by rules, but part, indeed the most important part, was left to anything like mere chance would not be a model

[29] Kant, *Critique of the Power of Judgment*, ed. Paul Guyer, trans. Paul Guyer and Eric Matthews (Cambridge: Cambridge University Press, 2000), §46, 5:307; pagination as in *Kant's gesammelte Schriften*, vol. 5, ed. Wilhelm Windelband (Berlin: Georg Reimer, 1913).

[30] Ibid., §46, 5:307.

[31] Ibid., §53, 5:303.

of rational activity. Second, while a natural way of mapping a conception of artistic production as partly rule-governed and partly not on to the kind of mimetic or representational art that Kant takes as paradigmatic would be to treat the invention of the content for a work of art as a matter of inspiration but the mastery of the medium for its expression as a matter of mere convention, Kant makes it clear that, in truly successful art, genius lies in the invention of both the content and the form for its expression; genius, "as a talent for art . . . presupposes a determinate concept of the product, as an end, but also a representation (even if indeterminate) of the material, i.e., of the intuition, for the presentation of this concept."[32] But, third and most important, Kant supposes that the pleasure in all beauty is intersubjectively valid – that is, that under ideal conditions any beautiful object ought to please all observers of it – and thus that a beautiful work of art, as the product of intentional activity, aims to produce an intersubjectively valid response and judgment; thus, a work of art aims to be a rule for all, something that all ought to find beautiful or otherwise appropriately satisfying.[33] A work of art must not just be produced in accordance with certain rules, but must itself be a rule, something that all should find satisfying.

But why should genius be necessary to achieve such a result? Why can't an artist simply follow known rules in order to produce an object that will be exemplary, or itself a rule for the pleasure of all? The answer to this lies in Kant's account of beauty itself, according to which our pleasure in beauty lies not in the sheer fact of mimesis or its adornment, as in a theory such as Gerard's, but in the free play of the cognitive powers of imagination and understanding induced by a beautiful object, a play that is experienced by us with a sense of contingency, and thus precisely as the freedom of the beautiful object from visible constraint by determinate concepts or by known rules for its form and matter, which would play the same role as determinate concepts. In the introduction to the *Critique of the Power of Judgment*, Kant asserts his view first as a thesis about "subjective purposiveness" in the representation of nature. Here he expresses his view by means of his contrast between "determining" and "reflecting" judgment, where the former seeks to find a particular to which to apply a given concept while the latter seeks to find a concept that is not given

[32] Ibid., §49, 5:317.

[33] I use this expression to leave room for the possibility that art may seek to satisfy otherwise than through beauty, for instance, through sublimity. Kant himself sees sublimity as a characteristic of nature rather than art, but of course he is rarely followed in this regard.

to apply to a particular that is.[34] In the case of the judgment of beauty, however, the model of reflecting judgment must be understood loosely, because reflection on the perception of the object leads to a sense of comprehension that cannot be captured by any determinate concept at all, although on the basis of such an indeterminate comprehension of the object the concept of beauty itself can ultimately be applied to it:

If pleasure is connected with the mere apprehension (*apprehensio*) of the form of an object of intuition without a relation of this to a concept for a determinate cognition, then the representation is thereby related not to the object, but solely to the subject, and the pleasure can express nothing but its suitability to the cognitive faculties that are in play in the reflecting power of judgment, insofar as they are in play, and thus merely a subjective formal purposiveness of the object.[35]

Kant then equates this "subjective purposiveness" with beauty, adding, what he will subsequently defend, that such a response is universally valid:

That object the form of which (not the material aspects of its representation, as sensation) in mere reflection on it (without any intention of acquiring a concept from it) is judged as the ground of a pleasure in the representation of such an object – with its representation this pleasure is also judged to be necessarily combined, consequently not merely for the subject who apprehends this form but for everyone who judges at all. The object is then called beautiful.[36]

In the central section of the "Analytic of the Beautiful" that he calls the "key to the critique of taste," Kant characterizes this play of cognitive faculties as a free play: "The state of mind in [the] representation [of a beautiful object] must be that of a feeling of the free play of the powers of representation in a given representation for a cognition in general," and again adds that, since a judgment of beauty claims universal validity for the pleasure in such a state of mind, "This state of a **free play** of the faculties of cognition with a representation through which [a beautiful] object is given must be able to be universally communicated," that is, "valid for everyone."[37] A successful work of art is thus one which pleases us precisely because both its content and its form induce a free play of

34 Kant, *Critique of the Power of Judgment*, First Introduction, V, 20:211; published Introduction, §4, 5:179.

35 Ibid., Introduction, VII, 5:189–90.

36 Ibid., 190.

37 Ibid., §9, 5:217. The interpretation of this section is highly controversial. For my account of how it needs to be untangled, see "Pleasure and Society in Kant's Theory of Taste," in Ted Cohen and Paul Guyer, eds., *Essays in Kant's Aesthetics* (Chicago: University of Chicago Press, 1982), pp. 21–54. For a rejection of my account, see Hannah Ginsborg, "Reflective Judgment and Taste," *Nōus* 24 (1990): 63–78.

our imagination and understanding in a way that cannot appear to be dictated by any determinate concept or rule, but which is nevertheless itself a rule or norm for everyone in the sense that, under ideal circumstances, it should please everyone by inducing the same pleasure in the free play of these cognitive faculties. In natural beauty, such as that of a flower or a sunset, it is the form of an object produced by nature without human intervention that induces this free play of imagination and understanding; artistic beauty must be both produced by rational human activity and not produced in accordance with a visible rule, so Kant construes it as the product of nature working through the medium of a human being to produce something that is not visibly rule-governed but yet is itself a rule for the pleasure of all.

This analysis of artistic beauty entails that truly successful art must always possess what Kant calls "exemplary originality":[38] originality, because the successful work of art can never appear to have been produced in accordance with a rule but must always strike us with an element of contingency or novelty; yet exemplary, because it must at the same time strike us as pleasing in a way that should be valid for all. Originality by itself, to be sure, is easy to achieve: just make something that departs from all known rules and models. Of course, in this way a lot of nonsense will be produced, so what Kant calls "original nonsense" is easy to come by. The trick is to produce exemplary originality, objects which, "while not themselves the result of imitation . . . must yet serve others in that way, i.e., as a standard for judging,"[39] or objects that strike us as original in appearing to depart from known rules and models but which can themselves be pleasing to all or a rule for all. Thus, in Kant's view, all truly successful art must be the work of genius.

This characterization of successful art makes the reception of art a delicate matter. First, since the essence of the response to any form of beauty is the feeling of the free play of imagination and understanding, a successful work of art must be an expression of the free play of imagination and understanding that has occurred in the artist, but yet leave room for a sufficient degree of free play of imagination and understanding in the members of its audience for them to take pleasure in the object – which depends, after all, precisely on their experiencing of the freedom of their own cognitive powers, not on their knowledge that the artist exercised such freedom. The work of art must be the product of intentional activity,

[38] Kant, *Critique of the Power of Judgment*, §46, 5:308.
[39] Ibid.

audience that will in fact include not only the mere consumers of their art, who are never given Kant's account of aesthetic response as free play, mere or merely passive consumers, but also those producers of art who will succeed them as they have succeeded their own predecessors.

This double task is difficult to accomplish, and the true genius is always a rare "favorite of nature." Leaving aside the question of how often works of genius will find their ideal audience, ready to meet the freedom of the artist's imagination and understanding with that of their own, Kant suggests that the majority of artistic producers following and responding to any example of genuine genius will fall into two camps: on the one hand, there is likely to be a "school" of followers, other artists seeking "a methodical instruction in accordance with rules, insofar as it has been possible to extract them from those products of spirit and their individuality," who may well descend to mere "aping" (*Nachäffung*), copying "everything, even down to that which the genius had to leave in, as a deformity," and even more likely losing the very spark of originality that made the work of genius exemplary in the first place; on the other hand, work of genius will also inspire "**mannerism**," that is, "mere **individuality** (originality) in general, in order to distance oneself as far as possible from imitators, yet without having the talent thereby to be **exemplary** at the same time."[44] In other words, since works of genius are naturally models and provocations for others yet genius is rare, the majority of what is inspired by works of genius is likely to consist of work that is exemplary but lacking originality on the one hand, or original without being exemplary – original nonsense rather than exemplary originality – on the other.

So Kant's theory of genius does not suggest, as its contemporaries did, that genius is simply a rare capacity to discover ideas and forms for their expression which, once discovered, will be understood and appreciated by all in exactly the same way. Kant's story is more complex. First, while every work of art in striving for beauty also strives for universal validity, at the same time, since beauty itself depends on the feeling of the free play of the cognitive faculties of its perceiver, every successful work of art must also generate a variety of responses. To be sure, such variety in the *content* of different individuals' responses to the same work of art might be compatible with a uniform *level* of satisfaction in the work, but in practice even that will undoubtedly be difficult to attain. Second, as someone who must be both exemplary and original, an artistic genius will provoke three kinds of response among his or her artistic successors: a school

44 Ibid.

of copiers, for whom the work will be exemplary in everything except its originality; mannerists, who will be provoked to originality without producing anything exemplary; and, in rare cases, other geniuses, whose work must necessarily depart from that of their predecessors in some essential respects. Thus, Kant's conception of genius guarantees that the history of art will be one of variety in response as much as agreement in valuation; constant upheaval in forms of artistic success; and, inevitably, great amounts of waste, academic on the one hand and mannerist on the other. This has the ring of truth,[45] something that every age ought to remember as it complains about its flood of second-rate art: there really is no other way in which the occasional works of genius, which tend to be the only ones we remember from past epochs, thereby making genius seem more prevalent in the past than in the present, could emerge.

To be sure, in the end Kant seems reluctant fully to embrace the implications of his own account of genius. Having analyzed genius in a way that guarantees a perpetual sequence of both experimentation and waste in the history of art, he suddenly asks what must happen when there is a clash between genius and taste, and asserts:

> If anything must be sacrificed in the conflict of the two properties in one product, it must rather be on the side of genius: and the power of judgment, which in matters of beautiful art makes its pronouncements on the basis of its own principles, will sooner permit damage to the freedom and richness of the imagination than to the understanding.

In other words, "Taste, like the power of judgment in general, is the discipline (or corrective) of genius."[46] Kant attempts to justify this assertion, so reminiscent of Gerard's insistence that "to render genius complete, fertility and regularity of imagination must be united,"[47] by suddenly aligning genius with imagination, and taste with judgment or understanding, and then maintaining that in any clash between these faculties the latter must surely be privileged over the former. But since throughout his argument Kant has argued that both genius and taste depend upon harmony between imagination and understanding, this new alignment is unexplained. Kant's thesis that, if necessary, taste must clip the wings

45 Everyone will have their own favorite examples of artistic waste. My most striking experience of academic waste came at the Prado, where three rooms of splendid work by Velázquez are followed by twice as many filled with his lackluster imitators, and the half-dozen rooms of brilliant Goyas are followed by numerous and uninteresting Goyesques.

46 Kant, *Critique of the Power of Judgment*, §50, 5:319–20.

47 See note 13.

of genius is probably better understood simply as another expression of his basic commitment to the intrinsic value of agreement in judgment itself, one that has manifested itself at other points in his argument as well.[48] But, although Kant structures the whole "Critique of the Aesthetic Power of Judgment" as an explanation of how we can reasonably claim intersubjective validity in judgments of taste, he never explains why it is so important that we actually be able to attain such agreement. He thus leaves us free to make our own judgment that, if the innovation of artistic genius can come only at the price of short- or long-term disagreement in our judgments of taste, the benefit may ultimately outweigh the cost.

3. The Value of Originality

Kant's account of genius makes variety and upheaval in the world of art inevitable, but as we have just seen he hesitates to embrace the limitation on our expectation of agreement in matters of taste that would seem to follow. Is there anything that could make the variety, upheaval, and even waste of artistic effort that must accompany the workings of genius seem valuable rather than lamentable? Here we can turn to a figure not usually mentioned in discussions of genius, John Stuart Mill (though we should keep in mind that Mill saw himself as the heir of Coleridge as well as of Bentham). Mill did not write a treatise on genius like an eighteenth-century divine, nor did he include a chapter on it in a systematic treatise, like a nineteenth-century aesthetician. But he uses the example of artistic genius to illustrate his arguments for the value of freedom of thought and expression in the central chapter 3 of *On Liberty* (1859). Like Kant, Mill conceived of genius as originality that is exemplary in its ability to stimulate others to originality as well, and part of its value is precisely that it does this:

> I insist thus emphatically upon the importance of genius, and the necessity of allowing it to unfold itself freely in both thought and in practice, being well aware that no one will deny the position in theory, but knowing also that almost every one, in reality, is totally indifferent to it. People think genius a fine thing if it enables a man to write an exciting poem, or paint a picture. But in its true sense, that of originality in thought and action, though no one says that it is not a

48 For example, Kant's exclusion of color and tone from the proper objects of taste simply because we are more likely to disagree in our responses to them than in our responses to spatial or temporal structure; see *Critique of the Power of Judgment*, §14, 5:223–5, and Paul Guyer, *Kant and the Claims of Taste*, 2d ed. (Cambridge: Cambridge University Press, 1997), pp. 199–210.

thing to be admired, nearly all, at heart, think that they can do very well without it. Unhappily this is too natural to be wondered at. Originality is the one thing which unoriginal minds cannot feel the use of. They cannot see what it is to do for them: how should they. If they could see what it would do for them, it would not be originality. The first service which originality has to render them, is that of opening their eyes: which being once fully done, they would have a chance of being themselves original.[49]

Of course, that genius is a stimulus to originality beyond itself will be no explanation of its value unless originality is valuable in itself, and that is what the larger argument of Mill's chapter 3 aims to establish. His argument falls into two parts: one, actually the second, in which this passage occurs, that originality has instrumental value; the other, that originality has intrinsic value. The argument that originality has instrumental value is simply that originality is the only source for new truths and practices, of which mankind is always in need: "There is always need of persons not only to discover new truths, and point out when what were once truths are true no longer, but also to commence new practices, and set the example of more enlightened conduct, and better taste and sense in human life."[50] This implies, along the way, Mill's recognition that both variety and change are inevitable features of the human condition, in tastes for art as well as in everything else, because the circumstances of individuals vary both within a particular period and over time, so that "at the maturity of his faculties" each individual must "find out what part of recorded experience is properly applicable to his own circumstances and character";[51] it could also be amplified, along the lines of Mill's argument in chapter 2, with the observation that new inventions in every sphere of human activity are necessary not only to help us discover new truths and practices and jettison those which are no longer valuable, but also to test and reaffirm those which are of continuing value. In these thoughts, it should be noted, Mill presumably does not use the case of artistic genius as just an analogue for creativity in more important areas of science and policy; it should surely be part of Mill's thought that new thoughts and practices important for human welfare can emerge through the fine arts as well as from anywhere else.

49 John Stuart Mill, *On Liberty*, in *Essays on Politics and Society*, vol. 18 of the *Collected Works of John Stuart Mill*, ed. J. M. Robson (Toronto and London: University of Toronto Press and Routledge & Kegan Paul, 1977), p. 268.

50 Mill, *On Liberty*, in *Collected Works*, 18:267.

51 Ibid., p. 262.

Beyond all this, however, Mill also argues for the intrinsic value of genius and originality, with a claim applicable to artistic genius as well as to any other form of human originality:

> It is not by wearing down into uniformity all that is individual in themselves, but by cultivating it and calling it forth, within the limits imposed by the rights and interests of others, that human beings become a noble and beautiful object of contemplation; and as the works partake the character of those who do them, by the same process human life also becomes rich, diversified, and animating, furnishing more abundant aliment to high thoughts and elevating feelings, and strengthening the tie which binds every individual to the race, by making the race infinitely better worth belonging to.[52]

In other words, the sheer variety of human beings and their products is something worth contemplating, perhaps the greatest thing worth contemplating, quite apart from the value of any particular productions – the sheer variety of human genius should be just as important to us as the value, intrinsic or instrumental, of any restricted canon of objects. This is perhaps Mill's most basic thought in *On Liberty*, and although he says nothing about the philosophical status of this premise, it might be suggested that it is itself an aesthetic thought – Mill's statement that it is through their variety and the variety of their productions "that human beings become a noble and beautiful object of contemplation" certainly exploits the terminology of classical aesthetics. But whatever the character of Mill's argument, it should be clear that the intrinsic rather than the instrumental value of genius, artistic or otherwise, lies precisely in the fact that it is a source of diversity rather than uniformity in human experience.

This passage of Mill might seem Emersonian in its elevated tone, but Mill's position is diametrically opposed to Emerson's. Emerson's thought is that every discovery of genius is a discovery of part of the single common human experience, the Over-soul that unites the individual souls of all. Mill's idea is that there is, at one level of abstraction, some one thing that is or should be common to all human beings – namely, their enjoyment of the spectacle of human diversity – but of course what is enjoyed *in concreto* is precisely the diversity rather than the uniformity of particular human experiences. There is no room for the thought of an Over-soul in Mill's empiricism, although there is certainly room for a common sense of the fascination of human diversity that could be developed by all enlightened persons.

52 Ibid., p. 266.

Putting Kant and Mill together, then, we might conclude that genius, as exemplary originality, is an engine of diversity and change as well as of universal validity in art, as elsewhere, yet that this is not merely a fact about human history and experience to be observed or even lamented, but rather something to be celebrated – itself one of the fundamental sources of satisfaction in human existence. Kant undermines the confidence of both his predecessors and his successors that the exemplarity of originality can be simply equated with uniformity of thought and feeling, but Mill portrays this result as itself an object of aesthetic satisfaction.

PART III

MOSTLY AFTER KANT

11

Pleasure and Knowledge in Schopenhauer's Aesthetics

Negative and Positive Pleasure

Schopenhauer is famous for his characterization of aesthetic experience in purely cognitive terms, as an experience in which consciousness of the manifold and ever-changing particulars of ordinary experience is superseded by cognition of the unique and timeless forms of objects of experience or objectifications of the Will,[1] which Schopenhauer calls "Platonic Ideas." In his words, aesthetic experience

> Is just the state that I described above as necessary for knowledge of the Idea, as pure contemplation, absorption in perception, being lost in the object, forgetting all individuality, abolishing the kind of knowledge which follows the principle of sufficient reason, and comprehends only relations. It is the state where, simultaneously and inseparably, the perceived individual thing is raised to the Idea of its species, and the knowing individual to the pure subject of will-less knowing, and now the two, as such, no longer stand in the stream of time and of all other relations. It is then all the same whether we see the setting sun from a prison or a palace.
>
> (*WWR* 1, §38, 96–97)[2]

[1] I capitalize "Will" when referring to the supra-individual metaphysical substratum of the world as Schopenhauer conceives of it, but use the lower-case "will" when referring to the phenomenon of individual volition as it presents itself through ordinary consciousness in the phenomenal realm. In fact, references to will in this ordinary sense of individual volition, which I will sometimes also designate as "our will" or "individual will," numerically predominate the other usage in this essay.

[2] References are to and translations from Schopenhauer's *World as Will and Representation*, tr. E. F. J. Payne (Indian Hills: Falcoln's Wing Press, 1958). References to Kant's *Critique of the Power of Judgment*, also to be cited frequently, are given by section number, followed

However, on first glance the pleasure of aesthetic response associated with this cognition of Platonic Ideas is entirely negative, consisting in relief from the incessant pain of the inevitably unfulfilled desires associated with ordinary consciousness of the manifold particulars of quotidian experience, and in nothing but that relief. But such a purely negative account of the pleasures of such an elevated form of cognition seems disappointing, and to treat aesthetic experience as indeed nothing but an anaesthetic: if all that cognition of Platonic Ideas has to offer us is relief from pain, it is not clear why the most refined art should be in any but merely contingent ways preferable to a good drug. Further, such an account of the aesthetic as offering relief from all effects of the will by means of the contemplation of Platonic Ideas seems to be not merely disappointing but particularly paradoxical when it comes to what Schopenhauer himself clearly regards as the highest of all art-forms and aesthetic objects, that is, music. For Schopenhauer characterizes music as "by no means like the other arts, namely a copy of the Ideas, but [as] a *copy of the Will itself*" (*WWR* 1, §52, 257). But this immediately raises the question, how can experience of a copy of the Will itself produce relief from the will, which is apparently the sole source of pleasure in all aesthetic experience? And if this question cannot be answered, is there then not a contradiction between Schopenhauer's general theory of aesthetic pleasure and the account of the particular art-form which he clearly cherished the most?[3]

To answer this and several other puzzles about Schopenhauer's cognitivist theory of aesthetic pleasure will require seeing Schopenhauer's account of the pleasure of cognition as rather more nuanced and complicated than is often recognized. On the account I will give, Schopenhauer's theory contains a positive element as well as a negative one, that is, a recognition that certain forms of cognitively significant experience are intrinsically pleasurable as well as affording relief from the pains associated with other forms of experience.[4] Recognition of the positive as well as

by volume and page as in Kant's *Gesammelte Schriften*, edited by the German Academy of Sciences (Berlin, 1900 –).

3 Such a tension must be obvious in, for example, the otherwise helpful exposition of Schopenhauer's aesthetics in Bryan Magee, *The Philosophy of Schopenhauer* (Oxford: The Clarendon Press, 1983), pp. 164–188. Magee claims that on Schopenhauer's view music "is the only art that articulates the noumenal will directly" (p. 184), but also describes Schopenhauer as holding that "we care so much about art" only "because it provides us with a release, if only momentary, from the prison we ordinarily inhabit" (p. 170), and does not ask whether knowledge of the noumenal Will as thing-in-itself provides such relief or, if not, whether there is some other pleasure inherent in it.

4 In recognizing both negative and positive pleasures, Schopenhauer's aesthetics is part of a well-established tradition. Both Burke and Kant had used versions of such a distinction

negative element in Schopenhauer's aesthetic cognitivism will also allow us to perceive some of the continuities between Schopenhauer's view and those of some of his most important predecessors, which the customary focus on the purely negative side of his theory may well obscure.

The Cognitivist Tradition in German Aesthetics

Let me begin, then, with a few words about the sorts of aesthetic theories prior to Schopenhauer's which we might regard as having defined the basic form of aesthetic cognitivism. In Germany, modern philosophy in general as well as modern aesthetics in particular began with Leibniz and Wolff. Neither one of these philosophers developed a free-standing aesthetic theory, but both revealed a certain shared conception of the nature of aesthetic experience and of the pleasure that we take in it in using examples to illustrate more general points in their philosophies, especially general claims about the nature of sensory or empirical knowledge. They appealed to the well-recognized experience of *je ne sais quois* in matters of taste to illustrate what they regarded to be the clear but confused nature of sensory perception in general as a cognitive state in which we have a clear recognition of the difference between one object and another without any distinct awareness of the particular characteristics that actually make the two objects distinct that a more refined or divine intellect than our own might enjoy. At the same time, however, they saw even such a confused form of thought, which might otherwise be thought to be a source only of distress, as a source of pleasure, insofar as it is the way, imperfect as it may be, in which the objective perception of the world can be communicated to us. Thus Wolff offered the famous definition of pleasure as the sensory perception of perfection.[5] Pleasure was thereby defined as the response to the recognition, or more precisely as itself the form taken by the recognition, of objective perfection, primarily in a metaphysical sense but then in a practical sense as well. On this account, however, the pleasurability of sensory experience in general or aesthetic experience in particular was not associated with the form or vehicle of

to explain the distinction between the beautiful and the sublime. See Edmund Burke, *A Philosophical Enquiry into the Origin of our Ideas of the Sublime and Beautiful*, Adam Philips, ed. (Oxford: Oxford University Press, 1990), Part I, sections III–IV, pp. 31–35; Immanuel Kant, *Critique of the Power of Judgment* §23, 5: 244–245. As we will see in the fourth section, Schopenhauer has a different way of explicating the distinction between the beautiful and the sublime, and uses the distinction between positive and negative pleasure much more broadly.

5 *Vernünftige Gedanken von Gott, der Welt, and die Seele des Menschen* (Halle, 1720) §404.

perception as much as with its content or object. Aesthetic experience was not thought of as pleasurable because of its logical or phenomenological features such as its clarity on the one hand and indistinctness on the other, but solely because of its content.

Alexander Gottlieb Baumgarten, usually reputed the founder of modern aesthetics because of his master's dissertation of 1735, *Meditationes philosophicae de nonnullis ad poema pertinentibus*,[6] wrote metaphysics in the Leibnizo-Wolffian vein, but effected a subtle transformation in the Leibnizo-Wolffian conception of aesthetic experience, one that indeed often went unnoticed by his own disciples such as Georg Friedrich Meier. For Baumgarten explained aesthetic pleasure as due not to the *sensory perception of perfection* but rather to the *perfection of sensory perception.* That is, Baumgarten agreed with the basic Leibnizo-Wolffian conception of sensory perception as a clear but confused awareness of that which could at least in principle be represented both clearly and distinctly by a more refined intellect, but did not infer from that characterization that the pleasure associated with sensory perception must therefore arise entirely in spite of the nature of sensory perception itself and only because of the content that is, however imperfectly, perceived. On the contrary, he held that the special nature of sensory perception as clear but confused is not an imperfection at all, but rather that it offers unique opportunities for cognition which could not be replicated by more purely conceptual cognition, and that in aesthetic experience we enjoy the exercise of this unique form of cognition in its own right and not merely because of some valuable content it may happen to convey. "The goal of aesthetics," he wrote, "is the perfection of sensitive cognition as such."[7] And the particular feature of sensory perception that is exploited for the unique pleasure of aesthetic experience, he held, is its *richness*, the possibility of conveying a lot of information through a single pregnant image, a possibility that is

[6] This work earns Baumgarten the status of founder because it was the first to introduce the term "aesthetics" (*aesthetica*) as a name for a special philosophical discipline; but that discipline had already been a recognized subject in professional philosophy in Britain for at least a decade, since the publication of Francis Hutcheson's first *Inquiry Concerning Beauty, Order, Harmony, Design* of 1725. While Baumgarten's work certainly constituted a major innovation in the German philosophical tradition and was to be of enduring influence for the better part of a century, the lively debate on the foundations of taste that had already begun in Britain means that his invention of the name for the new discipline cannot earn him credit for the invention of the discipline itself.

[7] *Aesthetica* §14; in Hans Rudolf Schweizer, *Ästhetik als Philosophie der sinnlichen Erkenntnis: Eine Interpretation der "Aesthetica" A. G. Baumgartens mit teilweise Widergabe des lateinischen Textes und deutscher Übersetzung* (Basel: Schwabe, 1973), p. 114.

sacrificed by logical or conceptual cognition for the sake of greater clarity. "The perfection of every sort of cognition arises from richness, magnitude, truth, clarity, certainty and the liveliness of cognition,"[8] he held, but whereas the richness of conceptual cognition arises from the way in which a concept can apply to many particulars precisely by sacrificing most of the detail that makes each unique, the richness of aesthetic objects arises precisely from the way in which they suggest an inexhaustible wealth of information and ideas that cannot be reduced to any simple concept. Although of course in the end Baumgarten made room for conventional pieties – under the category of "aesthetic magnitude" he explained our pleasure in the uplifting content of works of art – his revolutionary contribution lay in his recognition that aesthetic experience exploits the distinctive character of sensory rather than intellectual representation or cognition, and that we enjoy the exercise of this unique cognitive capacity in aesthetic experience at least as much for its own sake as for the sake of any content that is conveyed.

Much in the aesthetic theory of Immanuel Kant can be construed as an alternative to Baumgarten's conception of aesthetic experience, although there is much else in his theory that is clearly a direct development of Baumgarten's views.[9] Kant may well owe his general insistence on the overarching difference between intuitions and concepts in all knowledge to the example of Baumgarten's distinction between sensory and logical cognition, but he does not follow Baumgarten in associating what is characteristic about aesthetic experience with the unique formal features of intuition.[10] Nor, however, contrary to common characterization of Kant's aesthetics as non-cognitivist, does he dissociate the explanation of aesthetic experience from the value of cognition altogether. On the contrary, the heart of Kant's aesthetic theory is the explanation of aesthetic pleasure as due to the realization of the fundamental goal of cognition under non-standard conditions in which the realization of this goal cannot be taken for granted.

8 *Aesthetica* §22; Schweizer, p. 118.

9 In particular, the theory of aesthetic ideas in §49 of the *Critique of the Power of Judgment*, which presumably must have been at least an initial impetus to Schopenhauer's theory of the role of the Platonic Ideas in aesthetic experience, is a direct development of Baumgarten's leading idea of the richness of clear but confused sensory perception.

10 That association had been reserved, after all, to explain the unique contribution of space and time to all theoretical cognition; this is what underlies Kant's rejection of Baumgarten's conception of aesthetics as a special discipline concerning the beautiful at *Critique of Pure Reason* A 21/B 35–36.

The theoretical foundations of Kant's aesthetics have to be reconstructed from the two different introductions that Kant wrote for the *Critique of the Power of Judgment.* Most of the key premises are laid out in the Introduction that Kant published in the final text of 1790, where he argues that the feeling of pleasure is always connected with the attainment of a goal, and thus that an intersubjectively valid feeling of pleasure such as he will argue the feelings of the beautiful and the sublime to be must be associated with the attainment of an intersubjectively shared goal, such as he assumes in this context only the goal of cognition itself is. But further, Kant notes, such pleasure is "especially noticeable" only when there is something unexpected about the attainment of the goal in question.[11] And this additional condition is fulfilled when we are in the state which Kant characterizes as the "harmony" or "free play" of the cognitive faculties of imagination (which includes sensory intuition) and understanding, because, as Kant perhaps makes clearer in the originally drafted, so-called "First Introduction," which he did not use in the published work allegedly only on the grounds of its length, such a state represents satisfaction of the "subjective conditions for a cognition," or the unification of the sensory manifold presented by an object of experience, precisely in the absence of the condition which ordinarily guarantees the satisfaction of the goal of cognition, namely, the subsumption of the object of experience under some determinate concept.[12] This condition can be understood as one in which we have a sense of the unity of the manifold offered to us by an object that does not flow from the subsumption of that object under any determinate concept, a model which Kant develops for the specific case of art in the form of his theory of aesthetic ideas, which describes the ineffably rich way a work of artistic genius communicates to us an idea that cannot be exhaustively reduced to any ordinary concept.

In this theory, Kant does not follow Baumgarten in linking aesthetic pleasure directly to intuitions rather than concepts, but instead links such pleasure to a special state in which the understanding's general goal of finding unity in manifolds is felt to be satisfied by the sensory manifold offered to us by a work of nature or of art even and precisely when that manifold cannot be subsumed under any determinate concept. So he does not associate aesthetic pleasure with the achievement of a special

[11] *Critique of the Power of Judgment*, Introduction, Section VI, 5:187.
[12] *First Introduction to the Critique of the Power of Judgment*, Section VIII, 20:224.

kind of cognition, but rather with the use of the cognitive faculties and the realization of at least the subjective aspect of cognition under special circumstances, circumstances in which one of the ordinary requisites for cognition, the subsumption of objects under determinate concepts, is lacking. But he shares with Baumgarten the underlying impulse of aesthetic cognitivism, namely, the assumption that there is a powerful source of pleasure directly associated with the use of cognitive faculties and the achievement of cognitive goals, independent of any particular content of the object of such exercise of the cognitive faculties (although of course potentially enhanced by further values which may attach to the content). In other words, the key supposition of both of these pillars of the cognitivist tradition in German aesthetics is that the unique uses of our cognitive capacities which are paradigmatic for aesthetic experience are intrinsically and positively pleasurable.

Active and Passive Contemplation

It is precisely this underlying assumption which Schopenhauer's conception of aesthetic pleasure appears to deny. What I shall now argue, however, is that a similar assumption that there is a positive source of pleasure in cognition itself is not absent from Schopenhauer's thought, and some of the puzzles of his aesthetic theory, including the puzzle earlier mentioned about the possibility of our pleasure in music, can be resolved by recognizing this positive aspect of his cognitivism.

The quotation with which we began comes from a point in Schopenhauer's exposition of his aesthetic theory in the Third Book of *The World as Will and Representation* at which he is summing up the first stage of his discussion. This book begins, however, with a general characterization of the Platonic Ideas as the archetypes or forms of the species of particular objects in the world of appearance; those individuals are objectifications of the Will, which is on Schopenhauer's conception the underlying reality of appearance understood in terms of the phenomenon, human will, that most closely approximates it, and the Ideas thus represent the various possible forms or what Schopenhauer calls the "grades" of the objectification of the Will (*WWR* 1, §30, 169). Prior to making the explicit connection between the Ideas and aesthetic experience, Schopenhauer follows this initial general characterization of the Ideas with an initial and equally general characterization of the effect of contemplation of the Ideas on the will that does not yet mention art or the aesthetic. As this initial characterization raises several questions for the subsequent application to the aesthetic, it is necessary to have it before us in detail:

> The transition that is possible, but to be regarded only as an exception, from the common knowledge of particular things to knowledge of the Idea takes places suddenly, since knowledge tears itself free from the service of the will precisely by the subject's ceasing to be merely individual, and being now a pure will-less subject of knowledge . . .
>
> Raised up by the power of the mind, we relinquish the ordinary way of considering things, and cease to follow under the guidance of the forms of the principle of sufficient reason merely their relations to one another, whose final goal is always the relation to our own will. Thus we no longer consider the where, the when, the why, and the whither in things, but simply and solely the *what.* Further, we do not let abstract thought, the concepts of reason, take possession of our consciousness, but, instead of all this, devote the whole power of our mind to perception, sink ourselves completely therein, and let our whole consciousness be filled by the calm contemplation of the natural object actually present, whether it be a landscape, a tree, a rock, a crag, a building, or anything else. We *lose* ourselves entirely in this object, to use a pregnant expression; in other words, we forget our individuality, our will, and continue to exist only as pure subject, as clear mirror of the object, so that it is as though the object alone existed without anyone to perceive it, and thus we are no longer able to separate the perceiver from the perception, but the two have become one, since the entire consciousness is filled and occupied by a single image of perception. If, therefore, the object has to such an extent passed out of all relation to something outside it, and the subject has passed out of all relation to the will, what is thus known is no longer the individual thing as such, but the *Idea,* the eternal form, the immediate objectivity of the Will at this grade. Thus at the same time, the person who is involved in this perception is no longer an individual, for in such perception the individual has lost himself; he is *pure,* will-less, painless, timeless *subject of knowledge.*
>
> (*WWR* 1, §34, 178–179)

Here Schopenhauer suggests that because contemplation of the Ideas replaces attention to the particular objects that are the ordinary objects of desire, the subject is freed from desire and the pain attendant upon the impossibility of its fulfillment; and he suggests further that in focussing attention upon the Ideas the subject even loses awareness of its own individual identity, an awareness which Schopenhauer must thus be supposing is always grounded upon recognition of the distinction between the individual self and individual objects of perception, and in so losing all awareness of its individual identity the self seems to be freed of even the possibility of desire, which is always the desire of an individual subject for an individual object.

Whether it is at all plausible for Schopenhauer to ascribe such effects to the contemplation of Ideas, it seems at least clear what he wants to claim. On reflection, however, there are several puzzles about what he is claiming. First, although the passage ends by describing something like the loss of all individual desire and will, it begins with a description of contemplation as the consequence of an active, even violent adoption of a cognitive attitude by the individual mind – "knowledge tears itself free from the service of the will," and "raised up by the power of the mind, we relinquish the ordinary way of considering things." Yet it seems difficult to understand such decisive mental actions except as at least in part products of the individual will. Thus there seems to be an air of paradox about Schopenhauer's account. It is not mere contemplation which passively frees us from our will; rather we actively will to contemplate in order to free ourselves from our will. Not that there is actually a logical contradiction in such an idea – one could, after all, inflict a great pain upon oneself now in order to be free of all pain later, or freely choose to enslave oneself now and thus lose all freedom later – but there does seem to be something unsettling about it.

Further, the characterization before us seems to have several untoward consequences. First, the idea that we can free ourselves *for* contemplation by actively tearing ourselves away from our ordinary concerns and thus allowing what are ordinarily objects of individual desire to become objects for pure will-less and self-less knowing suggests that, since every object must embody some degree of the objectification of the Will, *any* object could become an object of aesthetic experience as long as our initial will to contemplate is sufficiently strong. Yet the fact that on a proposed characterization of the aesthetic attitude any object at all could become a proper object of this attitude is usually supposed to be a conclusive objection against that account of the attitude, or even against the very possibility of an aesthetic attitude theory altogether.[13] Second, the account appears quite unrealistic in ascribing a sort of mental heroism to all aesthetic transactions, that is, in suggesting that every experience of something beautiful presupposes a violent exercise of the will by means of

[13] See for example George Dickie, *Art and the Aesthetic: An Institutional Analysis* (Ithaca: Cornell University Press, 1974), p. 77. Of course, the potential ubiquity of the aesthetic attitude will be an objection against an account of it only if one supposes that the account is supposed to play some role in grounding some extensional distinction, such as that between art and non-art. Otherwise, the potential ubiquity of the aesthetic attitude implied by a given theory of it might well be thought to be a recommendation of that theory.

which the object is mentally wrenched from its ordinary context of desire and the freedom for contemplation created. At one point, Schopenhauer writes that art "plucks the object of its contemplation from the stream of the world's course, and holds it isolated before it" (*WWR* 1, §36, 185); but while that sort of active exercise of the will might be a plausible account of certain moments of genius or artistic revolution, it certainly seems too romantic to characterize every passing experience of natural beauty or art that has already been produced by someone else. On the contrary, it would seem to be the case that at least some if not many beautiful or aesthetically pleasing objects induce their response in us without any effort of our own will at all.[14] In Schopenhauer's own words, indeed, it seems natural to suppose that the "purely objective frame of mind" that he claims aesthetic pleasure to be is often quite passively induced, "facilitated and favored from without by accommodating objects, by the abundance of natural beauty that invites contemplation, and even presses itself on us" (*WWR* 1, §38, 197).

Considering these two objections together suggests that there is a tension or ambivalence in Schopenhauer's account between the idea that aesthetic contemplation is a state which always presupposes an effort of our will to free us from our ordinary concerns and the idea that it is a state that is passively induced in us by external objects and thereby produces rather than presupposes freedom from the will. Postponing consideration of any further objections to Schopenhauer's account, I would now like to turn to his defense by arguing that Schopenhauer is hardly unaware of the possibility of these two alternative interpretations of his basic idea. On the contrary, he clearly exploits the difference between them in order to provide an account of several of the most fundamental distinctions of aesthetic theory. Schopenhauer marks the theoretical distinctions between beauty and sublimity, natural and artistic beauty, and artistic creation and reception, among others, precisely by distinguishing their positions along an axis of activity and passivity. The active and passive conceptions of contemplation are thus not two incompatible conceptualizations of a single sort of experience, but are rather distinct but related phenomena that fall under Schopenhauer's general model of aesthetic experience even though they differ in important ways.

[14] This was precisely the reason for Hutcheson's classical characterization of the response to beauty as an internal sense. See *An Inquiry into the Original of our Ideas of Beauty and Virtue* (London: first edition, 1725; fourth, corrected edition, 1738), *Treatise I: Concerning Beauty, Order, Harmony, Design*, Section I, §§xiii–xiv.

Schopenhauer's Reconstruction of Traditional Aesthetics

Let us take first the distinction between the beautiful and the sublime, which was such a prominent feature of aesthetic theory from Addison to Kant. Schopenhauer's way of making this distinction was clearly influenced by Kant's, although it is ultimately set in a very different framework. On the one hand, Schopenhauer characterizes natural beauty precisely by the way in which naturally beautiful objects induce the state of contemplation and will-less knowing without any effort on the part of the individual subject:

> Transition into the state of pure perception occurs most easily when the objects accommodate themselves to it, in other words, when by their manifold and at the same time definite and distinct form they easily become representatives of their Ideas, in which beauty, in the objective sense, consists. Above all, natural beauty has this quality, and even the most stolid and apathetic person obtains therefrom at least a fleeting, aesthetic pleasure. Indeed, it is remarkable how the plant world in particular invites one to aesthetic contemplation . . .
>
> (*WWR* 1, §39, 200–201)

Here the apathetic person would appear to be precisely the person who does not himself in any way exercise his own will in order to enter into a state of contemplation, but is quite passively induced into that state by the objects presented to him, presumably by the lucidity of form and thus the accessibility of the Ideas in them. On the other hand, Schopenhauer equally explicitly characterizes the experience of the sublime by the effort of will that it takes to be able to contemplate the form of, or Ideas in, sublime objects:

> But these very objects, whose significant forms invite us to a pure contemplation of them, may have a hostile relation to the human will in general, as manifested in its objectivity, the human body. They may be opposed to it; they may threaten it by their might that eliminates all resistance, or their immeasurable greatness may reduce it to naught. Nevertheless, the beholder may not direct his attention to this relation to his will which is so pressing and hostile, but, although he perceives and acknowledges it, he may consciously turn away from it, forcibly tear himself from his will and its relations, and, giving himself up entirely to knowledge, may quietly contemplate, as pure, will-less subject of knowing, those very objects so terrible to the will . . . In that case, he is then filled with the feeling of the sublime . . . Thus what distinguishes the feeling of the sublime from that of the beautiful is that, with the beautiful, pure knowledge has gained the upper hand without a struggle . . . On the other hand, with the sublime, that state of pure knowing is obtained first of all by a conscious and violent tearing away from

the relations of the same object to the will which are recognized as unfavorable, by a free exaltation . . .

(*WWR* 1, §39, 201–202)

The difference between the beautiful and the sublime is then just that the latter requires a distinct, even conscious effort of the will in order to set aside the ordinary concerns of the will and thereby make possible contemplation of forms, whereas in the former the state of contemplation is achieved effortlessly and seems rather to cause than to presuppose liberation from the ordinary concerns of individual will. Schopenhauer does not incoherently suppose that the same state of mind is both active and passive; rather he supposes, quite coherently, that particular states of contemplation which are in some ways similar but in other ways different, and in any case numerically distinct, are sometimes reached more passively, sometimes more actively, and sometimes require more of an antecedent liberation from ordinary desires, and sometimes instead induce such liberation. And while it would in fact be logically possible even for the same objects to have these different effects on different occasions or different persons, assuming perhaps variations in the subjects rather than objects, Schopenhauer naturally enough assumes that these different effects will typically be correlated with phenomenologically different sorts of properties or objects (and thus different Platonic Ideas), such as light and darkness (*WWR* 1, §39, 203) or delicate ice crystals on a window-pane (*WWR* 1, §35, 182) and "immense, bare, over-hanging cliffs" (*WWR* 1, §39, 204) – in other words, typical examples of the beautiful and the sublime.[15]

Schopenhauer also exploits the difference between the active and the passive conceptions of contemplation in order to characterize the difference between aesthetic appreciation of nature and art. This contrast is clearest when we compare his remarks about natural beauty to his remarks about genius. In the case of natural beauty, as we just saw, it is the

[15] This is not the place for a detailed contrast between Schopenhauer's conception of the sublime and its Kantian antecedent. It will have to suffice to say that although Schopenhauer's account bears a great similarity to Kant's conception of the dynamically sublime (*Critique of the Power of Judgment* §28), they nevertheless differ in that for Schopenhauer the sublime frees one from concerns of the will altogether, while for Kant it is precisely the moral will, or the determination of the will by pure practical reason, which frees one from concerns that could influence the will only by inclination. The Schopenhauerian sublime, in other words, is an experience of liberation from the will altogether, while the Kantian sublime is an experience of the liberation of the will from inclination by pure practical reason.

object itself "that invites contemplation, and even presses itself on us" (*WWR* 1, §38, 197), and the subject need take no active role in preparing for this contemplation. Art, however, is described actively rather than passively: as we also saw earlier, "it plucks the object of its contemplation from the stream of the world's course, and holds it isolated before it" (*WWR* 1, §36, 185). This active rather than passive image of art becomes even more pronounced as Schopenhauer proceeds to describe genius, the concept which, in this again following Kant, he uses as the vehicle for his description of artistic creation. Genius is described precisely as the ability deliberately to disengage the will from its ordinary concerns in order to allow contemplation:

> Genius is the ability to leave entirely out of sight our own interest, our willing, and our aims, and consequently to discard entirely our own personality for a time, in order to remain *pure knowing subject*, the clear eye of the world; and this not merely for moments, but with the necessary continuity and conscious thought to enable us to repeat by deliberate art which has been apprehended . . . For genius to appear in an individual, it is as if a measure of the power of knowledge must have fallen to his lot far exceeding that required for the service of an individual will . . . This explains the animation, amounting to disquietude, in men of genius . . . This gives them that restless zealous nature, that constant search for new objects worthy of contemplation . . .
>
> (*WWR* 1, §36, 185–186)

Again there is that whiff of paradox in the idea of actively willing to set aside the will that we noticed earlier; but there can be no doubt that Schopenhauer describes genius in active terms: genius is an *ability* to leave ordinary concerns out of sight, to discard our own personality, to repeat by deliberate art, constantly to search, and so on.

The activity of the genius can be broken down into several aspects. First, the genius does not find the Platonic Ideas lying on the surface of things, but he has to seek them out by cognitive activity. "The man of genius requires imagination in order to see in things not what nature has actually formed, but what she endeavoured to form, yet did not bring about . . . Thus imagination extends the mental horizon of the genius beyond the objects that actually present themselves . . . " (*WWR* 1, §36, 186–7). But further, the work of art does not consist simply in "knowledge of the Idea," but in "communication" of it (187), and the second component of genius is both the will and the ability to find a vehicle for the communication of the Idea that contemplation has revealed to the artist to other persons as well. As Schopenhauer puts it, the genius can "retain that thoughtful contemplation necessary for him to repeat what is thus known in a voluntary and intentional work, such repetition being the work of art. Through this he communicates to others the Idea he has grasped" (*WWR* 1, §37, 195). As voluntary and intentional, the production of a work of art clearly requires an act of will in the ordinary sense, a decision and resolve, and the active exercise of human capacities, whether verbal as in the case of a poem or manual as in the case of a painting or sculpture. Thus even if its ultimate effect is the same sort of release from individual will that is induced by the contemplation of natural beauty as well, there can be no question that the production of artistic beauty is firmly anchored in the sphere of intentional human activity, and that among humans the genius is remarkable for his particularly high degree of both cognitive and indeed in many cases physical activity.[16]

This emphasis on the cognitive as well as the physical activity of the genius also provides the key for Schopenhauer's way of modeling the distinction between the creation and reception of art, or between artist and audience. Schopenhauer assumes that the ability to disengage the will and engage in contemplation must be "inherent in all men" in some degree, "as otherwise they would be just as incapable of enjoying works of art as of producing them" (*WWR* I, §37, 194), but that the difference between artist and audience lies precisely in the activity or passivity that characterizes the exercise of this inherent ability. The genius actively struggles to produce both his insight and the object by means of which to communicate it, but once having struggled to communicate the former through the latter he then facilitates the enjoyment of his knowledge by the rest of us, that is, makes it easy for us to see what was difficult for him, or allows us to be passive in that contemplation in which he had to be active. "The work of art is merely a means of facilitating that knowledge in which [aesthetic] pleasure consists . . . The artist lets us peer into the world through his eyes" (195). In other words, the genius and the

[16] Schopenhauer's conceptions of both art and genius stand squarely in the tradition of Kant. His emphasis on the intentional and voluntary nature of artistic production follows Kant's analysis of the concept of art in §43 of the *Critique of the Power of Judgment*, and his twofold analysis of genius as consisting in the capacity to discover both ideas and the forms for communicating them closely follows Kant's characterization of genius in §49 of the third *Critique*, where he stresses that genius consists in a talent for both the conception of aesthetic ideas as well as the expression of such ideas in "material, i.e., intuition for the exhibition of this concept" (5:317). The main difference between the two accounts is that Kant stresses the genius's *invention* of aesthetic ideas, whereas for Schopenhauer the genius uses all of the effort of his will ultimately to *discover* the Platonic Ideas that are inherent in the appearances of things.

ordinary person enjoy the same knowledge and ultimately enjoy the same respite from the incessant demands of ordinary desire and will that such knowledge affords, but the genius arrives at this knowledge by means of an active exercise of the will which the rest of us can then participate in passively.

In fact, Schopenhauer finally arrays artistic creation, the aesthetic enjoyment of nature, and the reception of art on a single spectrum of activity. The production of art through genius clearly requires the highest degree of activity; the reception or appreciation of art produced by others, however, requires not only a lower degree of activity than such production of art, but even a lower degree of activity than aesthetic response to nature. This is because in a work of art the Platonic Ideas have already been isolated out by the artist, and are presented to the rest of us on a platter, whereas in the case of natural beauty, although the objects are accommodating and inviting, there is still some work of abstraction to be performed before the Ideas can be entirely will-lessly contemplated. In Schopenhauer's words, "That the Idea comes to us more easily from the work of art than directly from nature and from reality, arises solely from the fact that the artist, who knew only the Idea and not reality, clearly repeated in his work only the Idea, separated it out from reality, and omitted all disturbing contingencies" (*WWR* 1, §37, 195). Thus human subjects are most active, both cognitively and otherwise, in the production of art, most passive in the reception and enjoyment of art, and fall in between in the perception of natural beauty because even the latter is not merely a matter of passive response to particulars but requires some cognitive effort of abstraction for the contemplation of pure forms.

Schopenhauer's emphasis on the passivity of the reception of art may not seem flattering to the modernist artist and the modernist critic, both of whom pride themselves on the possibility of artistic form challenging the audience rather than making things easy for it. The truth undoubtedly lies between the two positions: neither art that challenges its audience without gratifying it nor art that gratifies its audience without challenging it is likely to withstand the test of time. The very fact that Schopenhauer can suggest a spectrum of aesthetic response from the most active to the most passive, however, suggests that there may be no reason in principle why both the production and the reception of different works of art should not be seen to call for varying degrees of activity and passivity, thus allowing his theory to accommodate art that calls for both more and less from the audience and interpreter. But my aim here is not to assess the ultimate viability of Schopenhauer's aesthetics (that would obviously require major metaphysical surgery) so much as it is to use what would seem to be some of the most obvious objections to it in order to arrive at a better understanding of its complexity. I trust that it is clear by now, in any case, that Schopenhauer does not simply fail to distinguish between active and passive interpretations of his fundamental idea of the connection between contemplation and release from ordinary willing, but consciously exploits this distinction to provide his version of some of the most basic concepts of aesthetic theory.

Before leaving the issue of the active and passive entirely, I will note one other example of Schopenhauer's conscious exploitation of this distinction. I earlier mentioned a consequence of Schopenhauer's contemplative conception of aesthetic experience that is commonly alleged against it as an objection to any aesthetic attitude theory, namely, that on such an account any object is potentially an aesthetic object.[17] Schopenhauer is hardly unaware of this consequence of his basic theoretical model; on the contrary, he draws it quite explicitly himself: "Now since, on the one hand, every existing thing can be observed purely objectively and outside of all relation, and, on the other, the will appears in everything at some grade of its objectivity, and this thing is accordingly the expression of an Idea, everything is also *beautiful*" (*WWR* 1, §41, 210). Given his assumption of the overriding desirability of obtaining relief from the demands of the will by means of will-less contemplation, however, Schopenhauer could hardly see such a consequence as an objection to his theory of aesthetic experience, but would rather regard it as one of the theory's clearest strengths. Nevertheless, like any philosopher advocating a revisionary metaphysics, he does recognize the need to reconcile his theory with common sense, in this case the common assumption that there is a crucial difference between the beautiful and the aesthetically indifferent. He does this by again resorting to the distinction between the active and the passive inducement of contemplation, and recasting the ordinary distinction between the beautiful and the indifferent as a difference of degree rather than of kind: objects range from the most beautiful, which transport us into contemplation with virtually no effort at all, to the least

[17] It should be clear now that this would not imply that on Schopenhauer's account any object can therefore become a *work of art*; his account of art has held that works of art are products of voluntary and intentional human activity aimed at the communication of Platonic Ideas, a definition that is not satisfied by any natural or found object no matter how beautiful it might be.

but still potentially beautiful, which transport us into that state only with considerable effort on our own part. Thus he says:

> That even the most insignificant thing admits of purely objective and will-less contemplation and thus proves itself to be beautiful, is testified by the still life paintings of the Dutch . . . But one thing is more beautiful than another because it facilitates this purely objective contemplation, goes out to meet it, and, so to speak, even compels it, and then we call the thing very beautiful.
>
> (*WWR* 1, §41, 210)

Some things virtually compel us to contemplate them, thus leading us to abnegation of the will with almost no antecedent effort of our will, while other things we have to compel ourselves to contemplate, and they thus offer us relief from our will only after considerable antecedent effort of the will. On this account, then, the difference between what would commonly be regarded as beautiful and what would commonly be regarded as not is noticeable but never insuperable, and that is exactly how Schopenhauer should want it to come out.

In amplifying this point, Schopenhauer argues that the scale of beauty is actually correlated with the scale of cognitive adequacy in the objectification of the Will, a scale on which inorganic or lower forms of organic existence generally have a low degree of beauty because they manifest a relatively low-grade objectification of the Will, but on which the artistic representation of human form and conduct potentially has the highest degree of beauty because what is represented are the highest objectifications of the Will. In constructing such a scale of beauty, Schopenhauer is fulfilling a standard requirement of traditional aesthetic theory.[18] I will not discuss this theme in its own right, however, but only as it bears on the next issue I will take up.

The Pleasures of Knowledge

Thus I now return to another of the general objections to Schopenhauer's theory that I earlier raised, the objection that it characterizes aesthetic response in purely negative terms merely as relief from pain, and thus

[18] Both Kant and Hegel, for example, construct scales of the significance of art, Kant on the basis of the expressive potential of various artistic media (*Critique of the Power of Judgment* §51), though this has only a minor part in his aesthetic theory or even in his discussion of fine art, and Hegel on the basis of the cognitive potential of the different fine arts as stages in the sensuous embodiment of the Idea, the organizing thought of his entire *Lectures on Fine Arts*.

credits aesthetic experience with nothing that could not also be obtained from an adequate drug. The standard account of Schopenhauer's theory certainly presents it in this light,[19] and the idea that aesthetic experience is important only for an effect which could readily or perhaps even only potentially be obtained from other sources has certainly been taken to be a problem throughout contemporary aesthetic theory. What I would now like to argue, however, is that although Schopenhauer certainly stresses the negative pleasure of relief from the will that is afforded by contemplation of Platonic Ideas in much of his exposition, this is not in fact the only source of aesthetic pleasure that he recognizes. He also acknowledges an intrinsic and positive pleasure in the contemplation of those ideas themselves, a pleasure which cannot be readily be obtained from anything but aesthetic experience, and this should suffice to spare him from this objection.

Fairly early in his exposition Schopenhauer makes it clear that there are two elements in aesthetic experience:

> In the aesthetic method of consideration we found *two inseparable constituent parts*: namely, knowledge of the object not as an individual thing, but as Platonic *Idea*, in other words, as persistent form of this whole species of things; and the self-consciousness of the knower, not as individual, but as *pure, will-less subject of knowledge*. The condition under which the two constituent parts appear always united was the abandonment of the method of knowledge that is bound to the principle of sufficient reason . . .
>
> (*WWR* 1, §38, 195–96)

This does not imply, however, that there are two separate sources or kinds of aesthetic pleasure, but only that there are two conditions that need to be satisfied for the one and only kind of aesthetic pleasure to occur. Pure, will-less knowing of Platonic Ideas, this account suggests, produces the negative pleasure of relief from the incessant clamor of the will that has previously been described.

[19] See, for instance, D. W. Hamlyn, *Schopenhauer* (London: Routledge and Kegan Paul, 1980), p. 111; more recently, Terry Eagleton, *The Ideology of the Aesthetic* (Oxford: Basil Blackwell, 1990), pp. 162–163; and most recently, A. L. Cothey, *The Nature of Art* (London: Routledge, 1992), pp. 70–71. Two writers who come closer to recognizing the complexity I will now portray are Patrick Gardiner, *Schopenhauer* (Baltimore: Penguin, 1963), p. 196, and Michael Podro, *The Manifold in Perception: Theories of Art from Kant to Hildebrand* (Oxford: The Clarendon Press, 1972), pp. 100–104. Neither of these authors, however, is quite as explicit about Schopenhauer's positive theory of aesthetic pleasure as I am about to be.

As he continues the present passage, however, Schopenhauer suggests a more complicated picture:

> Moreover, we shall see that the *pleasure* produced by contemplation of the beautiful arises from those two constituent parts, sometimes more from the one than from the other, according to what the object of aesthetic contemplation may be.
>
> (*WWR* 1, §38, 196)

This suggests that acquaintance with the Platonic Ideas is not merely the necessary condition for achieving the state of pure will-less knowing, which is in turn pleasurable solely because it offers relief from the pain of ordinary willing, but rather that the contemplation of the Platonic Ideas is itself a source of pleasure in addition to being the precondition for pure will-less knowing, and that the pleasure of contemplation is to some degree independent of the pleasure of relief from the demands of desire, at least independent enough so that these two kinds of pleasure can be present in different aesthetic experiences in different amounts even if one never occurs in the total absence of the other.

Schopenhauer does not develop this suggestion in the remainder of his discussion of the beautiful in §38 or in his discussion of the sublime in §39, both of which focus on the negative pleasure of relief from the will whether that is achieved effortlessly or forcibly. Subsequently, however, Schopenhauer makes it clear that he does suppose that contemplation and relief from the will are two distinct sources of pleasure. In §41, he reiterates the distinction between the two components of aesthetic response:

> By calling an object *beautiful*, we thereby assert that it is an object of our aesthetic contemplation, and this implies two different things. On the one hand, the sight of the thing makes us *objective*, that is to say, in contemplating it we are no longer conscious of ourselves as individuals, but as pure, will-less subjects of knowing. On the other hand, we recognize in the object not the individual thing, but an Idea; and this can happen only in so far as our contemplation of the object is not given up to the principle of sufficient reason . . . , but rests on the object itself.
>
> (*WWR* 1, §41, 209)

In the next section, he then separates the pleasure of contemplation from the pleasure of relief from the will more fully and more firmly than before:

> I return to our discussion of the aesthetic impression. Knowledge of the beautiful always supposes, simultaneously and inseparably, a purely knowing subject and a known Idea as object. But yet the source of aesthetic enjoyment will lie sometimes rather in the apprehension of the known idea, sometimes rather in the bliss

and peace of mind of pure knowledge free from all willing, and thus from all individuality and the pain that results therefrom.

(*WWR* 1, §42, 212)

Here Schopenhauer does not say that there are two conditions for the occurrence of aesthetic pleasure, but that there are two different sources of such pleasure. Nor does he just suggest that these two sources can be present in different degrees on different occasions of aesthetic contemplation, but he asserts, apparently without qualification, that our pleasure in an aesthetic experience can sometimes be due to one cause and sometimes to the other. This would seem to make sense only if each of these sources can give rise to pleasure by itself, and that there are thus two different although not necessarily phenomenologically distinct sorts of aesthetic pleasure, which could be called positive and negative on account of their etiology. And this would imply that there is a pleasure in contemplation which is not merely identical to the pleasure of relief from the will, even if it typically leads to the latter, and thus that aesthetic experience is not simply fungible with anesthesia even if there are other sources of relief from the tyranny of the individual will besides aesthetic contemplation. Thus there is a positive aspect to the cognitivism of Schopenhauer's aesthetics which is clearly in the tradition of such predecessors as Baumgarten and Kant, even if Schopenhauer's conception of the ethical significance of the aesthetic – his account of the negative pleasure of relief from individual will, that is – is radically different from anything they would have contemplated or accepted.

Again Schopenhauer confirms his recognition of the complexity of aesthetic experience for us by grounding his version of a traditional contrast in aesthetic theory precisely on a distinction that we might initially have overlooked. In this case, he uses the distinction between negative and positive pleasures in cognition to differentiate lower and higher forms of beauty. The natural beauty of the inorganic and vegetable kingdoms as well as the beauty of forms of art rank relatively low, he argues, because in those cases the pleasure that predominates is just the negative pleasure of pure will-less knowing, that is, relief from the tyranny of will, whereas "if animals and human beings are the object of aesthetic contemplation . . . the enjoyment will consist rather in the objective apprehension of these Ideas that are the most distinct revelations of the will" (*WWR* 1, §42, 212). This ranking would be impossible if the objective apprehension of Ideas were merely the necessary condition for relief from the will. On the contrary, this ranking suggests that in the end relief from the will is not the most important benefit of aesthetic experience, but that the pleasure of contemplation is at least as great if not greater than the pleasure of mere relief.

The Paradox of Music

We are now in a position to consider the final question that was initially raised about Schopenhauer's apparently merely negative account of aesthetic pleasure, the paradox that aesthetic pleasure is supposed to arise entirely from relief from the pain of willing, but that music, which Schopenhauer clearly regards as the highest form of art and thus of all beauty, is nothing less than "a *copy of the Will itself*" (*WWR* 1, §52, 257). By claiming that music is a copy of the Will itself, Schopenhauer aims to avoid a simplistic mimetic theory of music, on which we enjoy flute trills because they imitate rippling streams and timpani rolls because they imitate rolling thunder, while still keeping music in the cognitive ballpark by claiming that it imitates a metaphysically deeper and more obscure reality (see also 261). But this still leaves the question, how can a copy of the Will offer relief from the will?

The complexity we have found in Schopenhauer's cognitivism now allows us to see that this is a question that Schopenhauer can and does answer at several levels. Schopenhauer stresses that music does not represent states of the will as individual occurrences in particular human lives, but as universals. "Therefore music does not express this or that particular and definite pleasure, this or that affliction, pain, sorrow, horror, gaiety, merriment, or peace of mind, but joy, pain, sorrow, horror, gaiety, merriment, peace of mind *themselves*" (*WWR* 1, §52, 261). This implies, first, that responding to a piece of music need not involve or invoke the individual will of the particular listener, perhaps even that it can distract the listener from the pains attendant on his own will. And there is no doubt that Schopenhauer does attribute such a palliative effect to music:

> The inexpressible depth of all music, by virtue of which it floats past us as a paradise quite familiar and yet eternally remote, and is so easy to understand and yet so inexplicable, is due to the fact that it reproduces all the emotions of our innermost being, but entirely without reality and remote from its pain.
>
> (*WWR* 1, §52, 264)

But as we have now seen, Schopenhauer does not in fact limit the pleasure of aesthetic experience to relief from one's private pain, so there is no reason why such negative pleasure should be the whole story about our enjoyment of music. And in fact what Schopenhauer clearly stresses the most in his account is not this sort of negative pleasure but the intrinsic pleasure of contemplative knowledge of the nature of Will and thus metaphysical reality itself. Thus, in discussing the contrast between harmony and melody in music, Schopenhauer stresses its necessity for understanding the complexity of reality, and in his treatment of melody in particular he gives a particularly intellectualist account, which asserts not that melody gives us greater relief from pain than any other aspect of music but that it gives us greater insight: "In the *melody*... I recognize the highest grade of the Will's objectification, the intellectual life and endeavour of man... In keeping with this, *melody* alone has significant and intentional connection from beginning to end" (*WWR* 1, §52, 259). Ranking melody over harmony on this ground would make no sense at all if intellectual insight itself were not a positive source of pleasure. And the claim that music is remote from the pain of reality which was cited a moment ago is only the preface to a description of the value of music in purely cognitive terms:

> In the whole of this discussion of music I have been trying to make it clear that music expresses in an exceedingly universal language, in a homogeneous material, that is, in mere tones, and with the greatest distinctness and truth, the inner being, the in-itself, of the world, which we think of under the concept of Will, according to its most distinct manifestation.
>
> (*WWR* 1, §52, 264)

Here there is no reference at all to music's power to alleviate pain, but a description of its cognitive significance which makes sense only on the assumption that cognition of universals is itself not just a source of pleasure but ultimately the source of the highest form of pleasure.

Schopenhauer's penultimate word on art in general further stresses the cognitive value that has become predominant in his account of music: "If the whole world as representation is only the visibility of the Will, then art is the elucidation of this visibility, the *camera obscura* which shows the objects more purely, and enables us to survey and comprehend them better" (*WWR* 1, §52, 266–7). Certainly such a remark makes sense only on the assumption that there is an intrinsic value, which within Schopenhauer's psychology can only be an intrinsic pleasure, in comprehension itself. Added to his account of how music can turn one's focus away from his own individual will, this is more than enough to resolve the apparent paradox in Schopenhauer's account of music.

But I think there is one more thing to be said about the paradox of will in Schopenhauer's account of art in general, something which is not explicitly mentioned in the account of music but which would apply to it above all else. This is a point which Schopenhauer makes, not repeatedly like most of his other points, but just once, in his treatment of the sublime. Here he suggests that there is a pleasure which is not just the cognitive pleasure of contemplation of the nature of reality through universals nor just the negative pleasure of relief from ordinary willing but a pleasure in the recognition of and indeed affirmation of the individual's underlying identity with a greater reality:[20]

> The vastness of the world, which previously disturbed our peace of mind, now rests with us; our dependence on it is now annulled by its dependence on us. All this, however, does not come into reflection at once, but shows itself as a consciousness, merely felt, that in some sense or other (made clear only by philosophy) we are one with the world, and are therefore not oppressed but exalted by its immensity.
>
> (*WWR* 1, §39, 205)

Here, like his nemesis Hegel but unlike the more Romantic Schelling, Schopenhauer does not suppose that art actually supersedes philosophy, but rather that aesthetic experience gives us an adumbration of truth which must ultimately be clarified by philosophy. But the truth of which philosophy thus gives us an adumbration is a truth about an identity with reality which is deeper than the superficial appearances which separate us from reality. And Schopenhauer does not characterize the recognition of this identity as merely relieving us from oppression, but as positively exalting us; we are not just relieved from the pain of being, but positively rejoice in being part of being itself. Thus the experience of art does not just allow us to escape from the pain of reality, like a drug, but occasions a joyful affirmation of our identity with reality that cannot readily be obtained anywhere else. And insofar as this account applies to music in particular, then, we would there enjoy not just relief from ordinary willing nor contemplation of the nature of Will in general but also, and perhaps above all, the identity of our individual selves and our individual wills with reality and Will in general.

20 This point is also suggested by Podro (*The Manifold in Perception*, p. 106), although without citation of this or any other supporting passage.

Whether plausible or not, this is surely no merely negative account of aesthetic pleasure, but a complex and ultimately affirmative account. Such an account of the complexity of Schopenhauer's aesthetic cognitivism would link it more closely to his successor Nietzsche's conception of the contrast yet equally inseparable connection between the Apollonian and Dionysian than might otherwise be thought. But that connection must be a story for another occasion.

12

From Jupiter's Eagle to Warhol's Boxes

The Concept of Art from Kant to Danto

In a recent book, Arthur Danto declares that he is both an "essentialist" and "an historicist in the philosophy of art" and claims that his essentialism has been as deep-seated as his historicism: "Now I would have taken the entire burden of... *The Transfiguration of the Commonplace,* to have been to underwrite essentialism in the philosophy of art, since that book takes as its program a definition of art which pretty much implies that there is, after all, a fixed and universal identity."[1] Danto thinks he needs to make this explicit in response to the perception of him as an anti-essentialist, someone who does not think there can be a single definition that can subtend the whole extension of what we now mean by the word "art" (and its equivalents in modern languages other than English). Indeed it may seem surprising that someone who has argued convincingly that objects can rightly be classified as art now that couldn't even have been conceived as art at an earlier time, while projects that at one time may have seemed the very essence of art, such as illusionistic painting and subsequently abstract painting, may have come to an end, could at the same time believe that there is a "fixed and uniform identity" or single definition of art that remains constant through all that change. Nevertheless, the position that Danto declares himself to hold is certainly coherent: to lend him a distinction borrowed from John Rawls, Danto could hold that the *concept* of art, that is, our most fundamental idea of what art is, has remained constant while *conceptions* of art, that is, views about what particular objects belong in the extension of the concept of art, have

[1] Arthur C. Danto, *After the End of Art: Contemporary Art and the Pale of History,* Bollingen Series 35 (44) (Princeton: Princeton University Press, 1997), 193.

changed even quite radically. In this essay, I want to support Danto's essentialism by showing that in its basic structure Danto's concept of art is very much in the tradition established by Kant's concept of art, in spite of all the differences in their conceptions of the extension of this concept necessitated by the development of the various arts themselves in the last two centuries. And since Kant himself surely did not conceive of his concept of art as revolutionary, but rather, as in the case of his moral philosophy, undoubtedly saw himself as using his novel understanding of the sources of human thought, feeling, and action to *save* common sense from equally common misconceptions,[2] the Kantian affinities of Danto's concept of art undoubtedly place it in a tradition far older than Kant. To lend at least a little further evidence to this claim of essential continuity, I will also show that we find a concept of art with considerable affinity to those of both Kant and Danto in the work of another recent but more traditional aesthetician, one who himself acknowledged a Kantian influence, namely, Monroe Beardsley.[3]

[2] For an elaboration of such an approach to Kant's moral philosophy, see my introduction to *Kant's Groundwork of the Metaphysics of Morals: Critical Essays,* ed. Paul Guyer (Lanham, MD: Rowman & Littlefield, 1998).

[3] In claiming that Danto's concept of art stands within the Kantian tradition, I am rejecting Danto's own historiography of the philosophy of art, since he thinks that Hegel was the first and "only figure in the history of aesthetics . . . to have grasped the complexities of the concept of art" (*After the End of Art,* 194). However, I believe that in making this claim Danto is confusing Hegel's greater recognition of the changing circumstances for the production and thus the conception of art with the complexity of the concept of art itself, which was already recognized by Kant and other eighteenth-century aestheticians, such as Moses Mendelssohn (see "The Perfections of Art: Mendelssohn, Moritz and Kant," chapter 4 of my *Kant and the Experience of Freedom: Essays on Aesthetics and Morality* [Cambridge: Cambridge University Press, 1993], 94–130). In rejecting Danto's historiography, I do not believe that I am rejecting anything significant in Danto's account of the concept of art itself. In Chapter 8 of *Kant and the Experience of Freedom,* I have also argued that Kant's philosophy of art, particularly his account of genius, provides a theoretical basis for a historical view of art as inherently changing that may be more like what we now think of as a Hegelian view than Hegel's own, for there is on Kant's account of genius no room for the thought that art can reach a stable and final *telos* at which point it must be superseded by other forms of knowing and becomes of no further historical significance; see "Genius and the Canon of Art: A Second Dialectic of Aesthetic Judgment," *Kant and the Experience of Freedom,* 275–303.

A second point: In calling Beardsley a "self-avowed Kantian," I am alluding to his own claim that in his account of "aesthetic experience" he "rel[ies] most heavily upon the work of John Dewey, Edward Bullough, I. A. Richards, and Immanuel Kant"; see Monroe C. Beardsley, *Aesthetics: Problems in the Philosophy of Criticism,* 2d ed. (Indianapolis and Cambridge: Hackett, 1981), 527n. 2. There will be more on Beardsley's concept of aesthetic experience later.

My claim of continuity may seem surprising for two reasons. On the one hand, there is an element that is fundamental to Kant's concept of the aesthetic in general and fine art in particular that goes unmentioned in Danto's and even Beardsley's accounts of art, namely, Kant's insistence that *pleasure* is essential to all aesthetic experience. On the other hand, Danto's concept of art in particular emphasizes the *intentionality* of art in a way that might seem difficult to reconcile with the *purposelessness* that seems to be an indispensable element in Kant's explanation of the pleasurableness of aesthetic response.[4] My discussion of Kant will address both these issues. First, I will show how Kant's theory of artistic genius serves to reconcile his own account of the essence of aesthetic experience with what he clearly regards as a traditional analysis of the intentionality of artistic production, the claim that fine art is what is produced out of an intention to provide *pleasure* of a certain kind: it is precisely by nature's gift of genius that the artist is enabled to go beyond the concepts and rules that are a necessary condition of all purposive activity to create the unexpected unity that in turn evokes the pleasurable play of imagination and understanding in the audience for the artist's work. Second, I will show that Kant's notion of pleasure is an abstract notion of a self-sustaining state of mind, and that his notion of our pleasure in the free play of imagination and understanding is essentially just that of a form of cognitive engagement that is self-sustaining in spite of its lack of any immediate practical benefit; I will then argue that what both Beardsley and Danto describe, in their different ways, as the state of mind that can and is intended to result from engagement with a work of art can be seen as an instance of Kant's concept of a free play of imagination and understanding that is self-sustaining in spite of its lack of any immediate practical benefit. Such a state of mind is clearly assumed by both of our contemporary authors to be deeply pleasurable, although that point may well have seemed too obvious to either of them to have needed to be made explicit.

4 See the Introduction to the *Critique of the Power of Judgment*, 189–90, and the Third Moment of the Analytic of the Beautiful, especially §§10–12, 219–23. Citations to the *Critique of the Power of Judgment* (hereafter referred to as *CPJ*) are given by their section and page number as they appear in vol. 5 of Kant's *Gesammelte Schriften*, ed. Royal Prussian (later German) Academy of Sciences (Berlin: Walter de Gruyter and predecessors, 1900 –). The text of the *Critique of the Power of Judgment* presented there was edited by Wilhelm Windelband. Citations to the so-called "First Introduction" to the *Critique of Judgment*, edited by Gerhard Lehmann in vol. 20 of the *Akademie* edition, are referred to as *FI*. Translations from both texts are my own.

1. Kant

The very possibility of art as a purposive human activity might seem to undermine Kant's definition of beauty, the traditional aim of art, as "the form of **purposiveness** of an object insofar as it[5] is perceived **without representation of a purpose**" (*CPJ*, §17, 236). It is surely to undercut the threat of paradox in his definition of fine art (*schöne Kunst*) as a "production through freedom" (*CPJ*, §43, 303) that is at the same time "without purpose" (§44, 306) that Kant amplifies this initial definition with his theory of "genius" as the capacity that produces fine art and of "aesthetic ideas" as its content: while each of these elements of Kant's treatment of art might be traced back to prior tradition, it is by his unique synthesis of them that Kant accomplishes his characteristic project of rescuing common sense from the self-contradiction or natural dialectic to which it is always liable.[6]

Indeed, Kant's view that the concept of art is threatened by a paradox that must be resolved by philosophical theory is signaled almost from the outset of the *Critique of the Power of Judgment* by his similarly apparently paradoxical concept of "dependent" or "adherent" *(anhängende, adhaerens)* beauty. Dependent beauty is contrasted to "free beauty": free beauty requires no concept of what an object ought to be, while dependent beauty does "depend on a concept" of an object "that stands under the concept of a particular purpose" (*CPJ*, §16, 229). Flowers, for example, are free beauties, because we are all pleased by the perception or representation of them independently of any knowledge of their biological function; but the beauty of a human being, a horse, or a building is not, because our response to such objects "presupposes a concept of the end that determines what the thing ought to be" (230). For example, an arsenal cannot appear beautiful if it has thin walls filled with large

[5] The antecedent for the feminine pronoun *sie* here translated as "it" must be the feminine *Form der Zweckmäßigkeit* ("form of purposiveness") rather than the masculine *Gegenstand* ("object").

[6] Kant might have taken the conception of genius from a source such as Alexander Gerard's *Essay on Genius* (1774) or other popular British works of the 1760s and 1770s (see Alexander Gerard, *An Essay on Genius,* ed. Bernhard Fabian [Munich: Wilhelm Fink Verlag, 1966], xi, xxiv–xli); and his conception of the "aesthetic idea" is certainly his reworking of Baumgarten's notion of aesthetic objects, paradigmatically poems, as clear but confused rather than distinct representations, "confused" in the sense of being dense with imagery rather than analytically explicit (*Meditationes philosophicae de nonnullis ad poema pertinentibus* [1735], e.g., §XV). But Kant's use of these commonplaces to explain how art can be both purposive and pleasurable at once has all the earmarks of the resolution of a natural dialectic that is at the heart of his philosophical method.

openings, because that would defeat the security required by its purpose, while a summer house, with its very different purpose, can only be beautiful if it does fit that description; a horse intended for racing can only be beautiful if has a large chest but slender legs; and the respect with which human beings must be considered because of their moral vocation is incompatible with what might otherwise be beautiful tattooing. Now it might seem as if Kant should say that a response to an object that presupposes a concept of what it ought to be is not a response to beauty at all, but at best a confused judgment of perfection (see *CPJ*, §15, 226–27); but he does not reject the concept of dependent beauty as a bad theory and instead speaks of dependent beauty as a proper although not pure (§16, 230) type of beauty. How can he do this? He can do this only if he is supposing that the constraints on the form and appearance of a kind of object that are imposed on it by a concept of its purpose are not sufficient but are at best necessary conditions for its beauty. Such conditions may suffice to prevent us from responding pleasurably to objects that do not satisfy them, but satisfying those conditions alone does not make an object beautiful; to be beautiful, an object must induce in us a free play of imagination and understanding that goes beyond anything dictated by the concept of its purpose, or perhaps even give us a sense of free play between those features in virtue of which it satisfies the concept of its purpose and other features of its form and appearance. In that case our pleasure in it is a pleasure in the free play between imagination and understanding, a harmony between the form we perceive in the object and the concepts we apply to it, and thus a genuine response to beauty.

Not all dependently beautiful objects are works of art, nor are all works of art dependent beauties. A beautiful human or horse is not a work of art, though much art may be applied to the former or go into the breeding of the latter; and, on the contrary, "designs *à la grecque*, foliage . . . on wallpapers" and musical "fantasias (without themes)" (*CPJ*, §16, 229) are all works of art, but our response to them is entirely free and unconstrained by any presuppositions about the purposes they ought to serve. Nevertheless, Kant's concept of dependent beauty can serve as the model for his concept of fine art, because in the most paradigmatic cases of fine art that Kant considers – works of literature, painting, sculpture, architecture, music with themes – we have determinate, conceptualizable expectations about both the purpose and the content of the work, yet respond with pleasure to the ways in which the form and appearance of the object both harmonize with such concepts yet go beyond anything that can be fully determined by them. Our aesthetic response to and judgment of paradigmatic works of art is not pure, where that means simple; it is complex, but all the more fittingly described as a free and harmonious play between imagination and understanding because of that complexity.

The model of dependent beauty should be kept in mind throughout Kant's explicit discussion of fine art (*CPJ*, §§43–53), because what Kant is attempting to do throughout this discussion is to show how our response to fine art can be free and thus genuinely aesthetic in spite of the layers of intentionality characteristic of our production of art and the layers of conceptuality characteristic of our reception of it.

Kant begins his discussion of fine art, in §§43 and 44, with an attempt to provide a formal definition of it, although he has said elsewhere that in philosophy definition should only come at the end, not at the beginning of an investigation.[7] Kant provides little argument for this formal definition of fine art, which suggests that he intends the novelty of his account to lie in the resolution of the paradoxes inherent in it, beginning in §45, rather than in the definition itself. The definition is given in two stages: in §43, Kant defines "art in general," and in §44 Kant further distinguishes "fine art" from merely "agreeable art." In §43, Kant locates the general concept of art by means of three criteria: first, art is a form of voluntary and purposive human production, guided by an antecedent representation of the object to be produced; second, however, the production of art requires skill, not merely knowledge (you cannot produce a work of art like a trick that everyone can do as soon as they are told how to do it);[8] and third, art as opposed to handicraft, or "free art" as opposed to "remunerative art" *(Lohnkunst)*, is a form of "play, i.e., an occupation that is agreeable in itself, rather than an occupation that is "unpleasant in itself . . . and attractive only because of its effect (e.g., the remuneration)" (*CPJ*, §43, 303–04). The last condition holds, Kant claims, even though "in all free arts something compulsory or . . . a **mechanism** is required," without which the "soul" of a work would be "bodiless and evanescent"; that is, in order to produce works of art, the rules of a medium, such as in the case of poetry prosody and meter, must be

7 See *Inquiry concerning the distinctness of the principles of natural theology and morals* (1764), passim.

8 Kant's examples: Following Columbus, you can make an egg stand on one end as soon as you are told how to do it (dent its bottom); but you cannot walk on a tightrope or even make a shoe just by being told how to do it.

mastered, even though acquiring this mastery may not be pleasant in itself but only in its effect (§43, 304; §44 will also add "knowledge of ancient languages" and other forms of expertise as conditions for the production of art the acquisition of which may not be intrinsically pleasurable). In §44, Kant expands upon this last criterion: "aesthetic" art is distinguished from "mechanical" art because it is intrinsically rather than merely instrumentally pleasurable, but there are two forms of "aesthetic art": merely "agreeable art," which aims to please merely through the sensations it arouses, and fine art, in which pleasure is to accompany representations "*as* **kinds of cognition**" *(Erkenntnisarten)* (305). Thus Kant concludes that "Fine art . . . is a kind of representation that is purposive in itself and, although without a purpose, nevertheless advances the culture of the powers of the mind for sociable communication" (306). In sum, then, a work of fine art is a product of voluntary and purposive human activity, guided by an antecedent representation of its object but requiring skill and not merely knowledge, which is both pleasurable in itself but also pleasurable because it advances the prospects for human communication.

There are many puzzles hidden in this definition, some of which Kant will subsequently address and some not. First, Kant's initial contrast between voluntary human production and other forms of pseudo-artistic production, such as the production of a complex form like that of a honeycomb by non-rational creatures like bees, needs to be unpacked. Kant describes human artistry as the causation of an object "a representation of which must have preceded its reality in its cause" and indeed one in which "the effect is **conceived** [*gedacht*] by the cause"; he also describes it as "production through freedom, i.e., through a capacity of choice that grounds its action in reason," and thus as a "producing cause" which has "conceived of an end, to which the object owes its form" (*CPJ*, §43, 303). But if the product of such activity is to be an object to which we can respond as beautiful, as inducing a pleasurable free play of imagination and understanding, then, as in the case of dependent beauty, neither the antecedent representation of the object or of an end to be achieved in or through it which are necessary conditions of its being a work of art can be seen as sufficient conditions for the form and appearance it actually has. A work of art, by this definition, must have a complex intentionality: it must have an intended end and an intended form, a form intended to be suitable for that end; but at the same time the rich particularity to which we respond must also transcend all such concepts of the object.

Explaining how this can be is clearly the point of Kant's subsequent discussion of genius as the source of fine art (§§46–49).

However, there are several puzzles about the definition that Kant does not subsequently resolve. One is that although §43 insists that the production of a work of art is intrinsically pleasurable, §44 describes the pleasure at which a work of fine art aims as one dependent upon the fact that such a work "advances the culture of the powers of the mind for social communication." This makes it sound as if a work of fine art is after all instrumentally rather than intrinsically pleasurable, that is, valued not for the character of the mere experience of it but rather because of some effect that this experience has on the conduct of our lives outside of the museum or theatre. Here Kant seems to be repeating a mistake or at least a misleading form of expression to which he succumbs elsewhere in the "Critique of Aesthetic Judgment," most notably in the section that is supposed to be its "key" (§9), where he suggests that the universal communicability of aesthetic response is the *cause* or *ground* of its pleasurability rather than merely a *property* of its pleasurability.[9] What he should say is that a work of fine art is one that is intended to please by calling forth a free play of harmony and imagination in all who are properly prepared to receive it, a response which, because it can be shared, can *also* advance the additional goal of strengthening the bonds of social communication and please us that way too. Kant should not have a problem at this stage of the book in arguing that fine art can have such a complex of pleasures as its goal, because in the discussion of the "empirical" and "intellectual" interests in beauty that immediately precedes the discussion of fine art (§§41 and 42) he has already made it clear that our pleasure in a beautiful object, whether natural or artistic, can be complex, at least in the sense of having multiple grounds. A work of art can please us *both* because it induces an intrinsically pleasing free play of imagination and understanding and because such a response is one we can take ourselves to share with others and be pleased about for that reason too; consequently, an artist can intend to please her audience both directly by inducing the

9 Part of the problem here is a threat of circularity, since Kant sets up the question of taste as one about what makes a pleasure universally communicable, and then can't very well answer that by arguing that it is its (the pleasure's) universal communicability which makes it pleasurable. See my *Kant and the Claims of Taste*, 2d ed. (Cambridge, U.K.: Cambridge University Press, 1997), 133–42, and "Pleasure and Society in Kant's Theory of Taste," in *Essays in Kant's Aesthetics*, ed. Ted Cohen and Paul Guyer (Chicago: University of Chicago Press, 1982), 21–54.

free play of imagination and understanding in each member of it and, less directly, by creating an occasion for sociable communication in her audience as a whole, which will be a further ground for each member's pleasure in the object.

Another puzzle in Kant's remarks about the pleasure that is the intended purpose of fine art is the fact that while §44 clearly suggests that the pleasure that is intended, whatever its ground may be, is one to be experienced by the intended *audience* of the work of art, the third condition listed in §43 makes it sound as if the pleasure aimed at in the production of art is the pleasure inherent in the act of production itself, that is, the pleasure of the *artist* rather than of the audience. Kant's claim in §43 seems troubling in other ways: his suggestion that "handicraft" is not an intrinsically pleasing activity but is pleasing only because of the prospect of financial reward is surely unfair to the experience of many craftspeople; and any suggestion that producers of fine art cannot also be pleased by the prospect of the rewards of riches and fame as well as by the intrinsic character of the production of their art is surely unrealistic. The latter, however, is not a serious problem, because as Kant himself well knows human intentionality can be and usually is complex, and an actual human agent can well intend an object or activity to be both pleasing and remunerative, indeed to be remunerative because it is pleasing. The question remains, however, *to whom* is the production of fine art supposed to be pleasing? Everything in Kant's account suggests that works of fine art, as a species of the beautiful, must be beautiful for the ideal audience of all humankind, and that any pleasure that the artist might take in producing the object would be irrelevant to its beauty or only minimally relevant insofar as the artist is also part of the larger audience for her work. But if the artist herself is too tormented to enjoy producing what everyone else does enjoy, so what? Kant makes no attempt to address this tension. But before dismissing his suggestion that the activity of the production of fine art must be intrinsically pleasing as just another one of Kant's misleading applications of his own more general theory, we might reflect on a point suggested by Kant's brief treatment of the role of criticism elsewhere in the *Critique* (§33, 284–85): precisely because there can be no *rules* for the production and therefore the judgment of beauty, Kant may mean to suggest, the artist's pleasure in her own production of her work – separated out from her pleasure in any prospect of reward or any other instrumental rather than intrinsic grounds of pleasure – may be her best or even only grounds for a reasonable expectation that her work will fulfill its objective of pleasing her audience. The artist may not *aim* to please herself by her work but may have to put herself in the place of her intended audience in order to judge whether she is succeeding in her aim of pleasing them.

Resolution of these puzzles, however, still leaves open the biggest question: how can Kant reconcile the (entirely common-sensical) definition of art as the intentional production of an object guided by the antecedent representation of it and aimed at least at the pleasure of its intended audience with his own account of the experience of beauty as above all that of a free and harmonious play of imagination and understanding induced by an object independently of the application of any determinate concept to it, *a fortiori* any concept of its intended purpose? Resolving this puzzle, as I have suggested, is the point of Kant's theory of genius.

The opening claim of §45 gives Kant's own formulation of the paradox: "One must be conscious that a product of fine art is art and not nature; yet the purposiveness of its form must appear to be as free of all compulsion from arbitrary rules as if it were a product of mere nature" (306). Art is a kind of intentional human production, like others apparently guided by concepts of both ends and means, yet Kant's fundamental account of aesthetic response assigns our pleasure in beauty to a free play of imagination and understanding, not determined by any concept, most plausibly induced by a natural form with no function or one of which we are ignorant. Initially, Kant seems to suggest we can resolve this paradox only by simultaneously acknowledging yet suppressing our recognition of the concepts and intentions that lie in and behind a work of art: "Art can only be called beautiful if we are conscious that it is art and yet it appears to us like nature" (306). The succeeding sections, however, resolve this paradox in two steps. First, Kant exploits the concept of genius, already popularized in both Britain and Germany, to argue that the creative activity of the artist is *guided* but not *determined* by concepts, thereby leaving room for the exercise of both skill and originality in the gap between the general constraints that are all that concepts can determine about an object and the particularity of form that can only be determined by the free play of imagination and understanding. Second, in his account of aesthetic ideas, his creative appropriation of Baumgarten's idea that beauty lies in the density of clear but confused perception, Kant turns from the analysis of the agency of the artist to that of its product, the work of art, to show how a work of art can embody concepts in both its form and content while yet leaving room for the free play of the imagination and understanding of the artist on the one hand and of the audience on the other.

Kant defines genius as "the talent (gift of nature) which gives the rule to art," or "the inborn disposition of the mind *(ingenium) through* which nature gives the rule to art" (*CPJ*, §46, 307). He derives the necessity of such a disposition from the fact that art must be intentional production in accordance with some antecedent conception of its product, using some mechanism for this production as well, yet must at the same time express the free play of the cognitive faculties of the artist and leave room for such a free play on the part of the audience. In his words, "every art presupposes rules, on the basis of which a product, if it is to be called artistic [*künstlich*], must first be represented as possible," but at the same time "[t]he concept of fine art does not permit the judgment on the beauty of its product to be derived from any rule that has a **concept** as its determining ground"; from this it follows that the antecedent rule necessary to the production of art cannot be the ordinary sort of rule furnished by a determinate concept, but can instead only be "nature in the subject giving the rule to art (through the harmony [*Stimmung*] of the subject's faculties" (307). This remark suggests that what nature provides which no determinate concept ever can is just that unity of form both with and within whatever constraints are implied by the concepts that apply to an object, in virtue of both its intended function and its content. This creates the sense of harmony going beyond any such concepts that is the basis for our pleasure in any case of dependent beauty.

In what sense is such a disposition a "rule"? What Kant next says is that the object produced out of genius is exemplary, or itself a rule for art: it provides *all judges* with a model *(Muster)* of what can be done and is thus a standard for judging other works of art (*CPJ*, §46, 308); it provides *subsequent artists* with a model to which they can aspire, though a model which they must not copy slavishly (*CPJ*, §47, 309–10). Rather than functioning like a rule *for the artist* herself, genius seems to be what takes her beyond all the rules that there may be for her art, whether those are "mechanical" rules for use of the medium or rules of thumb for success in that medium. For others, a work of genius is an exemplar or standard to aspire to, but for the artist genius seems to be simply an innate gift and source that cannot itself be derived from any precepts or rules; in Kant's words, genius "is 1) a *talent* for producing that for which no determinate rule can be given ... thus originality must be its foremost property," but yet 2) "its products must be at the same time models, i.e., *exemplary*, not themselves arisen through imitation but yet able to serve others as the standard or rule for estimation" (*CPJ*, §46, 307–08). However, since, as we have already suggested, even if the aim of art is not to please the artist herself, the artist has no rules to go on in determining how to please others except her success in pleasing herself; so genius may consist in an unusual talent in taking one's own pleasure as a rule for that of others, and perhaps in this sense genius might serve as a rule for the artist as well as her audience.

We can now amplify the initial Kantian definition of art as the intentional production of an object intended to yield pleasure in its audience, an object which may please both intrinsically and as an occasion for sociable communication. Now we can characterize the role of both artist and audience somewhat more precisely, and say that art is the intentional production of an object intended to produce and indeed set a standard for the harmony of imagination and understanding in its audience, both for its intrinsic pleasurability and for the sake of sociable communication, where, however, the production of such an object in turn requires an aptitude for the harmony of imagination and understanding in the artist that goes beyond anything derivable from all the rules and precepts for her art, necessary as those may be for the production of objects in that medium, and thus expresses the originality of the artist. This definition still focuses on the kind of activity that art is and the kind of response that it is intended to induce, leaving the work of art to be defined parasitically, merely as the object referred to in the definition of art. Kant's introduction of the concept of an aesthetic idea adds greater specificity to his concept of a work of art and, in so doing, fleshes out his conception of genius. In the theory of aesthetic ideas, above all, we see how concepts function as part of the material for the free play of imagination and understanding rather than as rules that predetermine our response to objects.

Pursuing a little further the etymological play which has already given him the concept of genius *(ingenium),* Kant suggests that what genius adds to a work of art beyond mere conformity to rules is "soul" or "spirit" *(Geist):* it is that which "sets the powers of the mind into a purposive swing, i.e., into a play which sustains itself and even strengthens the powers for it" (*CPJ*, §49, 313). He then says that the principle of such "spirit" is "nothing other than the faculty for the presentation of **aesthetic ideas**," and an "aesthetic idea" is immediately defined as "that representation of the imagination which occasions much thinking but without any determinate thought, i.e., *concept,* being adequate to it" (313–14). The capacity of genius is thus defined as the capacity to give a work of art its spirit by giving it a kind of *content* that goes beyond anything that can be grasped by determinate *concepts.* This suggests that the possibility of an artwork's successful manifestation of genius is in fact dependent on its being *representational* (as Kant has in fact assumed without argument in §48), for on this account it is in the content rather than the mere form of a work of art that genius is displayed.

This initial account of the notion of an aesthetic idea and of the gift of genius that produces it is too simple, however. Kant goes on to make clear that the notions of both aesthetic ideas and genius are complex. First, there are three elements involved in an artwork's exhibiting an aesthetic idea, not just one: an aesthetic idea is a "representation of the imagination" by means of which a work of art manages, on the one hand, to present a *rational idea,* even though a rational idea literally "lies beyond the limits of experience," and, on the other hand, to suggest what seems like an inexhaustible wealth of material for the imagination, "so much to think about that it could never be brought together in a determinate concept" (*CPJ,* §49, 314–15). These three elements are all visible in Kant's clearest account of his notion of the aesthetic idea: "In a word, the aesthetic idea is a representation of the imagination associated with a given concept, which is combined with such a manifold of partial representations in the free use of the imagination that no expression designating a determinate concept can be found for it, which therefore allows much that is unnameable to be added to a concept in thought, the feeling of which enlivens the cognitive faculties. . . . " (*CPJ,* §49, 316). Kant's examples suggest what he has in mind by these three components. First, a "rational idea," is an abstract notion, typically of moral significance, of something that is not given in our experience at all, such as blessedness, eternity, or creation, or of something whose full significance is apparently never exhausted in our experience, such as death or love (314). Such an idea might be thought of as the *content* of a work of art at the most abstract level, or its *theme.* Second, there is the overarching image or device of the imagination through which such an abstract theme is presented, such as the image of Jupiter as the embodiment of the idea of divine power and justice (315). Third, there is what Kant calls the wealth of "aesthetic attributes" associated with and suggested by the overarching image of the imagination, such things as "Jupiter's eagle with the lightning-bolts in its claws." Such things are not "logical attributes," because they are not properties specifically required by the analysis of any more general concept, but are associated with it more loosely; and although a notion such as that of Jupiter may have certain attributes characteristically associated with it, it seems to be Kant's thought that no such attributes are necessarily required by the ruling notion while yet an inexhaustible number may be suggested. Generalizing from these examples, we may suppose that the rational idea is the theme of a work; the middle term – which Kant sometimes treats as the aesthetic idea properly speaking – the general imaginative device, image, plot, symbol, etc., through which that theme will be conveyed; and the attributes of all those specifics – words, sounds, colors, images, and so on – by means of which the general form of the work succeeds in making its theme palpable to us and which are in turn suggested by that form. Then, Kant repeatedly suggests, it is the *interaction* of all these elements that sets the mind into a free but harmonious play, for example, by giving "the imagination occasion to spread itself over a multitude of related representations" or by animating "the mind by opening for it a prospect into a field of related representations exceeding any single point of view" (315). In other words, it is the interaction of theme or content with both the form and matter of the artistic presentation, all going beyond anything that could be derived by a rule from any determinate concept of either the content or the function of the work, that genius produces in its own mind and work; and this in turn induces a free play of cognitive powers in the audience for a work of art that must somehow feel as free as that in the genius herself, even though it occurs in response to the product of her work.

The same conclusion emerges from Kant's final statement of his conception of genius:

If after these analyses we look back upon the account of **genius** given above, we find: **first**, that it is a talent for art, not for science, in which clearly known rules precede and determine our procedure; **second**, that as a talent for art it presupposes a determinate concept of its product as end, thus understanding, but also a representation (even if indeterminate) of the matter, i.e., of intuition, for the presentation of this concept, thus a relation of imagination to the understanding; **third**, that it manifests itself not so much in the execution of the presupposed end in the presentation of a determinate *concept,* but rather in the delivery or expression of **aesthetic ideas**, which contain rich material for that aim, hence it allows the imagination to be represented as purposive in its presentation of the given concept in spite of its freedom from all direction by rules; finally, **fourth**, the unsought, unintentional, subjective purposiveness in the free accord of the imagination to the lawfulness of the understanding presupposes such a proportion and harmony of these faculties that cannot be realized by following rules, whether of science or mechanical imitation, but can only be produced by the nature of the subject.

(*CPJ*, §49, 317–18)

Genius lies in the ability to conceive of both a *content* or theme, a general *form* or approach, and a concrete, sensory *realization* for a work of art, all of which in their interaction create and express a free play of imagination and understanding in the artist and, in turn, call forth a similar state of mind in the audience for the resultant work of art.

In a moment we shall complete Kant's definition of art on the basis of these notions, but before we do so there is an obvious puzzle about Kant's claims that must be addressed. Throughout his discussion of fine art, Kant presupposes that paradigmatic works of art are *representational,* that is, they have a *content* or are *about* something, even though earlier in the book he had seemed to suppose that at least some works of art do "not represent anything, no object under a determinate concept" (*CPJ*, §16, 229), and certainly he has nowhere provided any argument that they *must* represent something. Further, in §49, Kant apparently presupposes not merely that works of art are always representational, but that they are always ultimately about ideas with some kind of *moral* significance. What is the basis of these presuppositions?

In order not to be disappointed here by an absence of arguments that we might think we have every right to expect, we should recall that throughout this discussion of art, Kant does not take himself to be radically revising an ordinary conception of art, but only showing how it can be saved from self-destruction. And except for some forms of absolute music, the importance of which was still controversial,[10] the art around Kant himself was all representational. Thus Kant would have felt no need to prove the typical representationality of art; rather, his task was to reconcile this non-controversial fact with his basic model of aesthetic response, indeed to show how that representationality can be exploited by his account to show just where the work of genius is done – in the room for play that lies between an abstract description of any work's theme or content and the specificity of its actual sensuous or imaginative form. Further, we can likewise take Kant to have just assumed rather than felt a need to prove that, because of the centrality of morality to human

[10] See Peter Kivy, *Music Alone: Philosophical Reflections on the Purely Musical Experience* (Ithaca: Cornell University Press, 1990).

concerns, most if not all human art typically touches on moral themes. His task, again, would not be to prove what all around him would have been taken for granted, but rather to show how that fact is compatible with his own account of aesthetic response, according to which nothing beautiful can manifest constraint by any determinate concept, *a fortiori* any determinate concept of morality. Kant's theory of aesthetic ideas then shows how a work of art can have a moral theme while still inducing a free play of imagination and understanding in its audience – although of course only a genius, through the gift of such harmony in his own powers of mind, can produce an object that can in turn produce such a response.

We can now formulate a final version of Kant's conception of art. Adding what has just been said about aesthetic ideas to what was previously said about genius, we can now cast our definition in the form of a definition of a work of art rather than of the capacity to produce art. Kant's definition of a work of art, then, would be something like this:

(1) an object voluntarily produced by a human agent, although by means of and as an expression of the free play of the agent's imagination and thought,
(2) with the intention of inducing a pleasure stemming from the free play of the cognitive powers, as well as further pleasures attendant upon that, such as pleasure in the communicability of such a state of mind,
(3) in an audience properly situated by its disinterestedness,[11] cultivation, and knowledge to so respond,
(4) in response to the interplay between the content or theme and general as well as particular features of sensuous and/or imaginative form of such an object.

Here a work of art is characterized as an object, produced out of the intentional and goal-directed but not determinately rule-governed activity of an artist, ultimately aimed at an end including the pleasure of an audience, which is in turn to result from the free play of imagination and understanding in that audience as a response to the expression of the free and original harmony of thought and sensuous presentation in the work of the artist.

[11] I have not presented evidence for this requirement, even in the indirect form in which I have hinted at the evidence for the following requirements of cultivation and appropriate knowledge, but it should be obvious from the basic tenets of Kant's aesthetic theory.

What now has to be shown is that in spite of obvious differences both between themselves and between them and Kant, such a relatively conservative aesthetician as Monroe Beardsley as well as an apparently more radical one as Arthur Danto have in fact continued to work with what is essentially the same concept of art, even though their conceptions of what particular objects belong in the extension of that concept have radically diverged from Kant's. Before I can show that, however, I must add a final word about Kant's concept of *pleasure,* which has been used without explanation throughout this exposition, for that is what is most noticeably absent from the more recent definitions of art. I shall ultimately argue that while the *word* "pleasure" may be missing from these contemporary accounts, in fact they continue to assume that art offers precisely what makes the experience of it pleasurable according to Kant.

Kant typically refers to the "feeling of pleasure and pain" in the singular (e.g., *CPJ,* §1, 204). He cannot mean that the feeling of pleasure is the same as that of pain, of course, but does seem to mean that each of these two is a phenomenologically unique sort of sensation. Thus he seems to think that what in the case both of pleasure and pain we might assume should be conceived of as a generic term, subsuming a variety of phenomenologically distinct kinds of feelings, is instead a unique feeling that can arise in a variety of contexts. Our pleasures in "the agreeable, the beautiful and the good," he states, are only "three different relations of representations to the feeling of pleasure and displeasure" (*CPJ,* §5, 209), not three qualitatively distinct kinds of feeling. Further, this assumption that there is a single sort of pleasurable feeling that may arise from a variety of causes plays a not unimportant role in some of Kant's arguments, even some of his most appealing arguments; in particular, his compelling view that particular judgments of taste are always liable to error and that no defense of the universal validity of taste should obscure this fact is supported by his assumption that in order to make such a judgment we must assign a single sort of feeling as an effect to one of several possible causes – an empirical judgment that, as empirical, is always liable to error (*CPJ,* §38, 290).

But Kant never actually argues that all pleasures (or pains) are instances of a phenomenologically singular kind of feeling, or even that pleasure is a feeling at all. His only attempts to give anything like a general characterization of pleasure (and pain), even while retaining the language of "feeling," are always at a higher level of abstraction and define pleasure and pain only in terms of their effects, by means of what we might now call functional definitions rather than by phenomenological descriptions. Thus he writes:

> An explanation [*Erklärung*] of this feeling considered in general, **without regard to the distinction whether it accompanies sensory sensation, reflection, or the determination of the will,**[12] must be transcendental. It can thus go like this: **Pleasure** is a state of the mind, in which a representation is harmonious with itself, as a ground either for preserving this state of mind itself (for the state of mutually assisting powers of mind in a representation preserves itself), or for bringing forth its object.... One readily sees that pleasure or displeasure, since they are not kinds of cognition, cannot in themselves be explained, and are felt, not understood, that one therefore necessarily can explain them only through the effect that a representation has on the activity of the powers of the mind by means of this feeling.
>
> (*FI*, VIII, 231–32)[13]

A pleasurable state of mind is simply any state of mind that one endeavors to preserve or renew, while an unpleasant state of mind is any which one tries to avoid or escape, presumably by avoiding or removing the presence of the object that causes it, but if that is not possible then by depriving the object of its usual effect (e.g., by anaesthesia in the literal sense of the word). This functional characterization undoubtedly needs refinement: particular occurrences of certain pleasures, e.g., sexual or gustatory pleasures, may only be enjoyable for relatively short periods of time separated by suitable intervals, and perhaps no pleasure can be enjoyed indefinitely; but it may still be characteristic of all pleasures that they create a desire if not for their continuous, then at least for their repeated enjoyment, while no pain ever creates a desire for its repeated experience. (If it does, then we say it has become a perverse sort of pleasure.)

Thus we can talk of pleasure without assuming that all pleasure involves some single identifiable sensation, or any special kind of sensation at all: where an activity is engaging or self-sustaining, a condition in which we wish to remain rather than one we wish to escape, then it is pleasurable, and all that we need mean by calling it pleasurable is that it is an engaging or self-sustaining form of activity. Perhaps we should add to this

12 That is, whether the object of the pleasure is the agreeable, the beautiful, or the good.

13 Similarly, in the published text of the *Critique* Kant states that "[t]he consciousness of the causality of a representation in respect of the state of the subject as one of **preserving** it in that same state can here designate in general what is called pleasure, while displeasure is that representation which contains the ground for determining the state of representations to their opposite (warding them off or getting rid of them)" (*CPJ*, §10, 220).

account, in light of Kant's discussion of disinterestedness, and as an explication of what is meant by the term "*self*-sustaining," that an activity is paradigmatically pleasurable when it is the quality of the experience of it that grounds the disposition to continue or renew that state, and not the expectation of some benefit extrinsic to the quality of the experience of the activity itself. On such an account, then, calling the free play of imagination and understanding pleasurable would not mean that it produces some unique and distinctive sensation, like a particular smell or taste, but just that it is an engaging, self-sustaining form of mental activity, one which – subject to appropriate qualifications – we want to preserve or repeat independently of any other interests in or benefits expected from the object that produces this state. Consequently, calling the experience of a work of art pleasurable would just mean that its form and content afford us the opportunity for an engaging and self-sustaining free play of imagination and understanding, a state that we wish to sustain because of the quality of this experience itself, independent of any further benefits it may bring, although it may in fact have further benefits.

What we will now see is that contemporary definitions of art continue to assume that works of art, no matter how different they may look or sound from anything that Kant could have imagined, offer us the opportunity for an engaging and self-sustaining free play of our cognitive powers – perceptual, intellectual, and above all imaginative. That such a state of mind is pleasurable, and that if it were not it would make no sense for us to go to the effort of creating or experiencing such objects is obvious, perhaps too obvious even to need stating, but is nonetheless implied by contemporary definitions of art. I will argue this first in the case of Beardsley and then in the case of Danto.

2. Beardsley

In the 1980 "Postscript" (actually a foreword) to the second edition of his *Aesthetics: Problems in the Philosophy of Criticism*,[14] Monroe Beardsley proposes a definition of art – more specifically, of a work of art – which he had not been willing to offer in the first edition. There, Beardsley

[14] Monroe C. Beardsley, *Aesthetics: Problems in the Philosophy of Criticism*, 2d ed. The first edition was published in 1958 by Harcourt, Brace and World (New York). The second edition of the work is a photographic reproduction of the first with only the new "Postscript" added in the position of a foreword. All my parenthetical citations of Beardsley in this section will refer to this work: Roman numerals refer to the second edition "Postscript," and Arabic numerals cite passages from the main text common to both editions.

had aimed at a definition of a general concept of "aesthetic object" that would make no reference to the intentional production of art by human beings so that our aesthetic judgments, even our judgments about what is an aesthetic object, would not depend upon problematic judgments about often inaccessible human intentions. But by the time of the second edition Beardsley had come to feel that his original scruples about an intentionalistic judgment were "overstated" and that it would be reasonable to appeal to intentions in defining an aesthetic object: "an artwork is an arrangement of conditions intended of being capable of affording an experience with marked aesthetic character – that is, an object (loosely speaking) in the fashioning of which the intention to enable it to satisfy the aesthetic interest played a significant causal part" (xix). This definition is squarely in the tradition of Kant's concept of art, refining it in some regards, although containing some of its elements only implicitly. (1) Beardsley's abstract term, "arrangement of conditions," might make it clearer than any term Kant had used that a work of art can be an event or state of affairs other than an enduring physical object; thus, it leaves room for the recognition of kinds of art Kant could not have envisioned, such as cinema or performance art, as well for all the arts other than the plastic arts, such as literature, music, or dance, which Kant of course did recognize. (2) While Beardsley does explicitly state that a work of art is the product of intentional activity, unlike Kant he leaves it implicit that this is the intentional activity of human beings rather than of, for example, bees;[15] but he clearly takes himself to be talking about human intentional activity throughout. (3) While explicitly specifying the overarching intention with which a work of art is produced as that of "affording an experience with marked aesthetic character" or of satisfying "the aesthetic interest," Beardsley's definition clearly leaves us dependent upon an antecedent account of that "character" or "interest," just as Kant's definition of art depended upon his preceding account of beauty and our response to it. (4) Finally, Beardsley's definition leaves implicit what Kant's preceding discussion of aesthetic judgment makes explicit, namely, that the intention to produce art must be an intention to produce a certain kind of experience in a certain kind of audience, one which receives the object with an appropriate background and expectations, that is, one which has an "aesthetic interest" it expects the object to satisfy. Thus, making

[15] He does make this explicit later: "Whatever other criteria we would need to use, a work of art is certainly something deliberately fashioned by human effort – it is a *work*, it is the product of *art*, or skill, at least in the traditional sense of the term" (59).

explicit what Beardsley had left implicit, we can expand his definition into one like Kant's: a work of art is (1) an object in the most general possible sense produced by a human being (2) with the intention of inducing (3) an experience of a certain kind, namely, "an experience with marked aesthetic character," in (4) a properly situated audience.

These elements correspond to the elements included in Kant's definition of a work of art as we saw it emerge through his discussion. All that is missing is the condition that an artwork is intended to produce a certain kind of *pleasure* in its intended audience, namely, pleasure in the free play of imagination and understanding. But an examination of what Beardsley means by "an experience with marked aesthetic character" will show that this phrase refers to an engaging and self-sustaining play of our cognitive powers, a condition that is so obviously pleasurable and prized by us for that reason that Beardsley may have felt that its pleasurability hardly needed to be stated. Be that as it may, since all that is required by Kant's definition of pleasure is that a pleasurable state of mind be engaging and self-sustaining, what Beardsley describes as an experience of marked aesthetic character is pleasurable in Kant's sense, and thus the intention which on Beardsley's account defines a work of art is an intention to produce aesthetic pleasure as Kant has described it.

As already observed, Beardsley's definition of an artwork presupposes a definition of "experience of a marked aesthetic character" or "aesthetic interest." In the original argument of his book, he arrived at such a definition only gradually (as Kant himself recommends), rejecting traditional models for such a definition and replacing them with an "objectivist" approach, which tries to identify aesthetically relevant properties of various kinds of aesthetic objects and only subsequently to define aesthetic experience as experience of *those* sorts of properties. Thus the first chapter of the book is entitled "Aesthetic Objects," and the next 300 pages are devoted to an examination of the various media of the arts. However, we can shortcut this discussion by taking what Beardsley rejects as alternative *approaches* to the definition of aesthetic experience as just incomplete *parts* of such a definition, and arrive at a definition of "experience of a marked aesthetic character" using Beardsley's material that will, again, reveal that his subsequent definition of art is squarely in the Kantian tradition.

At the end of the first chapter of his book, Beardsley considers and rejects three sorts of proposed definitions of "aesthetic object" before introducing his own candidate. These are three forms of what Beardsley classifies as "Psychological Definitions of 'Aesthetic Object'" (60), and then opposes to his own "The Objective Definition" of aesthetic object (63).

Beardsley's objections to the three "psychological definitions" fail, however, if these are considered aspects of rather than alternatives for a single definition; if they are taken as aspects of a definition that also includes his "objective approach," then what they yield is, in fact, the definition of an "experience of a marked aesthetic character" that is required by his definition of an artwork.

The three "psychological" kinds of definitions that Beardsley considers are definitions in terms of *motive, effect,* and *attitude.* In the first kind of definition, it is proposed that "an 'aesthetic motive' be distinguished from other motives, which would then usually be called 'practical' in a broad sense, including intellectual, religious and moral purposes," and an aesthetic object would then be an object produced out of whatever motive remains, such as that of "self-expression." Such a definition, Beardsley comments, would be "a genetic or intentionalistic definition" (60). Beardsley claims that there are several problems with this kind of definition. First, it requires an independent answer to the question "What psychological states and processes are generally, or universally, involved in acts by which aesthetic objects are produced?" Second, we may not know with what intentions a given object was produced at all, or alternatively we might well know that an object that we respond to as an aesthetic object was produced with non-aesthetic intentions. Finally, "the intentionalistic definition" seems too broad or "arbitrary": it can take in not just a surrealist or abstract painting, but a book or record jacket as well (61).

The second kind of psychological definition of "aesthetic object" is one "in terms of its *effects*": an aesthetic object would be one that "produces a certain kind of experience – say, a feeling of intense repose" (61). Against this kind of definition, Beardsley suggests two kinds of objections. First, he simply asserts again that we must be able to "define 'aesthetic object' independently of its psychological effects" in order to avoid question-begging, and, second, he claims that we have to do so in order to "keep the normative element out of [the] discussion," or to leave room in the category of aesthetic objects for unsuccessful ones.

The third form of psychological definition is one "in terms of our approach to it, or our attitude toward it": "we would first distinguish a certain sort of attitude towards things, the aesthetic attitude, and then we would say that any perceptual object may be an aesthetic object if we take it that way, or treat it as such as approaching it with an aesthetic attitude" (62). The problem with this kind of definition seems to be that it is a "relational one," thus that "nothing is aesthetic or nonaesthetic in itself" but instead becomes an aesthetic object or not depending on how it is approached. This suggests that what may be aesthetic object for one culture or even one person need not be one for the next, and at least the latter possibility would certainly introduce an untenable level of relativity into the definition.

To all of these "psychological" definitions, Beardsley opposes what he calls "The Objective Definition." This is not a definition at all, but is simply the approach that Beardsley proposes to carry out in the rest of his book by identifying "a set of characteristics that all aesthetic objects possess, though no other objects have them all . . . for example, [that aesthetic objects] present themselves as bounded segments of phenomenal fields, and have internal heterogeneity but with enough order to make them perceivable as wholes" (63). Such an approach, he thinks, will avoid the problems of the psychological definitions. In particular, it won't attempt to identify aesthetic objects by reference to some psychological phenomenon, the recognition of which presupposes a prior identification of aesthetic objects.

However, the kinds of characteristics Beardsley here calls "objective" can in fact only be identified by appeal to human psychological dispositions: what counts as heterogeneous, what counts as perceivable as a whole, even what counts as a phenomenal field, cannot be characterized in perceiver-neutral terms, but only in terms of an object's effects on human perceivers. There can be no escaping from "psychological" definition even in what Beardsley calls an "objective" definition. At the same time, the defects that Beardsley alleges to find in the psychological approaches in terms of motive, effect, and attitude can be remedied if we understand them not as alternative definitions of the concept of an aesthetic object, but rather as aspects of the complex framework of both the artist's and audience's intentions and expectations in the experience of art, to be referred to in any adequately complex definition of art. On such a definition, a work of art is (1) an object or objective condition produced by a human agent (2) with the intention – the "motive" – of inducing in (3) an appropriate audience – one receiving it with the right "attitude," or background and expectations – (4) a certain kind of pleasure – an "effect" – namely, a pleasure in the free play of cognitive faculties induced by such properties of the form and content of the object and their interplay as its "internal heterogeneity" and perceivability as a whole – that is, Beardsley's "objective" features, understood, however, as features that can in fact be specified only as ones characteristically capable of producing certain kinds of response in human perceivers.

Seeing Beardsley's "objective" and "psychological" definitions as working together to yield a single, complex definition of art undercuts his objections to the "psychological" definitions considered separately. First, taking the psychological components together rather than separately, thus understanding the motive of the artist to be that of producing a certain kind of pleasurable experience in an appropriately situated audience, frees the definition from parasitism on a presupposed identification of aesthetic objects, although not, certainly, from dependence on an informative notion of the aesthetic experience that is intended. And reflection on intentions and their potential complexity obviates Beardsley's other complaints. That we might not know with what intention a work was actually produced is itself not an objection to a definition that calls for intentionality, unless one makes the unwarranted assumption that any good definition must always be able to be applied to specific cases with certainty. Further, the threat of uncertainty will be diminished if we acknowledge two well-known facts about intentions: first, they don't always need to have been consciously formulated by an agent, in the terms that we would use, for it to be reasonable for us to impute them to that agent; second, we often or perhaps usually act with multiple intentions. Thus, if we *respond* to an object such as a cave painting or icon with a free play of imagination and understanding, it may be perfectly reasonable for us to suppose that our response is not accidental, that is, that even if the painter did not have our concept of art and was making these images for religious or magical purposes, we are nevertheless responding to aspects of the work the maker put there with an implicit intention to please by calling forth a free play of imagination and understanding in any audience for the object. Of course, if our description of an aesthetic intention was available to the maker of an object, it is all the more plausible that he made his object with that intention as well as with others: for example, the complexity of intentionality certainly allows a commercial artist to conceive of himself as making both a surrealist painting and a salable record jacket (contrary to Beardsley's supposition that this would be problematic). In fact, it would be a very strange commercial artist who did *not* conceive of his activity in such terms, and because of the complexity of intentionality "commercial artist" is not an oxymoron. Recognizing the complex intentionality imputed to an object by calling it a work of art makes room for the cases that seem problematic to Beardsley when his "psychological" definitions are considered in isolation.

The problems of the possibility of aesthetic failure and of relativity that Beardsley mentions also fall before the complexity of the intentionality postulated by the definition of art. First, if a work of art is one produced with the *intention* to please an appropriately situated audience in a certain way, it does not follow that the work actually pleases: the conditions for its actually pleasing may be missing in either the audience or the artist – in Kant's terms, the artist may lack the necessary genius to succeed in her intention, or the audience may lack the appropriate disinterestedness. This is, of course, true of all intentional action: an object intended to Φ is not necessarily an object that actually does Φ; it need only be produced with a reasonably grounded expectation of Φ-ing in appropriate circumstances. Thus a work of art need not be an object that actually pleases an actual audience; it need only be reasonably intended to please an appropriate audience in an appropriate way. And this does not introduce relativism, as Beardsley also fears, for while there may indeed be all sorts of variation in how different audiences actually respond to a particular object, that does not mean that the object was not intended to have a particular kind of effect on an appropriately situated audience.

What now remains to be seen is that the effect that is intended on the revised Beardsleyan definition is in the tradition of the Kantian concept of the free play of imagination and understanding. This becomes clear at the end of Beardsley's book, in his penultimate chapter 11 on "Aesthetic Value," when he states: "The sort of thing you can do with an aesthetic object is to perceive it in a certain way, and allow it to induce a certain kind of experience. So the question, 'Is *aesthetic object* a function-class?' is only a somewhat pedantic way of asking an old and familiar question, which we have long postponed: 'Is there such a thing as *aesthetic experience*?'" (526). He then argues that there is such a thing, descriptions of which "some writers have obtained by acute introspection, and which each of us can test in his own experience" (527). He then characterizes this experience in terms that could also be used to characterize the free play of imagination and understanding. Unlike Kant, Beardsley does not, at least at first, explicitly insist upon the pleasurability of such experience; but what he describes nevertheless satisfies the Kantian characterization of pleasure, namely, that of a form of experience which is engaging and self-sustaining without further reference to extrinsic benefits. Also, unlike Kant, he does insist that his characterization of this form of experience is empirical; but Kant has no good reason to resist this characterization, and in any case any claim for the apriority of his characterization of aesthetic response itself plays no part in his use of this characterization in his analysis of the concept of fine art, so is irrelevant for our present purposes.

According to Beardsley, "nearly everyone will agree" to the following characterization of aesthetic experience. First, "an aesthetic experience is one in which attention is firmly fixed upon heterogeneous but interrelated components of a phenomenally objective field – [e.g.,] visual or auditory patterns, or the characters and events in literature." In such an experience "we are deeply absorbed" in the properties of an object and their interrelation, such as "the tension of a visual design," and our "experience differs from the loose play of fancy in daydreaming by having a central focus" (527). This certainly sounds like a play of cognitive powers which involves rich materials for the imagination but at the same time satisfies the understanding's standing interest in unity.[16] Second, Beardsley says that the aesthetic experience is one "of some intensity," or that "Aesthetic objects give us a concentration of experience" (527). This again stresses the satisfaction of the understanding's standing interest in unity even in the face of a diversity of materials; and Beardsley also echoes Kant's suggestion that such an experience can seem both lawful yet free when he paraphrases his notion of "concentration" by suggesting that aesthetic experience "marshall[s] the attention for a time into free and unobstructed channels of experience" (528). Finally, Beardsley makes the Kantian heritage of his characterization of aesthetic experience even more explicit when he says that its remaining features "may both be subsumed under *unity*": these features are, third, that aesthetic experience "is an experience that hangs together, or is coherent, to an unusually high degree" – it has "continuity of development . . . a sense of overall providential pattern or guidance, an orderly cumulation of experience, toward a climax"; and, "Fourth, [that] it is an experience that is unusually complete in itself" (528). All of these terms seem like so many ways of capturing Kant's notion of a free yet lawful play of the mind with materials offered by the imagination yet satisfying the understanding's desire for unity.[17]

Beardsley does not immediately say that such a form of experience is pleasurable in itself, without regard to any further benefits it may bring

[16] See especially *FI*, VIII, 20:221–5.

[17] In calling this emphasis on unity "Kantian," I hardly mean to imply that Kant was the first to explicate aesthetic experience in terms of unity and variety (one need only go back as far as Hutcheson for an immediate predecessor); what is novel about Kant's characterization is its combination of the recognition of unity with the idea of the *free play* of the imagination, as well as the insistence that this has to be recognized subjectively and is not to be implied by any objective description of the object. Beardsley may be unclear about the latter point, but his insistence on both unity of focus and "free and unobstructed channels of experience" is genuinely Kantian.

us;[18] perhaps that is so obvious that he feels it needs no statement. Rather, his next step is to argue that his characterization allows for a comparative evaluation of aesthetic experiences themselves, since properties like intensity and focus admit of degrees; but in summing up this brief discussion he uses terms that are virtually the same as those used in Kant's "explanation" of pleasure. The magnitude of aesthetic experience, he says, is a function of the unity and intensity of the experience and the "range or diversity of distinct elements that it brings together": "For the more unified the experience is, the more of a whole the experience is, and the more concentratedly the self is engaged; the more intense the experience, the more deeply the self is engaged; the more complex the experience, the more of the self is engaged, that is, the more wide-ranging are its responses, perhaps over a longer time" (529). The essence of the aesthetic experience, *a fortiori* the basis for the comparison of aesthetic experiences, is that it is one in which the mind is *engaged* with the interrelated properties of its object for nothing but the sake of this experience; the duration of this experience is a natural consequence of this self-sustaining engagement. By Kant's account, this is what constitutes the pleasurability of experience. Several pages later, it comes as a bland understatement when Beardsley finally mentions that "aesthetic experience" as he has described it is a "kind of enjoyment" (534). As Kant's definition of pleasure if not some of his other claims implied, there is no need to postulate a specific sensation of pleasure: an engaging form of self-sustaining activity, as both Kant and Beardsley have described aesthetic experience to be, is what we mean in talking about pleasure.

We can now return to the definition of artwork with which Beardsley opened the second edition of his book. For Kant, as we saw, a work of art is ultimately defined as (1) an object freely produced by a human agent, by means of and as an expression of the free play of his imagination and understanding, with the intention of (2) yielding a pleasure stemming from the free play of the cognitive powers, as well as further pleasures such as pleasure in the communicability of such a state of mind, (3) in an audience properly situated by its disinterestedness, cultivation, and knowledge to so respond (4) by means of the interplay between its content or theme and general as well as particular features of its sensuous and/or imaginative form. For Beardsley, as we have now seen, an artwork is (1) an arrangement of conditions (2) produced by intentionally

[18] Such extrinsic benefits of aesthetic experience are the subject of the final chapter of his book, which we might say stands under the sign of Schiller rather than Kant.

guided human art or skill (Kant's 1) with (3) the intention or motive of producing the effect of pleasure (Kant's 2) in (4) an audience receiving the object with the right approach or attitude (Kant's 3) by means of the experience of the focus, concentration, coherence, and completeness of the experience of the phenomenal field afforded by the object (Kant's 4), an experience which by its very nature is engaging and self-sustaining and therefore pleasurable. All the terms of the definitions are the same: there is an agent with an intention or "motive" to produce the "effect" of a characteristic form of pleasurable engagement in an audience in the right "attitude" to receive the "objective qualities" of the arrangement of conditions produced by the agent with that intention.

3. Danto

From the outset of his career in aesthetics,[19] Arthur Danto has stressed that what makes an object a work of art is nothing necessarily perceptible in the object itself, but rather its place in an "artworld" – that is, a conceptual, interpretative framework intended by the artist and understood by the audience, not a sociological context of museums, galleries, curators, dealers, collectors, and critics.[20] This has been the lesson of his "method of indiscernibles": what makes an object a work of art is not just its immediately perceivable properties, which it may well share completely with something that is not a work of art at all, but the framework of concepts and intentions within which it is situated. Danto has written as if this concept of art is as revolutionary as the novel artworks to which it applies, Duchamp's *Fountain*, Andy Warhol's *Brillo Boxes*, and other works of conceptual and avant-garde art (typically visual art) produced throughout the twentieth century. But we have now seen that at least since Kant the conceptual framework within which a work is created – the intentions of the artist including the intended response of the audience – has always been at least a necessary condition for the definition of art; no one has assumed that something can be judged to be a work of art or responded to as a work of art just on the basis of its immediately perceivable properties. To this Danto might well reply that traditional thinking

[19] See "The Artworld," *Journal of Philosophy* 61 (1964): 571–84.

[20] That is, the "artworld" as envisioned in George Dickie's "institutional analysis" of art; see Dickie, *Art and the Aesthetic: An Institutional Analysis* (Ithaca: Cornell University Press, 1974), chap. 1, esp. 35–7.

about art still requires a place for beauty which his account, responsive to twentieth-century realities, abolishes. What I want to argue now is that even here there is less difference between Danto and the tradition than may initially meet the eye: Danto's conception of the response to art as primarily an activity of interpretation is, if not identical to, then at least an instance of, the Kantian concept of the free play of imagination and understanding. The basic idea of the intended response to art as one involving the play of thought and not merely perception is one that Danto shares with Kant as well as with a more traditional contemporary aesthetician such as Beardsley.

For the sake of brevity, I am going to use a formalization of Danto's definition of art provided by Noël Carroll. According to Carroll,

> Stated formulaically, the theory of art that Danto propounds . . . maintains that something *X* is a work of art if and only if (a) *X* has a subject (i.e., *X* is about something) (b) about which *X* projects some attitude or point of view (this may also be described as a matter of *X* having a style) (c) by means of rhetorical ellipsis (generally metaphorical ellipsis) (d) which ellipsis, in turn, engages audience participation in filling-in what is missing (an operation which can also be called interpretation) (e) where the works in question and the interpretations thereof require an art-historical context (which context is generally specified as a background of historically situated theory).[21]

Let us stipulate to the accuracy of Carroll's formalization of Danto's definition. I want to argue two things about this definition. First, although two key elements of what we can now, after our discussion of Kant and Beardsley, call the standard definition of art are not explicitly mentioned in this version of Danto's definition – above all, the intentional activity of the artist and the pleasure of the audience – they are clearly presupposed or implied by what Danto does explicitly mention, the projection and reception of an object requiring interpretation. Second, although the response to art that Danto's account canonizes, the activity of interpretation, may seem more particular than the abstract notion of the free play of the cognitive faculties that is central to Kant's account, it is both a good example of that idea and indeed the instance of that generally described activity that Kant himself assumes is canonical for fine art; at the same time, not only in Kant but in Danto as well the activity of interpretation may have to be considered only an example of a more general notion of the free play of the cognitive powers in order for

[21] Noël Carroll, "Essence, Expression and History: Arthur Danto's Philosophy of Art," in *Danto and His Critics*, ed. Mark Rollins (Oxford: Basil Blackwell, 1993), 79–106, at 80.

the concept of art in which it figures to accommodate comfortably the whole of what Danto as well as Kant recognizes as the extension of the concept of art.

I will begin by showing that although Danto's definition of art does not explicitly include all of the elements of the Kantian definition, it clearly presupposes whatever it omits. As we saw, Kant defines a work of art as (1) an object produced by a human agent with the intention of pleasing (2) by inducing a free play of the cognitive powers (3) in an appropriately situated audience (4) through the interplay of the properties of the object produced, above all by the interplay of form and content in the object. Conditions (a), (b), and (c) in Danto's definition clearly play the role of condition (4) in the standard definition – they characterize the interacting aspects of the work of art to which an audience can respond. Conditions (d) and (e) correspond to conditions (2) and (3) in the standard definition – condition (e) refers to (3), what is the appropriate situation for the audience to respond to a work of art, and condition (d) characterizes (2) the response of the audience in terms of a use of cognitive powers. Condition (1) of the standard definition, that a work of art is an object intentionally produced by a human agent in order to produce a certain response in an audience, is not explicitly mentioned, but is clearly presupposed throughout Danto's account: the idea of an object for interpretation is certainly the idea of an object intentionally produced by a human agent with the aim of inducing a certain kind of response. Finally, although Danto's account makes no explicit mention of the *pleasure* at which all art aims on the standard account, it implies it, because the interpretative activity postulated by its condition (d) is clearly a paradigmatic example of the kind of engaging and self-sustaining state of mind that satisfies the Kantian definition of pleasure. As we will see in the final part of this section, however, the pleasurable activity of interpretation or free play with the interrelation between form and content that both Danto and Kant assume is central to fine art can in fact only be an example of a more general concept of the appropriate response to art.

It may be obvious that for Danto a work of art is the product of a human being operating with a complex structure of intentionality, including a conception of what response is to be produced in an audience, a conception of the means by which such a response may be induced, and perhaps a further conception of an end or ends to be achieved through producing the intended response in an audience. The device by which Danto structures his argument throughout *The Transfiguration of the Commonplace,* the non-sense-perceptible distinction between artworks and "mere real things," always assumes that an artwork is a product of intentional human activity where the structure and character of the intentionality framing and guiding that activity is precisely the non-sense-perceptible element that distinguishes the artwork from the mere real thing. This holds true whether the distinction is between a product of non-human forces and a product of human intentionality, such as the difference between a paint splash that resembles Rembrandt's *Polish Rider* and the *Polish Rider* itself,[22] or between a human artifact produced (supposedly) without artistic intention and one that is produced with such an intention, for example, Brillo cartons in a supermarket storeroom and Andy Warhol's *Brillo Boxes* originally displayed in the Stable Gallery.[23] What makes the difference between the artwork and the non-artwork in these cases is not just that the artwork is an artifact of a kind that is always a product of human intentional activity, for although that is true of works of art it is true of most of the non-artwork counterparts that Danto imagines as well. What makes the difference is that the artist intends his product to have a certain kind of meaning, to illustrate an art theory, and so on, a kind of intention which is missing in the production of, say, an ordinary shipping carton for Brillo boxes, thoroughly intentional as the production of the latter also is. So Danto clearly presupposes that a work of art is an object produced by a human being with a certain kind of intention, indeed an intention of calling forth a certain kind of interpretative activity on the part of an audience, and that a work of art cannot even be recognized as such without an acknowledgment of that intention. (Interpreting an object as a work of art is presupposed by all further interpretation of it.)

Danto himself stresses this point when he is emphasizing the rhetorical character of artworks:

> It is an analytical truth that rhetoric is itself an intentional activity, and that beings only of a certain sort are capable of it. If true this implies an important relationship between work and artist. That is, there is an implicit reference to the fact

[22] See Arthur Danto, *The Transfiguration of the Commonplace* (Cambridge, Mass: Harvard University Press, 1981), 31.

[23] This example has figured in Danto's writing on philosophy of art since its beginning; see *The Transfiguration of the Commonplace*, 44, 208, and *After the End of Art*, 35, and many other passages. At least some of the original *Brillo Boxes* are now on display in the Philadelphia Museum of Art, where the idealization involved in Danto's use of this example becomes evident: Warhol's boxes could certainly not be mistaken by anyone with normal vision or touch for ordinary supermarket-bound packing cartons, although Danto may still be quite right that what makes Warhol's boxes art (if they are) does not depend on any of the differences between them and ordinary packing cartons that are sense-perceptible.

that someone is trying to move one rhetorically to the extent that one responds (perhaps mistakenly) to the work. "Intentional" does not entail "consciously" of course, and there may be room for a theory that refers art to the unconscious of the artist without this in any way changing the conceptual relationships between art and its intentions: metaphors have to be *made*.[24]

This passage implies that an artwork is a human artifact, produced intentionally as all such artifacts are, but produced with additional layers of intentionality as well: on the one hand, the kinds of intentions that constitute meanings, the subject-matter of rhetoric, on the other, an intention to produce a certain effect in an audience by means of these meanings, in this case "moving" them. Now notice Danto's observation that an act's and its product's being intentional does not entail that all aspects of that intentionality are conscious to the agent. We might well suppose that the intended meaning of a sign or symbol is typically conscious to its producer, although perhaps not every aspect of the meaning is; we do not have to assume that a framework of art theory within which an object is being produced is necessarily conscious to the artist, nor that the artist consciously thinks of his intended effect on an audience, such as moving them – these may all be taken for granted rather than consciously considered by the artist.

One thing still missing from Danto's concept of art is any explicit reference to the artist's intention to *please* his audience by inducing in it a characteristic form of experience or mental activity. Yet that does not imply any fundamental departure from the traditional definition, for if in fact the kind of response the artist does intend, whether that is *described* as interpretative activity of a certain kind or an effect of rhetoric such as being moved, *is* typically pleasurable, then by Danto's own account it may be perfectly reasonable to consider the production of pleasure part of the artist's intention, even if it is not a conscious part of that intention. Perhaps it is precisely the most obvious consequences of our actions that do not need to be a conscious part of our intentions: the pleasurability of engaging in interpretative activity may be so obvious that the aim of producing such pleasure almost never needs to be a conscious part of our intention when we are producing an object that needs interpretation with the intention that it be interpreted. I assume that in never explicitly discussing pleasure throughout *The Transfiguration of the Commonplace*, Danto is just taking the pleasurability of interpretative activity to be so obvious as never to need to be a conscious part of the artist's intentions

[24] *The Transfiguration of the Commonplace*, 175.

in producing an artwork, but taking it to be a fundamental part of the intentionality of art just for that reason.

I now turn to a further point of connection between Danto's definition of art and the traditional one. On Carroll's account, recall, Danto treats a work of art as something that (a) has a content (b) about which it expresses a point of view (c) by means of rhetorical devices such as ellipsis which in turn (d) need to be interpreted or filled in by the intended audience of the work, an audience which (e) must be appropriately situated for such interpretation by sharing an art-historical context with the author of the work. Condition (e) could certainly use further discussion: one might have to introduce further constraints on the appropriateness of the situation of the audience, such as its disinterestedness, to bring (e) into line with the conception of this situation intended in the traditional definition of art, but at the same time one might have to add emphasis on specific, historically contextualized knowledge to bring the traditional conception of an appropriately situated audience in line with condition (e).[25] But I will not take the space to do that. Instead, I want to comment a bit further on conditions (a) through (c). These represent Danto's argument in the final chapter of *The Transfiguration of the Commonplace* that works of art always express their content and an attitude toward it by means of metaphor and in a style that is a creature of its time, not available at any other time, yet unique to the artist even in his time. This claim raises many issues, but all I will say here is that Danto's concepts of metaphor and style can be understood as concepts of the interplay between form and content in artworks to which audiences respond, in the most general terms, with a free play of imagination and understanding.

This comes out in Danto's accounts of both metaphor and style. "A metaphor," he says, "presents its subject and presents the way in which it does present it."[26] This is to say that a metaphor is not just any way of conveying an idea or an opinion, but a way in which something is conveyed by the vehicle of presentation as well as by the semantic content of what is presented – to say that "men are pigs" is not just to say that they are greedy and messy, but to convey this along with the emotional reactions that the speaker and intended hearers have to pigs and not

[25] See Hume's discussion of "prejudice" in "Of the Standard of Taste" for recognition of this requirement in the tradition: a critic who is free of "prejudice" is one who can place "himself in that point of view which the performance supposes" (*Essays Moral, Political and Literary* [Oxford: Oxford University Press, 1963], 245).

[26] *The Transfiguration of the Commonplace,* 189.

just to anything greedy and messy. But this is just to say that in the use of metaphor – or in the use of all the artistic devices for which metaphor itself is a synecdoche – what we respond to is not just the content presented but also the form of presentation and the interplay between them. This is just what Kant assumes when he argues that in a work of artistic genius we respond with a free play of imagination and understanding to the interplay between the content of a work (rational idea), the overarching form of the work (aesthetic idea), and the particularities of the realization of that form (attributes). Likewise, on Danto's conception of style what we respond to in responding to the style of a work is the interplay between the content and the form of the work, although in this case an interplay between form and content that we also associate with the individuality of the author.

Danto's conception of style is also in the Kantian tradition of genius. Danto observes that the word "style" derives from *stilus,* the Latin word for a writing instrument, and infers from this that the term originally referred to the evidence in a piece of writing of the instrument by which it was made.[27] More generally, style signifies not just the evidence of the instruments that have been used to make a work, but the expression of the individuality of the maker who used those instruments in his own way as well. Again, this can be considered a matter of the interplay between form and content: in responding to style, we respond not just to an idea the work conveys, but to the features of the medium and form by which the content is conveyed, and the interplay between them, where these features as well as their interplay can in turn be seen as an expression of the individuality – or, in Kantian terms, genius – that has produced the work.

In arguing that the audience for a work of art responds to it by interpreting such features as its use of metaphor and its style, Danto is thus arguing that the audience for an artwork responds to the interplay of content and form, a response which is itself a free play of cognitive powers that is engaging and self-sustaining and thus, it goes without saying, pleasurable. We must now ask, however, whether artworks must always be defined as constituting metaphors, and as calling for the specific kind of interpretative response that metaphors require, thus whether the kind of interpretative activity Danto has in mind is as broad as Kant's concept of the free play of imagination and understanding.

[27] See ibid., 197.

At the outset of the *Critique of the Power of Judgment,* Kant focuses on cases of beautiful objects – natural objects and works of art like decoration and absolute music – that have no content, that represent nothing designated by any determinate concept (*CPJ,* §4, 207). As we saw, however, he subsequently assumes that all works of art represent something or have a content; then, in introducing a scheme for the classification of the arts based on their capacity to represent content – an heir to Lessing's distinction between poetic and plastic arts and a predecessor of Hegel's grand scheme of the arts – he even makes the gratuitous assumption that *all* beautiful objects, those in nature as well as those produced by human art, "may be termed the expression of *aesthetic ideas*" (*CPJ,* §51, 320). The assumption that even natural beauties express aesthetic ideas plays no role in any subsequent argument offered by Kant, not even in his account of the beautiful as the symbol of the morally good (§59), and can safely be ignored. The claim that works of art always have a content that can be associated with if not captured by a concept, however, is a premise for further argumentation – namely, the classification of the arts – though as we also saw Kant does not give it any special support. In an age that had not yet invented abstract painting or concrete poetry, the unargued assumption that all art has a content may not have seemed problematic. Nevertheless, Kant did mention the case of "fantasias" and "all music that is not set to words" (*CPJ,* §16, 229), and he should have recognized that the free play we enjoy between content and form in the case of works which do embody aesthetic ideas is only a special – even if by far the most frequent – case of the general concept of the free play of imagination and understanding. The mind will play with content as well as form when both are there – play with making and interpreting metaphors, for instance – but can play with and over formal features alone or form and matter even when there is no content, as in absolute music. Perhaps, as Kant also suggests, the mind cannot play as long – that is, pleasure cannot sustain itself as long – with objects that have no content as it can with works that do have content, especially moral content (*CPJ,* §52, 326); this is not incompatible with the basic idea of aesthetic response as pleasurable because self-sustaining – as Beardsley suggested, mental states such as focus and concentration do admit of different degrees and presumably therefore different durations as well. But this does not change the basic fact that the concept of the harmony of imagination and understanding is quite general, and while in the case of many artworks it may be induced and be intended to be induced through interplay between form and content, it can be induced and be intended to be induced by interplay between other aspects of perceivable objects and their conceptual context as well.

It seems as if Danto too would have good reason to think of the intentional production of and interpretative response to the interplay between what is presented and how it is presented as a special case of something more general. Even within the field of visual arts, which is what Danto most often has in mind, he recognizes that there is no single project for any physical medium. Indeed, at least in one recent book, Danto insists that what he has meant by the "end of art" thesis that he has proposed since *The Philosophical Disenfranchisement of Art* (1986)[28] is just that certain projects within certain arts, such as the projects of illusionistic painting and then self-referential painting – painting the point of which is to exemplify and explore the medium of painting as such – have, for a variety of internal and external reasons, exhausted their possibilities for novelty and thus for a certain kind of interest, namely, interest in their progression, although of course people will still continue to do many things with paint, including works in those genres and many others, perhaps some as yet unimagined. Although his general argument is that anything produced in any form of art must be accompanied by some form of non-sense-perceptible art theory, Danto gives no reason why the expression of content by rhetorical means should be a part of all these possibilities he is now prepared to countenance. Outside of the visual arts, Danto certainly never attempts to make the case that all forms of art involve content and therefore engage us through their rhetoric; he offers no argument, for instance, that music cannot engage us and be intended to engage us by formal features alone, or perhaps by an interplay between form and mood where it is not, however, in any meaningful sense *about* that mood. (Beethoven's Ninth Symphony may be *about* freedom, at least in its final movement, but the *Appassionata* sonata is not *about* passion, though it may be quite passionate and expressive of passion.) Thus, it seems that Danto too should recognize the creation of rhetorical expression for meaning and the interpretative response to that as one common and perhaps predominant form of what is intended in art, but there is no reason why he should not see that as an instance of something more general.

If this is so, then the definition of art with which Danto is really working – the definition that has remained single and uniform

[28] Arthur C. Danto, *The Philosophical Disenfranchisement of Art* (New York: Columbia University Press, 1986).

throughout the history of art, while its extension has constantly changed – should be something like this:

Something *X* is a work of art if and only if

(a) *X* is an object produced by a human agent that has and was meant to have a form and a subject (or something else that can interact with its form)
(b) about which *X* projects an attitude or point of view (or expresses the unique genius of its author in some other way)
(c) by means of rhetorical ellipses or the many other devices
(d) that can engage audience participation in interpretation (or engage the imagination and understanding of an audience) in a way that is engaging and self-sustaining and therefore pleasurable
(e) where the occurrence of such interpretation or other forms of cognitive play may presuppose an understanding of an historical context (and other constraints on the appropriate situation of the audience).

This definition is, to be sure, more cumbersome than its initial version, but indicates that objects intended to engage and please us by means of their interplay between form and content are in fact only a special case of the more general class of objects intended to please us by engaging our cognitive powers of imagination and understanding in a free and harmonious, engaging, and self-sustaining play. That is how art has always been intended to please, no matter what other functions it may also have been intended to serve and no matter whether a message, even a message about the nature of art itself, is part of what we play with and are intended to play with. At least from Kant to the present, I hope we can now see, there has been no essential disagreement about this concept of art.[29]

[29] I would like to thank David Hills for his exceptionally detailed and helpful comments on an earlier draft of this essay.

13

The Value of a Theory of Beauty

Mary Mothersill's Beauty Restored

Her publishers surely would have disliked quotation marks in the title of her wonderful book. Of course it is not beauty itself which Mary Mothersill hopes to restore. Rather, she aims to revive the concept of beauty, and to return it to the center of our attention, whence it had been displaced by the false modesty of the ordinary language philosophers and the incomplete cognitivism of the linguists of art, the fundamental connection between aesthetic merit and pleasure itself. A student of the eighteenth century, when the plain fact of our pleasure in it finally became the basis of a secular justification of our attachment to natural and artistic beauty, cannot but welcome Mothersill's essay. In these remarks I would only like to add that there may be even wider room and deeper need for a theory of beauty than Mothersill allows.[1]

On Mothersill's account, aesthetic theory must face the Kantian task of showing how the two truths which she calls the "First Thesis" and the "Second Thesis" can fit together and thereby render the judgment of taste at least logically possible (pp. 86–7). The First Thesis is that there are no noninnocuous *principles* of taste of the form "Whatever has property Φ is *pro tanto* beautiful" where the predicate Φ is not just another name for beauty or some more specific aesthetic merit (p. 164). The Second Thesis is the premise that individual judgments of beauty are "genuine" (pp. 135–44), no mere expressions of inner state but claims about individual objects in the external world. The project of restoring "beauty"

[1] Immanuel Kant, *Critique of the Power of Judgment*, trans. J. C. Meredith (Oxford University Press, 1952): Preface, 5: 170 (pagination as in the *Akademie* edition). Mothersill's book is *Beauty Restored* (Oxford: Clarendon Press, 1984).

is to dispel the apparent antinomy of these two theses by providing an analysis of beauty which shows how judgments of taste can be genuine without being derivable from noninnocuous generalizations.

Mothersill clears the ground for her proposal with a rejection of the attack on the possibility of aesthetic theory conducted by a number of philosophers of the 1950s and 1960s. This attack depended on a misunderstanding of the First Thesis: the "anti-theorists" objected to mostly unnamed traditional theorists that there were no determinate rules for the creation or judgment of beautiful objects, and concluded from this that there could be no such thing as a theory of beauty; but this conclusion followed only because they confused *principles* of beauty with a *theory* of beauty, and thus denied what more traditional theorists had never maintained – all the while continuing to help themselves to the supposition that there were certain "good-making characteristics." In fact, traditional theory, as in Croce, was more inclined to maintain the uniqueness of beautiful objects or genuine artistic expression and thereby ground rather than deny the First Thesis. Since Kant, if not before, the tradition had sought a theory of beauty which, like the Aristotelian account of the just, would be "both enlightening and just, but . . . not prescribe anything remotely comparable to a litmus-paper test" to determine the beauty of particular objects (see especially pp. 135–44).

Of course, it is unlikely that the anti-theorists just confused principles and theories and so simply failed to notice that there was no substantive disagreement between themselves and more traditional theorists. So what explains their misunderstanding? A prominent part of Mothersill's explanation is that the anti-theorists were moved by the traditional idea of a parallel between aesthetics and ethics; but instead of conceiving of ethics as providing ideals of virtue or action which can be applied correctly only by the mature individual of good judgment, they pictured an ethical theory precisely as a definition of the good or right which yields determinate rules for action or reaction in all conceivable circumstances of human practice. With such a conception of ethical theory, they could not but conclude that aesthetics fails to satisfy the only acceptable model for a theory of value in general.

Such a conception of ethical theory, really no more Kantian than Aristotelian but in the British tradition of both utilitarianism and intuitionism, surely played a role in the attack upon aesthetic theory, but cannot be the whole story. Two other prejudices of the period must also have influenced the anti-theorists. First, the verificationist theory of meaning, according to which the meaningfulness of a term is dependent on the existence of rules for its application to objects of experience, must have made them suspicious of such a general conception as that of beauty; for if such a general concept cannot directly yield determinate rules for its own application, then it may begin to look as if there is really no general concept for aesthetics at all. And if even more particular concepts of aesthetic appraisal, such as the dainty and the dumpy, could not be associated with any procedures for the verification of their application, then so much the worse. Second, the positivist equation of scientific *explanation* and *prediction* must have motivated the doubt that even if there was a general *concept* of the beautiful there could be any informative *theory* about it; for clearly no proposed *explanation* of our aesthetic appreciation suffices to yield any particular *predictions* of our aesthetic predilections. In sum, it could hardly have been easy for aestheticians in the hey-day of positivism, whether logical or ordinary and express or tacit, to embrace the First Thesis, the equation of meaning with rules for verification, and the equation of explanation with rules for prediction, and still to suppose that there could be a meaningful and even explanatorily significant concept of beauty. Only once these two dogmas of positivism began to be relaxed might it once again have seemed respectable to offer a general theory of beauty.

I doubt whether Mary Mothersill would disagree with such an extension of her diagnosis of anti-theory. But removal of these positivist constraints may leave room for more theory of beauty than Mothersill's analysis of the concept provides. A brief sketch of her account may help us see where it needs amplification.

I

A theory of beauty must work within the boundaries (p. 170) imposed by the First Thesis, that there are no aesthetic principles of the form "Anything which is Φ is beautiful," and the Second Thesis, that individual judgments of the form "This *x* is beautiful" – where whatever general *term* is used to pick out *x* will not imply a *principle* entailing the further predication of beauty – are genuine claims to objective validity. The meaning of the First Thesis requires little explanation, and in a way the thesis also requires little argument: no one has ever mounted a plausible argument against it, few have ever tried, and even the anti-theorists themselves have provided suspiciously few examples of the kinds of "theories" that would imply such rules. The Second Thesis requires more explication. Mothersill devotes much of her chapter on the Second Thesis to the *normative* aspect of judgments of taste – the difference between a mere *avowal* of personal pleasure and a *verdict* binding on an audience wider than oneself; and here she quite rightly seeks a middle ground between the proto-emotivism of Santayana, according to which for all its normative sound the judgment of taste is just a misleading expression of personal pleasure, and the excessive moralism of Kant, according to which the judgment of taste actually conceals a *command* for the agreement of others. I will return to this important issue, but now we must consider Mothersill's overall analysis. This seems to be that a genuine judgment of taste is an assertion that an individual object has pleased me and promises to do so again, subject to four conditions. (1) This assertion is an expression of my *conviction* as opposed to mere opinion, which can thus withstand reflection on my qualifications to appreciate the object and the acceptability of the conditions under which I have appreciated it, and can even be connected with procedures by which my conviction can be tested. (2) This assertion can have discernible impact on my overall body of beliefs and implications for my own behavior, that is, it does not simply represent an epiphenomenal episode of pleasure but can affect my plans and action of various cognitive and practical kinds. (3) Moreover, it is intended to express the contingent truth that it is something about the object of my pleasure which pleases me, (4) as well as intended to have some kind of normative implication for others, though surely not a command that others must also like the object or even a claim which is defeated by the evident disagreement of others. Mothersill's argument for this characterization I find somewhat obscure. She does acknowledge that the Second Thesis may seem less secure than the First, but associates insecurity about it primarily with the unclear normative import of judgments of taste. Otherwise, she seems content to rest with the view that this thesis, like the other, is not a self-evident but is an *obvious* truth which is not provable, but then again is not intended as an *axiom* of a theory of beauty which it entails; it simply provides a natural boundary on our aesthetic theorizing which could in principle be overthrown by a powerful theory – but has hardly been so to date (p. 168).

Mothersill's next step is the identification of a "standing concept" of beauty, a conception of it which is taken for granted in "critical discussion of the arts" as the concepts of knowledge and action are assumed in our first-order scientific and practical discourse, and which, although it is certainly open to philosophical reflection, explanation, and even refinement, is no more open to dissolution through philosophical objection than it is dependent upon philosophical support to begin with. This standing concept of beauty provides a pre-theoretical identification of the *object* of aesthetic judgment complementing the constraints on the *judgments* of taste themselves which are expressed by the First and Second Theses. The three "commonly accepted truths" (p. 275) which constitute the standing concept of beauty are (1) that "Beauty is a kind of good," something which "in contexts of deliberation and choice counts as a plus" (p. 262) though not a plus against which no minuses can be set; (2) that "Items of any sort may be beautiful" (p. 265), by which is meant not that any *particular* can properly be seen as beautiful, but rather that there are no ontological *kinds* – such as "images, shadows, reflections, dreams [and] fictions" (p. 265) – but also, presumably, no more natural kinds as well – such as, say, wines, women, and songs – among which beautiful particulars cannot be found; and finally (3) that "Beauty is causally linked to pleasure and inspires love" (p. 271), that both the perception and the production of beauty cause pleasure among a variety of producers and audiences in a variety of ways.

The first of these truths is basically self-evident. The second may be understood as the complement of the First Thesis which holds that no noninnocuous classification is a *sufficient* condition of beauty, while the present claim is that no such classification is a *necessary* condition of beauty. Though the beauties of maidens, pots, and pictures may be interestingly different, no theory of beauty which pretended to prove *a priori* that one of these kinds of things *couldn't* be beautiful would be plausible. It is the third component of the standing concept of beauty, the claim that beauty in an object is the *cause* of a notable pleasure in it, that calls for some of Mothersill's most subtle argumentation and that ultimately points the way to the theory of beauty itself.

Mothersill undermines three philosophical objections to the otherwise natural assumption that beauty is a property in an object which causes feelings of pleasure in those who observe it. First, it has been held that the causal relationship requires an effect which is an event of change from an antecedent state of affairs, but our pleasure in a beautiful object is not any sort of event; pleasure is not an inner episode like pain but some sort of attitude or even a way of conducting an activity. Second, it is held that causality is a contingent connection between two discrete states of affairs, and so requires that the otherwise appropriate characterizations of the cause and the effect reflect their logical independence; yet beauty and pleasure are no more logically independent, than, say, pleasure and fulfillment of desire. If the fulfillment of desire *logically* entails pleasure, it cannot *cause* it, and likewise beauty is actually too closely connected with pleasure to *cause* it. Finally, it is insisted that cause and effect must each be instances of repeatable kinds, states of affairs between which there can be law-like regularities; but then any assumption of a connection between the beauty of an object and its uniqueness will be precluded.

Philosophers as profound as Kant have felt the force of these objections,[2] and Mothersill's refutation of them is masterly. She rejects the arguments, especially the Rylean arguments, against the supposition that pleasure really is any sort of inner episode at all on a number of grounds: pleasure is in fact sufficiently distinct from the rest of our experience of an object to be abstracted from it and sometimes even to interfere with it; pleasure need not be synchronous with the activity that produces it – it may linger on after our encounter with the object is over, or even come to our notice only then; and our several pleasures are not merely ways of talking or otherwise behaving, but inner states which may at least sometimes be hidden and have to be inferred (pp. 282–3). Second, although the "answer to the question, 'What is the cause of your current pleasure?' is often obvious and unmistakeable" (p. 301), this does not mean that the connection between cause and effect is other than contingent; there is no logical necessity that a beautiful object invariably and obviously please, any more than there is in fact a logical necessity that the fulfillment of desire actually produce the pleasure expected from it. Beauty and the fulfillment of desire almost always please, and it is almost always evident that they are the causes of the pleasures they produce, so the inference from cause to effect is almost always routine. But the exceptional is not the logically impossible, and the connection between beauty and pleasure, like that between fulfillment of desire and pleasure, is in fact a contingent causal connection even if it hardly ever fails or even fails to be obvious.

This brings us to the objection that a beautiful object is too unique to be the proper subject of a causal generalization. Here Mothersill's answer is that the uniquely pleasing character of a beautiful object is not in fact *logically* unique; it is logically possible that an object please in virtue of a property which as a matter of fact it does not share with every or even any other member of its natural kind, but which it could share with objects "indistinguishable" from it "under standard conditions of observation" (p. 343–5). In fact, in cases in which an object that has aesthetically satisfactory reproductions, or in allographic arts, where the work of art is intended to exist only in a reproducible form, repeated occurrence of the property which pleases is actual and not just logically possible. Rembrandt's etching "View of Amsterdam" certainly differs in a myriad

[2] Ibid., §2.

of ways from "The Three Trees," and either may be said to please precisely in virtue of features which render it unique in comparison to the other; but one print of "The Three Trees" may also – *ceteris paribus* – please precisely in virtue of the same property which makes another print of that etching beautiful. A beautiful object pleases in virtue of a property which is aesthetically unique but which satisfies the logical requirement of repeatability derived from the Humean analysis of causation.

Such a property is what Mothersill calls an "aesthetic property" and is the heart of her final analysis of the concept of beauty. She approaches her definition through Aquinas's description of beauty as that *cujus apprehensio ipsa placet.* From the premise that beauty pleases only through *apprehensio* comes the requirement that pleasure in a beautiful object can only be caused by considerable, even studied acquaintance with the individual object, and neither from any general classification under which the object may fall nor from an indeterminate "context of pleasure," that is, an overall situation instead of an individual – an evening at the opera rather than the opera itself. From the adverb *ipsa,* however, Mothersill derives a further requirement of particularity: what causes the specific pleasure of beauty is not just an individual object in a more complicated context, the opera in the midst of all the distractions attending its performance, but something particular in the object itself, an "aesthetic property." This is the unique constellation of the more ordinary properties of the object – colors and shapes or words and chords – which, although a critic may be capable of referring to it only by general terms for ordinary properties, is actually shared only with the class of possible or actual objects perceptually indistinguishable from the beautiful object at issue. Thus, for instance, *The Burial of the Conde Orgaz* may please because of "the steeply rising and falling curve" traced by the outlines of the figures in its foreground (pp. 336–8), but a geometrical equivalent of that curve on a blackboard or a page of Hogarth, or maybe even in another painting by El Greco, wouldn't necessarily please equally or at all – it's *that* line outlining *those* figures with *those* colors creating *that* mood that pleases. With this notion of an "aesthetic property," Mothersill then proposes a triad of definitions, required to make epistemological space for the differences between merely taking something to be beautiful, finding it beautiful, and the object's really being so, which culminates in the definition that

Any individual is beautiful if and only if it is such as to be a cause of pleasure in virtue of its aesthetic properties (p. 347).

This appearance of the word "aesthetic" in the *definiens* should raise the hackles of the anti-theorist. But when it is recalled that a definition of the beautiful is to enlighten without providing a litmus-test and when both the extended defense of the causal status of beauty as well as the elaborate characterization of an aesthetic property are kept in mind, it will be seen that this definition does in fact encapsulate a considerable amount of enlightenment.

Nevertheless, this definition does not go as far as we can to explain the causal link between beauty and pleasure or as far as we must to justify the normative aspect of judgments of taste.

II

Mothersill defends the assumption that beauty causes pleasure from the objections to it, but does not try to explain *why* aesthetic properties *should* cause pleasure. Nor does she say why she ventures no such explanation. Clearly she is put off by the spectacular failure of Kant's attempt at a *transcendental deduction* of an *a priori* principle of aesthetic judgment and even a necessarily true version of the First Thesis itself (p. 116), and possibly thinks that any attempt to venture beyond differentia to an actual explanation must come to such a sorry end. I certainly agree with her that Kant falls far short of his goal of showing that aesthetic pleasure is just as necessary a consequence of the basic faculties of human cognition as, say, causal judgment itself and that the communicability of a correct judgment of taste is just as secure an assumption as that of the objective affinity of nature itself. Nevertheless, certain issues left open by Mothersill's analysis of beauty call for an explanatory theory. Aesthetic properties need not cause pleasure; the ugliness of an object may also lie in a property shared only with others perceptually indistinguishable from it. So why should aesthetic properties ever be a cause of pleasure at all? And what explains the difference between those which are and those which on the contrary cause displeasure, aversion, or even just indifference instead of attachment? Further, what about criteria for the latter discrimination? Of course, Mothersill has disavowed litmus-paper tests for judgments of beauty, but her defense of the Second Thesis certainly implies that my judgment that an object is beautiful may be subjected to reflection which can secure me in the belief that the judgment is genuine, that the object does not just happen to please me right now but promises to please me again and even to please at least some others on some suitable occasions.

What form does this reflection take? In isolation, Mothersill's definition would leave room for me to assure myself only that I feel pleasure and that my pleasure has been caused by an aesthetic property. But if aesthetic properties are not necessarily beautiful, how can that be sufficient? On what basis do I judge that an aesthetic property which pleases me today will not seem ugly tomorrow? or that an aesthetic property which pleases me and promises to continue doing so will please you? In other words, why do some aesthetic properties promise pleasure and how does one know when that promise is being made?

Released from its self-imposed burden of providing a transcendental deduction for an *a priori* principle as well as from a later generation's demand that a meaningful explanation of our pleasure in beauty issue in verifiable rules which can actually serve to predict aesthetic preferences, perhaps Kant's explanation of our pleasures in the beautiful and sublime can answer more of these questions than Mothersill allows. Here is Kant's account. Our linguistic intuition tells us that judgments of taste are not intended just to report personal preferences, but are rather meant to express some kind of claim, whether ideal prediction or quasi-command, to the assent of others – Mothersill's Second Thesis. Yet at the same time it seems an obvious fact of human nature – though not, as Mothersill has persuasively argued, any kind of necessary truth – that pleasure is connected with the fulfillment of some aim or objective. How are these intuitions to be reconciled and transformed into a theory? Leaving aside details, mistakes, and anachronisms, Kant's idea is that an object strikes us as beautiful when, all things considered – that is, either leaving aside or going beyond whatever classifications it may seem natural to impose upon it – it seems to satisfy our underlying desire for cognitive unity in our manifold of representations by effecting a harmony between imagination and understanding, and that an object strikes us as sublime when, under similar conditions, it satisfies our equally basic aim of harmony between imagination and reason even though it must override some of the customary constraints of the imagination. In such a case, there is after all an objective to be satisfied, though not one which the object satisfies automatically in virtue of any classification of it, and thus the occurrence of pleasure is not inexplicable; but at the same time, precisely since the satisfaction of the underlying cognitive objective is not rendered obvious by any conceptualization or classification of the object, it is also explained why this satisfaction does not seem routine, a condition under which, as Kant emphasizes, pleasure, even if theoretically necessary, would hardly be noticeable.[3] The occurrence of our pleasure in the beautiful or sublime is thus ascribed to a subjective mechanism, the harmony of imagination and understanding or imagination and reason, which can reasonably be expected to work in others as well as ourselves, and to a relation between an external object and that mechanism which, though it can be made to fit the Humean paradigm of lawlikeness only with the introduction of something like Mothersill's "aesthetic properties," is still clearly causal. It is, after all, the form of the object – not of course in the restricted sense of its shape rather than its color and content, but in the enriched sense of all that and more, anything and everything about it by means of which our representations of it can be "posited and ordered"[4] as long as that order strikes us as free[5] – which sets our faculties into harmony and causes us pleasure.

If one supposes that there can be truth-conditions for concepts like beauty and sublimity only if there are determinate and precise warrants for the application of "beautiful" and "sublime," this will not seem like much of an analysis of those concepts; and if one insists that an explanation issue in predictions this will not seem like much of an explanation. But if these requirements are relaxed, then this Kantian theory of taste can provide some needed supplementation of Mothersill's analysis of beauty.

I cannot understand Kant's theory of the harmony of the faculties except as a venture into psychology – arm-chair psychology, if one insists, or concert-hall or gallery psychology. Nor can I reconcile the freedom of the imagination postulated by this theory with the rule-governed character of self-consciousness required by the *Critique of Pure Reason*'s theory of transcendental apperception except by interpreting the theory of taste as precisely the kind of psychological theory which the theory of apperception *cannot* be. The premises that humans find pleasure in the satisfaction of their aims, but only if the latter seems somehow contingent and unexpected, and the postulation that beautiful objects produce a mental state which unexpectedly strikes us as satisfying a cognitive objective and thus please us, seem matters of psychological fact rather than transcendental epistemology. Thus there is no prospect for Kant's truly *a priori* principle of taste or for his "modal versions" of the First and Second Theses

3 Ibid., V, 5: 187–8.
4 Immanuel Kant, *Critique of Pure Reason*, trans. Norman Kemp Smith, Second ed. (London, 1933): A 20/B 35.
5 Kant, *CPJ*, §22 GR, 5: 240–1.

(pp. 86–7, 116–17). But it is still a virtue of Kant's theory that it attempts to provide some theoretical support for the pre-theoretical insights from which it starts. On Mothersill's account, the assumptions that judgments of beauty are genuine claims with objective import but independent of any determinate classifications of objects or principles of taste can be defended from theoretical objections but cannot themselves be given any theoretical defense. Indeed, the crucial concept of the final analysis of beauty, that of aesthetic property itself, is given logical expression but no theoretical derivation, for its discussion too really comprises a defense from theoretical objections to its use in a causal context but no deduction of any sort. In Kant, the relations between intuition and theory are more complex. On the one hand, to be sure, Kant poses the problem of taste with an appeal to our pre-theoretical intuitions about private preferences and public tastes, and likewise writes as if the disinterestedness of taste were common knowledge which self-evidently entails the freedom of beauty from a concept of the object, and his venture into speculative psychology surely derives some support from these facts which we all take ourselves to know just by knowing what we mean when we're talking about taste. Yet at the same time Kant clearly believes that these pre-theoretical intuitions just pose the problem of taste, and that they are by no means immune from skeptical objections until they are themselves deduced from a theory of aesthetic response and judgment. That judgments of taste cannot be grounded on concepts and must instead be occasioned by as many features of the objects as freely and therefore apparently uniquely dispose our cognitive faculties to their enjoyable harmony or free play – in a word, by aesthetic properties of individual objects – may be something which has to be defended from theoretical objections, but it is also a theoretical consequence of Kant's theory of the subjective conditions of human cognition. Pre-theoretical insights may provide boundaries for our aesthetic analysis, but a theory of taste in turn provides a deduction, even if not a transcendental one, of our title to the land within these boundaries.

Kant's theory also explains why some but only some aesthetic properties will please us and thus lead to a judgment of beauty. On the one hand, the property of an object which gives us aesthetic pleasure must be an aesthetic property, logically shared with the class of indistinguishable counterparts but not captured by any ordinary general term, precisely because our pleasure in the satisfaction of our underlying goal of cognition is noticeable only if that satisfaction is not predictable by any classification of an object which entails that it must satisfy any more determinate purpose, practical or cognitive. So beauty must at least be an aesthetic property. But on the other hand, this is only a necessary but not a sufficient condition. Only aesthetic properties can render our sense of cognition of them radically contingent, but certainly not every aesthetic property will give us any sense of cognitive accomplishment at all. It's hard to quantify over aesthetic properties (p. 353) but presumably the vast majority of them will either escape our notice altogether or else strike us as cognitively dissonant rather than harmonious. Kant's theory imposes a dual condition on beautiful objects – they must please us through an apparently contingent satisfaction of our cognitive objectives. This condition can be satisfied only by aesthetic properties, but it is not necessarily satisfied by all aesthetic properties. Thus there is some explanatory connection between aesthetic properties and aesthetic pleasure but not one which explains too much.

This alleged explanation of our pleasure in beauty might seem open to a ready objection. Kant's theory of the harmony of the faculties, after all, is nothing but a translation of the older image of unity amidst variety as the object of taste into the language of the subjective faculties of imagination and understanding, coupled with an overreaching attempt to make the uniformity of human thought a necessary truth rather than a happy accident. Yet it is obvious that for any object, no matter how formless or misshapen it may seem, there is at least one description under which it will satisfy the requirement of unity amidst variety, or, in Kantian terms, at least one empirical concept adequate to unify the manifold which the object presents. Doesn't this render the Kantian theory explanatorily, let alone criterially, hollow? Won't every object, not just some objects of any natural kind but every last object, have to come out beautiful on this account?

As long as it is kept in mind that we are not dealing with *a priori* principles but with human psychology, and as long as the possibility of meaningful explanation is separated from that of determinately applicable rules for prediction, this objection can be set aside. If we were looking for rules which could be applied by a machine, surely the condition of unity amidst variety could be satisfied by some easy description of any particular object; and if we were looking at the world from some god's eye point of view, perhaps every object would strike us as self-evidently unified. But on the Kantian account of aesthetic response, we are certainly not looking at the world from such a point of view, and the description of the object of taste as a unity amidst variety is not meant to furnish a decision-procedure for judgments of taste. Though it is logically and metaphysically possible to describe every object as presenting some unity amidst its variety, it is equally a fact of human psychology that not every object *strikes* us as unified apart from any concept we are immediately inclined to apply to it. And the causal explanation of our pleasure in beauty says that an object will please us if it unexpectedly *strikes* us as unified, or if it *feels* like it is satisfying our cognitive objective, not just if there is some logically or metaphysically possible point of view from which it *could* be seen as unified.

The Kantian theory of aesthetic response also offers some model for the kind of aesthetic reflection which might produce or confirm our confidence in a genuine judgment of beauty. On Mothersill's account, it seemed as if one could only assure oneself that one felt pleasure in an aesthetic property, and this didn't seem adequate to ground any kind of promise of pleasure if there was no evident reason why the same aesthetic property one is inclined to associate with one's pleasure on one occasion should please others or even oneself on another occasion. On Kant's account, there is room for an additional consideration – if reflection suggests that an object is causing pleasure because its aesthetic property is subjectively satisfying the general aim of cognition, then one has some reason to believe that one is not taking pleasure in an aesthetic property which might strike one as ugly another time or displease someone else; one will see some reason why this aesthetic property but not others should please.

To be sure, Kant's initial presentation of his theory does not suggest that the phenomenon of unexpected cognitive accomplishment can have criterial as well as explanatory significance. Rather, Kant actually provides a theoretical argument for the intuitive view that judgments of taste can be justified only by the *via negativa*, by the exclusion of idiosyncrasies as well as both private and public interests. This is because he argues, on the one hand, that pleasure and pain are the only necessarily noncognitive forms of consciousness, and therefore that the existence of the not strictly cognitive harmony of the faculties can be manifest to consciousness only in the occurrence of the feeling of pleasure, but that, on the other hand, there is no qualitative difference among different feelings of pleasure, thus no self-evident distinction between feelings of pleasure produced by sensory gratification, the satisfaction of practical reason, or the harmony of the faculties. Therefore the occurrence of the harmony of faculties, the proper cause of pleasure in the case of a correct judgment of beauty, is not manifest to consciousness, and can only be inferred from the absence of alternative causes of pleasure. When he gets beyond the simple cases of natural beauty or decorative art that provide his paradigms in the "Analytic of the Beautiful," however, and presents his more complicated theory of our pleasure in the fine arts, Kant seems to depart from this *a priori* phenomenology and assume that we can actually have a direct sense of free and therefore merely subjective cognitive satisfaction. Perhaps in the pleasant contemplation of a rose or an arabesque we can imagine that the harmony of the faculties is itself in some sense sub- or pre-conscious, and that all that we are actually conscious of is the object on the one hand and our feeling of pleasure on the other. But, for example, when an artwork expresses an aesthetic idea, it is hard to believe that "the flight" of the imagination "over a whole host of kindred representations that provoke more thought than admits of expression in a concept determined by words"[6] is not meant to be a unique kind of manifestly cognitive but not rule-governed experience, a quasi-cognitive quality of experience that is to some degree phenomenologically distinct from the pleasurability of the experience and which can thus be recognized and not just inferred to be the cause of one's pleasure. So extended, the theory of the harmony of the faculties as the cause of pleasure in aesthetic properties might not merely add some explanatory content to Mothersill's analysis of the concept of beauty, but also provide some criteria – though no decision-procedure – for the reflection which she associates with the genuineness of judgments of beauty.

III

I now suggest that there is need as well as room for a theory and not just an analysis of the beautiful. This is because justice cannot be done to the normative component of a judgment of taste without appeal, at least in a significant range of cases, to a theory of the beautiful which can sustain a burden of responsibility in making a claim upon the aesthetic attention of others.

Mothersill recognizes that there is a difference between even a sincere *avowal* of pleasure in an object and a *verdict* that it is beautiful (pp. 91–4), and does suggest that the normative implication of a verdict of taste requires some form of justification. Yet she forcibly argues that Kant has gone too far in construing the normative aspect of the judgment of taste as any sort of *command* that others find beautiful what I find such, creating some kind of *obligation* to be pleased by beauty in them. But her own

[6] Ibid., §49, 5: 315.

characterization of the norm appropriately connoted by a judgment of taste is vague. Surely I am not to command that others enjoy the beauties that I do, let alone sit in judgment upon the tastes of others like some pope or Pope (p. 216). But neither am I just to sincerely avow my own pleasures to others; I have more than a general burden of sincerity in critical communication, and it seems to me that Mothersill gives short shrift to a perfectly serious dimension of responsibility in issuing judgments of taste.

I certainly agree that Kant fails to defend his suggestion that "the judgment of taste [can] be exacted from everyone as a sort of duty."[7] Indeed Kant cannot very well argue that pleasure can be commanded when he insists that even love cannot be; and his suggestion that the cultivation of taste *may* assist in the development of a moral disposition hardly seems strong enough to justify such a command – nothing less than an argument that taste is a unique and indispensable aid to morality would really seem to justify an exaction of agreement in taste. However, as Mothersill herself suggests, there is a more modest conception of the judgment of taste: while I may not reasonably *command* that you like an object, I can certainly *commend* it to you (p. 217). To commend something is to perform a speech-act, thus in the realm of practice, and at least in principle subject to the constraints of morality. But more specifically, to commend is not just to risk influencing your beliefs in ways that may have unforeseen consequences for your actions, which is true in the case of any indicative speech-act, but is to offer you fairly clear motivations for action, and thus certainly subject you to standards of responsibility. In commending a show or performance to you, I may well be fairly explicitly recommending that you spend some of your finite time, energy, or money in one way rather than another; and you will have good ground to resent it if I have no good ground for doing so, and even do so without a thought of such grounds. Though Mothersill mentions the responsibility involved in commending objects to others in passing (pp. 31, 79, 224), she does not say enough about it.

To be sure, the standard of responsibility for critical utterances cannot reasonably be set as high as standards of responsibility are elsewhere. In Western democracies, at least, the consequences of ill-advised aesthetic choices are not likely to be incarceration or incapacitation, and neither a professional critic nor each of us in our aesthetic recommendations should be held to the same standard of considered judgment required in

[7] Ibid., §40, 5: 296.

matters of life and death. Nevertheless, the costs of a night at the opera, a journey to a distant cathedral, or even a weekend afternoon spent at the museum without a child who has been in day-care all week are not negligible, and one would like to think that those who recommend such costs to us will not do so irrationally or even just thoughtlessly. To put this point in professional terms, what was always so offensive about the image of self-appointed members of the art-world baptizing objects as candidates for appreciation without any particular theory of aesthetic appreciation was not the metaphysical or conceptual problem of speech-acts performed without any qualifications or constraints for their performance, but rather the moral problem of claims upon our thought and action being made without any consideration for our own interests and pleasures. But to satisfy these moral claims, a theory of beauty may often be required.

I do not mean to suggest that a critic can issue responsible recommendations only if possessed of a unique and correct theory of beauty; even in moral judgment, after all, we require only that the conscientious agent have what he takes on due reflection to be a good reason for his action, not that he be right in so taking it. Nor is it even obvious that for every responsible recommendation *some* theory of pleasure is required. There are clearly a variety of ways in which we might reasonably commend objects of taste to each other. Nevertheless, appeal to a theory of taste may be required to justify many of our aesthetic recommendations.

Though Addison and Hume saw the need to commend the "pleasures of imagination" themselves, let us leave that aside and consider authorial and critical recommendations of particular objects. What form do such commendations take, and how can a theory of beauty help sustain them?

A) Sometimes an individual object will be offered by its producer or commended by a critic, paid or volunteer, to a general public; here a reason to expect good value will surely be wanted, and both artist and art-critic may reasonably be required to have a good reason to promise pleasure to others. Even if the critic's product is not itself a work of art, that the artist also bears the critic's burden of having some reason to impose his work upon our attention is clear. In the case of the philosophical artist, perhaps even more than in the case of the critic, a theory of beauty itself may provide that reason; particularly the inventor of a new genre or the pioneer of a new medium can be expected to have some kind of theory as to why his product should please us like other more traditional works have. And while the model of conscience suggests that such a theory cannot reasonably be required to be unimpeachable, the same model also suggests that we can require it to be considered; not every artistic manifesto will discharge the responsibility incumbent upon such demands on our attention, but only such as have either some self-evident plausibility or some serious reflection behind them.

B) More often, however, an artist or critic will not recommend a work to our attention by directly subsuming it under an explicit theory of beauty. Rather, the object is likely to be associated with an artistic or cultural tradition the value of which may be presumed, and recommended to us as sharing in that value. Even here, however, a theory explaining the value of the artistic tradition may well be needed to sustain the claim that the object is connected to what is really valuable in its predecessors. A critic who associates an abstract presentation of the picture plane with the great representational painting of the past may not make much of a case for his abstractions unless he can explain the centrality of the picture plane in our appreciation of those older paintings. Of course, there are an infinite number of relations which it is logically possible to construct between one stretched and colored canvas and another; relevant connection with a tradition of beauty may require a theory of that beauty and not just some accidental resemblance. Connection with an accepted artistic tradition will probably almost always be required to supplement a theory of beauty, given the indeterminateness of the latter, but cannot simply substitute for it.

C) In many cases, an object will not actually be recommended to a general public, but to a more specific one. When Hume says that "At twenty, Ovid may be the favorite author, Horace at forty, and perhaps Tacitus at fifty,"[8] he should not be thought to surrender his defense of standards of taste – by which he of course means paradigms, or paragons, not principles. For such a comparison is not like an assertion of equality between Ogilby and Milton; it does not reduce taste to idiosyncratic preference, but only suggests that some beauties may be apparent, or at least most salient, to persons in a certain restricted but certainly shareable position – at a certain stage of life, in a certain kind of relationship, and so on. But there will still be a genuine reason why anyone in such a position should take pleasure, and the kind of pleasure associated with other beautiful objects, in such a case; and it will be incumbent upon the critic to have such a reason available. That is, it is not just that Ovid appeals

[8] David Hume, "Of the Standard of Taste," in *Essays Moral, Political, and Literary* (Oxford University Press, 1903): 250.

to a common interest of twenty-year olds and Tacitus to one of fifty-year olds; Ovid and Tacitus both have genuine aesthetic merits, but their beauties are most salient to persons in the different positions described. Of course, in this case a critic may also have the additional responsibility of making the intended audience of his recommendation plain: if there are differences in their best audiences, then Tacitus and Ovid should not be equally recommended to all, or Tacitus, say, recommended in the same way to the twenty-year old as to the fifty-year old.

D) Finally, one other kind of case. Hume often emphasizes that the appropriate aesthetic response to an object may require some form of connection to a particular community of taste. When he explicates the requirement that a qualified critic "must preserve his mind free from all *prejudice*," it turns out that he does not mean that the critic must free himself from all presuppositions whatever and approach the objects mindlessly (to borrow an image from Mothersill); it means he must approach a work from the *right* point of view, free from *alternative* preconceptions that would indeed be prejudicial for his perceiving the merits that the object really has to offer. Thus, "a critic of [a work from] a different age or nation . . . must have all these circumstances in his eye, and must place himself in the same situation as the audience, in order to form a true judgment."[9] This actually suggests two different situations. In some cases, a work created from one point of view is commended to an audience with another; art from a religious age is still commended in secular times, an artist's expression of his own personality is offered to others of quite different frames of mind, yet some claim is made that it is worth the effort of assimilating the alien point of view. In other cases, a work is recommended within a certain community, though not necessarily to those who stand beyond its membership. In these cases, it might seem, no general theory of beauty could possibly have a place, for it is precisely in virtue of its particularity that an object is commended – the particular insight it offers into another mind or culture, the particular shared taste that differentiates one community from another rather than assimilating it to the other.

But even in these kinds of cases responsible commendations may have to be grounded in a serious theory of beauty. If the recommendation to enter into another point of view is not that there is insight into archaeology, sociology, or psychopathology to be so derived, but an *aesthetic pleasure*, a perception of *beauty*, then there must be some reason to

[9] Ibid., p. 244–45.

suppose that this alien expression is in fact beautiful though this may be obscured if the object is approached with inappropriate preconceptions about culture, religion, or personality. Indeed, the more alien the viewpoint of the object being commended is to that of the audience to whom it is commended, the more obvious it is that the commender should have an *aesthetic* reason for his recommendation; and the more alien is the *tradition* of beauty to which the commended object belongs, the more obvious will it be that the recommendation must be grounded in some more general *theory* of beauty.

Consider now the second kind of case, where shared pleasure in an object is commendable precisely because of the additional bonds of sociability it creates within a particular community. Here one might think of the model of "in" jokes, which create a sense of community precisely because they are *not* universally shared. Many eighteenth-century theorists were impressed by this value especially in art. But the social explanation of our pleasure in a beautiful object is circular, and its recommendation even within a particular community will be hollow, unless the object can please *as beautiful* – it is the perception of its beauty, after all, which it is so pleasant to share. In the other case, the joke had better be *funny* if it is to become "in." Here again, the purely extensional approach cannot stand alone. An object cannot be commended *simply* as standing in a certain tradition, or as part of a certain individual or communal point of view, but the tradition or point of view itself must be commended as of genuine aesthetic merit. Backing up such a commendation may well push the critic towards the expression of a serious theory of beauty.

I hope that my profound sympathy with Mary Mothersill's restoration of beauty has remained apparent throughout. I have only wanted to suggest that a recognition of the genuine even if hardly capital burden of responsibility we undertake in offering critical commendations may often be satisfied only by some theory of beauty, and that by looking further into the causal connection between aesthetic properties and the pleasure they surely do cause we may discern something more of the shape of such a theory.

Bibliography of Works Cited

Kant, Immanuel: Modern Editions and Translations

Kant, Immanuel. *Kant's gesammelte Schriften.* Edited by the Royal Prussian (later German and Berlin-Brandenburg) Academy of Sciences. 29 volumes. Berlin: Georg Reimer (later Walter de Gruyter & Co.), 1900 –.

Kant, Immanuel. *Critique of Aesthetic Judgment.* Translated by James Creed Meredith. Oxford: Clarendon Press, 1952 (originally 1911 and 1928).

Kant, Immanuel. *Anthropology from a Pragmatic Point of View* (1798). Translated by Mary J. Gregor. The Hague: Martinus Nijhoff, 1974.

Kant, Immanuel. *Lectures on Logic.* Translated and editied by J. Michael Young. Cambridge: Cambridge University Press, 1992.

Kant, Immanuel. *Practical Philosophy.* Edited and translated by Mary J. Gregor. Cambridge: Cambridge University Press, 1996.

Kant, Immanuel. *Religion and Rational Theology.* Edited and translated by Allen W. Wood and George di Giovanni. Cambridge: Cambridge University Press, 1996.

Kant, Immanuel. *Lectures on Ethics.* Edited by Peter Heath and J. B. Schneewind, translated by Peter Heath. Cambridge: Cambridge University Press, 1997.

Kant, Immanuel. *Lectures on Metaphysics.* Edited and translated by Karl Ameriks and Steve Naragon. Cambridge: Cambridge University Press, 1997.

Kant, Immanuel. *Critique of Pure Reason.* Edited and translated by Paul Guyer and Allen W. Wood. Cambridge: Cambridge University Press, 1998.

Kant, Immanuel. *Critique of the Power of Judgment.* Edited by Paul Guyer, translated by Paul Guyer and Eric Matthews. Cambridge: Cambridge University Press, 2000.

Kant, Immanuel. *Theoretical Philosophy after 1781.* Edited by Henry Allison and Peter Health. Translated by Gary Hatfield, Michael Friedman, Henry Allison, and Peter Health. Cambridge: Cambridge University Press, 2002.

Other Sources and Secondary Literature

Abrams, M. H. *The Mirror and the Lamp: Romantic Theory and the Critical Tradition.* Oxford: Oxford University Press, 1953.

Addison, Joseph, and Richard Steele. *The Spectator.* Edited by A. Chalmers. Eight volumes. Boston: Little, Brown and Company, 1869.

Alison, Archibald. *Essays on the Nature and Principles of Taste.* Two volumes. Second edition. Edinburgh: Bell & Bradfute et al., 1811.

Allison, Henry E. *Kant's Theory of Taste: A Reading of the* Critique of Aesthetic Judgment. Cambridge: Cambridge University Press, 2001.

Ashfield, Andrew, and Peter de Bolla, eds. *The Sublime: A Reader in British Eighteenth-Century Aesthetic Theory.* Cambridge: Cambridge University Press, 1996.

Baumgarten, Alexander Gottlieb. *Meditationes philosophicae de nonnullis ad poema pertinentibus (1735)/ Philosophische Betrachtungen über einige Bedingungen des Gedichtes,* parallel Latin and German texts edited by Heinz Paetzold. Hamburg: Felix Meiner Verlag, 1983.

Baumgarten, Alexander Gottlieb. *Metaphysica* (1739). Parallel Latin and German passages in *Texte zur Grundlegung der Ästhetik,* edited by Hans Rudolf Schweizer. Hamburg: Felix Meiner Verlag, 1983.

Baumgarten, Alexander Gottlieb. *Aesthetica* (1750–58). Frankfurt an der Oder, 1750–58; reprint, Hildesheim: Georg Olms, 1961. Modern edition, edited by B. Croce, Bari: J. Laterza, 1936. Selections, with an introduction and parallel German translations, in Hans Rudolf Schweizer, *Ästhetik als Philosophie der sinnlichen Erkenntnis: Eine Interpretation der "Aesthetica" A. G. Baumgartens mit teilweise Widergabe des lateinischen Textes und deutscher Übersetzung.* Basel and Stuttgart: Schwabe, 1973.

Bäumler, Alfred. *Das Irrationalitätsproblem in der Ästhetik und Logik des 18. Jahrhunderts bis zur Kritik der Urteilskraft.* Second edition. Tübingen: Max Niemeyer, 1967.

Beardsley, Monroe C. *Aesthetics: Problems in the Philosophy of Criticism.* Second edition. Indianapolis and Cambridge: Hackett Publishing Company, 1981.

Berkeley, George. *Alciphron, or the Minute Philosopher.* In *The Works of George Berkeley, Bishop of Cloyne.* Edited by A. A. Luce and T. E. Jessop. Volume 3. Edinburgh: Thomas Nelson & Sons, 1950.

Bernstein, Jay M. *The Fate of Art: Aesthetic Alienation from Kant to Derrida and Adorno.* University Park: Pennsylvania State University Press, 1992.

Blair, Hugh. *Lectures on Rhetoric and Belles Lettres.* London: W. Strahan, 1783.

Brandt, Reinhard. "Die Schönheit der Kristallen und das Spiel der Erkenntniskräfte. Zum Gegenstand und zur Logik des ästhetischen Urteils bei Kant." In Reinhard Brandt and Werner Stark, eds., *Autographen, Dokumente und Berichte: Zu Edition, Amtsgeschäften und Werk Immanuel Kants, Kant-Forschungen,* vol. 5. Hamburg: Felix Meiner Verlag, 1994, pp. 19–57.

Budd, Malcolm. "Delight in the Natural World: Kant on the Aesthetic Appreciation of Nature. Part 1: Natural Beauty." *British Journal of Aesthetics* 38 (1998): 1–18. Reprinted in Budd, *The Aesthetic Appreciation of Nature: Essays on the Aesthetics of Nature.* Oxford: Clarendon Press, 2002, pp. 24–47.

Budd, Malcolm. "The Pure Judgment of Taste as an Aesthetic Reflective Judgment." *British Journal of Aesthetics* 41 (2001): 247–60.

Bürger, Peter. "Critique of Autonomy." In Kelly, *Encyclopedia of Aesthetics*, Vol. I, pp. 175–8.

Burke, Edmund. *A Philosophical Enquiry into the Origin of Our Ideas of the Sublime and Beautiful.* Second edition, with Introduction on Taste. London: Robert and James Dodsley, 1759. Modern editions by J. T. Boulton (London: Routledge and Kegan Paul, 1958) and Adam Phillips (Oxford: Oxford University Press, 1990).

Carroll, Nöel. "Art and Ethical Criticism: An Overview of Recent Directions of Research." *Ethics* 110 (2000): 350–87.

Carroll, Noël. "Essence, Expression and History: Arthur Danto's Philosophy of Art." In Mark Rollins, ed., *Danto and His Critics.* Oxford: Basil Blackwell, 1993, pp. 79–106.

Carroll, Noël. "Hume's Standard of Taste." *Journal of Aesthetics and Art Criticism* 43 (1984): 181–94.

Cavell, Stanley. "Aesthetic Problems of Modern Philosophy." In Cavell, *Must We Mean What We Say?* New York: Charles Scribner's Sons, 1969. Updated edition, Cambridge: Cambridge University Press, 2002, pp. 73–96.

Cavell, Stanley. *The Claim of Reason.* New York: Oxford University Press, 1979.

Caygill, Howard. *Art of Judgement.* Oxford: Blackwell, 1989.

Cohen, Ted, and Paul Guyer, eds. *Essays in Kant's Aesthetics.* Chicago: University of Chicago Press, 1982.

Coleridge, Samuel Taylor. *Biographia Literaria, with his Aesthetical Essays.* Edited by J. T. Shawcross. 2 vols. Corrected edition. Oxford: Oxford University Press, 1954.

Cothey, A. L. *The Nature of Art.* London: Routledge, 1992.

Crawford, Donald W. *Kant's Aesthetic Theory.* Madison: University of Wisconsin Press, 1974.

Crowther, Paul. "The Claims of Perfection: A Revisionary Defence of Kant's Theory of Dependent Beauty." *International Philosophical Quarterly* 26 (1986): 61–74.

Crowther, Paul. *The Kantian Sublime: From Morality to Art.* Oxford: Clarendon Press, 1989.

Danto, Arthur C. "The Artworld." *Journal of Philosophy* 61 (1964): 571–84.

Danto, Arthur C. *The Transfiguration of the Commonplace.* Cambridge, Mass.: Harvard University Press, 1981.

Danto, Arthur C. *The Philosophical Disenfranchisement of Art.* New York: Columbia University Press, 1986.

Danto, Arthur C. *After the End of Art: Contemporary Art and the Pale of History.* Princeton: Princeton University Press, 1997.

Danto, Arthur C. *The Abuse of Beauty: Aesthetics and the Concept of Art.* Chicago and LaSalle: Open Court, 2003.

De Man, Paul. "Phenomenality and Materiality in Kant." In Hugh J. Silverman and Gary E. Aylesworth, eds. *The Textual Sublime: Deconstruction and Its Differences.* Albany: SUNY Press, 1990, pp. 87–109.

Derrida, Jacques. "Economimesis." *Diacritics* 11 (1971): 3–25.

Devereaux, Mary. "Protected Space: Politics, Censorship, and the Arts." *Journal of Aesthetics and Art Criticism* 51 (1993): 207–15.

Dickie, George. *Art and the Aesthetic: An Institutional Analysis.* Ithaca: Cornell University Press, 1974.

Du Bos, [Jean-Baptiste,] Abbé. *Critical Reflections on Poetry, Painting and Music.* Translated by Thomas Nugent, from the fifth edition. London: John Nourse, 1748.

Eagleton, Terry. *The Ideology of the Aesthetic.* Oxford: Blackwell, 1990.

Emerson, Ralph Waldo. *Essays and Lectures.* Edited by Joel Porte. New York: The Library of America, 1983.

Faas, Ekbert. *The Genealogy of Aesthetics.* Cambridge: Cambridge University Press, 2002.

Ferry, Luc. *Homo Aestheticus: The Invention of Taste in the Democratic Age.* Translated by Robert de Loaiza. Chicago: University of Chicago Press, 1993.

Franke, Ursula, ed. *Kants Schlüssel zur Kritik des Geschmacks: Ästhetische Erfahrung heute – Studien zur Aktualität von Kants "Kritik der Urteilskraft."* Sonderheft des Jahrgangs 2000 der *Zeitschrift für Ästhetik und Allgemeine Kunstwissenschaft.* Hamburg: Felix Meiner Verlag, 2000.

Gadamer, Hans Georg. *Truth and Method.* Translated by Garrett Barden and John Cumming. New York: Seabury Press, 1975.

Gardiner, Patrick. *Schopenhauer.* Baltimore: Penguin, 1963.

Gaut, Berys. "Art and Ethics." In Berys Gaut and Dominic McIver Lopes, eds., *The Routledge Companion to Aesthetics.* London: Routledge, 2001, pp. 341–52.

Gerard, Alexander. *An Essay on Taste.* London: A. Millar, 1759.

Gerard, Alexander. *An Essay on Genius.* London: W. Strahan, 1774.

Gerard, Alexander. *Versuch über das Genie.* Translated by Christian Garve. Leipzig: Weidmanns Erbe und Reich, 1776.

Ginsborg, Hannah. "Reflective Judgment and Taste." *Nous* 24 (1990): 63–78.

Ginsborg, Hannah. "Lawfulness without a Law: Kant on the Free Play of Imagination and Understanding." *Philosophical Topics* 25 (1997): 37–83.

Gottsched, Johann Christoph. *Versuch einer critischen Dichtkunst vor die Deutschen.* In Gottsched, *Schriften zur Literatur.* Edited by Horst Steinmetz. Stuttgart: Philipp Reclam, 1972.

Guyer, Paul. *Kant and the Claims of Taste* (1979). Second edition. Cambridge: Cambridge University Press, 1997.

Guyer, Paul. "Pleasure and Society in Kant's Theory of Taste." In Cohen and Guyer, *Essays in Kant's Aesthetics,* pp. 21–54.

Guyer, Paul. *Kant and the Experience of Freedom.* Cambridge: Cambridge University Press, 1993.

Guyer, Paul. "Kant's Conception of Fine Art." *Journal of Aesthetics and Art Criticism* 52 (1994): 175–85. Reprinted as chapter 12 in the second edition of *Kant and the Claims of Taste.*

Guyer, Paul, ed. *Kant's Groundwork of the Metaphysics of Morals: Critical Essays.* Lanham: Rowman & Littlefield, 1998.

Guyer, Paul. "Dependent Beauty Revisited: A Reply to Wicks." *Journal of Aesthetics and Art Criticism* 57 (1999): 357–61.

Guyer, Paul. *Kant on Freedom, Law, and Happiness.* Cambridge: Cambridge University Press, 2000.

Guyer, Paul. "The Unity of Nature and Freedom: Kant's Conception of the System of Philosophy." In Sally S. Sedgwick, ed., *The Reception of Kant's Critical Philosophy.* Cambridge: Cambridge University Press, 2000, pp. 19–53.

Guyer, Paul. "From Nature to Morality: Kant's New Argument in the 'Critique of Teleological Judgment'." In Hans Friedrich Fulda and Jurgen Stolzenberg, eds., *Architektonik und System in der Philosophie Kants.* Hamburg: Felix Meiner Verlag, 2001, pp. 375–404.

Guyer, Paul. "Ends of Reason and Ends of Nature: The Place of Teleology in Kant's Ethics." *Journal of Value Inquiry* 36 (2002): 161–86.

Guyer, Paul. "Kant's Deductions of the Principles of Right." In Mark Timmons, ed., *Kant's Metaphysics of Morals: Interpretative Essays.* Oxford: Oxford University Press, 2002, pp. 23–64.

Guyer, Paul, ed. *Kant's Critique of the Power of Judgment: Critical Essays.* Lanham: Rowman & Littlefield, 2003.

Guyer, Paul. "Kant's Principles of Reflecting Judgment." In Guyer, *Kant's Critique of the Power of Judgment: Critical Essays,* pp. 1–60.

Guyer, Paul. "Purpose in Nature: What is Living and What is Dead in Kant's Teleology?" In Dietmar Heidemann and Christina Engelhard, eds., *Warum Kant Heute?* Berlin: Walter de Gruyter, 2004, pp. 383–413.

Hamlyn, D. W. *Schopenhauer.* London: Routledge & Kegan Paul, 1980.

Haskins, Casey. "Autonomy: Historical Overview." In Kelly, *Encyclopedia of Aesthetics.* Vol. I, pp. 170–5.

Hegel, Georg Wilhelm Friedrich. *Hegel's Aesthetics: Lectures on Fine Arts.* Translated by T. M. Knox. 2 vols. Oxford: Clarendon Press, 1975.

Heidemann, Dietmar H., and Kristina Engelhard, eds. *Warum Kant heute? Systematische Bedeutung und Rezeption seiner Philosophie in der Begenwart.* Berlin: Walter de Gruyter, 2003.

Henrich, Dieter. "Kant's Explanation of Aesthetic Judgment." In Henrich, *Aesthetic Judgment and the Moral Image of the World: Studies in Kant.* Stanford: Stanford University Press, 1992, pp. 29–56.

Herman, Barbara. *The Practice of Moral Judgment.* Cambridge, Mass.: Harvard University Press, 1993.

Hudson, Hud. "The Significance of an Analytic of the Ugly in Kant's Deduction of Pure Judgments of Taste." In Ralf Meerbote, ed., and Hud Hudson, associate ed., *Kant's Aesthetics, North American Kant Society Studies in Philosophy,* vol. 1. Atascadero: Ridgeview Publishing Co., 1991, pp. 87–103.

Hume, David. *Essays Moral, Political and Literary.* Oxford: Oxford University Press, 1963.

Hume, David, *An Enquiry Concerning the Principles of Morals* (1751). Edited by L. A. Selby-Bigge, third edition revised by P. H. Nidditch. Oxford: Clarendon Press, 1975.

Hume, David. *The Natural History of Religion and Dialogues Concerning Natural Religion* (1779). Edited by A. Wayne Colver and John Valdimir Price. Oxford: Clarendon Press, 1976.

Hume, David. *A Treatise of Human Nature* (1739–40). Edited by L. A. Selby-Bigge, second edition revised by P. H. Nidditch. Oxford: Clarendon Press, 1978.

Hume, David. *A Treatise of Human Nature* (1739–40). Edited by David Fate Norton and Mary J. Norton. Oxford: Oxford University Press, 2000.

Hutcheson, Francis. *An Inquiry into the Original of Our Ideas of Beauty and Virtue.* Fourth edition. London: D. Midwinter, et al., 1738. Modern edition, with an introduction and notes, by Peter Kivy. The Hague: Martinus Nijhoff, 1973.

Jones, Peter. *Hume's Sentiments: Their Ciceronian and French Context.* Edinburgh: Edinburgh University Press, 1982.

Jones, Peter. "Strains in Hume and Wittgenstein." In Donald W. Livingston and James T. King, eds. *Hume: A Re-evaluation.* New York: Fordham University Press, 1976, pp. 191–209.

Kames, Henry Home, Lord. *Elements of Criticism.* Edited by Abraham Mills. New York: Huntington & Savage, 1849.

Kant, Immanuel: Individual Works

Kant, Immanuel. *The Only Possible Basis for a Demonstration of the Existence of God* (1763). In *Theoretical Philosophy, 1755–1770.*

Kant, Immanuel. *On the Form and Principles of the Sensible and Intellectual World* [Inaugural Dissertation] (1770). In *Theoretical Philosophy, 1755–1770.*

Kant, Immanuel. *Groundwork for the Metaphysics of Morals* (1785). In *Practical Philosophy.*

Kant, Immanuel. *Metaphysical Foundations of Natural Science* (1786). In *Theoretical Philosophy after 1781.*

Kant, Immanuel. *Critique of Practical Reason* (1788). In *Practical Philosophy.*

Kant, Immanuel. First Introduction to the *Critique of the Power of Judgment* (1789). In *Critique of the Power of Judgment.*

Kant, Immanuel. *Religion within the Boundaries of Mere Reason* (1793). In *Religion and Rational Theology.*

Kant, Immanuel. *Metaphysics of Morals* (1797). In *Practical Philosophy.*

Kelly, Michael, ed. *Encyclopedia of Aesthetics.* 4 vols. New York: Oxford University Press, 1998.

Kennick, William. "Does Traditional Aesthetics Rest on a Mistake?" *Mind* 67 (1958): 317–34.

Kern, Andrea. *Schöne Lust: Eine Theorie der ästhetischen Erfahrung nach Kant.* Frankfurt am Main: Suhrkamp Verlag, 2000.

Kivy, Peter. "Hume's Standard: Breaking the Circle." *British Journal of Aesthetics* 7 (1967): 57–66.

Kivy, Peter. *Music Alone: Philosophical Reflections on the Pure Musical Experience.* Ithaca: Cornell University Press, 1990.

Kneller, Jane. "Disinterestedness." In Kelly, ed., *Encyclopedia of Aesthetics.* Vol. 2, pp. 59–64.

Korsmeyer, Carolyn. "Hume and the Foundations of Taste." *Journal of Aesthetics and Art Criticism* 35 (1976): 201–15.

Kristeller, Paul Oskar. "The Modern System of the Arts" (1951). In his *Renaissance Thought II: Papers on Humanism and the Arts.* New York: Harper & Row, 1965, pp. 163–227.

Lessing, Gotthold Ephraim. *Laokoön, oder über die Grenzen der Malerei und Poesie* (1766). In *Lessings Werke.* Edited by Kurt Wölfel. 3 vols. Frankfurt am Main: Insel Verlag, 1967.

Livingston, Donald W., and James T. King, eds. *Hume: A Re-evaluation.* New York: Fordham University Press, 1976.

Lohmar, Dieter. "Das Geschmacksurteil über das faszinierend Häßliche." In Parret, ed., *Kants Ästhetik – Kant's Aesthetics – L'esthétique de Kant*, pp. 498–512.

Magee, Bryan. *The Philosophy of Schopenhauer*. Oxford: Clarendon Press, 1983.

Makkreel, Rudolf. *Imagination and Interpretation in Kant: The Hermeneutical Import of the Critique of Judgment*. Chicago: University of Chicago Press, 1990.

Mandelbaum, Maurice. "Family Resemblances and Generalizations Concerning the Arts." *American Philosophical Quarterly* 2 (1965): 219–28.

McFarland, John D. *Kant's Concept of Teleology*. Edinburgh: Edinburgh University Press, 1970.

Meerbote, Ralf. "Reflection on Beauty." In Cohen and Guyer, *Essays in Kant's Aesthetics*, pp. 55–86.

Meerbote, Ralf, and Hud Hudson, eds. *Kant's Aesthetics. North American Kant Society Studies in Philosophy*, Vol. 1. Atascadero: Ridgeview Publishing Co., 1991.

Mendelssohn, Moses. *Philosophical Writings*. Edited by Daniel O. Dahlstrom. Cambridge: Cambridge University Press, 1997.

Mill, John Stuart. *On Liberty* (1859). In *Essays on Politics and Society. The Collected Works of John Stuart Mill*, edited by J. M. Robson. Volume 18. Toronto and London: University of Toronto Press and Routledge & Kegan Paul, 1977.

Monk, Samuel H. *The Sublime: A Study of Critical Theories in XVIII-Century England*. Second edition, with a new preface. Ann Arbor: University of Michigan Press, 1960.

Moore, G[eorge] E[dward]. *Principia Ethica* (1903). Revised edition, with introduction by Thomas Baldwin. Cambridge: Cambridge University Press, 1993.

Mothersill, Mary. *Beauty Restored*. Oxford: Clarendon Press, 1984.

Osborne, Harold. "Hume's Standard and the Diversity of Taste." *British Journal of Aesthetics* 7 (1967): 50–6.

Parret, Herman., ed. *Kants Ästhetik – Kant's Aesthetics – L'esthétique de Kant*. Berlin: Walter de Gruyter & Co., 1998.

Podro, Michael. *The Manifold in Perception: Theories of Art from Kant to Hildebrand*. Oxford: Clarendon Press, 1972.

Rind, Miles. "Can Kant's Deduction of Judgments of Taste Be Saved?" *Archiv für Geschichte der Philosophie* 84 (2001): 20–45.

Rogerson, Kenneth F. *Kant's Aesthetics: The Roles of Form and Expression*. Lanham: University Press of America, 1986.

Rousseau, Jean-Jacques. *Reveries of a Solitary Walker*. In *The Collected Writings of Rousseau*, edited by Roger D. Masters and Christopher Kelly. Volume 8. Hanover and London: University Press of New England, 2000.

Rush, Fred L., Jr. "The Harmony of the Faculties." *Kant-Studien* 92 (2001): 38–61.

Santayana, George. *The Sense of Beauty: Being the Outline of Aesthetic Theory*. New York: Charles Scribner's Sons, 1896.

Sartwell, Crispin. "Art for Art's Sake." In Kelly, *Encyclopedia of Aesthetics*, Vol. I, pp. 118–21.

Savile, Anthony. *Aesthetic Reconstructions: The Seminal Writings of Lessing, Kant, and Schiller*. Oxford: Blackwell, 1987.

Scarré, Geoffrey. "Kant on Free and Dependent Beauty." *British Journal of Aesthetics* 21 (1981): 351–62.

Schaeffer, Jean-Marie. *Art of the Modern Age: Philosophy of Art from Kant to Heidegger.* Translated by Steven Rendell. Princeton: Princeton University Press, 2000.

Schaper, Eva. *Studies in Kant's Aesthetics.* Edinburgh: Edinburgh University Press, 1979.

Schiller, Friedrich. *On the Aesthetic Education of Man, in a Series of Letters.* Edited and translated by Elizabeth M. Wilkinson and L. A. Willoughby. Oxford: Clarendon Press, 1967.

Schopenhauer, Arthur. *The World as Will and Representation.* Translated by E. F. J. Payne. Two volumes. Indian Hills, Colorado: The Falcon Wing's Press, 1958.

Seel, Gerhard. "Über den Grund der Lust an schönen Gegenständen: Kritische Fragen an die Ästhetik Kants." In Hariolf Oberer and Gerhard Seel, eds. *Kant: Analysen – Probleme – Kritik.* Würzburg: Königshausen & Neumann, 1988, pp. 317–56.

Shaftesbury, Anthony Ashley Cooper, Third Earl of. *Characteristics of Men, Manners, Opinions, Times* (1711). Edited by Lawrence F. Klein. Cambridge: Cambridge University Press, 1999.

Shier, David. "Why Kant Finds Nothing Ugly." *British Journal of Aesthetics* 38 (1998): 412–18.

Smith, Adam. *The Theory of Moral Sentiments.* Edited by A. L. Macfie and D. D. Raphael. Oxford: Oxford University Press, 1976.

Stolnitz, Jerome. "On the Origins of 'Aesthetic Disinterest'." *Journal of Aesthetics and Art Criticism* 20 (1961): 131–43.

Stolzenberg, Jürgen. "Das Freie Spiel der Erkenntniskräfte: Zu Kants Theorie des Geschmacksurteils." In Ursula Franke, ed., *Kants Schlüssel zur Kritik des Geschmacks: Ästhetische Erfahrung heute – Studien zur Aktualität von Kants "Kritik der Urteilskraft," Sonderheft des Jahrgangs 2000 der Zeitschrift für Ästhetik und allgemeine Kunstwissenschaft.* Hamburg: Felix Meiner, 2000, pp. 1–28.

Strube, Christian. "Das Häßliche und die 'Kritik der ästhetischen Urteilskraft': Überlegungen zu einer systematische Lücke." *Kant-Studien* 80 (1989): 416–46.

Vitruvius. *The Ten Books of Architecture.* Translated by Morris Hicky Morgan. Cambridge, Mass.: Harvard University Press, 1914.

Walton, Kendall. *Mimesis as Make-Believe: On the Foundations of the Representational Arts.* Cambridge, Mass.: Harvard University Press, 1990.

Weitz, Morris. "The Role of Theory in Aesthetics." *Journal of Aesthetics and Art Criticism* 32 (1956): 27–35.

Wenzel, Christian. "Kant Finds Nothing Ugly?" *British Journal of Aesthetics* 39 (1999): 416–22.

Wicks, Robert. "Dependent Beauty and the Appreciation of Teleological Style." *Journal of Aesthetics and Art Criticism* 55 (1997): 387–400.

Wittgenstein, Ludwig. *Philosophical Investigations.* Translated by G. E. M. Anscombe. Second edition. New York: Macmillan, 1968.

Wolff, Christian. *Vernünftige Gedancken von Gott, der Welt und der Seele des Menschen.* New edition. Halle: Renger, 1751.

Index